African security in the
twenty-first century

MANCHEStER
1824
Manchester University Press

African security in the twenty-first century

Challenges and opportunities

**STEPHEN EMERSON AND
HUSSEIN SOLOMON**

Manchester University Press

Copyright © Stephen Emerson and Hussein Solomon 2018

The right of Stephen Emerson and Hussein Solomon to be identified as the authors of this work has been asserted by them in accordance with the Copyright, Designs and Patents Act 1988.

Published by Manchester University Press
Altrincham Street, Manchester M1 7JA, UK
www.manchesteruniversitypress.co.uk

British Library Cataloguing-in-Publication Data is available

ISBN 978 1 5261 2273 5 *hardback*
ISBN 978 1 5261 4371 6 *paperback*

First published by Manchester University Press in hardback 2018

This edition published 2019

The publisher has no responsibility for the persistence or accuracy of URLs for any external or third-party internet websites referred to in this book, and does not guarantee that any content on such websites is, or will remain, accurate or appropriate.

Typeset in Sabon and Gill by
Servis Filmsetting Ltd, Stockport, Cheshire

Contents

List of figures, maps, tables and text boxes	vi
Foreword	vii
List of abbreviations	x
1 Understanding the security environment	1
2 Thinking about security	16
3 Identity conflict	35
4 Failing states	62
5 Terrorism and extremism	86
6 Trafficking in drugs and small arms	116
7 Health and disease	144
8 Resource conflict and the environment	169
9 The African response	194
10 The international response	215
11 The future of African security	250
Bibliography	260
Index	287

Figures, maps, tables and text boxes

Figures

1 The African health challenge	154
2 Regional economic community diagram	205

Maps

1 Africa, Nations Online Project	xii
2 Colonial Africa, 1950 CIA administration map	19

Tables

1 Religious identification in sub-Saharan Africa, 1920–2020 (%)	44
2 Key terrorist groups in Africa	96
3 UN/AU peacekeeping missions in Africa	227

Text boxes

1 Case study: the myth of "Somalia"	70
2 Case study: the Guinea-Bissau epicenter	123
3 The future of the Nile River: regional confrontation or cooperation?	180

Foreword

This is a book about "African" security and, as such, it examines and analyzes the nature of the current environment, as well as the key challenges and opportunities facing the entire continent. This, by definition, includes the five countries—Algeria, Egypt, Libya, Morocco, and Tunisia—that comprise North Africa. The reasoning goes beyond simply geographic correctness. While these five countries do share common political, cultural, and historical links to the Arab Middle East, they also share powerful linkages to their sub-Saharan African brethren. In the past, the primary emphasis was on longstanding economic, political, and social links: think of the pre-colonial trans-Saharan caravan trade, ideological support for the anti-colonial liberation struggle, or the importance of the Nile River as the lifeblood of Egyptian society. Security, however, is one link that has come rushing to the fore in the new century, and the security of North Africa and its people is now, more than ever, tied to the security challenges of the wider continent.

Moreover, the African security challenge now transcends national and sub-regional borders across all of the continent and thus to rely on artificially drawn and outdated conceptual boundaries of an Arab North Africa and a black sub-Saharan Africa that separate the two and their shared challenges is to deny this twenty-first-century reality.

There is a growing acceptance and acknowledgement of this reality. The United States' creation of Africa Command in 2007 brought together for the first time all the countries of Africa (with the exception of Egypt) under a single organizational structure for implementing American military policy and for providing security assistance. International organizations working in Africa now routinely view the security implications of crime, drug and arms trafficking, disease, migration, and refugee flows from a continental perspective. With Morocco's rejoining of the African Union in January 2017 after a 33-year absence, all of the continent's sovereign nations will be represented in the forum. Likewise, the North African bloc comprises one of the African Union's five sub-regional structures for advancing economic and security cooperation. Inter-regional cooperation on matters of instability and the rise of terrorism and extremism has also boosted political and security ties across the pan-Sahel between both North and sub-Saharan African countries.

This does not mean one should treat the entire continent as a monolithic block, because it is not. Africa, as we shall see, is a highly diverse place with various countries and sub-regions facing a broad spectrum of threats and challenges. All threats and challenges are not the same across the continent. Some of these—identity conflict, poverty, underdevelopment, disease, and environmental degradation—are more widespread and endemic than others, which tend to be clustered into self-delineating zones of conflict and violence. Some are rooted in a very specific historical and socio-economic context that increases their intensity and significance. Others pose more of a threat because of globalization and the fragile nature of the modern state. Many are often highly complex and intertwined with other challenges that further muddle the waters. But all ultimately affect the continent's overall security and stability that in turns helps shape Africa's impact on the global security environment.

The authors employ a human security approach to not only examine and analyze these challenges, but also to assess the effectiveness of solutions and progress so far in addressing these challenges. This approach is critical to understanding the true meaning and context of security in Africa by asking questions such as: security for whom and security for what? For in the Africa of today, security is more about advancing freedom of fear and freedom of want by empowering individuals and communities and having truly accountable governments. Importantly, this mandate calls for moving beyond ruling regimes and militaries as the sole arbitrators of security by calling for a more inclusive societal approach to building security.

While the critics of the human security approach may deem it overly broad in its definition and too encompassing to be effectively used as a theoretical framework, we believe this perceived weakness is actually one of the approaches' primary strengths. In blurring the traditional stark divide between security and development, human rights, and quality of life the notion of security becomes more relevant and policy prescriptive. This is especially important for Africa, where more conventional perspectives of security fall short in addressing the vast array of interdependent and non-traditional challenges—ranging from communal resource conflict, pandemic disease, and environmental degradation to transnational crime, terrorism and extremism, and failing states—facing the continent and its people. Moreover, with its focus on securing individuals and communities first and foremost rather than regimes, state structures, and institutions, the human security model is a bottom-up approach to security that taps into a broader and more diverse collection of stakeholders, putting the onus of responsibility on Africans themselves for ultimately defining and addressing their own security needs.

In the pages that follow, this book looks at the key security challenges facing the continent now and in the coming decades. It does so in the context of Africa's history, culture, and a still evolving security paradigm in an increasingly globalized world; all of which make the continent one of the most dynamic and difficult security environments. In doing so, this book seeks to challenge more traditional security constructs, which the authors deem as being woefully inadequate to meet the real security needs of African countries and their citizens.

In the concluding pages various ongoing and proposed solutions to these challenges at the local, regional, and international level are examined and assessed. All are works in progress. Still progress is being made, albeit not at the pace and extent that many in and outside of Africa had hoped to see, and much more work still needs to be done. What is telling, however, is the rising acknowledgement that Africa is not solely to be seen as a venue for problems or as an exporter of global security threats. For now is has truly become an integral part of the global solution to these challenges, working with fellow Africans and with international partners to establish its rightful place as a valuable contributor in building international security. It will be a long and difficult journey, but one that has finally begun.

Abbreviations

ACOTA	African Contingency Operations Training and Assistance program
AFRICOM	US Africa Command
AMISOM	African Mission in Somalia
ANC	African National Congress (South Africa)
AQIM	Al-Qaeda in the Islamic Maghreb
ASF	African Standby Force (African Union)
ATS	amphetamine-type stimulants
AU	African Union
AUPSC	African Union Peace and Security Council
CAR	Central African Republic
CEMAC	Central African Monetary and Economic Community
CJTF-HOA	Combined Joint Task Force-Horn of Africa (United States)
DRC	Democratic Republic of the Congo
ECOWAS	Economic Community of European Union
G-8	group of eight industrialized countries
GDP	gross domestic product
GPOI	Global Peace Operations Initiative (United States)
GSPC	Salafist Group for Preaching and Combat
IGAD	Intergovernmental Authority on Development
IGO	international governmental organization
IS	Islamic State (formerly the Islamic State in Iraq and Syria)
MDG	Millennium Development Goals
NATO	North Atlantic Treaty Organization
NGO	non-governmental organization
OAU	Organization of African Unity (predecessor to the African Union)
OECD	Organization for Economic Cooperation and Development (Europe)

Abbreviations

P3+1	United States, United Kingdom, France, and Germany
PEPFAR	President's Emergency Program for AIDS Relief (United States)
REC	regional economic community
SADC	Southern African Development Community
SALW	small arms and light weapons
TFG	Transitional Federal Government (Somalia)
UIC	Union of Islamic Courts (Somalia)
UNCHE	United Nations Conference on the Human Environment
UNHCR	United Nations High Commissioner for Refugees
UNODC	United Nations Office on Drugs and Crime
USAID	US Agency for International Development
WHO	World Health Organization

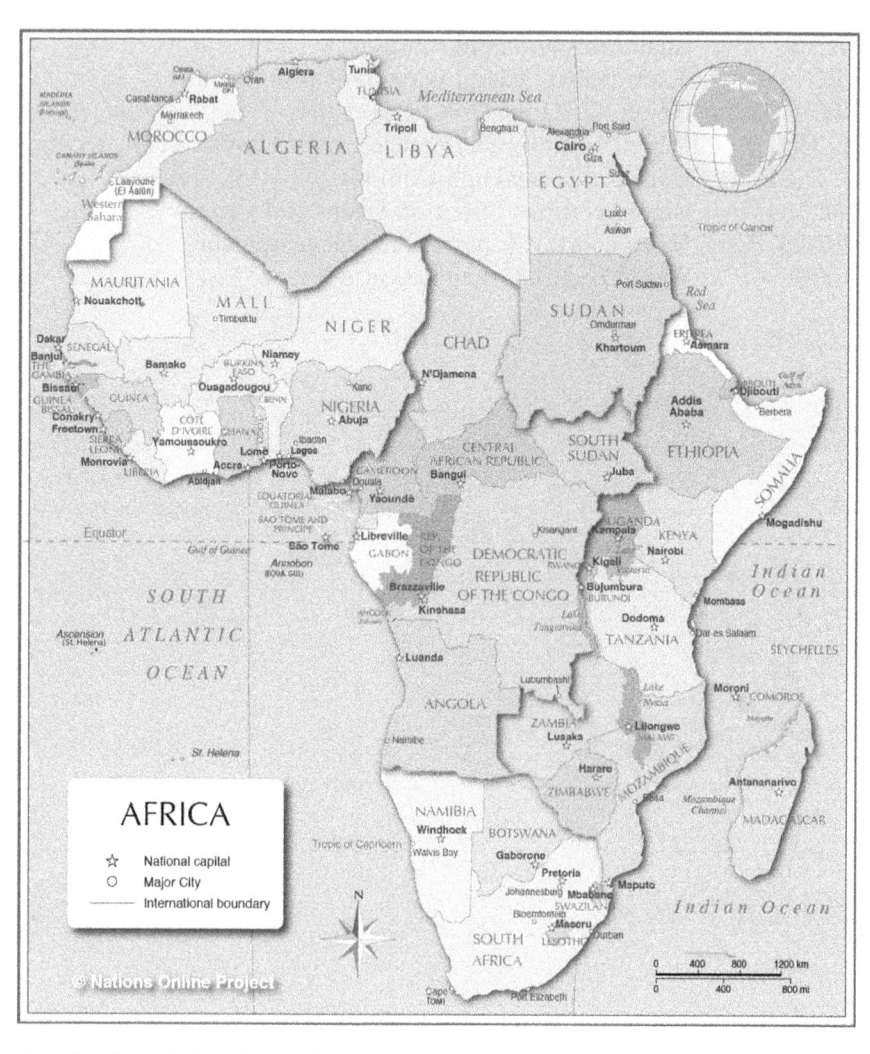

Map 1 Africa, Nations Online Project

1
Understanding the security environment

Long isolated from the rest of the world and more often than not neglected and deemed irrelevant, Africa with its fragile governments and institutions, abject poverty amid great resource endowments, and legacy of incessant violent conflict has become increasingly integrated into the global security architecture and its future security a rising concern for the United States and the international community. And while the continent has long been a setting for great power rivalries and has been highly susceptible to the political machinations of outside forces, it is now also viewed as a caldron and incubator of global instability and insecurity. Once ignored as strategically irrelevant, the Africa of the twenty-first century now, more than ever, matters to the rest of the world. Simply ignoring it is no longer an option, because in a globalizing world, insecurity anywhere is a threat to security everywhere. For the cost of failing to adequately address African security problems in the coming decades of this new century will come at a price, which African countries are increasingly incapable of paying, and the international community unwilling to shoulder.

The setting: a continent without equal

The African security environment of today is a dynamic one, characterized by a volatile mix of conflict, instability, and state weakness. It is also beset by a broad spectrum of traditional and non-traditional threats on the one hand, and yet home to an emerging regional* and international

---

* For the purpose of this book (and as it is commonly used in writing about Africa), the term "region" or "regional" generally refers to the *entire African continent*. The African Union is thus a "regional organization." It should be noted, however, that the word "region" can also be used to mean a specific geographic area or part of a country; for example, "the Ogaden region" of Ethiopia. The terms "sub-region" or "sub-regional" are used in this book to refer to various *geographic subdivisions of the African continent* or to geographically based organizations.

security consciousness and activism on the other. Meanwhile, the historical legacies of colonialism, authoritarianism, and the Cold War have left many African countries politically and economically underdeveloped and poorly equipped to meet the multitude of problems facing them. Specifically a chronic shortage of resources and institutional capacity have helped produce a security capacity gap—one of the most severe in the world—that is further exacerbated by endemic corruption and poor governance, thus making Africa one of the most singularly perplexing and challenging regions in the world today. It is the nature and wide range of these security challenges, as well as Africa's extreme vulnerability to them that undoubtedly caused the US National Intelligence Council's *Global Trends 2025* report to label the region as the one "most vulnerable to economic disruption, population stress, civil conflict, and political instability."[1]

While all regions of the world are by definition "unique" in their own right, the unequaled combination of Africa's geography, demography, historical development, and sheer magnitude of its political, economic, and social diversity place the continent and its people in a league of their own. At nearly 12 million square miles Africa's land mass is greater in size than the United States, China, Western Europe, India and Argentina and it is home to some of the largest countries in the world: The former Sudan, prior to the creation of South Sudan in 2011 and the Democratic Republic of the Congo (DRC), when combined would equal one-half the size of the United States. With currently more than one billion people, composed of thousands of ethnic groups (there are some 450 alone in Nigeria and the DRC) speaking some 2,000 languages, Africa is not only among the most populous region in the world, but it is certainly one of the most diverse, fastest growing, and youngest.[2] According to UN and CIA statistical estimates, Africa's projected population growth of more than 2 percent over the next five years will easily outstrip second place Asia by more than 2:1.[3] Of the fastest growing populations in the world today, 17 of 20 are now found in Africa and the continent's largest city, Lagos, Nigeria with more than 21 million people, is likely to become one of the five largest cities in the world by 2020.[4] These demographic trends will increase the continent's "youth bulge" (40 percent of the population is currently estimated to be under the age of 15) at a time when economic development in Africa threatens to fall even further behind other developing regions of the globe.

The Economic Community of West African States (ECOWAS), for instance, is a "sub-regional organization."

The continent is also home to many of the poorest countries on earth, many of which are the largest recipients of international development and humanitarian aid. Poverty is widespread and economies are struggling; half of all African countries have annual gross domestic products (GDP) under $12 billion—an amount about equal to the annual GDP of Mongolia—and fall in the bottom one-third of all global economies.[5] Of the 28 countries suffering from burdensome international debt that have fully qualified for assistance under the International Monetary Fund's Heavily Indebted Poor Countries initiative, 22 are found in Africa.[6] Infant mortality rates, which can be attributable to the high levels of poverty and inadequate health care in Africa, are also the highest in the world; 34 of the continent's 54 countries rank at the very bottom of the United Nation's under-five mortality rankings.[7] Despite the provision of some $25 billion annually in official development assistance from G-8 countries since 2009,[8] the situation shows little sign of improvement as ill-conceived programs, mismanagement, and rampant corruption undermine development efforts.

All of this in spite of Africa's abundance of natural resources. Recent oil and gas discoveries in the Gulf of Guinea and off the east coast of Africa, for instance, hold out the promise of significant economic development and an improved quality of life in some of the continent's poorest countries. However, lingering issues of corruption, mismanagement, and an equitable division of revenues often mean that this new found wealth will likely be squandered too and few lives improved. The prospects for overcoming these obstacles are not bright, however, as some of Africa's most historically resource endowed states—Angola, the DRC, Equatorial Guinea, Nigeria, and Sudan—have been some of the most poorly governed, corrupt, and divided countries on the continent. For example, Nigeria is believed to have lost over half the $600 billion it has earned from oil since the 1960s[9] and for all its national wealth, more than 80 percent of Nigerians survive on less than $2 per day.[10]

Africa's colonial past, with its tainted legacy of exploitation, elitism, and repression, has also helped contribute to the political, economic, and social fragmentation of the continent, thereby complicating efforts to address the continent's security challenges. Ill-suited and imposed colonial borders split communities and undermined cultural, social, and political cohesiveness. European divide-and-rule strategies inflamed ethnic, religious, and geographic tensions, as did prolonged violent anti-colonial struggles. This situation gave rise at independence to many artificial "nation-states" that tended to lack economic viability or any sense of nationhood, and were riven by societal conflict and/or were dominated by self-aggrandizing leaders and self-serving political parties that were largely unaccountable to the people they sought to govern. Heavy-handed attempts by central governments in the 1960s and 1970s at nation building in these fragmented societies too often backfired. The result was a steep upsurge in secessionist or irredentist movements, massive human rights abuses, violent repression, and civil conflict, as well as frequent international military interventions. Coups and counter-coups "in the name of saving the country" became a defining characteristic of the immediate post-independence period. The result is a political culture of authoritarianism and military rule that still simmers just below the surface even today.

Likewise, the continent's serving as a surrogate venue for superpower competition during the Cold War further disrupted and distorted Africa's political and economic development, as both Washington and Moscow pursued their own foreign policy and security agendas without regard to the seeds of instability that they sowed across the continent. Both sides' unquestioned support for "their" African dictators, escalating arms sales, and the use of African surrogates to fight proxy wars not only turned the continent into a superpower battlefield for decades, but further militarized and polarized African societies by fanning the flames of existing problems. From Ethiopia, Eritrea, and Somalia in the Horn of Africa, across much of Central Africa and into Angola, Mozambique, and Zimbabwe in the south, the legacy of the Cold War still resonates today. Sadly it seems that there may well be a repetition of this Cold War dynamic with Beijing and Washington vying for influence.

Chronic conflict and instability
From domestic power struggles and clashes over national resources to competing territorial claims and irredentist and separatist movements, violent conflict is a constant and seemingly unavoidable feature of the African landscape. Despite recent strides in resolving some longstanding problems and an overall decline in violence since the end of the Cold War, violent conflict remains at the heart of Africa's security challenges and the continent is still home to most of the world's armed conflicts. According to the Human Security Centre, "at the turn of the twenty-first century more people were being killed in wars in this region than in the rest of the world combined."[11] A conservative estimate of Africans killed as a result of major conflicts since the early 1990s would probably exceed 5 million, with tens of millions more having been displaced from their homes and livelihoods. Maybe even more telling beyond Africa's high profile conflicts in Darfur, the eastern DRC, or Somalia are the tens of millions of people affected by the constant low-level violence that is a part of their everyday life. Whether it is conflict over

water and grazing rights in northeastern Uganda, communal violence in central Nigeria, press-ganged children in the tantalum mines of the DRC or drug-fueled violence on the streets of Johannesburg, the resulting high levels of fear and insecurity across the continent are surely the ultimate indication of African governments' inability to provide security for its citizens.

Alongside long-established sources of African conflict, such as ethnic or religious differences, or competition over scarce resources, a whole new set of globally driven forces outside the continent are also fueling the violence. For example, the worldwide proliferation of small arms and light weapons following the collapse of the Berlin Wall has made these the weapons of choice in civil conflicts, not only in Africa but across the globe. While these weapons are not in and of themselves the cause of conflict, their widespread availability, affordability, and lethality contributes to prolonging and intensifying violence. The mixture of old and new sources of conflict has created a continent seeped in violence, which by some estimates has cost African countries around $18 billion per year and an estimated $284 billion from 1990 to 2005—an amount equal to all the donor aid given over the same period.[12]

Another significant feature of African conflict is the increasing sub-regionalization of conflict, whereby domestic conflicts rarely remain so and thus spread from one country to the next, creating endemic zones of conflict. Factors such as transnational ethnicity, a common historical or cultural heritage, traditional migration patterns, and linked socio-economic development help facilitate the spread of domestic conflict across international borders. The Mano River Basin of West Africa, the Great Lakes region of Central Africa and Darfur's tri-border area with Chad and the Central African Republic (CAR) are all examples of this sub-regionalization of conflict. This problem is further complicated by inadequate or ineffectual resolution mechanisms that fail to comprehensively address both the domestic and transnational dimensions of these conflicts. In addition, these situations are also highly susceptible to exploitation and intervention by those outside Africa. Al-Qaeda, for example, has sought repeatedly to advance its own global agenda by internationalizing the conflicts in Algeria, Darfur, Mali, Nigeria, and Somalia, albeit with limited success. More recently, the Islamic State (formerly known as the Islamic State in Iraq and Syria, or ISIS) has been trying to expand its reach and influence into parts of North Africa, most notably into conflict-ridden Libya.

Unlike some other regions of the world, what is characteristically not present in Africa is an abundance of inter-state conflict. With rare exceptions, such as the Ethiopian–Eritrean border war of 1998–2000, African countries generally do not go to war with each other. When tensions do become seriously strained (as they often do), governments historically resort to the use of proxies or lend their support to armed opposition groups operating in the offending country, rather than rely on the direct use of conventional military power to solve their differences. This support can take the form of providing safe havens, granting freedom of movement within the hosting country, providing friendly media coverage, or increasing the provision of arms and equipment, intelligence support, or direct logistics assistance. The old maxim that the "enemy of my enemy, is my friend" certainly applies in Africa.

While this approach tends to defuse the likelihood of all-out inter-state war, it also usually leads to periods of protracted, low-intensity conflicts that can last for decades. Moreover, sponsoring governments can find it increasingly difficult to control and manage their surrogates over time as insurgent or opposition groups broaden their base of support and seek greater independence. The use of proxies as a foreign policy tool also complicates domestic conflict resolution efforts as it adds another external dimension (one commonly with a completely different set of priorities and objectives) to the original problem. Chadian–Sudanese relations over the years clearly reflect this trend, as Khartoum uses its support of anti-Chadian rebels to punish N'Djamena for its support of Darfur insurgents in a reinforcing cycle of violence in both countries. Proxy conflicts can also play out in third countries, as shown by both Ethiopia's and Eritrea's involvement in Somalia, where each side backs opposing Somali factions.

Finally, the problems of chronic conflict are further compounded by the existence across the continent of extremely weak governments and politically fragile, unstable states. This situation is partly the result of Africa's historical heritage, but it is also the by-product of African leaders and elites recklessly seeking to hold on to power at all cost. The upshot for many countries has been the formation of highly centralized and authoritarian, but institutionally weak governments that are lacking accountability and any significant degree of popular support. The "failed state"—defined as "one in which the government does not have effective control of its territory, is not perceived as legitimate by a significant portion of its population, does not provide domestic security or basic public services to its citizens, and lacks a monopoly on the use of force"[13]—being the most extreme case of government implosion. Although Somalia has become the poster child for state collapse in Africa, The Fund for Peace identified six African countries (Somalia, South Sudan, the CAR, Sudan, Chad, and the DRC) in its top eight countries in the world in 2016 as being the most vulnerable to instability and state failure.[14]

The shift away from one-party rule and the rise of democratic movements all across the continent in recent decades has been, without a doubt, one of the major watershed events since the end of the Cold War. In 2010 more than one-third of all African countries were electoral democracies in contrast to a mere handful ten years earlier and 62 percent were rated as "free" or "partly free," according to Freedom House civil liberties indices.[15] The 2011 people's revolutions in Egypt and Tunisia underscore the power behind this trend that has still yet to fully run its course in Africa. Nonetheless, many of these emerging African democracies are extremely fragile and face an uphill struggle to cope with social and political upheaval as they transition to more open and inclusive societies. Freedom House, in fact, reports that there are "more countries seeing declines in overall freedom than gains" in recent years and several African countries showed a decline in political rights and civil liberties since 2007, reversing several years of positive improvements.[16] Egypt, Ethiopia, and Kenya are cases in point, as they grapple to find the right balance of democracy and stability in their highly fragmented and conflict-prone societies.

The rise of non-traditional and transnational threats
A salient feature of the twenty-first-century African security environment has been the steady rise of a wide range of non-traditional and transnational threats, which mirrors a global trend in the evolving type and nature of threats facing the international community at large. The most alarming aspect of this new trend is the sheer volume and diversity of these emerging threats—that are in addition to more traditional threats already facing countries—and the added security burden it imposes. Nowhere is this truer than in Africa. Already poorly resourced and lacking the capacity to deal with most existing traditional security problems, African governments and institutions are on the verge of being overwhelmed with this new set of challenges. Nonetheless, it is in this new arena that Africans and the international community must focus their attention, for herein lie some of the most serious long-term threats to peace and stability.

The most prominent of these in Africa are:

- *Terrorism.* While terrorism has been a persistent feature of domestic conflicts in Africa for some time, the new danger lies in the growing internationalization of the threat across the continent or what some, like Jakkie Cilliers, see as "a melding of domestic and international terrorism" to reshape the face of African terrorism.[17] Beginning in the early 1990s in Algeria and arriving in full force in 1998 with the bombing of the American embassies in Kenya and Tanzania, Africa moved into the limelight as a venue for the emerging struggle between the West and international jihadists. Even more alarming is a rising fear that the continent's facilitating environment—weak states, economic and political marginalization, deep societal divisions, and potentially sympathetic populations—is providing a fertile breeding ground for the growth and export of not just African, but also international, terrorism as well. The powerful rise since 2007 of both locally grown and international violent jihadist groups, such as Boko Haram, splinter groups of al-Qaeda in the Islamic Maghreb, or the Islamic State, are evidence of the seriousness of this evolution. The quickening pace of globalization clearly appears to be facilitating this trend, as Africa increasingly becomes part of the larger global security environment and its set of challenges.

- *Criminal trafficking in drugs and small arms.* Likewise, the rising tide of globalization and the associated diffusion of technology into the far corners of the world, including Africa, have stimulated an explosion in international criminal activity. Nowhere is this more apparent than in West Africa. Long known for its extensive sub-regional criminal networks, West Africa has now become a key global hub for drugs, arms, and human trafficking, as well as for money laundering and financial fraud, according the United Nations.[18] Other parts of the continent are affected too. The illicit Africa-wide trade in small arms is reported to be a $1 billion-a-year business;[19] localized conflicts, underdevelopment, and a climate of corruption that helps sustain non-state actors, particularly armed militia groups, has fueled the growth of criminal activity in recent years. Even more worrisome have been the growing links between criminal and terrorist organizations in parts of West and North Africa and the serious implications this has for security.[20]

- *Pandemic disease.* Once simply categorized as health and quality of life issues, deadly pandemic diseases, such as HIV/AIDS, malaria, and tuberculosis, have come to the forefront of the non-traditional, transnational security challenges facing African countries today. Sub-Saharan Africa is the most severely affected HIV/AIDS region of the world, having nearly 70 percent of the worldwide total of 36.7 million people infected in 2015; 73 percent of AIDS-related deaths in 2015 were in Africa.[21] Several million more Africans—many of them women and young children—also die each year from the combined impact of AIDS, malaria, and tuberculosis. Beyond the human

cost, the impact on economic development, societal relationships, and human security is profound, and contributes directly to reinforcing the cycle of poverty, social fragmentation, and government weaknesses.
- *Demographic and environmental pressure.* Whether through disruptions to Africa's fragile ecosystem, economic pressures, or unrelentingly conflict, millions of Africans have been forced to abandon their homes and seek safety and a better life elsewhere. These increasingly dramatic population shifts can be highly localized or felt several thousand miles away, but more worrisome is their increasing frequency. Conflict and the accompanying deprivations have historically been responsible in Africa for fueling refugee flows and displacing people; Sudan's conflicts over the years, for example, have produced some 1.5 million refugees and over 4 million internally displaced persons. But rising demographic pressures and an overly stressed ecosystem are increasingly becoming critical factors. While certainly significant from an economic development perspective, these uncontrolled—and largely unmonitored—population movements complicate efforts to address other linked security problems, such as terrorism, resource and civil conflict, criminal activity, and pandemic disease.

What is most striking about the above list is the sheer complexity and diversity of these new threats and the additional burden they place on African governments. The rapid pace of globalization has certainly been instrumental in driving these trends, as has the continent's evolving integration into the global security architecture. Both trends show no signs of abating. Some security problems, such as sub-regional conflict, small arms proliferation and drug trafficking, pose a clear and present danger to governments and their citizenry and thus require immediate attention. Other problems, such as those associated with health and the environment, present more of a long-term challenge to security. Unfortunately, the need to address both current needs and future threats will put a further strain on Africa's already limited security capability.

Africa is certainly in dire need of a fresh approach to its security challenges—one that moves away from an outdated, state-centric focus heavily dependent on centralized traditional security organs, such as the military, and to a broader based, bottom-up approach with an emphasis on improving governance, development and strengthening civil society. For the Africa of the twenty-first century to be secure, it will require new thinking to face up to the challenges of a new century.

Emerging twenty-first-century security trends

Without a doubt Africa is changing. The final decade of the twentieth century in retrospect will be seen as a major watershed for the continent because it set the stage for the transformation of Africa—for better or for worse. The ending of Cold War-fueled conflicts, the increasing pace and reach of globalization, the emergence of new non-Western economic and political centers of power, the rising tide of democratic reform, and the shifting nature of global conflict and competition are driving a vast international transformation. Nowhere is this more so than in Africa. These forces of change—when viewed in concert with the continent's projected demographic explosion, a rising global dependence on African raw materials (and potential new markets) to help fuel future economic expansion, and the growing probability of the continent becoming an exporter of security problems and not simply a setting for chronic instability—are dramatically altering Africa's place on the world stage.

Long seen as isolated and peripheral to the rest of the world, the continent is gaining new importance—and strategic relevance—as an integral part of the arising twenty-first-century global security architecture that cannot be ignored. While this realignment undoubtedly will have enormous impact on the governments and people of Africa, its more telling impact in the decades ahead is likely to be on those outside the continent—outsiders, who must be increasingly willing to acknowledge this new reality and be accepting of the need to take a fresh approach to helping Africans create a more peaceful and secure future. As such, the continent finds itself likely to become a laboratory for the security challenges of the twenty-first century, both in terms of spawning new problems and in testing new solutions. As Pliny the Elder observed long ago, "*Semper aliquid novi Africam adferre*"—Africa always brings us something new.[22]

There are several emerging trends that merit watching, as they will almost certainly play a major role in both shaping the security challenges of tomorrow and in efforts to provide solutions today. These include:

- A decline in widespread, large-scale armed conflict, but other factors will continue to drive low-intensity conflicts across the continent. Despite an uptick in the death toll since 2013, there has, nonetheless, been a significant shift away from large-scale armed conflicts. Large-scale violence in 2017 is concentrated in a handful of countries—Libya, Nigeria, Somalia, South Sudan, and Sudan—and frequently spills over into neighboring countries. Thus, as Jakkie Cilliers notes,

"Africa as a whole is much less violent and more stable now than at the end of the Cold War."[23] The broader trend is toward low-level, festering conflicts that will be kept generally in check, but certainly have the potential to flare up into larger-scale violence and instability at any time.
- Non-traditional and transnational threats are growing and undoubtedly will replace large-scale violent conflict as the most persistent type of security challenge in the coming decades. These threats will run across the entire security threat spectrum from the high end of presenting an immediate threat, such as terrorism and drug trafficking, to the low end of being a longer-term threat, like pandemic disease and environmental degradation. Moreover, there is a high potential for some of these non-traditional threats to merge together over time into new, more powerful challenges to security.
- Traditional tools of state security, most notably the heavy reliance on militaries, are becoming increasingly ineffective and irrelevant for addressing the new security environment. This will mean a further diminishing of the role of the state and of the utility of force or coercion in addressing security concerns. An expansion of non-state and international actors in the African security sector is an inevitable result.
- The proliferation of threats is causing the security gap in Africa to widen and this will exert greater strain on national, regional, and international resources. Even with the inclusion of new actors and increased attention by the international community, resources are likely to prove inadequate to address all of Africa's future security requirements. This will necessitate experimentation with radical new approaches to security at all levels of society.
- Africa's steady integration into a globalized security architecture increases the possibility that the continent will shift from being an isolated and insulated security environment to playing a greater role in shaping future global security challenges. Events in Africa will, then, have more of a direct bearing on the rest of the world than ever before. Ignoring the continent will simply not be an option in the future.

While many of the continent's current security problems are rooted in the past, others clearly reflect the direct impact of rising globalization and Africa's greater integration into the world. All, however, pose a serious challenge to peace and security. As the old neo-colonial security model of control, repression, and state preeminence was ineffective at best and counterproductive at worst, Africans have clearly recognized the need to develop a better—and different—model, one that addresses not only their old existing problems, but the looming challenges of the twenty-first century too. Without a fundamental reassessment of the meaning of security in the modern age and how this security is delivered, this cannot happen. This will require the development of a new security paradigm that is grounded in human security concepts, acknowledges Africa's role in international security, and uses multiple synergistic strategies in achieving its goals. The future of African security depends on the success or failure of this endeavor.

The harsh reality is that there will never be enough resources available in Africa to tackle all the continent's security problems. It is imperative that the international community becomes a real partner in building African security, not simply out of altruism or humanitarianism, but out of global necessity. This, however, needs to be done in a more coordinated and cooperative fashion and within the security framework that Africans are constructing. Merely doing more of the same by throwing more money and resources at problems or using outdated approaches will not only be ineffectual, but will invariably produce frustration and disillusionment at the inability to solve anything. The United States in particular must break free of its traditional security construct and not just talk the talk of human security but actually restructure its engagement in Africa to walk the walk. Despite all the US rhetoric about the need for enhancing human security and using a "3D approach" (defense, development, and diplomacy) in implementation, the American military remains at the forefront of US security engagement in Africa today. As Africans have learned, using old security tools to delivery human security in the new century will not work. Now the United States must learn, and more importantly embrace, this same lesson.

Lastly, without political reform and improving governance in Africa, none of the above is likely to happen. Efforts already underway across the continent—both at the government and popular level—to promote greater accountability and transparency need to be encouraged and pursued with unwavering political commitment. Africa's leaders and people know what should be done and now they need to move forward in putting their houses in order. It will undoubtedly be difficult. It will certainly be chaotic, but it will also be necessary. Political commitment will be required from the international community too. The road to internal reform in Africa and building security will be a long and arduous one that will require patience, persistence, and, most of all, a long-term outlook—things that are, unfortunately, often in short supply.

Conclusion

Through an examination of the broad spectrum of security threats and challenges—from civil conflict and failing states to issues of criminal trafficking, health, and the environment—this book paints a complex picture of the diverse African security landscape and the enormity of the task before African and global leaders. Not all 54 African countries or even the continent's various sub-regions face the same challenges or face them to the same degree, but in all these places Africans are seeking to build more secure and stable societies. Only time will tell if they are successful. Although no one can predict the future with any degree of certainty, the future for Africa and its people will surely be one of both continuity and change. From colonialism to the Cold War and beyond, issues of security have dominated the continent's development and determined its place in the world. So, too, are the opening decades of a new century giving rise to fresh challenges and unresolved problems where Africa will be at the forefront of discovering new solutions to what are increasingly becoming globalized challenges and threats.

Notes

1. National Intelligence Council, *Global Trends 2025: A Transformed World* (Washington: US Government Printing Office, November 2008), p. vii.
2. Times Books, 'Africa', in Times Books, *The Times Comprehensive Atlas of the World* (London: Harper-Collins, 12th edn, 2008).
3. United Nations Department of Economic and Social Affairs, Population Division, *World Population Prospects: The 2012 Revision* (New York: United Nations, 2013), accessed at http://data.un.org on February 22, 2017; CIA, *The World Factbook* (Washington, DC: Central Intelligence Agency), accessed at www.cia.gov/library/publications/the-world-factbook/rankorder on February 22, 2017.
4. United Nations Department of Economic and Social Affairs, Population Division, *Excel Tables—Population Data 2015* (New York: United Nations, 2015), accessed at http://esa.un.org/unpd/wpp/Excell-Data/population.htm on February 22, 2017; J. Campbell, 'This is Africa's new biggest city: Lagos, Nigeria, population 21 million', *The Atlantic* (July 10, 2012), accessed at www.cia.gov/library/publications/the-world-factbook/rankorder on February 22, 2017.
5. World Bank, 'Gross domestic product 2015', *World Development Indicators Database* (October 2016), accessed at http://databank.worldbank.org/data/download/GDP.pdf on February 22, 2017.
6. International Monetary Fund, 'Debt relief under the heavily indebted poor countries (HIPC) initiative', *International Monetary Fund Factsheet*

(February 2010), accessed at www.imf.org/external/np/exr/facts/hipc.htm on February 22, 2017.
7. United Nations, 'Under-five mortality rankings', *UNData*, accessed at http://data.un.org on February 22, 2017.
8. OECD, 'Development aid rose in 2009 and most donors will meet 2010 aid targets', *Financing for Sustainable Development* (Development Co-operation Directorate, 14 April 2010), accessed at www.oecd.org/document/0,3445,en_2649_34447_44981579_1_1_1_1,00.html on February 22, 2017.
9. National Public Radio, 'Documenting the paradox of oil, poverty in Nigeria', *Weekend Edition Sunday* (July 6, 2008), accessed at www.npr.org/templates/story/story.php?storyId=92155119 on February 22, 2017.
10. *Vanguard*, 'Nigeria: country's per capita income drops, now $2,748' (February 15, 2010).
11. Human Security Resource Centre, *Human Security Report 2005* (New York: Oxford University Press, 2005), p. 4.
12. D. Hillier, 'Africa's missing billions: International arms flows and the cost of conflict', *Oxfam.org Briefing Paper* (International Action Network on Small Arms, Oxfam International and SaferWorld, October 11, 2007), pp. 1 and 9, accessed at www.oxfam.org/sites/www.oxfam.org/files/africas%20missing%20bils.pdf on February 22, 2017.
13. Fund for Peace, *The Failed States Index 2006*, accessed at http://fsi.fundforpeace.org/rankings-2006-sortable on February 22, 2017.
14. Fund for Peace, *Fragile State Index 2016*, accessed at http://fsi.fundforpeace.org/rankings-2016 on February 22, 2017.
15. Freedom House, 'Global erosion of freedom', *Freedom in the World 2010*, accessed at www.freedomhouse.org/report/freedom-world/freedom-world-2010 on February 22, 2017.
16. *Washington Post*, 'Around the world, freedom is in peril' (July 5, 2010); A. Puddington, 'Freedom in retreat: Is the tide turning?' *Freedom in the World 2008*, p. 10, accessed at https://freedomhouse.org/report/freedom-world-2008/essay-freedom-retreat on February 22, 2017.
17. J. Cilliers, 'Terrorism and Africa', *African Security Review* 12:4 (2003), 101.
18. UN Office on Drugs and Crime, *Transnational Organized Crime in the West African Region* (New York: United Nations Publication, 2005), p. iii.
19. United Nations, 'Illicit small arms trade in Africa fuels conflict, contributes to poverty, stalls development', *United Nations Information Service DC/3032* (June 27, 2006).
20. *The Telegraph (UK)*, 'Revealed: How Saharan caravans of cocaine help to fund Al Qaeda in terrorists' North African domain' (January 26, 2013); *Forbes.com*, 'The secret of Al Qaeda in Islamic Maghreb Inc.: A resilient (and highly illegal) business model' (December 12, 2013), accessed at www.forbes.com/sites/kerryadolan/2013/12/16/the-secret-of-al-qaeda-in-islamic-maghreb-inc-a-resilient-and-highly-illegal-business-model/ on February 22, 2017; *allAfrica.com*, 'North Africa: AQIM partners with

Colombian drug cartel' (December 5, 2014), accessed at http://allafrica.com/stories/201412060088.html on February 22, 2017.
21 UNAIDS, 'Global HIV statistics', *UNAIDS Fact Sheet* (November 2016), accessed at www.unaids.org/sites/default/files/media_asset/UNAIDS_Fact Sheet_en.pdf on February 22, 2017.
22 *The Oxford Essential Quotations Dictionary—American Edition* (New York: Berkley Books, 1998), p. 88.
23 J. Cilliers, *Conflict trends in Africa: A turn for the better in 2015?* (Institute for Security Studies, November 4, 2015), accessed at www.issafrica.org/iss-today/conflict-trends-in-africa-a-turn-for-the-better-in-2015 on February 22, 2017.

2

Thinking about security

Africa, as we have seen, is a very challenging, diverse, and complex security environment, and how the continent achieves security amidst this situation remains one of the most pressing questions of the day. Perspective matters here. How governments, institutions, and societies view the key elements of "security" lie at the heart of this debate. So too is it influenced by Africa's colonial and post-independence history, which has shaped the lives and attitudes of its current leadership. Just, if not more important, is the continent and its people's willingness to embrace new definitions and concepts about the meaning of security in the twenty-first century, because these ideas will ultimately provide a framework for moving forward.

In recent years the human security approach has gained widespread acceptance as the future of security in Africa. Its comprehensive approach and inclusiveness is critical in an increasingly globalized world where the continent plays a greater security role and takes on more responsibilities. While certainly not a panacea for all of Africa or the world's security ills, the debate over human security and its effectiveness goes a long way in advancing our understanding of how best to achieve a better and more secure life for the people of the continent in the decades ahead. In the pages that follow, the evolving Africa security paradigm is explored in light of the diverse and varying threats facing not only the continent, but the greater international community, now and in the decades ahead. In doing so, it seeks to challenge more traditional security constructs, which are deemed woefully inadequate to meet the real security needs of African countries and their citizens in a globalized and interdependent world.

The evolution of security thinking in Africa

Paradoxically, as much as Africa and its current problems are often rooted in the past, the continent today finds itself squarely at the forefront of new security thinking and has become a test bed for innovative approaches and strategies. Africa is clearly changing. Out of necessity its governments, people, and institutions are also being forced into a fundamental reassessment and rethinking of the very nature and meaning of security. Security for whom? And for what? The answers to these types of questions will undoubtedly require breaking away from historical and Western security constructs as the continent struggles to find its own path. It will be a difficult journey and one filled with great obstacles and setbacks. Much of this process, however, is already underway and producing some positive signs, but the ultimate success or failure of Africa's security realignment is likely to be tied directly to a growing global acceptance of an evolving and more expansive view of security, as well as the willingness to employ different tools. Simply doing more of the same is not an option.

The colonial experience
As with a number of current African issues, the colonial legacy has had a direct and profound bearing on the development of African concepts of security and on their relationship with the state and its exercise of power. While the modern colonial era can be traced to the 1884–85 Berlin Conference during the European scramble for Africa, its roots and implications clearly go back several hundred years earlier to the first establishment of European toeholds on the continent. Although largely a byproduct of the Age of Discovery, the creation of coastal European enclaves as way stations to the east and then later to facilitate trade and commerce between Europe and Africa opened the door to a new era in relations between the two continents. Central to this relationship were notions of security and, more to the point, externally imposed perceptions of security that would come to define European-African relations well into the twentieth century.

While the colonial period in Africa has customarily been viewed as an outlet for European imperialist expansion, as well as Europe's search for wealth and new markets, two important characteristics of colonialism—defense of territory and maintaining control—would come to form the crucial underpinnings of colonial involvement on the continent. Moreover, these features would later become the accepted building blocks of African security in the post-independence era. This legacy has helped to create a modern-day peace and security architecture that is largely state-centric and serving the self-interests of political elites, which is directly at odds with the notion of human security.

Flowing out of the Berlin Conference were the de facto principles of effective occupation and control. These formed the basis for establishing colonial territorial claims and thereby defusing potentially explosive situations arising over the intense European competition for colonies in Africa. Although the conference only officially addressed coastal territorial rights, the so-called "hinterland theory" recognized that "a power in possession of coastlands was entitled to claim the exclusive right to exercise political influence for an indefinite distance inland," according to Sir Frederick Lugard's correspondence.[1] This in turn formed the basis for the ensuing scramble in the remaining years of the nineteenth century by European nations eager to establish a physical presence in the interior of the continent. While some effort was made to coopt local African rulers into ceding control of their land, military might was the most commonly wielded tool of colonial expansionism. Whether through French "administrative tours" (long-range military patrols) across the Sahara, British punitive expeditions, or Portuguese pacification programs, the far reaches of the African interior and their indigenous populations fell before the onslaught of European imperialism. By the early years of the twentieth century nearly all of Africa had been neatly carved up among the powers of Europe; only Liberia and Ethiopia maintained any degree of independence.

Once the European nationalistic euphoria of the initial conquest was over, however, the real challenge came in administering and safeguarding these new empires. The harsh economic reality was that these colonies, with few exceptions, were expensive for metropolitan powers to maintain and defend. Securing colonial borders from other European interlopers, establishing even a rudimentary administrative structure, developing a basic economic infrastructure, and ensuring control over often restless new African subjects were costly both in terms of money and manpower. For example, the pride of French colonialism, Algeria, had a colonial budget deficit of 93 million francs in 1910 (about $450 million in today's dollars) and France spent ten times more administering its Saharan territories than it collected in annual taxes.[2] Thus, self-sufficiency and security became the primary order of the day. For colonial administrators this meant the formation of locally recruited colonial armies and native police forces to replace more expensive metropolitan troops and police.

Although the specific style of governance varied from one European power to the next, near absolute power over the daily running of the colony was ultimately vested in the hands of governors-general (or their equivalent) and their senior military commanders on site. This melding of political and military power, moreover, tended to create highly militarized and authoritarian governing structures where the use of force or coercion was seen as essential to ensuring the safety, good order, and security of the colony. The result was an institutionalized culture of state violence that extended across colonial Africa—from the more "benevolent" firm hand of the British in West and East Africa to the outright brutality and cruelty of the Belgians in the Congo, onto the ruthless genocide by the Germans in Southwest Africa. Accordingly, under European colonialism the state itself became the referent of security with its safety and survival being the preeminent concern against any internal or external threat to its continued existence or functioning. Regardless of the colonial power in charge, there was never a question as to how far the state was willing to go to ensure its own security. As a popular colonial saying of the time reflects, "Whatever happens we have the Maxim gun and they [the Africans] do not."[3]

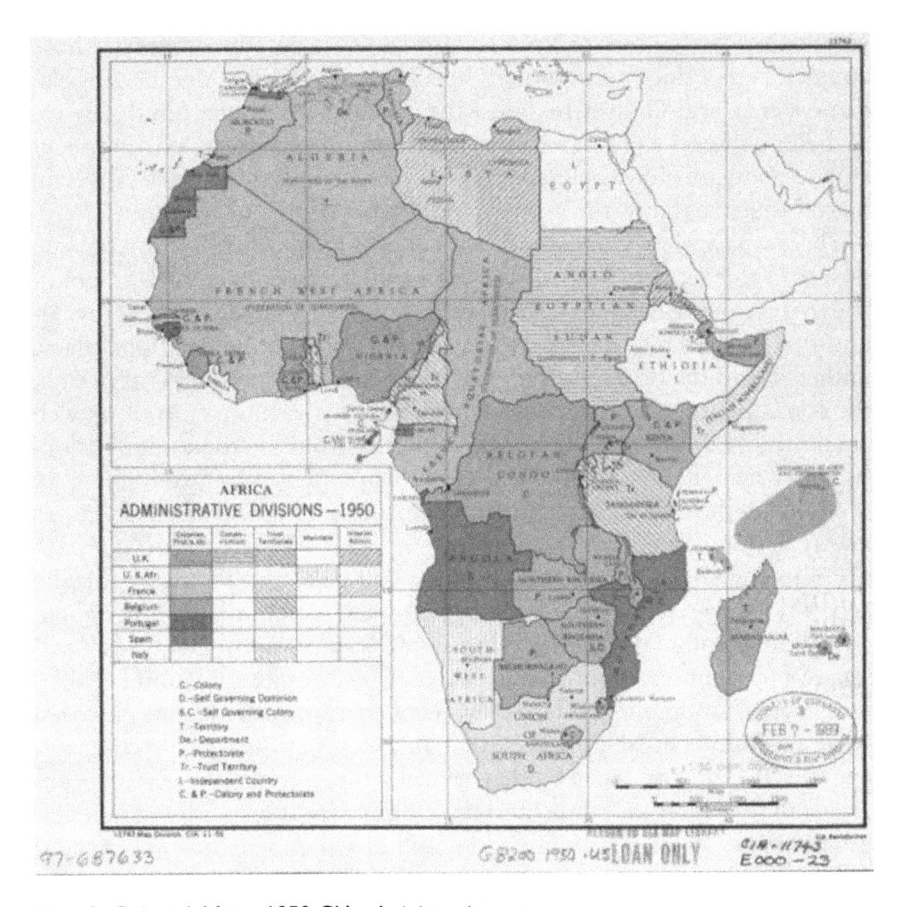

Map 2 Colonial Africa, 1950 CIA administration map

Post-colonialism: from state security to regime security

While the dawn of an independent Africa beginning in the late 1950s brought with it momentous political, social, and economic changes, it did not bring about a fundamental change in the African security construct. The state continued to be viewed as the foci of security. Not only did this model go unchallenged, but the accompanying colonial security apparatus that new African governments inherited at independence was widely accepted lock, stock, and barrel. Ironically, many of the very same security mechanisms used by colonial authorities to suppress African nationalism and imprison its leaders were unquestioningly adopted by the new rulers. Secret police, intelligence organizations, ethnically recruited militaries, and emergency security legislation were to become the new face of African security in the immediate post-independence era. This was especially true for countries such as those in British and French West Africa, East and Central Africa, or the Sudan, which achieved their independence without protracted armed struggles. In contrast, those countries emerging out of violent liberation struggles—Algeria, Angola, Cape Verde and Guinea-Bissau, Mozambique, Namibia, South Africa, and Zimbabwe—were more likely to overhaul or reform existing security structures. Nonetheless, even in these cases there was powerful inertia to leave things the same to maintain a degree of continuity.[4]

There was a very practical side to this continued centralization of state power in the security sector too. For newly independent African countries, overcoming decades or even centuries of deliberate colonial divide-and-rule policies required more than the unveiling of new national flags, anthems, and the other trappings of independence. It required above all, the consolidation of power and control where a vacuum existed, as well as the ability to maintain territorial integrity from the forces of division. In this, the inherited colonial security structures were well suited to accomplish the task through the use of existing administrative structures and type of governance.

Following the euphoria of attaining self-rule, the key task to take center stage was actually creating a nation-state out of highly fragmented and divided colonial societies that, with few exceptions, lacked any real sense of a common heritage, national identity, or unity. Nation building was indeed a monumental task as nascent African governments grappled with a whole host of problems that threatened to tear their countries apart, but that had been hidden beneath the colonial veneer of peace and stability. Internal ethnic and geographic divisions within countries, political and social marginalization, and growing demands for broader political and economic enfranchisement all began to boil to the surface, giving rise to mounting domestic unrest and separatist or irredentist movements. Even a partial list of countries on the verge of imploding shortly after independence is telling: widespread ethnic violence in Nigeria, Rwanda, and Burundi; a secessionist rebellion in southern Sudan and the Congo's Katanga uprising; full-scale civil war in eastern Nigeria; and growing irredentism in southern Senegal's Casamance region and Ethiopia's Ogaden region (the latter of which would escalate into a full-blown insurgency and drag Ethiopia and Somalia into war in the 1970s). To many leaders the harsh remedy to these challenges would appear to lie in the maintenance of a powerful central governmental authority and the unhesitating willingness to unleash the full might of the state against the forces of instability and disintegration.

Exercising centralized political power, let alone control, was easier said than done. The end of colonial rule opened the floodgate of national politics with all sorts of cultural and ethnic associations, religious sects, geographical groupings, workers unions, student groups, and business interests—all of whom were seeking a greater voice and the long anticipated benefits of independence. Political parties and self-promoting politicians mushroomed overnight. And so too did the political chaos that ensued. With more demands on the state than national resources could accommodate, political parties became locked in bitter power struggles and political gridlock soon set in, fueling popular frustration and unrest over government's inability to deliver the anticipated fruits of independence. For the sake of the country and its security, strong action needed to be taken to break these political impasses. Increasingly the solution came in the form of military interventions, which tended to be well-received initially by the population, in ousting unpopular civilian governments. Between 1956 and 1980, African militaries intervened more than 50 times.[5] Military regimes, however, were usually no more successful at governing than their civilian counterparts, leading to a cyclical pattern of alternating military and civilian governments in many African countries.

The other centralized control model came in the form of the one-party state and personalized rule. In the name of promoting national unity and ending divisive politicking, smaller, often geographically or ethnic-based parties were either coopted or coerced into merging with the country's dominant party and its established leadership. This not only led to the institutionalization of the one-party state, but reinforced the personal position of many pre-independence political leaders as head of their party and head of state. Rule in these countries became increasingly personalized. Loyalty to the party (manifest in the form of unwavering allegiance to the party's leader) was equated with loyalty to the state. Accordingly, any opposition to the first was seen as treason against the other. Under this system, power and control came to be concentrated in the hands of the "big men" of Africa: Houphouet-Boigny of the Ivory Coast, Eyadema of Togo, Bongo of Gabon, Mobuto of Zaire, Qadhafi of Libya, Nimeiri of Sudan, and Mugabe of Zimbabwe.

The one-party state's authoritarian model also served to cement the military's relationship with the ruling party, much along the lines of the old political-military alliance of colonial days. African militaries provided the internal security necessary for sustaining these regimes in power and in turn were appropriately rewarded for their loyalty through favorable defense budgets, arms purchases, and inclusion at the top of the social hierarchy. This was even true in some of the most economically impoverished countries that could ill-afford the luxury of devoting scarce resources to the military, because in the end survival of the regime was seen as synonymous with survival of the state.

Rise of the human security paradigm

The ending of the Cold War, the swelling tide of global democratic reform, and the search for a new world order in a drastically changed world energized those calling for a critical review and reevaluation of the fundamental meaning of security. By the mid-1990s this movement had given birth to a novel security perspective grounded in the belief that domestic conflicts, not interstate wars, posed the primary threat to international peace and security. Most future threats and challenges, they claimed, would emanate not from other states, but increasingly from within the states themselves. Moreover, these new threats and challenges were likely to arise from non-traditional sources (like poverty, health, and lack of education) and the growth of powerful non-state actors (such as insurgents, militias, and criminal syndicates) and thus demanded a broadening of the definition of security. For the ordinary citizen this meant that "security symbolized protection from the threat of disease, hunger, unemployment, crime, social conflict, political repression and environmental hazards."[6] This attendant shift in thinking also called for a moving away from a state-centric perspective of security to a new people-centric view of security. "From an exclusive stress on territorial security to a much greater stress on people's security" and "from security through armaments to security through sustainable human development," according to the United Nation's groundbreaking 1994 Human Development Report.[7] Ultimately, the state was no longer "the sole referent of security" and security had become "an all-encompassing condition in which individual citizens live in freedom, peace, and safety and participate fully in the process of governance."[8]

This type of rethinking the meaning of security in an increasingly interdependent and globalized post-Cold War world gave a voice to those seeking to chart a new course for building national security beyond traditional reliance on the state and its institutions and toward empowering broader societal elements to create a more peaceful and secure environment. And thus, the human security paradigm was born. Former UN Secretary-General Kofi Annan summed up this new way of thinking by saying:

> Today, we know that "security" means far more than the absence of conflict. We also have a greater appreciation for nonmilitary sources of conflict. We know that lasting peace requires a broader vision encompassing areas such as education and health, democracy and human rights, protection against environmental degradation, and the proliferation of deadly weapons. We know that we cannot build freedom on the foundations of injustice. These pillars of what we now understand as the people-centered concept of "human security" are interrelated and mutually reinforcing.[9]

Fundamental to the human security paradigm, as Annan noted, is the belief in an expansive and broad definition of security that puts the well-being of a society's people first, over and above the structural needs of the state. "That people should enjoy without discrimination all rights and obligation—including human, political, social, economic and cultural rights—that belonging to a State implies."[10] While acknowledging the necessity of the state to defend territory, maintain public order, and safeguard institutions, proponents of human security believe that this is not enough to secure true security in a modern globalized age. Under this construct, true security of the state rests not with regimes, but with the people. Security of the state and security of its population are inseparable and simply different sides of the same coin. A state can have all the trappings of security, but with the absence of basic human rights—life, liberty, and opportunity—for its citizens, there can be no real security. Human security requires an inclusive and integrated approach to problem solving that utilizes a variety of methods and national stakeholders (especially those outside the traditional security establishment) to produce a peaceful and secure environment. Moreover, the emphasis on broad societal inclusion makes it a highly decentralized and bottom-up process to building security.

Essential to this people-centric pillar of human security is the political and socio-economic empowerment of people and communities so that they can "make informed choices and ... act on their own behalf" to "find new ways to participate in solutions to ensure human security for themselves and others."[11] This bottom-up approach is critical to advancing security, not only by empowering multiple elements of society to assume a greater role in their own security, but also in building state legitimacy through popular engagement and giving people a stake in the system. The latter is especially true when the heretofore marginalized or under-represented segments of society are engaged, and when popular empowerment is combined with the state's traditional role of providing a protective structure: a mutually reinforcing human security mechanism is put in place.

Another major pillar of the human security construct is its interdependent and inter-locking relationship with human development. Poverty alleviation, adequate health care, educational opportunity, and improvement in the general quality of life are not just significant development challenges, but critical security challenges as well. Impoverished and marginalized populations with little hope of a better future are a threat not only to themselves, but also to the greater society in which they reside. Thus, within the context of the human security paradigm, advancements or failures in one are tied to advancements or failures in the other; human development cannot take place without security, and human security does not exist without development. This symbiotic connection is also reflective of the people-centric, bottom-up approach fundamental to creating human security, where the emphasis is on enhancing security at the individual and community levels. Or, more simply put, security is a fundamental component of everyday life and anything that threatens it is a security threat.

This latter point is worth highlighting as it is both a strength and weakness of the human security paradigm. Human security is a broad and all-encompassing construct. "Anything which degrades [people's] quality of life—demographic pressures, diminished access to … resources, and so on—is a security threat" and "anything which can upgrade their quality of life … is an enhancement of human security."[12] According to the United Nations Development Programme, human security encompasses economic security, food security, health security, environmental security, personal security, community security, and political security.[13] This makes it a highly multi-dimensional and complex concept that cuts across many critical issue areas and, as such, is a very utilitarian and multi-disciplinary tool. And this can be overwhelming, say critics.[14] If human security is "about everything," then it is really about nothing and is far too broad a concept that lacks real world context. This is especially true when prioritizing policies and threats, they argue. Not everything can be a priority, and efforts to translate human security principles into successful human security policies have, indeed, been challenging. Nonetheless, its appeal as a useful framework for moving beyond traditional concepts of security continues to grow and multiple countries such as Canada, Japan, Norway, and the United Kingdom now have foreign policies rooted in human security principles.

The post-Cold War security environment has evolved away from large-scale inter-state conflict and conventional threats to national sovereignty toward a world of increasingly globalized, interconnected, and transnational security challenges. These challenges are growing and they are more multi-dimensional and non-traditional than ever before. They threaten not only the stability and existence of the state but of societies themselves. And this, in turn, requires a far-reaching reconceptualization of the meaning of security that is more evocative of this new security environment. The human security paradigm was born of this need.

African security in theory and practice

In the human security construct, many African governments, regional organizations, communities, and individuals found not only a theoretical framework for redefining the meaning of security, but also a practical roadmap for addressing the continent's current and emerging challenges in a post-Cold War world. While not without its shortcomings, this construct has proven its worth in providing a useful way forward for those who have embraced it. That the implementation of human security in Africa will continue to evolve into its own unique character is without question, just how this evolution takes places remains to be seen.

Political buy-in

For Africans this new view of security was a welcome breath of fresh air. It redirected the focus of security away from an association with propping up colonialism, rationalizing regime security, or excusing military and authoritarian rule. Moreover, it signaled the opportunity to make a clear break with the past. The concept of security was shifting beyond the state to the people, where many long believed the answers to the continent's security challenges reside. Likewise, in moving away from a more traditional and narrow view of security, there was widespread optimism that practical solutions to many of Africa's problems could be found—problems that the state-centric approach to security had proved incapable or unwilling to address. Not surprisingly, Africans have been at the forefront of implementing human security principles to address the continent's existing and emerging challenges.

Beyond simply calling for a shift away from the state's preeminent role in security, reform of the state itself became a central theme of those pushing a human security approach in Africa. It called for a break with the past model that equated the state's ability to exercise control over its people with effective security. This was especially relevant for Africans given the often repressive nature of the state in fueling or sustaining internal conflict rather than mitigating it. Thus, in the view of human security advocates, the state itself can present one of the most serious threats to the nation's peace and safety. Weak African states, in particular, often resort to extra-legal measures to gain and/or retain political power. According to Cilliers, "Indeed, internal repression by governments is a greater cause of human suffering and abuse than any other."[15] Flawed governance, corruption, political marginalization, and lack of transparency all need to be effectively addressed to achieve a measure of societal security. Accordingly, the type and nature of state involvement in the security sector was just as, if not more, important than its capability to exercise control and defend territory. While the state certainly has a vital role to play in ensuring national security it must be an accountable one, working in harmony with the society as a whole.

From this theoretical perspective the nation's security was no longer the exclusive preserve of the military and other traditional security services. Representatives of the people in the form of grassroots organizations, community leaders, civil society groups, non-governmental organizations (NGOs), political parties, and other non-traditional security-related governmental departments (such as health, education, and development) needed to play a part too. Thus, greater public participation in the security sector is essential—making the state "part of a dynamic and seamless policy network" that works to achieve a "common objective of promoting human security."[16] This, however, would require a fundamental realignment of the state and an opening of the political process that is easier said than done in Africa, as we shall see.

While commonly seen in the West as part of the wider academic debate over the future meaning of security in the post-Cold War era,[17] the human security model resonates in Africa largely because of its practical application in tackling a whole host of seemingly intractable problems—such as ethnic violence, failing states, and extremism, which have eluded traditional security approaches and mechanisms—as well as its potential to address new and emerging non-traditional and transnational security challenges of the twenty-first century.

The marked decline in Africa since 1999 of inter-state armed conflict[18]—and with it the traditional external threat to state sovereignty—signaled a turning point for African governments and institutions because it brought to light a wide variety of existing and emerging problems that they were ill-equipped or incapable of handling. Doing more of the same to address this new security environment was simply not an option. Moreover, as the preeminent security organ of the state, African militaries were now expected to assume a diverse set of new roles, from peacekeeping and counterterrorism to crime prevention, humanitarian assistance, and protecting the natural environment—all tasks which militaries were rarely trained, equipped, or structured to perform. With most African countries already hamstrung by limited resources, the security capability gap was bound to widen even further with the addition of these new responsibilities, unless other actors and mechanisms were brought to bear. With the human security construct Africans found a useful tool to engage other elements and sectors of society to meet this challenge. All has not been plain sailing though, as governments under pressure from rising threats find themselves increasingly drawn back to a more traditional state security approach.

The implementation challenge
Even with strong political buy-in and a useful conceptual framework, the road to effective implementation across the continent has been a difficult one, largely because of resource constraints, conflicting international and/or domestic priorities, overdependence on militaries, and faltering democratic and security sector reform efforts.

Resource constraints
There are not enough domestic, regional, or international resources to address all of the continent's security challenges effectively. Resource constraints are a reality of Africa—both present and future. There will never be enough money, equipment, expertise, or training available to go around. Finding ways to implement human security initiatives in a heavily resource-constrained environment is one of the most pressing challenges facing African governments, sub-regional and regional organizations, and the international community. And most important, simply having "more" (i.e. money, equipment, expertise, or training) is not the answer. Finding better and more effective ways to utilize the resources available is paramount, which is no easy task, and many solutions have significant unintended consequences.

For example, the expansion of human capital inputs in the form of greater popular participation and engagement of civil society has been beneficial in terms of addressing socio-economic security challenges, such as poverty, chronic food shortages, infectious diseases and malnutrition, environmental degradation, identity conflict, and the repression of human rights. Nonetheless, these efforts have generally not been accompanied by increased budgets. There are some notable exceptions of course, particularly in the health arena with respect to HIV/AIDS and anti-malaria programs, but domestic spending and international assistance has not kept pace with this heightened level of engagement. Despite pledging to commit 15 percent of their annual budgets to health care spending to achieve health-related Millennium Development Goals in 2001, only four African countries have succeed, while 30 countries spend less than 10 percent, according to a recent study.[19] Moreover, "a number of countries [in 2010] allocate a lower proportion of their budgets to healthcare" than before 2001.[20] Thus, the existing finite pool of resources now has to be shared up among a growing number of actors, stretching limited resources even further.

Likewise, by seeking to address security threats in a comprehensive and holistic manner—a key principle of human security approach—prioritization becomes exceedingly difficult. Stemming ethnic conflict may be the goal, for instance, but addressing underlying structural problems of resource competition, migration patterns, political disenfranchisement, or poverty make resource prioritization a Herculean task. Who gets what and how much? Where and when should scarce resources be allocated? How is coordination handled and how are responsibilities defined? These are all critical questions that need to be answered as a strategy is put in place. In a heavily resource-constrained environment like Africa the margin for error is a terribly unforgiving one.

Conflicting priorities

Ironically, the substantial financial and technical engagement of foreign governments, international organizations, and NGOs often complicates implementation and hinders strategic planning. Their engagement is a double-edged sword. Foreign actors may have conflicting security priorities or agendas that are at odds with recipient countries. This foreign assistance can come with strong strings attached that leave little flexibility and may undercut or distort an existing strategy. Unfortunately, this can create the all too typical situation in Africa of "if you funded it, we will do it," the Western emphasis on counterterrorism in recent years being a prime example.

Even where there is general agreement between donors and recipients concerning priorities, the external assistance may be too heavily focused on a single issue or interest. Take, for instance, advancing health security. The United States has spent nearly $50 billion since 2003 or about $3.7 billion per year to help fight HIV/AIDS in Africa with great success.[21] Deaths have decreased by almost 60 percent since their peak to less than 800,000 per year in 2015, according to the World Health Organization.[22] In contrast, however, the United States spends just over $220 million per year—6 percent of HIV/AIDS spending—to promote access to clean water, improve hygiene, and fight preventable water-borne disease in Africa.[23] This despite the fact that water-related diseases and poor sanitation are responsible for 3.4 million deaths worldwide (the bulk in Africa and Asia) each year and that diarrheal diseases are one of the leading causes of death for children under five in Africa.[24]

Likewise, domestic politics, internal divisions, and poor governance can also distort strategic planning and the setting of national priorities. Human security programs, no matter how well conceived, are not immune to the give and take of domestic politics, or to graft and corruption. This can often bring about poorly thought-out, conflicting, underfunded, or unsustainable initiatives that are motivated more by political or economic factors than in advancing human security objectives. Poor governance, lack of transparency, and outright corruption can make a bad situation even worse when it comes to setting priorities. And this can be especially damaging where national resources are severely constrained.

The case of the 1999 South African arms deal is a prime example. While controversy continues to surround senior government officials, the African National Congress (ANC) party, and foreign suppliers in the awarding and terms of contracts under the $4.8 billion Strategic Defence Package nearly two decades later, the focus here is on the strategic disconnect between the ground-breaking 1996 White Paper on National Defence and the political decision to move forward on the arms deal in the first place. This first post-apartheid White Paper recognized "the profound political and strategic consequences of the ending of apartheid" and that the government's priority was one of "addressing poverty and socioeconomic inequalities" through the Reconstruction and Development Programme, which "stands at the pinnacle of national policy and, consequently, defence policy."[25] The document was laced with human security references, acknowledging "a reorientation of thinking on 'security' and 'threats to security' ... [as] the non-military dimensions of security have gained prominence."[26] It identified a range of non-military threats to the country in the form of "personal insecurity and social instability," endemic crime, and continuing criminal and social violence, as well as those sub-regional threats in the form of "environmental destruction, the spread of disease, the burden of refugees, and cross-border trafficking in drugs, stolen goods and small arms."[27] Importantly, the White Paper concluded that "the absence of a foreseeable conventional military threat provides considerable space to rationalize, redesign and 'rightsize' the SANDF [South African National Defence Force]."[28]

Thus, it came as a surprise to many defense analysts and social advocates when the South African government approved the purchase of

R30 billion worth of ships, submarines, helicopters, and fighter aircraft in November 1998. As one social activist involved in the Defence Review noted, "We argued that poverty eradication through massive public investment in education, health, housing and job creation was post-apartheid South Africa's priority, not more weapons for a country that had no conceivable foreign military threat."[29] The decision also came at a time when ANC party leaders claimed the country could not afford to provide the anti-retroviral drug AZT to tens of thousands of HIV-positive pregnant mothers.[30] Clearly there was a serious strategic disconnect between the threat environment described in the White Paper and the conventional military tools being purchased as the means to address these threats. Just as clear is the power of domestic political and economic factors to reshape the human security agenda into something far removed from its original objectives.

Overdependence on the military

Despite the strong political buy-in and widespread support for implementing human security initiatives across the continent, African governments and institutions are still overly dependent on militaries to achieve their goals. This also reflects, in our view, a subconscious traditional mindset that continues to see state-centric tools as the most effective means of building security. (The same criticism also applies to many Western governments—notably the United States—as we shall see later on.)

Historically, African militaries are usually the strongest and best resourced institution in most countries. Even as the threat of interstate conflict has declined markedly, military spending on equipment and training has soared since 2004. Algeria's defense budget hit $10 billion in 2014 and Angola's increased by more than one-third in 2013 to $6 billion, overtaking South Africa as the largest in sub-Saharan Africa.[31] Two out of three African countries have substantially increased their military spending, with military expenditures growing by 65 percent since 2001, according to data from the International Peace Research Institute.[32] Thus, it is natural for governments to turn to them not only for their security expertise, but also for their resource capability.

This situation creates a Catch-22 for implementing human security. The more governments and African institutions rely on militaries to advance security, the fewer resources are available to non-traditional security actors, and so their effectiveness declines. As these non-traditional actors become less capable, governments increasingly turn to their militaries. Thus, the belief that militaries are the only real effective security tool becomes a self-fulfilling prophecy. This is not to say that

African militaries haven't changed and increased their non-conventional capabilities. They have. More so than ever, African soldiers, sailors, and airmen are engaged in unilateral and multilateral counterterrorism, peacekeeping and stability, and humanitarian operations. They are actively involved in building roads, protecting the environment, fighting criminal networks, and supporting local health care efforts. Nonetheless, this begs the central question: Are they the best tool for the job? Moreover, if the human security approach requires facilitating individual and community involvement from the bottom up then this level of top-down military dependency is likely to prove counterproductive.

Faltering democratic and security sector reform
The democratic reform movement and the push for greater political inclusiveness that began in the 1990s have been instrumental in stoking the fires of human security initiatives and security sector reform in general. But momentum has slowed in recent years and much of this progress is in danger of being reversed. Freedom House reports the number of African countries it identifies as "Not Free" rose from 35 percent to 43 percent from 2006 to 2016, reflecting the slide downward by several countries previously listed as "Partly Free."[33] Democratic setbacks and political violence have occurred in Burundi, Congo, Rwanda, and Uganda recently, as leaders manipulate term limits to remain in power; and across parts of North Africa where popular frustration lingers over the failure of the 2011 Arab Spring to bring about drastic changes to dysfunctional regimes. Likewise, the battle against militant Islamists and efforts to counter the spread of global jihadist incursions into Africa have resulted in heavy-handed government crackdowns in places like Egypt, Ethiopia, and Kenya, which undermine individual freedoms and rights.[34] In 2016 half of the bottom 12 countries with the worst aggregated scores for political rights and civil liberties were found in Africa.[35]

The persistent threat of violent Islamic extremism and sub-regional instability, along with an Arab Spring backlash shows no signs of abating anytime soon. This, in turn, has led to a growing number of governments reverting to an authoritarian focus on regime security and away from the inclusionary principles of human security. Moreover, the West's preoccupation with advancing its counterterrorism agenda in Africa has signaled its tacit acquiescence to this shift, which often comes at the expense of promoting democratic reforms and human rights. Security sector reform suffers too, because civil society groups and NGOs find it increasingly difficult to question government counterterrorism programs or see a role for themselves in these new security initiatives. The result is a further reallocation of resources back toward traditional security actors like the military, police, and intelligence services.

Conclusion

Still coping with the legacy of widespread insecurity and violence during the Cold War, the continent now finds itself struggling under the weight of the added burden of an entirely new set of globalized, non-traditional security challenges. With most African countries already crippled by limited resources and capacity, the security capability gap is bound to widen with the addition of these challenges unless other actors and mechanisms are brought to bear. This will require an overhauling of traditional definitions and ways of thinking about security.

In the human security construct African governments have found such a framework to do just that. By bringing together a broad spectrum of stakeholders into the security sector, for the first time governments are able to: expand their human resource base beyond the military and security services; tap into expertise in non-traditional security areas, such as health delivery, public education, and agricultural development; and better develop and coordinate a comprehensive national strategy for tackling their country's problems. Moreover, this approach holds out the prospect of making more effective and efficient use of the limited resources at hand. In addition to having better capability to deal with the broad array of emerging security threats in Africa, the new security paradigm has the distinct advantage of directly linking development with security. National development was not simply a by-product of national security, but at its very essence an indispensable feature of human security itself. Thus, economic opportunity, poverty alleviation, educational advancement, and an improved quality of life were not the result of national security, but key elements upon which that security was built.

While the human security construct has not proved to be the Holy Grail in solving all the problems of a long suffering continent, it certainly has brought about a rethinking of the real meaning of security in an increasingly globalized world. It has also expanded opportunities for popular participation in such a critical arena that was long the sanctum of a privileged few. In gaining widespread acceptance as the way forward in Africa, human security principles are helping to redefine the role of the state and providing new hope to a continent struggling to achieve peace and security for its people in the face of monumental challenges.

One thing, however, is becoming apparent: Africa will no longer be simply a mere setting for others' security challenges, but increasingly will become a significant factor in driving global security requirements itself.

Notes

1 R. Brooke-Smith, *The Scramble for Africa* (Basingstoke: Macmillan Education, 1987), p. 43.
2 D. Porch, *The Conquest of the Sahara* (New York: Fromm International, 1986), p. 8.
3 Hilaire Belloc, *The Modern Traveller*, cited in *The Oxford Essential Quotations Dictionary—American Edition* (New York: Berkley Books, 1998), p. 343.
4 In a stranger instance of this, Ken Flower, the head of Rhodesian intelligence and many of his white staff went on to serve under Robert Mugabe—a man they had tried to assassinate on several occasions—following Zimbabwean independence in 1980.
5 P. McGowan, 'African military coups d'etat, 1956–2001: Frequency, trends and distribution', *Journal of Modern African Studies*, 41:3 (2003), 351.
6 United Nations Development Programme, *Human Development Report 1994* (New York: Oxford University Press, 1994), p. 22.
7 Ibid., p. 24.
8 Commission on Human Security, *Human Security Now* (New York: Commission on Human Security, 2003), p. 3.
9 R. McRae and D. Hubert, *Human Security and the New Diplomacy: Protecting People, Promoting Peace* (Montreal: McGill-Queen's University Press, 2001), pp. xix–xx.
10 S. Ogata, 'Inclusion or exclusion: Social development challenges for Asia and Europe' (Statement of Mrs Sadako Ogata, U.N. High Commissioner for Refugees at the Asian Development Bank, April 27, 1998), accessed at www.unhcr.ch/refworld/unhcr/hcspeech/27ap1998.htm on February 23, 2017.
11 Human Security Unit, *Human Security in Theory and Practice* (New York: United Nations Trust Fund for Human Security, 2009), p. 7.
12 R. Thakur, 'From national to human security', in S. Harris and A. Mack (eds) *Asia-Pacific Security* (Sydney: Allen & Unwin, 1997), p. 54.
13 United Nations Development Programme, *Human Development Report 1994*, pp. 24–5.
14 See, for example, S. Fukuda-Parr and C. Messineo, 'Human security: A critical review of the literature', *CRPD Working Paper No. 11* (January 2012), accessed at https://soc.kuleuven.be/web/files/12/80/wp11.pdf on February 23, 2017; R. Christie, 'Critical voices and human security', *Security Dialogue* 41:2 (April 2010), 169–90; T. Owen, 'Human security—conflict, critique and consensus', *Security Dialogue* 35:3 (September 2004), 373–87.
15 J. Cilliers, *Human Security in Africa: A Conceptual Framework for Review* (Pretoria: African Human Security Initiative, 2004), p. 11.

16 S. Tadjbakhsh and A. Chenoy, *Human Security: Concepts and Implications* (New York: Routledge, 2007), p. 238.
17 W. Dorn, 'Human security: An overview' (Paper prepared for the Pearson Peacekeeping Centre, undated), accessed at http://walterdorn.net/23-human-security-an-overview on February 23, 2017.
18 Human Security Report Project, *Human Security Report 2013* (Vancouver: Human Security Press, 2013), p. 3, accessed at www.hsrgroup.org/human-security-reports/2013/text.aspx on February 23, 2017.
19 KPMG Africa, 'Expenditure on healthcare in Africa' (December 12, 2012), accessed at www.blog.kpmgafrica.com/expenditure-on-healthcare-in-africa/ on February 23, 2017.
20 Ibid.
21 President's Emergency Plan for AIDS Relief website, 'PEPFAR funding' accessed at www.pepfar.gov/documents/organization/252516.pdf on February 23, 2017.
22 World Health Organization, 'Number of deaths due to HIV/AIDS', *Global Health Observatory*, accessed at www.who.int/gho/hiv/epidemic_status/deaths_text/en/ on February 23, 2017.
23 United States Agency for International Development, *Fiscal Year 2014: Safeguarding the World's Water* (Washington, DC: USAID, July 2015), p. 8.
24 *Voice of America*, 'WHO: Waterborne disease is world's leading killer' (October 29, 2009); World Health Organization, 'Children—reducing mortality' *Fact Sheet* (January 2016), accessed at www.who.int/mediacentre/factsheets/fs178/en/ on February 23, 2017.
25 South African Department of Defence, 'White paper on national defence for the Republic of South Africa' (May 1996), accessed at www.dod.mil.za/documents/WhitePaperonDef/whitepaper%20on%20defence1996.pdf on February 23, 2017.
26 Ibid.
27 Ibid.
28 Ibid.
29 T. Crawford-Browne, *ECAAR-SA Annual Report* (November 17, 2011), accessed at http://accountabilitynow.org.za/ecaar-sa-annual-report-terry-crawford-browne/ on February 23, 2017.
30 *AVERT*, 'History of HIV/AIDS in South Africa', accessed at http://hivsa.com/?q=content/hiv-aids-south-africa on February 23, 2017.
31 *The Economist*, 'Arms and the African' (November 23, 2014).
32 Ibid.
33 Freedom House, *Freedom in the World 2006* and *Freedom in the World 2016*, accessed at https://freedomhouse.org/report/freedom-world/freedom-world-2006 and https://freedomhouse.org/report/freedom-world/freedom-world-2016 on February 23, 2017.
34 Ibid., p. 11.
35 Ibid., p. 4.

3

Identity conflict

A basic feature of the universal human condition is the need to find commonality with others and form larger associations at the individual, group, and community level, and this is at the heart of the concept of identity. A variety of factors, ranging from physical attributes, language, and culture to societal norms and structures work to promote a self-awareness and self-consciousness of sameness with a larger collective. A significant positive benefit resulting from this shared identity is the ability to provide protection and security against outside threats. It can also, however, create the basis for an "us" against "them" type of mentality whereby anything emanating from outside the group's shared identity is automatically viewed with suspicion or seen as a potential threat.

Probably nowhere else in the world is group identity—be it ethnic, racial, religious, sectarian, or communal—so closely associated with persistent, and even genocidal, violence than in Africa. "Over half of the top twenty countries in the world where people are most under threat of genocide or mass killing are in Africa," noted the Minority Rights Group International in 2008.[1] And high-profile events would appear to confirm this assessment: Rwanda 1994, Darfur 2003, Kenya 2008, Nigeria 2010, the CAR in 2013–14, Ethiopia in 2016, and South Sudan 2013–present. But is Africa really so different? Is there something inherently unique to the continent or the African experience that makes it so seemingly vulnerable to this type of violence? More importantly, can anything be done to eliminate this long-standing threat to peace and security?

The often patronizing response by many outsider observers is that all conflict in Africa is tribal or that "tribal conflicts are fragmenting Africa's nations" with the unspoken acceptance that identity-related violence is simply a way of life.[2] "It is Africa, after all," so goes the common refrain. This dismissive and simpleminded view not only ignores the complex nature of African conflict, but excuses the political and economic culpability critical to fueling and sustaining the problem of ethnic, racial, religious, sectarian, or communal violence across the continent. More to the point, the world at large has witnessed a significant upsurge in identity conflict in recent decades—from the Balkans of the 1990s to the current reminders in the central Asian republics of the former Soviet Union, India, Iraq, and even China. Everything old is now new again. The reality is that demographic pressures, rapid globalization, and increasing competition for scarce resources are breathing new life into identity conflict, not just in Africa but around the globe. What makes Africa especially vulnerable to this type of security challenge, however, is not the intensity or pervasiveness of these types of conflicts, but rather the difficulties African countries have in defusing this type of violence through the creation of effective conflict resolution mechanisms.

The African context: the role and importance of identity

On the surface the concept of identity in Africa may appear to be quite straight forward. However, decades of research have shown it to be multifaceted, often ambiguous, and the product of competing (and frequently contradictory) social and historical forces.[3] Most of all, identity in Africa is not fixed or static, but is a dynamic concept that is directly tied to the political, social, economic, and historical development of the continent and its people. While certainly not without controversy, understanding the importance and role of key elements of identity are essential prerequisites to exploring the roots of identity conflict in Africa today and its implications for security.

In the African experience, identity has served as both a survival and self-protection mechanism, first within rural society and later within an urban setting. Although great cities, city-states, and even large empires were a significant feature of pre-colonial African history, the continent remained primarily rural and sparsely populated. Small, scattered, and generally isolated populations were a defining characteristic of the pre-colonial period. The unit of identity for most Africans was first and foremost the family, followed by kinship ties, and then the village. These relationships not only helped to define individuals and their place in society, but also acted as a safety net in times of famine or provided a ready defensive mechanism when faced with an external threat. With some notable exceptions, such as the trans-Sahara caravan trade, Islamic pilgrimage routes across West Africa or the trading coastal communities of East Africa, contact with, or knowledge of, the outside world was highly limited. Thus, identity in the pre-colonial era tended to be a very narrowly defined and personalized concept that was highly localized and independent of the larger world outside the village environs.

All this began to change with the onset of European colonialism that began in earnest in the nineteenth century. The resulting growing contact with a world outside the village, economically driven population shifts to nascent urban areas, and the rise of new European and African centers of trade, wealth, and power produced a greater awareness of differences. Colonial authorities for their part too contributed to changing notions of African identity through their simplistic efforts to make sense of complex and diverse African societal relationships by streamlining and 'inventing' new versions of identity to align with their administrative policies. "It was only under European colonial rule that ... introduced the concept of individual, personal identity, together with its collective counterparts, culturally and linguistically distinct tribes and nations," according to Carola Lentz.[4] A good example of this in practice was the "uniting" of various distinct and independent groups in southwest Nigeria by British colonial authorities to produce a new "Yoruba identity"—something that heretofore had not existed. Likewise, African elites, eager to maintain (or even expand) their position and power, often became willing tools in this endeavor by reinterpreting traditions, customs, and even history to align with the colonial perspective of African identity. This was especially true in British governed colonies, whose use of indirect rule necessitated the existence of an African administrative structure built largely along identity lines.* The end result was an increasingly fluid and adaptive concept of African identity that was to become a powerful tool of political manipulation and mobilization, first by colonial rulers and later by post-independence leaders.

Ethnicity
Even after more than five decades of highly publicized debate by everyone from anthropologists, sociologists, and psychologists to political scientists, civil leaders, and politicians over the meaning (and even

---

* "Indirect rule" (more common in British-ruled Africa) refers to the use of existing, or sometimes reinvented, local African structures and leaders by European colonial administers to govern their colonies. This contrasted sharply with the system of "direct rule" (more common in French- or Portuguese-ruled Africa), which was a highly centralizing style of colonial administration. Here European colonial officers were directly responsible for governing territory and people, and overseeing all services down to the lowest levels of administration either personally or with the assistance of their handpicked local African surrogates. In practice the two administrative styles often overlapped and most colonies experienced a mixture of both approaches during colonial rule.

existence) of ethnicity in Africa, the concept remains one of the most highly charged, divisive, and controversial aspects of discussions of identity. It also, nonetheless, lies at the heart of identity conflict today and is an indispensable element of any discussion or analysis of the subject. Moreover, it continues to capture the attention of the outside world and the international media that too often views the continent's security problems as rooted in ancient hatred manifesting itself as primeval "tribalism."

But what then really is "ethnicity?" And what role does it play today in defining identity for Africans?[5] A useful starting point in answering these questions might begin with what ethnicity is or is not. Ethnicity is not a primordial or natural trait of people or social groups. It is not predetermined nor is it permanent, but "multi-layered ... situational, circumstantial and contingent."[6] It is not "an essentialist attribute of the African," but simply one part of African identity.[7] Although anchored in a common culture, language, and kinship structures, ethnicity today is not a prescriptive element of identity that exists independently of local historiographies and external forces. Nor is it the historical remnant of African traditional societies' failure to modernize. Moreover, it is not a static concept that operates within clearly defined social and geographic boundaries, but is an evolving part of individual and group identity responding and adapting to both positive and negative change. As Crawford Young astutely noted, "Ethnicity is ultimately experienced, performed, and enacted by individuals who have a range of choice."[8] Most of all ethnic identity is not the same as tribal identity—a rural-based identity centered on small, simply organized, genealogical groupings who share a common ancestry that owe personal allegiance to an individual leader. Ethnicity, however, is often manipulated to maintain or secure power and wealth. John Lonsdale calls this ethnic manipulation "political tribalism," which he defines as "the instrumental use of ethnic identity in political competition with other groups." And he goes on to point out that "ethnicity is always with us," but "tribalism is contingent upon political intention and context."[9]

Then what exactly is the meaning of ethnicity in today's Africa? First and foremost, despite all its flaws and ambiguity ethnicity is a significant—and often powerful—element of social identity that creates an "us versus them" frame of reference for both individuals and groups. It has a distinctly urban appeal, yet it exists in rural areas as well. Throughout the continent it exists in varying degrees, waning and waxing as to time, place, and context. Thus, it is an extremely malleable and constantly evolving form of identity that is highly situational with respect to location, events, and needs. Ethnic identity also is not homogenous nor tightly confined, but rather spills over into other aspects of social identity, such as religion, occupation, or geographic location, which are part of multiple and overlapping individual and group networks. Although externally imposed perceptions of African identity, colonial policies, and labor migration patterns nurtured the rise of modern-day ethnicity, it now has a distinctly African character that is just as much shaped by internal forces as the outside world.

As a modern concept ethnicity fulfills several important roles and functions, such as serving basic individual needs, mobilizing people, allocating group power and resources, and as a forum for building political accountability that have a direct bearing on African identity and conflict.

First, it provides a mechanism through kinship structures for meeting the basic needs of people that the state either failed to provide under colonialism or has been largely incapable of providing since independence. These often complex modern-day relationships give the individual "a clear identity ... from which he expects his basic security needs to be met," according to Peter Ekeh,[10] who goes on to list these needs as protection against violence, socialization and the raising of children, social welfare of the individual and family, and funeral and burials (which includes care for those left behind).[11] This is especially important in urban settings where newly arriving economic migrants find themselves in strange and often confusing cosmopolitan settings. They are far removed from their familiar and established support networks, yet these new migrants are in need of securing some measure of safety and security. Ethnicity through extended kinship networks often helps to fill this void. Moreover, it helps bolster an association, even if subconsciously, between one's ethnic identity and their own personal or group security.

Second, even with its sometimes artificial and transit character, ethnicity remains an extremely powerful mobilization tool. Its ready-made structure with strong internal linkages, and common sense of identity and purpose, as well as the ability to reward loyalty, facilitate mass and rapid mobilization by ethnic elites. Paradoxically, ethnic mobilization has both the power to unite, as well as to divide. Critically, as Chabal and Daloz underscore, is that "the political significance of ethnicity is thus *almost wholly a function of the circumstances* in which the question of such an affiliation becomes more salient."[12] On the one hand it can serve as a rallying point for the building of a common and larger group consciousness by otherwise disjointed communities and has been employed as a nation-building tool. Ethnic identity was able to provide a measure of surrogate political identity, such as with the Wolof in Senegal or the Kikuyu in Kenya, in the run up to independence.[13] On the other hand ethnicity can be divisive, pitting one group against the other and stoking the fires of a zero-sum competition for scarce national resources. While the inherently competitive "us versus them" nature of ethnicity isn't necessarily bad for society, its radicalization by political leaders can unleash the dark side of ethnicity. Political tribalism fueled by fear, ignorance, and propaganda can easily explode into a genocidal violence of the most base kind. One does not have to look far for examples: Biafra 1967–70, Zimbabwe's Matabeleland 1983–84, Rwanda 1994, and Zaire/DRC 1993–2003.

In the absence of (or sometimes in spite of) effective political mechanisms for distributing power and resources within a society, competing ethnically defined patronage networks function as an alternative allocation system. This concrete ability to reward loyalty to the group through patronage politics is a key underpinning of ethnicity's popular appeal. The rewards may be quite tangible, such as government business contracts or government jobs, or they could be more symbolic, like the elevation to a prominent cultural position within the group. While these types of client-patron relationships have long been an established feature of African society, it is the over aggressive pursuit of power and resources for one's own group by ethnic entrepreneurs—whatever the consequences for other groups or the state—that is the driving force of political tribalism.[14] And where there is political tribalism, there is sure to be ethnic conflict.

Finally, although initially used as a tool of colonial control and administration, ethnicity has come to be seen as a highly useful means of enforcing political accountability and legitimacy on those who govern or who seek to represent the interests of their ethnic constituency. This "moral ethnicity", as termed by Lonsdale, sees ethnicity as forming the basis of a social contract between ethnics and their representatives.[15] Loyalty to leaders and elites is rewarded in turn with political accountability and obligation to the masses. Ethnicity, rather than being simply the divisive factor fueling inter-ethnic competition, can also be seen as an opportunity to define internal ethnic group values and may be among the "most fruitful sources of nationally active citizenship," according to Lonsdale.[16] It imposes a social burden and responsibility beyond the competition for access to power and resource on the individual, as well as on the group. Thus, it represents a potent counter to political tribalism and the manipulation of ethnicity to advance the parochial interests of elites.

Race
In sharp contrast to the voluntary and shifting nature of ethnic identity, racial identity is a genetic inheritance, although a racial consciousness

Identity conflict

can also be shaped by societal factors. The mixed race "Coloureds" of South Africa, for example, developed their own racial (and ethnic) identity over time, which was later codified as a separate "racial group" under the apartheid structure. Anthropologically speaking, however, there are in reality only three indigenous racial groupings in Africa today—Caucasoid, Negroid, and Bushmanoid—that historically fall within well-defined geographic areas.[17] A very prominent racial dividing line between African Caucasian and Negroid groups runs west to east, south of the Sahara Desert into Sudan before curving southward toward the Kenyan-Somali border. To the north of this line are primarily Arab, Berber, and Semitic people (Caucasian), while to the south Bantu groups (Negroid) are in the majority. The Bushman people (a distinct separate racial grouping, also known as the San) are few in number and are confined exclusively to parts of southern Africa along with an enclave of some five million Caucasian descendants of European settlers. In terms of sheer numbers, Negroid groups have historically comprised the bulk of the continent's population; over 70 percent in the post-World War II period.

Once at the very center of African identity discussions, issues of racial identity have now been largely subsumed by other factors with some notable exceptions—the Sudan–South Sudan divide for instance. The demise of the role of race as a primary differentiating factor in shaping African identity has been driven by two major trends: 1) The enormous population explosion in sub-Saharan Africa; 2) The end of colonialism, including the demise of apartheid South Africa.

In 1970 the population of Africa was nearly 370 million, but in the decades since, the continent has seen nearly a tripling of growth that had pushed the population to nearly 1.2 billion people in 2015, according to the most recent UN figures.[18] Even more startling is that this dramatic growth has taken place in spite of the ravages of the HIV/AIDS pandemic, chronic health care delivery problems, wars, drought, and famine that have afflicted the continent over the past four decades. While there have been some significant Caucasian population increases in pockets across North Africa (primarily Egypt and Algeria), as well as the Horn of Africa (Ethiopia), by far the bulk of this growth has occurred in Negroid sub-Saharan Africa that now accounts for over 80 percent of the continent's people.[19] Although starting from a low base, both Niger and Chad saw their populations more than triple since 1970, while Kenya's and Uganda's growth was even more impressive in increasing by 4.1 times over the same period.[20] This growth and the accompanying population shifts across old racial fault lines in West and Central Africa, as well as the Horn, has created a more homogenous black African identity across the continent even among non-Negroid groups.

Likewise, the end of European colonialism—where race was a (if not the) defining feature of the colonial experience in determining power, wealth, and social standing—removed a key differentiating element of African identity and source of conflict. This was even more so in South Africa, where the question of race was the lynchpin of apartheid doctrine for nearly 50 years. Despite efforts to promote multi-racialism, armed liberation struggles in settler and apartheid societies (Algeria, Angola, Kenya, Mozambique, Rhodesia, and South Africa) tended to have a strong racial overtone given the direct correlation between race and political power. The rallying cry of the youth wing of the Pan Africanist Congress—"one settler, one bullet"—signaled dramatically the movement's public rejection that white South Africans had any legitimate role to play in the struggle and should be forced to leave the country or die. The ultimate success of African independence struggles, however, eliminated most of these overtones, instead replacing them with an evolving new nationalist identity.

Once the overwhelming focus and defining characteristic of African identity, race now plays an increasingly secondary role to other factors such as ethnicity, language, religion, and even occupation in shaping modern identity. That being said, there are several key flashpoints particularly along the historical Caucasian-Negroid fault line where race does remain an important factor in reinforcing societal cleavages that inflame identity conflict. Race acted as a further differentiating element in Sudan's historic north–south conflict between the Arab-Caucasian-Muslim north and the African-Negroid-Christian/animist south prior to South Sudanese independence. And it continues to be a subtle factor in inflaming Sudan–South Sudan relations. Race also plays a role in Mauritania, Mali, and Niger, where domestic unrest over the years has been fueled by feelings of racial discrimination and neglect at the hands of either a ruling Arab-Caucasian or African-Negroid government in these countries. The trend, however, is clearly one of diminishing the importance of race within Africa, while at the same time maintaining a strong racial identity outside of the continent.

Religion
Like many places in the world, religion plays a powerful role in shaping personal and community identity in Africa. But unlike much of the world, religion in Africa still continues to shape nearly all aspects of everyday life; "the importance of religion in any attempt to understand African life in all its social, economic, and political aspects cannot be overemphasized"[21] and it crosses all socio-economic and ideological divides. African societies and their attendant problems tend to reflect

this indispensable and inseparable feature of their identities to drive internal and external relationships for better or worse. Thus, religious identity in Africa has within it the immense power both to bridge differences or fuel societal divisions. This can often mean the difference between peaceful coexistence and violent confrontation.

Nearly all the major religions of the world can be found in Africa, but three religious traditions are predominant: Christianity, Islam, and indigenous religious beliefs and practices (commonly referred to as "African traditional religions").[22] It is important to bear in mind, however, the wide variety and diversity of Christian and Islamic practices across the continent, which often results in unique Africanized or localized versions. This, in turn, has given rise to multiple sectarian splits, and internal tensions, within both religions. Moreover, it is not uncommon to see a melding of mainstream religious beliefs with elements of African traditional religions; results from a Pew Research Center survey "suggest that many Africans are deeply committed to Islam or Christianity and yet continue to practice elements of traditional African religions."[23]

Together Christianity and Islam accounted for over 93 percent of religious affiliation on the continent in 2010, and in 2017 there are estimated to be some 587 million Christians and 492 million Muslims in Africa, according to Pew Research Center data projections.[24] Despite the rough numerical balance between the Christian and the Muslim communities, geographic and historical factors have created a religious fault line that sharply divides Islamic Africa from Christian/animist Africa. Running eastward from Guinea and Sierra Leone on Africa's Atlantic coast, and arcing across the Sahel through northern Nigeria and into tropical Sudan, the line abruptly sweeps north of the Ethiopian highlands before curving southward again into eastern Ethiopia and Somalia and then down the east African coastline into Tanzania and northern Mozambique. To the north of this line Muslims outnumber Christians by more than 100:1, while the reverse is generally true south of this fault line.[25] There are some notable exceptions, with southwestern Nigeria and parts of the Great Lakes Region, as well as South Africa and many of the Indian Ocean islands, supporting significant pockets of Muslims. In contrast Egypt and parts of Eritrea still contain sizeable Coptic Christian communities. Nonetheless, recent demographic trends and religious survey results show a hardening, not lessening, of this historical dividing line. According to the Pew Research Center, "neither Christianity nor Islam is growing significantly in sub-Saharan Africa at the expense of the other; there is virtually no net change in either direction through religious switching,"[26] although long-term projections based on higher

Table 1 Religious identification in sub-Saharan Africa, 1920–2020 (%)

	Christianity	Islam	Traditional beliefs
1920	14	15	70
1930	18	19	62
1940	21	20	58
1950	25	22	52
1960	35	24	40
1970	49	25	25
1980	51	26	22
1990	53	28	18
2000	58	28	13
2010	57	29	13
2020*	58	31	10

*Estimated

Muslim community birth rates show Islam's share gaining some five percentage points in sub-Saharan Africa by 2050.[27]

Religious affiliation has long been a critical factor in forming identity in Africa, but it has assumed a special importance since mid-2000 given the rise of violent religious extremism across the continent. Not surprisingly in the post-September 11 world, much of this focus has centered on the polarizing Christian–Muslim divide that appears to be fueling and sustaining multiple conflict situations in Africa. In several strategically important countries, such as Nigeria and the DRC, at least half those interviewed agreed that conflict between religious groups is a very big problem in their countries.[28] In the former Sudan the Muslim–Christian/animist divide clearly played a defining role in the north–south conflict and continues to complicate Sudan–South Sudanese relations. In addition, some of the fastest growing religiously divided societies on the continent—Nigeria and Ethiopia, for example—lie directly along this fault line. Even more pointedly, it is projected that by 2050 more than 40 percent of all Christians and close to 30 percent of all Muslim in the world will live in Africa,[29] thus increasing the influence of the continent on the global religious stage.

Finally, it is also important to note that religious-inspired conflict in Africa extends beyond the Christian–Muslim divide to include intra-religious sectarian divisions as well. The historic spread of Islam across the continent resulted in the creation of a wide range of sectarian communities from Shi'ism and Sufi sects to Afro-Sunnism and Wahhabist/Salafist fundamentalists that for the large part lived in relatively peaceful coexistence. Since the turn of the new century, however, there has been a sharp rise in more militant and extremist forms of Islamism in Africa that has given rise to intra-Muslim strife. In particular, violent jihadists from Algeria and the pan-Sahel across to Somalia and even into South Africa have demonstrated an uninhibited willingness to confront non-Muslims and Muslims alike to advance their cause and beliefs. The evolution of Nigeria's Boko Haram group in the northeast part of that country, from religious protest to violent secession and the accompanying widespread path of death and destruction, is one of the more extreme instances of inter-religious conflict. (Boko Haram's evolution into a terrorist group will also be discussed later in Chapter 5.) It should be kept in mind too that many of these sectarian conflicts are further subsumed into more encompassing identity, political, and socio-economic conflicts.

Geography
Geographic ties—both actual and ancestral—often work in tandem with other defining characteristics to anchor one's personal and communal identity. A geographic identity is not only determined by actual physical residence, but also by one's sense of origin and extended family and kinship ties that may go back generations to a very specific personal homeland. In Africa a "sense of place" is profoundly rooted in a person's links to a physical and spiritual homeland, whether the person actually resides there or not. Ties to the land of one's family and ancestors are highly valued, even among long-time urban dwellers, because they are irrevocable and constant. Unlike other more fluid aspects of identity, these ties can provide a great sense of security and grounding in an otherwise changing world.

Not only does geography work to shape personal and communal identities, but also plays a powerful role in intensifying other associated identity factors like ethnicity, language, and customs. This reinforcing characteristic of geographic ties can even continue after people physically relocate to another location, as they continue to maintain real and imagined ties to their previous locale. Thus, it is not unusual in Africa to find geographic identity references to individuals and communities even long after their resettlement to other regions. For example, despite their presence in Cote d'Ivoire long before Ivoirian independence, the two million Mossi people residing in the country are commonly known as "Burkinabe" given their historical geographic ties to Cote d'Ivoire's northern neighbor, Burkina Faso. This label over the years has been a factor in fueling north–south political tensions within the country over questions of Ivoirian identity and citizenship; the internationally recognized winner of the 2010 presidential elections, Allassane Quattara, was barred from previous elections on the grounds that his parents came from Burkina Faso.[30]

Although it is fundamentally primordial in nature as a source of identity formation, economic development, urbanization, and globalization have combined to strengthen, not lessen, the importance of geographic ties in today's Africa. The strong pull of economic opportunities, the psychological attraction of urban areas, and enhanced real time communications have fed a massive modern-day movement of people from rural to urban areas, across national and sub-regional borders, and even between continents. The result of these intra-national and international migratory patterns in many cases has been the creation of scores of newly transplanted communities outside their traditional homelands. This can present a dilemma. On the one hand, these transplanted communities provide a sense of common identity and sense of belonging to immigrants in a strange environment. But on the other hand, these identity ties act to highlight and reinforce differences with the indigenous population. This can make social integration exceedingly difficult and in extreme situations result in violent conflict between the two communities. Deadly xenophobic attacks on Mozambican, Zimbabwean, and other African immigrants in South Africa in 2008, 2015, and 2017 demonstrate just how quickly things can spin out of control.

Scope and nature of the problem

As noted previously, parts of Africa continue to be violent and dangerous places, and violent conflict is an inescapable part of the continent's security landscape. If one agrees with Stuart Kaufman's assessment that "identity conflicts are, and will remain for decades to come, the most important source of international violence and war in the world,"[31] then Africa and its people are likely to be at the epicenter of this maelstrom. In many ways African conflicts do mirror similar macro trends and patterns around the globe, but in other ways the scope and characteristics are uniquely African. Without a doubt, post-Cold War efforts to drive down the number and deadliness of armed conflicts around the world have been remarkably effective, according to the Human Security Project.[32] This has been true for Africa too. Reported battle deaths fell to less than 5,000 annually by 2011,[33] reflecting a drastic decline since 1999 when the last of the continent's most deadly and long-running Cold War-fueled conflicts finally came to an end.

Since 2011, however, the continent has witnessed a reversal of this downward trend, with ever increasing death tolls thanks to a handful of high-intensity conflicts fed by the terrorist insurgency in northeast

Nigeria that has spilled over into neighboring countries, an on-again off-again civil war in South Sudan and associated violence in neighboring Sudan, a resurgence of the al-Shabaab terrorist group in Somalia, and the continuing violent chaos in Libya in the aftermath of the overthrow of the Qaddafi government. While 2014 was the bloodiest year in sub-Saharan Africa since 2004 with some 35,000 conflict deaths, only five countries—Nigeria, South Sudan, Somalia, Sudan, and the CAR— accounted for 83 percent of the toll.[34] Moreover, the total number of African conflicts has remained relatively constant, averaging 13–14 per year since 2010 with high-intensity conflicts accounting for a little more than one-third of all conflicts.

Thus, for the overwhelming majority of African countries smaller, low-intensity conflicts are more the norm. In addition, many of these conflicts are persistent, domestically fueled ones where issues of identity are an important factor in fueling and sustaining them. Not surprisingly then, it is difficult to avoid hearing or reading about some form of identity conflict in Africa and it would seem as if no part of the continent is free from this type of violence. But what is the reality? And, moreover, how widespread is identity conflict and what is fueling and sustaining this type and level of violence?

What is identity conflict?

Given the formidable role and importance of identity in African societies as we have seen, it should come as little surprise that threats to individual or group identity can easily be perceived as threatening the very survival of the broader collective. These threats can come in the form of challenges to values, beliefs, and customs or through discriminatory practices and the denial of legitimacy, but they are ultimately rooted in perceptions—both real and imagined—that appear to challenge the very existence of the individual's, community's, or group's sense of self and of belonging. And when survival is at stake, conflict is too often the result. Moreover, identity conflicts tend to be highly destructive affairs that release pent up passions and demonize their opponents. As Jay Rothman points out, "identity and conflict are passionate forces indeed. They are two of the most engaging features of human life. When they are combined, the result is a combustible mixture that can either destroy or create, depending on how the mixture is handled."[35] It is this highly personalized and psychological aspect of identity conflicts that often makes them exceedingly difficult to resolve.

Simply viewed, identity conflict is violence between one or more groups over an actual or perceived threat to the continued maintenance and/or survival of group identity. This identity may be grounded in a shared ethnicity, race, religion, or common belief system, language, shared culture and history, geography, or occupation that tends to foster an "us versus them" mentality. These conflicts are "usually intransigent and resistant to resolution," as they are "deeply rooted in the underlying individual human needs and values that together constitute people's social identities, particularly in the context of group affiliations, loyalties, and solidarity."[36]

Identity conflict can play out in various forms, but most commonly in Africa, it manifests itself as ethnic, religious, or communal violence. As Crawford Young points out, this type of violence "inevitably incorporates discourses of difference" and this "escalates mutual fears, anxieties, and insecurities; communally targeted violence inscribes memories of ineffable loss of kin and fellow ethnics, and inspires dreams of vengeance."[37] Even more alarming is the problem of identity conflict where multiple identity references become mutually reinforcing societal cleavages. The north–south divide in the former Sudan being the most extreme example, where racial (Caucasian/Negroid), religious (Muslim/Christian and animist), cultural (Arab/African), historical (slavers/slaves), and geographical (arid and semi-arid/tropical) identities repeatedly divide along the same fault lines to create an extremely powerful, and seemingly intractable, identity conflict. Although the most common form of conflict pits two or more identity groups against each other, the state itself can also be seen as posing a threat to a group if it is seen as a surrogate of a competing group. The latter usually occurs in exclusionary political and social systems where an elite identity group seeks to control the levers of power within a state at the expense of other groups. Yet, as Kaufman points out, identity conflict is ultimately a form of symbolic politics that uses concepts and myths of identity for political mobilization and manipulation purposes[38] and thus there is nothing inevitable or preordained driving identity violence.

Resolving identity conflicts once they occur, however, has proved challenging in Africa. Although the initial violence can usually be traced to a very specific catalyst, identity groups often have difficulty articulating specific demands for redressing the underlying source of their grievances. Intangible group grievances over "lack of respect," "legitimacy" or "belonging" are tricky to translate into concrete issues. The inherently antagonistic "us versus them" attitude of identity groups makes compromise seem like capitulation. The challenge in these situations, according to Rothman, is to redirect the discussion away from points of division and toward areas of common needs and motivations; changing the dynamic from a divisive "us" versus "them" attitude to a shared "we" attitude.[39] Of course this is easier said than done.

Especially in Africa, where national resources are rarely adequate to meet all societal demands, there is a long history of exclusionary political systems, and there is a lack of transparency and belief in judicial objectivity. Nonetheless, when done correctly, conflict mitigation and resolution mechanisms have proven effective in diminishing—although not eliminating—prospects for future identity conflict.

How widespread is identity violence?
Although identity violence in Africa is certainly a reality, commonly held perceptions about its role in conflict, its frequency, and intensity are often distorted. Simply labeling conflicts as ethnic, racial, religious, or communal is usually not only misleading, but can obscure and diminish the importance of other factors fueling the violence. Moreover, a single-minded focus on issues of identity at the expense of other underlying causes can complicate conflict resolution efforts.

At the peak of post-Cold War violence in 1991 the overwhelming majority of the thirteen major, high-intensity armed conflicts underway reflected the playing out of Cold War-fueled and sustained civil wars, local power struggles, and the dying days of apartheid. While issues of identity, particularly of ethnicity, were certainly elements in many of these conflicts they played a secondary or even tertiary role to other drivers of conflict. This was true given instances of a sharp ethnic, racial, religious, or geographical divide (or a mixture of all these) between government and rebel forces. For ultimately, the conflicts in such places as Angola, Ethiopia, Liberia, Mozambique, Sudan, and Zaire were more about the struggle over state control or state formation rather than an intense display of identity violence. The southern Sudanese rebels of the Sudanese Peoples Liberation Army were not so much fighting to uphold their identity as black, non-Muslims from the south, but for greater autonomy and freedom, as well as economic independence from the central Sudanese government in Khartoum. Likewise, the civil wars in Angola, Ethiopia, and Liberia were more about the struggle for political power and ultimate control of the state and less about Ovambo-Mbundu, Amara-Tigray, or Krahn-Gio ethnic rivalries. This is not to say that identity politics played no factor in the violence of the early 1990s, as the conflicts in Rwanda, Burundi, and Senegal's Casamance region clearly demonstrate, but that other drivers of conflict were more significant.

What then is the role (or non-role) of identity in African conflict today? First and foremost, nearly all new conflicts appear to include some significant element of identity violence. Specifically, ethnic or religious identification has played an ever increasing role in shaping and energizing modern-day African conflicts—ones that are now often characterized by ethno-political, ethno-economic, sectarian, separatist or communal violence. Just as important, identity is rarely the only factor underpinning any conflict. Nonetheless, it is frequently used as a powerful agent for social and political mobilization by those seeking to advance a broader agenda. This makes identity violence extremely difficult to control and contain once unleashed because of its ability to stoke the fires of already existing political or socio-economic cleavages. Not surprisingly, identity-laced conflicts are complicated to resolve and tend to persistent for years or even decades.

They are, however, not the most deadly form of conflict in Africa today. Violent conflict arising out of chronic political instability, state failure, resource competition, and terrorist insurgencies has proven to be far deadlier. High-intensity conflicts are more likely to be rooted in these factors rather than in identity. Think of the legacy of the war-torn eastern DRC that killed some 45,000 per month from 2003 to 2006,[40] the ongoing violence and chaos in Somalia and Libya following state implosion, or the deadly toll in northeastern Nigeria beginning in 2009 that has now surpassed 15,000 dead.[41] Of course identity-related conflicts can, and sometimes do, spin out of control; the most graphic example being the 1994 Rwandan ethnic genocide that left more than 800,000 dead. And in December 2016 UN Secretary-General Ban Ki-moon "feared that genocide was about to start in South Sudan" as the country teetered on the brink of ethno-political civil war.[42] Thus, there is always the danger of low-intensity identity conflict situations morphing into deadlier high-intensity conflicts.

Finally, often overlooked is the role of identity conflict in undermining a sense of personal or community security and this strikes at the very heart of human security—freedom from fear. More so than many other forms of violent conflict, identity conflict manifests itself in highly personalized terms and presents a direct and immediate threat to the well-being of individuals and communities. In pitting neighbor against neighbor and dividing communities, this type of violence undermines an essential building block of human security. Rebuilding trust in the aftermath of such conflicts can be done (witness Rwanda); however, the task is time consuming and fraught with obstacles as tensions often simmer under the surface for years.

Some past manifestations
While there are dangers inherent in trying to pigeonhole complex African conflicts as driven by any single overarching factor, the issue of identity often plays more of a crucial role than many perceive in shaping the political and socio-economic dynamics of conflict.

Nigeria

Communal identity violence has been a longstanding problem for Nigerian society, but for the past 15 years much of the conflict has centered on the states of the "middle belt"—particularly, Plateau and Kaduna states—where glaring religious and ethnic identities collide violently. Jos, the capital and largest city in Plateau State, has been at the center of the conflict that until the outbreak of major violence in September 2001 had "always been viewed as a peaceful city" and a place "where diverse communities had coexisted peacefully for years."[43] Changing demographics from Nigerians fleeing violence elsewhere in the country to Jos, as well as intense political and economic competition, however, set the stage for an unrelenting cycle of violence. Major bloodletting in September 2001, May 2004, November 2008, in the early months of 2010, January–April 2014, and again at the beginning of 2016 left tens of thousands dead, displaced entire communities, destroyed dozens of churches and mosques, and produced a climate of distrust and insecurity all across the state.

While there are no official numbers for those killed, a 2004 government study reported that 53,787 people had died in Plateau State as a result of communal-related violence between September 7, 2001 and May 18, 2004 alone.[44] Subsequent reporting from Human Rights Watch and other sources indicate that the death toll across central Nigeria had probably swollen to more than 60,000 by 2016.[45] The British-based NGO Mercy Corps estimated that the conflict has cost Nigeria more than $14 billion from 2012 to 2015 alone by impeding market development, deterring investment, and stifling economic growth.[46] Repeated efforts by local officials and community leaders to defuse the situation have met with only limited success given the perceived lack of justice and human rights abuses by security forces brought in to stem the violence.

The fierce fighting has pitted Hausa-Fulani Muslims against several Christian ethnic groups in a bitter cycle of attack and retaliation. Both sides have suffered enormously and there is clearly enough blame to go around. Although commonly viewed by the media as simply a religious conflict between Christians and Muslims, the violence is really about the struggle for local political and economic power between two distinct communities and how political and community leaders have manipulated identity for their own ends. As a 2010 government commission on the violence pointed out, religion was not the cause of the violence, but "was exploited by some individuals and groups to gain political popularity and support."[47] Thus, religious differences are but one, albeit a highly visible one, of the dividing factors. A more important identity is that of "indigenes" and "settlers," whereby indigenes or original inhabitants are granted special rights under Nigerian law at the expense of settlers, many of whom have lived in Plateau State for generations.[48] While neither group is monolithic in ethno-religious terms, Christianity tends to be the dominant religion among the non-Hausa-Fulani indigenes and Islam the dominate religion among the Hausa-Fulani settlers.[49] Likewise, disputes over land ownership and land use between herders and farmers have fueled tensions. Here again the fault line generally divides Fulani herders from other ethnic farming groups. The result has been warring communities that are split along multiple, but reinforcing, sources of identity—identities that are then violently mobilized in the quest for political and economic dominance.

The implications of this ongoing conflict are significant not only for the future of Nigerian society, but for African identity conflict in general. Certainly the most important lesson one takes away is the extreme fragility of Nigeria's pluralist society and how the expansion of federalism and increase in regional autonomy following the end of military rule in 1999 may have indirectly sown the seeds for bitter, violent communal conflict. In fact, institutional structures (such as the indigene law) have served to deepen community divisions rather than serve to bridge differences. With more than three-quarters of the country's GDP flowing through state and local governments,[50] the political competition for control of these levers of power have never been higher. Meanwhile, rising demographic pressures in Africa's most populous country, endemic corruption, and widespread poverty have created an explosive situation. All too often, superficial issues of identity provide the spark that ignites pent up frustration and feelings of alienation into destructive communal violence. The extreme nature of the identity violence in central Nigeria also provides a potent reminder of the power of reinforcing identity cleavages, where the social, political, and economic fault line repeatedly falls in the same place creating two very distinct communities with little to no overlapping identities. Not only then are these communities more easily mobilized, but political and economic interests can more readily be camouflaged as a threat to group survival.

Chad

The spillover of the Darfur conflict from neighboring Sudan into eastern Chad, which would devolve into full-scale civil war by 2006, clearly demonstrates the critical transnational character of identity conflict and the intertwining of domestic and international politics.

Chadian President Idriss Deby rose to power in 1990 as the head of an ethnically based Zaghawa insurgency operating out of Darfur with the support of Sudan, Libya, and French intelligence. Although the

Zaghawa comprise less than 3 percent of the Chadian population, the estimated 325,000-strong community straddles the Chadian–Sudanese border, and transnational familial and clan ties have historically been very strong. In the decades following his seizure of power, Deby relied on a network of ethnic patronage in government and the military to ensure the backing of key Zaghawa leaders.

Not surprisingly Deby, under growing pressure from Chadian Zaghawa leaders to assist his fellow kinsmen under attack in Darfur in 2003, began actively supporting the Darfuri rebels against Khartoum; Sudanese Zaghawa then comprised a majority of the fighters, including those in the Justice and Equality Movement and within factions of the Sudanese Liberation Army. Khartoum in turn unleashed its Arab militias on eastern Chad and stepped up its support to anti-Deby forces within Chad, including the ethnically based Tami rebel movement and breakaway factions within the Zaghawa community. Soon the fighting in Chad escalated into full-blown civil war in 2006–8 when several rebel factions—supplied with Sudanese weapons and equipment—united to launch high-profile attacks on the Chadian capital. Deby survived this onslaught, thanks to timely French military intervention, and in turn stepped up his support to Darfuri rebels. By 2009 the war had become a protracted low-intensity transnational conflict that was fed by repetitive cycles of attacks and retaliation, inter- and intra-ethnic violence, and constant recriminations between Khartoum and N'Djamena. It was only in 2010 that the fighting came to an end after Deby and Sudanese President Omar al-Bashir agreed to reconcile and stop supporting Darfuri and Chadian rebels respectively. Nonetheless, the situation in Chad today remains tenuous with unresolved social tensions, an entrenched ethnic patronage system, and Deby's heavy-handed authoritarian rule.

Somalia

Although deposed in 1991, General Mohamed Siad Barre's legacy of manipulating Somali clan identity as a foundational source of political power provides the backdrop for much of the ongoing instability in Somalia today.

As early as 1972, the Barre regime began to install a Soviet-style system of appointing political commissars to the armed forces, administrative institutions, and social organizations. Soon after, however, the regime began to substitute ideology for clanism as the criteria for such appointments, favoring three clans from the Darod clan-family, resulting in the clandestine code name 'MOD' given to the regime. The M (Marehan) stood for the patrilineage of the President, O (Ogaden) for that of his mother, and D (Dulbahante) for that of his principal son-in-law and head of the National Security Service. Moreover, this clan-klatura within state institutions was exported into rural society after the Ogaden War (1977–78) with devastating effect as Barre pursued brutal divide-and-rule policies by arming so-called loyal clans and encouraging them to wage wars against rebel clans. The long-term damage caused by this identity manipulation of clan consciousness in Somalia during the Barre years has almost certainly contributed to the ensuing chaos and the inability of civil society to rebound when Barre fell from power.

These examples highlight several important lessons for our understanding about the nature of identity violence in Africa today. First and foremost, shared ethnicity may serve as an extremely effective conduit for spreading and escalating conflict beyond its domestic roots because "ethnicity connects people in ways that transcend political boundaries and national borders, and members of an ethnic group tend to identify at a regional level as opposed to a national level."[51] With conflict on the continent becoming increasingly sub-regional in nature, the transnational nature of many ethnic groups—and of group identity in general—is likely an important, but often overlooked factor in the regionalization of conflict. Secondly, group identity isn't always homogenous but is subject to divisions and factionalism. This is even true with respect to a shared ethnic identity (as in the case of Zaghawa), where internal divisions can occur over competing interests and "ethnic groups can invest loyalty where it pays the highest desired returns."[52] Moreover, individual leadership and the rewards associated appear to be more of a decisive factor in determining group loyalty than the intangible elements of a shared group identity. Third, although the dangers of identity manipulation by local politicians are well-known, little attention has been paid to the ability (or inability) of international actors to use identity mobilization as a tool for advancing their own foreign policy agendas. Finally, the presence of multiple, and often overlapping, conflicts beyond identity underscores the enormous challenge in bringing about peace and reconciliation.

Implications for security

The links between identity, violent conflict, and insecurity in Africa are well established and pervasive. Moreover, they play a defining role in how the continent and its often violent landscape is perceived by the outside world, and thus to many, African conflict has become synonymous with identity violence. While certainly a mistakenly simplistic view of the complex nature of African conflict, it is also true that improved security—and particularly human security—cannot become a reality until the issue of identity conflict is more effectively addressed.

Human security is fundamentally about people and securing their freedom from fear and persecution, ensuring their personal safety, and providing them with economic opportunities. It begins at the very basic level of the individual and rises to the level of the state's obligations and responsibilities. Likewise, as we have seen, identity is an individual and group based concept that seeks among other things to ensure survival and provide protection. Thus, the ultimate goal of safeguarding the individual (and by extension the group or community too) and human security is the same. Despite sharing this common goal, the "us against them" mentality inherent in building group identity can be very detrimental to building security for the society as a whole. If identity is used by leaders as a polarizing force or is manipulated to inflame tensions in the pursuit of personal agendas or political and economic power, then it is clearly destabilizing and presents a dangerous challenge to the nation's security. If, on the other hand, identity concepts are used constructively to emphasize areas of commonality and shared interests then it can be a powerful force in building a pluralistic and inclusive society.

In examining the relationship between identity conflict and security challenges of the new century, several important linkages stand out as likely to have a direct bearing in shaping the future of the continent and its people: a) persistent low-level multifaceted conflicts becoming the norm; b) rising transnational threats that are heavily influenced by environmental and demographic changes; c) the diminishing utility of force in building security; and d) the growing relevance and importance of the non-traditional security sector.

As noted earlier, the data over the last two decades show a clear historic downward trend in the deadliness of armed conflicts in Africa. Large-scale, armed inter- and intra-state conflict is becoming a thing of past, to be replaced by more numerous, low-level, and diverse types of violence. Although these new-century conflicts produce fewer deaths (with some exceptions) and are less of a direct threat to the state, their seeming intractability poses a long-term challenge to peace and stability. Moreover, they still have the potential of exploding quickly into larger-scale violence given the appropriate catalyst. Identity violence and associated communal conflicts fall into this category.

The resulting challenge is in peacefully resolving these types of identity conflicts. Some countries, however, have proven successful in reducing conflict or the potential for conflict. Politically inclusive and open societies that respect the rule of law and have even modest economic growth tend to be more successful in defusing the most overt forms of identity violence. Unfortunately, many of these same societal characteristics are in short supply in Africa.

Although traditionally seen as an internal or domestic challenge, identity conflict—like other types of African conflict—is becoming increasingly transnational in nature and is neither constrained nor explained in solely domestic terms. Thus, transnational identities pose a significant security challenge to both domestic and sub-regional security. Transnational ethnic groups have long been viewed with suspicion by governments, especially in civil war situations where they have the ability to provide cross-border support and sanctuary to their kinsmen. The widespread use during the Cold War of transnational ethnic groups as proxy armies only served to reinforce these suspicions and rationalize wholesale discrimination against them. While a highly visible component in some conflicts—ethnic Somalis battling Ethiopian forces in the Ogaden, Jola seeking succession in the Casamance region of Senegal, or Tuaregs rebelling in Mali and Niger—the transnational aspect of identity conflict is now widening to include other aspects of identity. Transnational conflict has moved beyond ethnicity in the new century. Religious or geographic identification, for instance, is increasingly becoming more of a rallying factor in regionalized conflicts and these are harder in general to defuse given the usual dearth of effective transnational conflict resolution mechanisms.

Likewise, identity-fueled conflicts tend to highlight socio-economic and political grievances. Poverty, lack of education and health, inadequate economic opportunity, corruption, or poor governance all come to the fore. Moreover, the use of force as a response has limited utility here. While militaries and police forces can obviously help quell the violence, they are patently ill-equipped to implement the types of reforms necessary to address the cause of violence in the first place. Only by moving outside the traditional definition of state security can governments begin to build the necessary institutions and tools that enhance security at the individual and community level. This will, out of necessity, entail an acceptance of the expanded role of NGOs, civil society, and local initiatives in the security sector because these structures are best suited for mobilizing people across existing identity lines. By building new cross-cutting identities that emphasize shared interests and common societal objectives, identity violence can be replaced with identity security.

Threats to national security in Africa are more likely to arise from within states than from external sources. They feed off people's sense of inequality, injustice, distrust in government, and lack of empowerment. But most of all they are nurtured by an atmosphere of fear, as well as the perceived inability of the state to provide protection and ensure safety for its citizenry. Identity conflict is rooted in that fear and distrust. True security lies in alleviating that fear and distrust at the most basic level of the individual. Building trust and confidence in the state to provide this type of security is the challenge and it will require both a top-down all-of-government approach, and the active involvement of civil society to achieve. Failure to do so will rarely result in genocidal mass murder (Rwanda being an exceptional case); however, it will inevitably weaken the state and make it exceedingly vulnerable to other security threats.

Conclusion

With a few notable exceptions—Libya, Nigeria, Somalia, South Sudan, and Sudan—the overall historic level of large-scale armed conflicts and conflict-related deaths in Africa have been declining for some time. Moreover, large-scale, intense conflicts are likely to be increasingly replaced by more numerous, smaller-scale, and persistent identity-related conflicts over the coming decades. Major population growth and the associated competition for scarce resources, increased mobility of populations, the effects of rising globalization on attitudes and ideas, and the struggle for political and economic inclusion will strengthen—not diminish—the role of identity in Africa. As an integral part of African society, identity, and particularly perceptions of self-identity, have always mattered greatly and will continue to do so. Although identity is infrequently the sole driver of conflict, aspects of identity violence cannot be easily separated from other forms of complex conflict. Identity has never been a static concept, however, and the changing nature of African identity will accordingly require a constant reassessment of its role and impact on African conflict.

Ethnic-related conflict is likely to continue to garner most of the world media's attention, but other forms of identity conflict will pose a more serious threat to peace and stability in the future. Religious and geographic based identity factors, for instance, are rising in importance as components of twenty-first-century conflicts, and their influence are only likely to expand. The global spread of religious extremism and the associated problem of terrorism over the past decade has heightened awareness of religious divisions and elevated religious identity to a new level in Africa, which is fueling suspicion and distrust among religious communities as a Pew survey highlights.[53] Likewise, powerful demographic changes and the pull of new economic opportunities are encouraging wholesale shifts in population movements both within countries and across entire regions. These trends will undoubtedly spur greater interaction between divergent and alien communities and locals. This will significantly raise the potential for more identity-related violence unless appropriate conflict prevention and mitigation mechanisms are developed and put in place.

As we have seen, identity violence occurs all across the continent to varying degrees, but some countries and sub-regions appear to be more susceptible than others. The colonial legacy of divide-and-rule, ethno-religious favoritism, and the formation of artificial states at independence continue to provide fertile ground for identity conflict. So too will many new trends. For instance, booming population growth in Ethiopia, Egypt, and Nigeria, when combined with stagnating economies, high levels of poverty, poor governance, and exclusionary political systems, will almost certainly make these countries more vulnerable to identity conflict. Other flashpoints are likely to occur along the pronounced racial and religious fault line cutting across West Africa to the Horn and down the east coast of the continent. The CAR, Chad, Mali, Mauritania, Niger, and Kenya will probably witness periods of rising identity-related violence in the coming decades. (In the case of South Sudan and Sudan this is already happening.) Not all countries along this fault line will see more identity-fueled violence. Some, such as Tanzania, with proven track records of defusing high levels of domestic identity conflict will probably see an overall decrease in violence. The bulk of African countries, however, will fall into the second tier where economic and political power struggles will continue to be disguised as identity conflicts and manipulated by political entrepreneurs in an effort to gain or maintain power. Countries struggling with democratic reforms or changes of old-line regimes, such as Cameroon, Guinea, Ivory Coast, and Zimbabwe, are especially vulnerable to this type of manipulation. One only has to be reminded of the events in Kenya in 2008 to see the explosiveness of the situation.

Identity is an integral part of modern African society and, as such, plays an important role in shaping modern conflict. It is not going away. Politicians and leaders will continue to use issues of identity to advance their own and their group's interests because it works. Thus, the biggest challenge for African countries is how best to manage identity conflict and put in place mechanisms for effective mitigation and resolution. Turning the "us versus them" mentality into a shared "we" attitude will be a difficult challenge. It will require an all-of-government approach that spans the spectrum of human security, as well as the active involvement and support of NGOs, civil society, and local citizens from the bottom up to make it work. Leaders of all stripes must be willing to set aside their individual and group differences in the quest for long-term stability. This will be difficult, but it also will be necessary for African peace and security.

Notes

1 *VOA*, 'Most Under Threat of Genocide and Mass Killing Are in Africa' (February 28, 2008).
2 *The Los Angeles Times*, 'African continent tormented by tribal conflicts' (March 23, 1986).
3 G. Murdock, *Africa: Its Peoples and Their Culture History* (New York: McGraw-Hill, 1959); L. Kriesberg, *Social Inequity* (Hemel Hempstead: Prentice Hall, 1979); T. Gurr, *Minorities at Risk: A Global View of Ethnopolitical Conflict* (Washington, DC: US Institute of Peace, 1993); R. Werbuer and T. Ranger, *Postcolonial Identities in Africa* (Cape Town: University of Cape Town Press, 1997); S. Bekker, M. Dodd, and M. Khosa, *Shifting African Identities* (Pretoria: Human Sciences Research Council, 2001); P. Burke and J. Stets, *Identity Theory* (New York: Oxford University Press, 2009).
4 C. Lentz, 'Tribalism and ethnicity in Africa: A review of four decades of Anglophone research', *Cahiers des Sciences Humaines* 31:2 (1995), 319. M. Mamdani, *Citizen and Subject: Contemporary Africa and the Legacy of Late Colonialism* (Princeton, NJ: Princeton University Press, 1996) also looks at the issue of invented identity and traditions under his bifurcated state framework.
5 This brief discussion can only begin to scratch the surface of the ethnicity debate and will address only a few of the most salient points of the extensive body of academic literature, which have a direct bearing on our examination of the security implications of ethnicity. For a more in-depth overview, see C. Lentz, 'Tribalism' and ethnicity in Africa', pp. 303–28; D. Horowitz, *Ethnic Groups in Conflict*, 2nd edn (Berkeley, CA: University of California Press, 2000); B. Berman, D. Kyoh, and W. Kymlicka (eds), *Ethnicity and Democracy in Africa* (Oxford: James Currey Publishers, 2004).
6 C. Young, *Ethnicity and Politics in Africa* (Boston: Boston University African Studies Center, 2002), p. 9.
7 P. Chabal and J. Daloz, *Africa Works: Disorder as Political Instrument* (Oxford: James Currey Publishers, 1999), p. 58.
8 C. Young, 'Deciphering disorder in Africa: Is identity the key?' *World Politics*, 54 (July 2002), 551.
9 J. Lonsdale, 'Moral ethnicity and political tribalism' (April 21, 2008), accessed at http://kenyaimagine.com/index/php?view=article&catid=266%3Aintern on February 24, 2017.
10 P. Ekeh, 'Individuals' basic security needs and the limits of democracy in Africa', in Berman, Eyoh, and Kymlicka (eds), *Ethnicity and Democracy in Africa*, p. 31.
11 Ibid., p. 34.
12 Chabal and Daloz, *Africa Works*, p. 58, emphasis added.
13 R.H. Bates, 'Ethnic competition and modernization in contemporary Africa', *Comparative Political Studies*, 6:4, 457–84.

14 B. Berman, D. Eyoh, and W. Kymlicka, 'Ethnicity and the politics of democratic nation-building in Africa', in Berman, Eyoh, and Kymlicka (eds), *Ethnicity and Democracy in Africa*, p. 5.
15 J. Lonsdale, 'Moral and political argument in Kenya', in Berman, Eyoh, and Kymlicka (eds), *Ethnicity and Democracy in Africa*, p. 75.
16 Ibid.
17 Murdock, *Africa: Its Peoples and Their Culture History*, pp. 7–12.
18 United Nations Department of Economic and Social Affairs, Population Division, *World Population Prospects: The 2012 Revision* (2015), accessed at http://esa.un.org/wpp/unpp/p2k0data.asp on February 24, 2017.
19 Ibid.
20 Ibid.
21 A. Moyo, 'Religion in Africa', in A. Gordon and D. Gordon (eds), *Understanding Contemporary Africa* (Boulder, CO: Lynne Rienner, 2007), p. 317.
22 African traditional religions is a catch all classification for those indigenous religious practices that adhere to a belief in a supreme being, believe in individual spirits that inhabit natural objects and phenomena, believe in life after death, practice ancestor worship, maintain a religious structure and hierarchy, acknowledge sacred places, and practice elements of witchcraft and magic. See Moyo, 'Religion in Africa', pp. 319–26 for a useful overview.
23 The Pew Forum on Religion and Public Life, 'Tolerance and tension: Islam and Christianity in sub-Saharan Africa' (April 15, 2010), p. 2, accessed at www.pewforum.org/datasets/tolerance-and-tension-islam-and-christianity-in-sub-saharan-africa/ on February 24, 2017.
24 The Pew Forum, 'The future of world religions: population growth projections 2010–2050' (April 2, 2015), accessed at www.pewforum.org/2015/04/02/sub-saharan-africa/ on February 24, 2017 and 'The global religious landscape' (December 18, 2012), Table: Religious composition by country accessed at www.pewforum.org/2012/12/18/global-religious-landscape-exec/ on February 24, 2017.
25 The Pew Forum, 'Tolerance and tension', p. 2.
26 Ibid., p. 3.
27 The Pew Forum, 'The future of world religions'.
28 The Pew Forum, 'Tolerance and tension', p. 9.
29 The Pew Forum, 'The future of world religions'.
30 C. Chogugudza, 'Ethnicity main cause of instability, civil conflict and poverty in Africa', *AfricaResource* (January 8, 2008), accessed at www.africaresource.com/essays-a-reviews/politics/478-ethnicity-main-cause-of-instability-civil-conflict-and-poverty-in-africa on February 24, 2017.
31 S. Kaufman, 'Social identity and the roots of future conflict' (NIC 2020 discussion paper, October 2003), p. 1, accessed at www.au.af.mil/au/awc/awcgate/cia/nic2020/kaufman_panel2_nov6.pdf on February 24, 2017.
32 Human Security Report Project, *Human Security Report 2013*, p. 3.
33 Ibid., Figure 4.13: State-based conflicts and battle deaths in sub-Saharan Africa, 1989–2011, p. 94.

34 AfricaCheck, 'Factsheet: Conflict-related deaths in sub-Saharan Africa', *Factsheets and Guides*, accessed at https://africacheck.org/factsheets/conflict-related-deaths-in-sub-saharan-africa/ on February 24, 2017.
35 J. Rothman, *Resolving Identity-Based Conflict in Nations, Organizations, and Communities* (San Francisco: Jossey-Bass Publishers, 1997), p. xi.
36 Ibid., p. 6.
37 Young, 'Deciphering disorder in Africa', p. 556.
38 Kaufman, 'Social identity and the roots of future conflict', p. 3.
39 Rothman, *Resolving Identity-Based Conflict*, pp. 42–4.
40 Human Security Report Project, *Human Security Brief 2007* (Vancouver: Human Security Research Group, 2008), p. 22.
41 *Washington Post*, 'The brutal toll of Boko Haram's attacks on civilians' (April 3, 2016).
42 *Reuters*, 'U.N. chief fears genocide about to start in South Sudan' (December 16, 2016).
43 Human Rights Watch, 'Jos: A city torn apart', *Human Rights* Watch, 13:9A (December 18, 2001), p. 5, accessed at www.hrw.org/report/2001/12/18/jos/city-torn-apart on February 24, 2017.
44 *BBC News*, 'Nigeria clashes: 50,000 killed' (October 7, 2004).
45 *Reliefweb*, 'Nigeria: Escalating communal violence' (April 14, 2014); 'Estimated number of people killed in inter-communal violence in Plateau and Kaduna states, Nigeria, January 2010–November 2013', accessed at http://reliefweb.int/map/nigeria/estimated-number-people-killed-inter-communal-violence-plateau-and-kaduna-states-nigeria on February 24, 2017; *BBC News*, 'Making sense of Nigeria's Fulani-farmer conflict' (May 5, 2016).
46 Ibid.
47 *Daily Trust*, 'Nigeria: The presidential panel report on Jos crises' (September 2, 2010).
48 The distinction is critical as 'in practice the two groups effectively have different rights, resulting in discrimination and inequalities of access in many areas. The impact has been felt particularly in education and employment [including senior federal and state positions], where an informal two-tier system appears to operate.' Human Rights Watch, 'Jos: A city torn apart', p. 22.
49 Ibid., p. 5.
50 *BBC News*, 'Nigeria violence in Jos: Q & A' (March 8, 2010).
51 J. Sany and S. Desai, 'Transnational ethnic groups and conflict: The Zaghawa in Chad and Sudan', *Conflict Trends*, 2 (ACCORD, 2008), p. 26.
52 Ibid., p. 29.
53 The Pew Forum, 'Tolerance and tension'.

4

Failing states

States are the only contemporary political organizations that enjoy a unique legal status under international law—sovereignty—and are deemed to possess an exclusive monopoly on the legitimate use of force within their borders. While the modern nation-state[†] has existed for more than 350 years, states today are much more varied in their capacity, capability, and composition than ever before. They are also more numerous than they were half a century ago, and the range of their population sizes, physical endowments, wealth, productivity, delivery systems, ambitions, and attainments is subsequently much more extensive than they once were. Likewise, the rise of powerful non-state actors in the post-Cold War period has severely undermined the traditional role and legitimacy of the state.

A central feature of the state is to provide for the delivery of public goods (such as security) to its citizenry, and states fail to function as states when they can no longer do this. Others point to various litmus tests to determine state failure: an inability to perform key functions of a state; cannot or will not provide for domestic peace, law, and order, and good governance; or unable or unwilling to adhere to the terms of an implied social contract. The categorization of states simply as either functioning or failing, however, is akin "to throw[ing] a monolithic coat over disparate problems that require tailored solutions."[1] Thus, this approach tends to cloud, and even misleads clear analysis, due to the fact that the concept contains culturally specific assumptions about what a successful state should look like. Therefore it groups together disparate sorts of states with diverse problems, which leads to narrow

---

[†] While the terms "nation," "state" and "nation-state" have nuanced political science definitional differences that legitimately raise questions as to their applicability in the African context, for the simplicity of this discussion the basic term "state" is used throughout to identify a territory organized as a political structure that may (or may not) be inhabited by people sharing a common history, culture, and language.

and univalent policy prescriptions. Thus, a more complex view of state failure is needed, one that addresses a range of empirical state capabilities, which are grounded in the concept of "positive sovereignty" or the state proactively providing for citizens' needs.

And while the concept of "state failure" or "failing states" is much debated among academics (and will not be resolved here), the consequences of such failure are all too real, especially in Africa. Endemic violence, ethnic and religious tensions, rampant human rights abuses, rising terrorism and crime, along with a lack of legitimacy and political inclusion, as well as an inability to exercise effective control over territory are hallmarks of failing states. The Fund for Peace's 2016 Fragile States Index, for example, ranks six African countries—Somalia, South Sudan, CAR, Sudan, Chad, and the DRC—as the most in danger of collapse, and African countries account for 14 of the top 20 overall.[2] Tellingly, the DRC, Somalia, and Sudan, have ranked in the top ten every year since 2005. To compound matters still further, such regional powerhouses as Nigeria, Kenya, and Ethiopia also find themselves in the top 25 of the Index as their stability has declined.[3] Despite the weakness of many African states, however, their active involvement remains critical to advancing human security in the twenty-first century. Thus, the challenge in Africa is one of finding effective ways of strengthening the power of the state while at the same time diversifying its base of support and societal participation from the bottom up.

The failed state in context

For many centuries, societies and smaller groups have endeavored to form organizations that provide them with security, access to resources, social rules, and means of continuity,[4] but there are many different ways of typifying the pattern of relations among these political communities. Modern international society comprises the norms, rules, established practices, and institutions that govern the relations among sovereign states. David Armstrong claims that a sovereign state may be defined as a community occupying a defined territory within which it is able to exercise juridical independence.[5] Alex Thomson also defines a state as a set of political institutions that govern within a delimited territory.[6]

The Peace of Westphalia (1648) is still regarded as one of the most important multilateral treaties concluded in international relations to date and is often also referred to as the founding date of the modern state system with its embedded ideas, practices, and norms of modern statehood and sovereignty.[7] Since that time, states have been a central feature of the political landscape, but it was only during the twentieth century that gave rise to unprecedented growth. In the wake of the collapse of the Ottoman and Austro-Hungarian empires following the end of the First World War, there were 59 states; this number had reached 69 soon after the Second World War in 1950. A decade later, following the attainment of independence in much of Africa, there were 90 national polities recognized as states in the world. After many more African, Asian, and Oceanic territories gained independence, and the implosion of the Soviet Union, the number of states leaped to 191; and if one considers Taiwan as an independent state from China, the current number of recognized states stands at 196.[8]

Within the failed state literature, the decisive criterion of success rather than failure is based on the state's possession of positive sovereignty.[9] This concept is most closely associated with Robert Jackson and is based in turn upon Max Weber's ideal state. According to Jackson:

> Positive sovereignty ... presupposes capabilities which enable governments to be their own masters: it is a substantive rather than a formal condition. A positively sovereign government is one which not only enjoys rights of non-intervention and other international immunities but also possesses the wherewithal to provide political goods for its citizens. It is also a government that can collaborate with other governments in defence alliances and similar international arrangements and reciprocate in international commerce and finance.[10]

A successful state, therefore, does not only enjoy international legal or *de jure* recognition of its statehood, but the government and organs of the state also possess the capabilities to project and protect their authority throughout the entirety of its sovereign territory and consequently enter into collaborative arrangements with other states.[11] It is exactly this ability of the government and organs of a state to exert their authority and enter into international relations with other states that result in them acquiring *de facto* statehood too, distinguishing them from negatively sovereign states. If positive sovereignty is defined as a substantive rather than a formal condition, then negative sovereignty can be said to represent its exact opposite. Jackson defines negative sovereignty as "freedom from outside interference: a formal-legal condition," but nothing else.[12] Strong states are characterized by positive sovereignty and, conversely weak states are characterized by negative sovereignty. In short, the sovereignty of successful states is both *de facto* and *de jure*, whereas the sovereignty of failing states is solely *de jure*.

States exist to provide a decentralized method of delivering political (public) goods to the citizens living within their designated territory.[13] "Political goods" may be defined as those intangible and hard to quantify claims that citizens made on sovereigns before the birth of the modern state characterized above, and now make on the state.[14] They encompass expectations and conceivable obligations, inform the local political culture, and give content to the social contract between the ruler and the ruled. This is at the core of regime/government and citizenry interactions.[15] Robert Rotberg argues that strong states may be distinguished from weak ones, and weak states from failed or collapsed states based on their possession of positive sovereignty and their levels of performance in delivering crucial political goods.[16]

Underpinning each of the descriptions, therefore, are predetermined definitions of what constitutes a non-failed or successful state and what it is that failed states are failing to be. Thus, failed states have been described variously as those that "can no longer perform the functions required for them to pass as states;"[17] those that "cannot or will not safeguard minimal civil conditions for their populations: domestic peace, law and order, and good governance;"[18] or those in which "public authorities are either unable or unwilling to carry out their end of what Thomas Hobbes called the social contract."[19] And within these definitions one finds two common elements. The first is the identification of failed states as being either unable and/or unwilling to perform the functions that they should and the second encompasses what these functions are, namely the provision of welfare, law and order, and security.[20]

A fundamental flaw with this approach is the assumption that all states are essentially alike and therefore function in similar ways. States considered to be functioning are perceived as legitimate actors and worthy recipients of Western donor assistance, whereas those unable or unwilling to function according to the standard template tend to be regarded with some suspicion. This categorization of states as either functioning or failing by donors and policymakers is reductive, non-contextualized, and ahistorical. This in turn often results in aggregation of diverse states, cookie-cutter prescriptions for strengthening states, a strong emphasis on order over democratic discourse, and a Western value bias concerning the modern role of the state, according to Charles Call.[21] Accordingly, he warns of throwing a monolithic coat over disparate problems that ultimately require tailored solutions.[22]

A more realistic approach—especially for Africa—is to focus on the capacity of the state to provide the most crucial political goods to its citizenry. In the hierarchy of political goods, none is more critical and central to the success of the state than security, especially human security.[23] The state's primary function, therefore, is to provide the citizenry with the political good of security: to prevent cross-border invasions and infiltrations, and any loss of territory; to eliminate domestic threats to or attacks upon the national order and social structure; to prevent crime and any related dangers to domestic human security; and to enable citizens to resolve their disputes with the state and with their fellow inhabitants without recourse to arms or other forms of physical coercion. In turn, the delivery of a range of other desirable political goods becomes possible when a reasonable measure of security has been sustained. These include everything from essential personal freedoms (such as civil liberties and human rights), health care and education to the promotion of commerce and the development of physical infrastructure. Considered together, the state's capacity to deliver a range of political goods starting with security establishes a set of criteria by which states may be judged as strong, weak, or failed, according to Rotberg.[24]

Scope and nature of the problem

Since the end of the Cold War, Africa has struggled mightily with the problem of weak and failing states. And while many of the challenges facing the African state today—capacity, delivery, legitimacy, and cohesiveness—are not new, they were historically overshadowed by a superpower rivalry that propped up faltering African governments. State collapse, especially of an ally, was not an option for either the United States or Soviet Union during the Cold War. But once this source of external support was removed, African countries were forced to fend for themselves, and long suppressed problems quickly erupted, Somalia becoming the poster child for African state collapse by 1992.

It is difficult, however, to determine the extent to which the concept of state failure actually guides policy prescriptions. Or is the concept merely used as justification for punitive or intrusive interventions in states deemed to pose a security threat to the international community, and the West in particular? Morten Bøås and Kathleen Jennings, for example, point out that the use of state failure as a pretext for intervention has an interesting converse, which is that states not facing interventions are typically not referred to as failed, even when they share some or all of the characteristics ascribed to those so labelled.[25] This would suggest that the labelling of states as "failing," "weak," or "fragile" has less to do with a particular state's functioning and more to do with its ability and willingness to partner with Western countries in the West's efforts to guarantee its own security, access resources, or gain support for its security agenda.

As a case in point, Africa's strategic significance as posing a security threat to Western security interests was raised post-9/11. Then Assistant Secretary of State for Africa, Susan Rice, described Africa as the world's "soft underbelly for global terrorism."[26] Likewise, the *2002 National Security Strategy of the United States* also changed the calculus of Africa's strategic significance by identifying that "weak states ... can pose as great a danger to our [US] national interests as strong states." It continues and emphasizes that: "Poverty does not make poor people into terrorists and murderers. Yet poverty, weak institutions, and corruption can make weak states vulnerable to terrorist networks and drug cartels within their borders."[27] In addition, a rising concern for the CIA, that "vast stretches of ungoverned areas—lawless zones" were creating safe havens for extremists elements to recuperate and grow, focused renewed attention on the security threat posed by failing states[28]—so much so that the Pentagon soon launched an Ungoverned Areas Project, and a senior US State Department official called the challenge "one of the toughest ones this and future administrations will face."[29]

On a positive note, some countries, such as Cote d'Ivoire, Liberia, or Rwanda, once considered on the verge of state collapse have made significant progress over time in addressing many of their challenges. Others, such as Botswana and Senegal, have a long history of state stability thanks to visionary political leadership and the growth of responsive and inclusive institutions. Despite this good news, Africa remains a continent littered with states or quasi-states containing porous borders, widespread poverty, political alienation, religious radicalism, and repression, which have combined to create an environment that presents a serious security challenge to the continent and the international community.

As we noted earlier, the modern African state differs markedly from the classic Westphalian state, and indeed James Ferguson powerfully argues that "the state" may not actually refer to an actor in the African context at all. Rather he notes it is a name of a process tying together a multiplicity of formal and informal power relations.[30] Unlike a classic Westphalian state, its African counterpart importantly does not possess a monopoly of coercive force over its territory and activities normally associated with states (such as commerce and waging war); many of these activities are often exercised by non-state actors within the formal African state.[31]

William Zartman provides an interesting approach to analyzing state failure in Africa that is useful to our understanding. Rather than defining the nature of the phenomenon and then proceeding to examine its occurrence deductively, he reverses the procedure by developing an initial analysis inductively from a brief empirical review. Zartman suggests that to better understand the nature of state failure, one can return to the recognition of the two key phases of state failure as they occurred in Africa.[32]

The first phase came in the late 1970s and early 1980s when new regimes replaced the nationalist generation that brought about independence in such countries as Chad, Ghana, and Uganda. Unfortunately, these new regimes proved incapable of correcting the weakness of their predecessors and improving governance. This, in turn, undermined their legitimacy. Now deficient in resources, legitimacy, capability, and security, the state began to collapse.

The second wave came in the early 1990s, and is characterized by states made vulnerable when they constricted power, conducting governance for the benefit of a narrow, often ethnically identifiable few, alienating the general population.[33] Interestingly, this phase came at the same time as the second wave of democratization on the African continent and resulted in the rise of popular movements calling for a greater role by civil society. The most notable expression of this trend was the Sovereign National Conference that arose in 12 West and Central African countries. Here and in other parts of the continent, these popular movements helped to overthrow authoritarian rulers, rewrite constitutions, and implement multiparty elections. The degree and duration of state failure in these countries varied widely according to local conditions—a strong violent reaction in the DRC, Ethiopia, Liberia, Sierra Leone, and Somalia, yet a reasonably peaceful transition in the South African case.

From this analysis Zartman identifies nine overarching characteristics pertaining to state failure,[34] but we will focus our attention on just a few important themes that help to define the nature of the failed state in Africa today.

First, just as the state fails because it is too weak and lacking in capacity as to be incapable of functioning, so too the state can fail because it is so heavy-handed and authoritarian that it alienates and isolates itself from the general population. Often characterized by increasingly personalized rule and dependence on a narrow patronage group (often familial, ethnic or sectarian) these states project an image of strong centralized control that masks their fragility. Sudan under Nimeiri in the mid-1980s exhibited many of these characteristics that undermined state capacity and the legitimacy of his regime, while setting the stage for the future fragmentation of the territorial integrity of the state. Thus, donor policies designed to strengthen the power of the state without due concern for its base of support may ultimately do more harm than good and actually precipitate the weakening or even collapse of the state.

This brings up an important related point. State failure in Africa is neither tied to one single cataclysmic event nor is it even linear in nature. So too, the process of state failure can vary widely in terms of duration and intensity. It can span decades of slow decline in some instances or rapidly implode into chaos in others. Extreme cases, such as Somalia and the DRC, tend to garner the most visibility, but the steady erosion of state capacity in Nigeria or Zimbabwe can have just as serious—if not more—long-term implications for sub-regional stability and security.

Likewise, even the most severe state collapse does not necessarily mean societal collapse. Again there seems to be two typical scenarios: either the imploding state takes civil society down with it, or civil society pulls back into itself at the local level and makes do, performing resiliently and filling the gaps left by the state. In this latter scenario, civil society can revert to communal structures, elders, and traditional religious leaders, and ethnic identities. In either of these environments, people continue to find means of subsistence, trade and conduct business, and find alternative means of education and adjudication. As the most severe cases of state collapse have shown, African societies are highly resilient. Life goes on. Processes and individuals, albeit often local and informal, step in to fill the void more in keeping with Ferguson's view of state functions in Africa. The situation of the non-Westphalian state and the absence of any central authority, however, present a major obstacle for the conduct of international relations.

In these situations, the desire for a return to normalcy is a strong one. State collapse or a severe weakening of the state leaves a society hungry for a normal life, responsive government, and a source of legitimacy, and law and order. It also pushes neighboring states and global powers to assist in re-establishing order and preventing the spread of sub-regional instability. While the atmosphere for restoration is encouraging, the tendency is to support quick, top-down fixes rather than address the root causes of the collapse. And this may result in a more, not less, dysfunctional society for longer durations. It can also produce wild swings from one end of the political spectrum to the other. For instance, protest movements against a corrupt, inefficient, or self-serving state helped produce attempted Islamist takeovers in Sudan in 1989, Algeria in 1991, and Egypt in 2012, but the resulting backlash led to the reestablishment of authoritarian military-civilian governments.

Notably, failed or fragile states also tend to cluster together and produce broader pockets of sub-regional instability. This is fueled in part by the extensive economic, ethnic, communal, or religious ties that historically transcend African national borders and can facilitate the spread of instability to neighboring vulnerable states. Moreover, the resulting cauldron of instability often reinforces a violent cycle of state failure that ebbs and flows from one neighbor to the next, which complicates problem solving. Thus, neglecting to address state failure on a wider transnational basis will likely result in national solutions collapsing over time and returning the state to a condition as bad if not worse than before. The ongoing situation in the Horn of Africa and the eastern DRC clearly highlights the difficulty in creating effective transnational solutions to the problem of failing states.

What does this all mean for the future of the African state? First and foremost, the African state will not disappear. It is resilient, but it is also very different. As David Francis argues, the African state is "fundamentally different from the western-centric understanding of the state and statehood" and "is dynamic, incorporating indigenous and traditional norms of governance with the trappings of the Westphalian modern state."[35] And as such state reconstruction is not about replicating Western notions, but finding ways to more accurately reflect the reality of the African political and social environment. This will be a challenge not only for Africa but for the international community and the West in particular, who seem unwilling to abandon the Westphalian construct. For if they continue to focus only on this idealized notion of the state, any solution is merely temporary and it papers over rather than addresses the underlying problems. Success will be transitory and will ultimately facilitate a return to the chaos of the past. It will likely produce frustration, futility, and calls for disengagement. Rather it is better to leverage the African experience as a template for developing a new hybrid state that incorporates Western notions, but more appropriately also reflects the African notions of societal governance—leadership accountability, responsiveness, and advancing the greater good.

Case study: the myth of "Somalia"

Often cited as the very epitome of state collapse, Somalia has long been a contested concept even amongst Somalis. It embodies one of post-colonial Africa's worst mismatches between conventional state structures and indigenous customs and institutions.[a] During the nineteenth century, the United Kingdom, France, Italy, and Ethiopia laid claim on the Somali-inhabited territories in the Horn of Africa and divided "Greater Somalia" into five distinct political jurisdictions. One might assume then that Somalia possesses an excellent basis for a cohesive polity, given the fact that Somalis share a common ethnicity, culture, language, and religion. But in reality Somalis are divided by territorial borders and clan affiliations—the most important component of their identity.[b] The unification of the former British Somaliland and

---

[a] S. Kaplan, 'Rethinking state-building in a failed state', *The Washington Quarterly*, 33:1 (2010), 82.
[b] Ibid.

Italian Somaliland following independence on July 1, 1960 to form the Republic of Somalia still excluded Somali brethren from neighboring territories in what is today Djibouti, eastern Ethiopia, and northern Kenya. Somalia's current strife began in 1969 when General Muhammad Siad Barre overthrew elected president Abdirashid Ali Shermarke in a military coup. Since then Somalia has been characterized by bouts of civil and international war, resulting in profound instability that still persists today.

Somalia's political and economic development stagnated under the authoritarian socialist regime of President Barre, being characterized by persecution and the jailing and torture of political opponents, with the president inordinately favoring members of his own *Darod* clan-family.[c] Barre's unsuccessful attempt to conquer Ethiopia's Somali-inhabited region, the Ogaden, in 1977 led to a national crisis, which eventually contributed to internal dissent and civil war. Barre's regime collapsed in 1991 and the country fell further into a state of disarray and violent clan-militia warfare.

The Somali population—some 13–14 million, including Somalis living in neighboring countries—is divided into four major clans and a number of minority groups. Similar to tribal societies elsewhere in the Middle East, the clans use deeply ingrained customary law to independently govern their communities from modern state structures. There have been over a dozen Somali national reconciliation peace agreement attempts over the last two decades to reconstitute the state that existed when Barre came to power, but these agreements persistently fail due to clan rivalries and misrepresentation of all the clans in talks. From 1996–97, for example, the Sodere Conference in Ethiopia introduced the "4.5 formula"—a clever formula designed to enable fair power-sharing among the large Somali clan-families. However, it was regarded as a discriminatory and controversial policy at the cost of the smaller clans and minorities (the "0.5") and was later seen to create more problems among the Somalis than it solved.[d]

But what brought the collapse of the Somali state about? It is fundamental to note that the Somali state's failure originates from internal problems that cannot be fully addressed by the international response. The fact that the international response has been more concerned with the spill-over effects of state failure is illustrated from a historical perspective. Hussein Adam lists the main factors under eight headings—seven are considered to be essentially internal factors, with the eighth considered an external factor.[e]

[c] M. Ibrahim, 'Somalia and global terrorism: A growing connection?' *Journal of Contemporary African Studies*, 28:3 (2003), 283.
[d] Ibid., p. 284.
[e] H. Adam, 'Somalia: A troubled beauty being born', in William Zartman (ed.), *Collapsed States: The Disintegration and Restoration of Legitimate Authority* (Boulder, CO: Lynne Rienner Publishers, 1995), pp. 70–6.

Personalized rule. After assassinating President Sharmarke in a coup d'état in October 1969, General Mohamed Siad Barre, like many other African rulers, installed a personalized rule when he took over the Somali state which lasted to 1991. His prolonged dictatorial rule damaged and distorted state-civil relations and his final year in power was characterised by a civil war. Aid indirectly fuelled the civil war, and the withdrawal of aid by the international community led to the end of Barre's reign in January 1991 at the hands of the United Somali Congress.[f]

Military rule. Barre's dictatorial rule did not function in an institutional vacuum. Barre understood the need for states to be able to wield authoritative force. Soon after independence, the Somali army numbered a mere 3,000. The Soviet Union agreed to train and equip an army of 12,000 and by 1977 a 37,000-strong army entered the Ogaden War. By 1982 the numbers in the Somali army had grown to 120,000, and the army of liberation had been converted into a huge army of repression.[g] The military was also used to control other sectors of society.

From nomenklatura to clan-klatura. Nomenklatura involves appointing loyal political agents to guide and control civil and military institutions, and the introduction of the concept to Somalia by the Soviets involved politicisation of institutions that were beginning to function well, relying on education and training, technical competence, specialisation, and experience.[h] As early as 1972, the military regime began to appoint political commissars for the armed forces, administrative institutions, and social organisations. Barre soon began to substitute clanism for ideology as criteria for such appointments, favouring three sub-clans from the Darod clan-family.

From class rule to clan rule. Once Barre dropped scientific socialism as his guiding ideology, instead of resorting to Islam as President Jafaar Nimeiri did in the Sudan, Barre turned to clanism.[i] Hardly any members of his clan gained strong bourgeois connections during his reign, and promising clan members were plucked out of educational institutions to fill clan-klatura positions. Conversely, Barre sought to destroy the bourgeois element of other clans by sending members to jail or to exile abroad. The damage done to the Somali elite class partly explains both the total state collapse and the delay in Somali state renewal.

---

[f] T. Dagne and A. Smith, 'Somalia: Prospect for peace and U.S. involvement', in N. Fitzgerald (ed.), *Somalia: Issues, History and Bibliography* (New York: Nova Science Publishers, 2002), p. 2.
[g] Adam, Somalia: A troubled beauty being born, p. 71.
[h] Ibid., p. 71.
[i] Ibid., p. 72.

Poisoning clan relations. The clan-klatura havoc created within state institutions was exported into rural society.[j] After the Ogaden War (1977–78), Barre pursued brutal divide-and-rule policies by utilising his army to arm so-called loyal clans and encouraging them to wage wars against rebel clans. The damage caused by elite manipulation of clan consciousness contributed to the inability of civil society to rebound when Barre fell from power, and it is argued that it will take years still to heal these societal wounds.

Urban state terror. Young people started to disappear in regional cities like Hargeisa in the north of Somalia, considered rebel territory, during the early 1980s.[k] This phenomenon spread to other towns, eventually arriving in Mogadishu. During 1989 and 1990, Barre's clan-klatura forces massacred hundreds of religious protesters, and the vindictive terror-state that he created laid the basis for wars of revenge that postponed civil society's ability to create a successor state.

The campaign against the North. Northern Somalia (formerly British Somaliland) came to resent the South for various reasons.[l] At independence and unification in 1960, the South monopolised all key positions: president, prime minister, commander of the army and head of the national police. The former prime minister of the North, Mohamed Ibrahim Egal, merely became minister of education in the unity government. The conflict between the North and the South generated low-intensity demands for distributional benefits within the political system, which, when unsatisfied, escalated into the current high-intensity demand for separate statehood and independence for Somaliland once the Barre regime collapsed.

External factors. Military, technical, and financial foreign assistance played a key role in prolonging the life of the Barre regime.[m] Somalia's geographic position on the Red Sea and Indian Ocean has long attracted foreign interests. Early in Barre's rule, the Soviet Union provided substantial military and economic assistance, including fuel, supplying financing for project local costs that helped cushion the Somali economy from international economic conditions. After 1977, the Americans replaced the Soviets in providing armaments—unlike the Russians, sending mostly defensive arms—and during the 1980s, about $100 million of economic aid per year. Barre also managed to manoeuvre Somalia into the Arab League in 1974 resulting in the regime benefitting significantly from Arab petrodollar assistance.

---

[j] Ibid., p. 73.
[k] Ibid., p. 73.
[l] Ibid., p. 74.
[m] Ibid., p. 75.

The government coup in 1991 left a political vacuum, and after fifteen years of chaos, characterized by the outbreak of civil war between the tribal warlords, a fundamentalist Islamic group emerged in early 2006, gaining unprecedented support from many citizens.[n] The Union of Islamic Courts (UIC), a loose confederation of regional judiciary systems, defeated the ruling CIA-backed warlords that controlled Mogadishu in June 2006, becoming more politically powerful and relevant than the rival Transitional Federal Government (TFG) based in Baidoa.[o] For many Somalis, the UIC appeared to be the long-sought solution to years of state collapse, reason enough to support the Islamists.[p] Although the UIC did not enjoy any form of democratic legitimacy, it nevertheless provided a higher level of security and a modest economic upsurge.[q]

Although al-Shabaab was not active and did not control any territory until 2007–8, the primary objective of this group was irredentism and to establish the "Greater Somalia" under Islamic law or *Shari'a*. The Ethiopian invasion of Somalia in December 2006 led to the disintegration of the UIC system, and while the UIC leadership moved to Eritrea, al-Shabaab's secretive leadership slowly took control over the resistance movement.[r] After being exiled, the UIC split into separate factions. Many Somalis then joined the fight against Ethiopian occupation.

The strategic significance of al-Shabaab to the United States was raised in 2008, when the then Secretary of State Condoleeza Rice designated al-Shabaab as a Foreign Terrorist Organization and as a Specially Designated Global Terrorist.[s] Al-Shabaab only formally joined the ranks of al-Qaeda in February 2012, when the *emir* (leader) of al-Shabaab, Ahmed Abdi Godane, proclaimed that he "pledged obedience" to al-Qaeda head, Ayman al Zawahiri, in a joint video.[t]

Apart from frequent suicide attacks carried out by al-Shabaab in Mogadishu and elsewhere, al-Shabaab carried out the twin suicide bombings in Uganda's capital, Kampala. This attack killed 76 people watching the 2010 football World Cup final and was in response to Uganda's involvement in contributing

[n] M. Simpson, 'An Islamic solution to state failure in Somalia', *Geopolitics of the Middle East*, 2:1 (2009), 33.
[o] M. Shank, 'Understanding political Islam in Somalia', *Contemporary Islam* (2007).
[p] K. Menkhaus, 'The crisis in Somalia: Tragedy in five acts', *African Affairs*, 106:204 (2007), 371.
[q] A. Kasaija, 'The UN-led Djibouti peace process for Somalia 2008–2009: Results and problems,' *Journal of Contemporary African Studies*, 28:3 (2010), 265.
[r] T. Dagne, *Somalia: Current Conditions and Prospects for a Lasting Peace* (Washington, DC: Congressional Research Services Report, October 2010), p. 5.
[s] C. Rice, 'Designation of al-Shabaab', *Office of the Coordinator for Counterterrorism* (March 18, 2008), accessed at www.state.gov/j/ct/rls/other/des/143205.htm on 28 February 2017.
[t] *Al Jazeera*, 'Al Shabaab "Joins Ranks" With Al Qaeda' (February 10, 2012).

(along with Burundi) the bulk of the African Union Mission in Somalia that deployed in February 2007.[u]

The fifteenth attempt since 1991 to restore central governance in Somalia saw the birth of the TFG in 2004. This was the product of protracted negotiations rather than elections.[v] Reflecting the influences of the clan-based society of Somalia, the TFG adopted the "4.5 formula," evenly dividing representation in parliament amongst the four main clan-families (the *Darod*, *Hawiye*, *Dir*, and *Digle-Marifle*), plus five minority constituencies. From its founding in 2004 until June 2005, the TFG had to meet in neighboring Kenya out of security fears. From June 2005 until February 2006, the parliament did not convene, and convened again finally on Somali soil in the western city of Baidoa in February 2006.[w]

The election of Sheik Sharif Sheik Ahmed, the former head of the deposed UIC, as the new president of an expanded TFG on January 31, 2009 resulted in dramatic changes in the political landscape of Somalia.[x] In March 2009, the TFG adopted a Somali version of *Shari'a*, challenging the legitimacy of al-Shabaab as the preferred vessel to Islamize Somalia. Despite substantial financial assistance and much other international help, the TFG remained largely confined to Mogadishu.

But after more than two decades of state collapse, Somalia made a number of commendable strides on the political front. In September 2011, a political roadmap was agreed upon by the major Somali constituencies, detailing the delivery of transitional milestones before the expiry of the TFG's mandate.[y] The international responses to the roadmap in the form of the London and Istanbul conferences once again illustrated the international community's increased interest in Somalia due to the perceivable security threat that state failure presents and the need to overcome failure in an attempt to secure their own security interests. The London Conference on Somalia on February 23, 2012—aimed at achieving a "Somali consensus" for international cooperation after the transition period—ended in August 2012 and attracted over 40 heads of states, including representatives from the United States, the United

---

[u] BBC News, 'Q&A: Who are Somalia's al Shabaab?' (October 5, 2012), accessed at www.bbc.co.uk/news/world-africa-15336689 on February 28, 2017.

[v] B. Hesse, 'The myth of "Somalia"', *Journal of Contemporary African Studies*, 28:3 (2010), 252.

[w] Ibid., p. 253.

[x] International Crisis Group, 'Somalia's divided Islamists,' *Africa Briefing No. 74* (Policy Briefing, May 2010), p. 6.

[y] K. Chitiyo and A. Rader, *Somalia 2012: Ending the Transition?* (Johannesburg: The Brenthurst Foundation Discussion Paper 4, 2012), accessed at www.thebrenthurstfoundation.org/files/brenthurst_commisioned_reports/ Brenthurst-paper-201204-Somalia-2012-Ending-the-Transition.pdf on February 28, 2017.

Kingdom and Turkey.[z] The Somali Federal Government emerged as the successor of the TFG.

In February 2017, Mohamed Abdullahi Mohamed (known as Mohamed Farmajo), a dual Somali-US citizen, defeated incumbent President Hassan Sheik Mohamud (2012–17) after two rounds of parliamentary voting. Amid threats of violence from al-Shabaab the election was generally peaceful, but somewhat tainted by reports of vote buying and corruption.[aa] Despite President Farmajo's optimism, he will confront many of the same challenges as his predecessor—the persistent al-Shabaab insurgency, Somalia's failed state status, and the government's continued heavy reliance on peacekeepers of the African Union Mission in Somalia.

[z] Ibid.
[aa] *allAfrica.com*, 'Somalia: Election heralds unexpected fresh start' (February 13, 2017), accessed at http://allafrica.com/stories/201702130819.html on February 28, 2017.

Implications for security

Both the process itself and the manifestation of the failed state phenomena in Africa have serious implications, not only for the future of statehood, but for the advancement of human security itself. For, as we have seen earlier, at the heart of our definition of human security is freedom from fear and freedom from want. However, if the state lacks the capacity to provide these things then security is severely compromised. Failed and failing states by definition lack the capacity to deliver public goods—most notably security—to their societies.

The loss of positive sovereignty as the state begins to fail directly compromises the territorial integrity of the state, its ability to maintain social order and structure, and to protect its citizenry. This, in turn, jeopardizes the state's legitimacy, its monopoly on the use of force with the rise of powerful non-state actors, and, moreover, its ability to function within the Westphalian system. This latter situation creates a severe security challenge for the international community because today's global security architecture is anchored within the Westphalian state structure and the continuation of this structure is seen as essential to a secure and stable world. Accordingly, states work together to enhance not only their domestic security, but international security as well. Without an effective state system there can be no true security and thus, by extension a failure of one means a failure of the other.

This interdependence, however, frequently complicates international efforts to reconstitute fragile and failing states because the systematic need for a central focal point incentivizes outsiders to prioritize strengthening the central authority of the troubled state, and this is the paradox of the failing state in Africa.

Too strong a state and too much concentrated power can feed state collapse by alienating and dividing society, stimulating fragmentation, and further weakening the state. Thus, while well-intended, this common top-down approach to redressing the problem of failing states in Africa by buttressing central government is often counterproductive. It is an imposed solution. It refuses to acknowledge the factors that fueled state collapse in the first place and hinders the evolution of domestic bottom-up solutions. Attempting to build long-term security on such a shaky foundation is usually a recipe for disaster, resulting in ineffective and expensive peacekeeping and stability operations and decades of frustration. Just as elsewhere in the world, the record of international nation building in Africa is a poor one—for every Liberia or Sierra Leone success there is a seemingly unsolvable DRC or Somalia.

Much more common in Africa than complete state collapse is the persistence of weak and fragile states that exercise limited functions. Their capability to deliver public goods is highly circumscribed by not only a serious lack of resources and expertise, but also as a result of questions over legitimacy, inclusiveness or political will, as well as competition from alternative centers of power and influence. Over time they tend to become increasingly reliant on coercive measures that only serve to further alienate the people. Not surprisingly in a post-9/11 world, the United States identifies weak and fragile states as posing a great danger to American national security interests—and Africa is full of these states. Largely because of their inability to exercise effective control over national territory and deliver critical public goods, these weak and fragile states present an enormous international, as well as domestic and regional, challenge to the security of the continent, its people, and the global community.

Cross-cutting security linkages
The inability of many African states to maintain control over parts of their national territory has created wide swathes of "ungoverned spaces" (or more accurately under-governed spaces) across the continent, which not only threaten the stability of these governments, but also facilitate an enabling environment for the rise and/or strengthening of a whole host of non-state actors ranging from international terrorist groups and transnational criminal cartels to violent religious extremists and armed separatist movements. Once established, the void of state power allows these groups to roam unfettered from government interference. They

may even begin to develop alternative political and economic power bases that directly challenge the supremacy of the state itself. While the rise and decline of alternative non-state centers of power and illicit activities on the periphery has been a historic feature of African states, the melding of international and domestic groups and their increasingly globalized agenda has become particularly worrisome to those both in and outside of the continent. Beginning in 2003, for example, the US intelligence community specifically started to highlight the challenge posed by "vast stretches of ungoverned areas—lawless zones, veritable 'no man's lands' ... where extremists movements find shelter and can win the breathing space to grow."[36] Within five years the elimination of these alleged illicit safe havens became a central element of US counterinsurgency, counterterrorism, counter-narcotics, stabilization, and peacekeeping operational strategies.[37]

While overstated, American fears that so-called ungoverned parts of Africa could become the "next Afghanistan" and serve as safe havens from which to recruit, plan, and launch terrorist operations against the United States and its allies led to the creation of the Combined Joint Task Force-Horn of Africa in 2002 and the Trans-Saharan Counterterrorism Initiative in 2005. Beyond direct action, these efforts were designed to build capacity, implement civic action programs, and promote stability in the Horn of Africa and the pan-Sahel. If, so the reasoning went, the United States could strengthen weak and vulnerable African states it could not only eliminate terrorist safe havens, but enhance local capacity to improve governance and economic conditions in marginal regions.[38]

More than a decade and billions of dollars later, the results of these efforts have been mixed at best. Thanks to international and African Union (AU) efforts, some progress has been made in Somalia and a process of de facto decentralization has produced stability in parts of the country. The independence of South Sudan has resulted in greater local autonomy and government responsiveness on the one hand, but has also exposed serious, violent social rifts within that society. Meanwhile, the CIA reportedly now lists at least five African countries—Libya, Mali, Mauritania, Nigeria, and Somalia—as potential safe havens and "external operations platforms" for Islamic extremists that require close monitoring.[39]

But most terrifying in recent years has been the dramatic rise and power of the Boko Haram Islamist movement in Nigeria and the threat it poses to central government authority. The movement, which represents the deadly confluence of radical Islam, international terrorism, and separatism, was once estimated to have controlled a 10,000 square mile tract (about the size of Belgium) in the northeastern part of Nigeria.

Repeated government efforts to crush the rebellion failed miserably to constrain its growth. In fact, Boko Haram gained considerable momentum, intensifying attacks on both the government and civilian populations since 2010 and threatened to destabilize not only Africa's largest economy and key oil exporting state, but several of Nigeria's neighbors as well. Thanks in large part to a powerful military coalition of Nigeria's neighbors in 2015, the central government and its allies were able to inflict severe defeats on the movement and recapture nearly all of the territory formerly under Boko Haram's control. But the movement—and the threat it poses to Nigeria and sub-regional security—is far from eliminated, as witnessed by Boko Haram's continued ability after its 2015–16 setbacks to strike towns and kill civilians in the northeast, as well as launch retaliatory suicide bombings and attacks in Cameroon, Chad, and Niger.

This latter point is worth emphasizing. One state's security vulnerability can quickly become another's and then another's, as problems fueled by state failure can spread beyond national borders. In today's globalized world, local problems rarely remain so—they become transnational ones. This is especially true in the African context. The spillover effect of state failure onto regional neighbors exemplifies the regionalization of insecurity in Africa today. In extreme cases this level of insecurity can create self-perpetuating regional clusters of weak and failing states that linger for years, if not decades. Failure to address problems on a wider transnational basis often results in national solutions collapsing over time and returning the state to a condition as bad if not worse than before. The situation in Liberia and Sierra Leone within the Mano River Basin in the 1980s and 1990s, the eastern DRC and its Great Lakes neighbors in 1990s and 2000s or modern-day Somalia, highlight the difficulty in crafting long-term solutions to the problem of failing states.

The predicament of state-centric solutions
Weak and fragile African states present a fundamental security dilemma: is the state part of the problem or part of the solution? The answer, of course, is both. And herein lies the challenge, especially for regional and international engagement. Weak or ineffective state political structures, divisive ruling elite policies, and institutional corruption are symptoms and drivers of state failure and are clearly part of the problem of instability and insecurity. Yet, the state and its existing—albeit flawed—institutional framework is too often seen as the only viable structure capable of providing true security. Approaches that rely on strengthening the state and governing regimes continue to dominate the response to weak and failing states and its associated security challenges.

This is especially true for the international community and how foreign governments and institutions have traditionally responded to state failure in Africa. The heavy reliance on a state centric engagement approach implies that the African state exists in the same way as its richer Western counterpart. Moreover, it assumes that capacitating African states with the requisite technical expertise and financial resources will serve to secure national security and thereby contribute to international security. But this engagement approach fails to recognize the often predatory nature of the state that equates regime security with national security and thus treats challenges to one as indistinguishable from challenges to the other. Ultimately, trying to strengthen a flawed structure will do little to enhance national (much less international) security and, more importantly, is more likely to further alienate elements within the society or drive them into the hands of government opponents or violent extremists.

A striking example of the pitfalls of state centric thinking is readily apparent when it comes to addressing the challenge of terrorism and extremist-inspired violence in Africa in the context of failing states. While widely acknowledged that long-term solutions to these problems require a broad-based societal approach that goes beyond governmental action to incorporate informal power structures and civil society engagement, the most common response by governments and their international allies is a state-centric approach that seeks to strengthen African militaries and the security organs of the state. The underlying rationale is that these traditional state structures are the only truly effective institutions or societal actors capable of addressing this challenge. Not surprisingly then, scarce resources and international assistance are directed heavily toward these institutions, which further undermines the capabilities of non-governmental structures, yielding a self-fulfilling prophecy. While this state-to-state approach to engagement is easy and routine, the challenge of terrorism and extremist-inspired violence in failing states is anything but easy and routine. Ultimately, non-traditional challenges such as these require a reconceptualization of the nature of the African state and its relationship to the society it seeks to safeguard.

Likewise, critical African regional and sub-regional institutions charged with enhancing security rely almost exclusively on a state model and structure too. The AU's peace and security architecture, for instance, is rooted in the state system and the effectiveness (or ineffectiveness) of states. It can only be as effective as its weakest members. Weak states result in a weak union of states and, by extension, the creation of ineffectual security programs and mechanisms because the state itself is often a large part of the security problem. The same can be said for the sub-regional economic communities, such as the Economic Community of West African States or the Southern Africa Development Community, that are viewed as the primary instruments for countering regional threats to peace and security. Nonetheless, issues of state sovereignty and excessive deference to regime wishes have repeatedly allowed national governments to veto collective action when they feel their own interests are at stake. During Burundi's recent political crisis, which many believed would plunge the country back into a bloody civil war, President Pierre Nkurunziza went so far as to threaten to fight peacekeepers, which he called "an invasion force," should they be deployed to his country without the government's permission.[40] President Nkurunziza apparently had support for his position among some African leaders who were reluctant to endorse such a move because "Burundi is a sovereign country," according to press reports.[41]

Clearly African states and a reliance on the state system with all its overt trappings of authority and power are part of the problem of insecurity. Rather than being an indicator of strength, the heavy-handed exercise of governmental power and repressive tactics all too often exacerbate, instead of mitigate, insecurity. Though states are part of the solution, they are not the sole option. Today, because of a heavily weighted state centric approach, there exists a sizeable disconnect between the language and intellectual acceptance of human security and its implementation in Africa. Part of this will undoubtedly require reinventing the modern African state; one that is more inclusive of the society, and with greater engagement from the bottom up. Finding the right balance in the context of each state's history, culture, and political background will be essential for both Africans and non-Africans alike.

Future trends
While weak and failing states have long been a part of the African security landscape, the continent and the global community must now come to terms with the permanent existence of the actual failed state as a new norm. Some failing states will implode and never recover. Libya is on a similar course and the eastern DRC has been a de facto autonomous region for decades. Not all weak or failing states are on an inevitable path to collapse and national disintegration though. Moreover, new states inevitably will arise from the ashes of the old post-independent state, the relative success of Somaliland and Puntland being cases in point. Nonetheless, the Africa Union and the international community will almost certainly continue to be wedded to nation rebuilding given their persistent reliance on the state as the central referent of security. This

mind set, moreover, will complicate other efforts to promote human security solutions to the challenge of weak and failing states.

At the other end of the spectrum, some weak African states are likely to make sustained progress on reinventing themselves as more representative of their people and societies and thus become less fragile and vulnerable. While advancements in democratic reforms, the creation of more representative institutions, and increased popular inclusion will undoubtedly suffer periodic setbacks, the process of political and socio-economic engagement from the bottom up is a critical one to recasting the role of the state. And this bodes well for improved human security and stability.

The vast majority of African states, however, will probably fall somewhere between these two extremes and their future is unclear. Some will make strides toward reinventing themselves, others will not. Those with a legacy of authoritarian leadership and emphasis on regime security, such as Algeria, Egypt, Ethiopia, and Zimbabwe for instance, are likely to be especially susceptible to state failure. Moreover, their continued dependence on traditional security mechanisms—the military, police, and intelligence organizations—to ensure state stability makes them particularly ill-suited to address twenty-first-century security challenges. These types of regimes are also less likely to embrace the human security paradigm and the use of non-traditional mechanisms to build security from the bottom up. The old model of a highly centralized, state-centric approach to security is increasingly becoming irrelevant and ineffectual in meeting the real needs of Africans.

Finally, as we shall see later on in this book, foreign governments and international governmental organizations (both at the bilateral and multilateral levels) are, however, loath to abandon the state-centric engagement model. Unwillingness to accept the failed state as a new norm will continue to fuel periodic episodes of state reconstruction initiatives—and failure. No amount of good will or money will be able to put some failed states back together. These efforts, moreover, are more likely to fuel a deterioration of the old state and its legitimacy. Knowing when not to intervene and the limits of intervention will be just as, if not more, important than the actual intervention itself, and this is likely to be challenging for both international and African actors alike.

Conclusion

While certainly not unique to the continent, the phenomena of weak or failing states is widespread and has more serious implications in Africa than anywhere else because of the crucial role the African state plays (or fails to play) in building human security at the national, sub-regional, and regional level. Despite the ongoing debate over the future of the African state and its relevance in an increasingly globalized world, the state still remains a key tool in shaping the African security environment and addressing the challenges of the twenty-first century. No matter how flawed, the state structure and system in Africa is not going away.

African states have been around a long time; many of the great kingdoms of pre-colonial Africa were able to exercise enormous power and their rulers had vast capabilities that we commonly associate with the modern-day nation-state. More often than not, they were no more "nations" than the African states of today. Governance and security came from the top down. Security was an imposed construct that was more about protecting the regime than protecting the society and delivering public goods. Rather than return to some romanticized view of the pre-colonial African state as the solution, it is better to extract the key features of the African historical experience that replicate democratic principles, inclusiveness, transparency, and responsiveness. Using these concepts as the building blocks of the new state–society relationship, the resulting bottom-up approach will more likely produce a truly Africanized state that has greater legitimacy and is more in tune with the needs of its people.

This will take a greatly changed mindset, yet the human security construct provides a useful roadmap. Human security flows from the bottom up and is widely inclusive of society, reflecting of a wide and, more importantly, diverse set of stakeholders. In contrast, the traditional state model often imposes its power from top down and can be very restrictive as to which elements of society it serves. Here security may be for the few and more aligned with protecting the regime or state itself. It is merely a perpetuation of the status quo. Thus, the debate over reforming the state to provide better security carries a connotation greater than governance or improving capacity. It is really about inclusion and building a more cohesive and responsive society that reflects the collective interests and well-being of the entire nation and its people. This is human security, and meeting its demands will require both vision and patience—two attributes that are often in short supply when addressing the challenge of failing states in Africa.

Notes

1 C. Call, 'The fallacy of the "failed state"', *Third World Quarterly*, 29:8 (2008), 1495.
2 Fund for Peace, *Fragile States Index 2016*.
3 Ibid.

4 K. Holsti, *Taming the Sovereigns: Institutional Change in International Politics* (Cambridge: Cambridge University Press, 2004), p. 28.
5 D. Armstrong, 'The evolution of international society', in J. Baylis, S. Smith, and P. Owens (eds), *The Globalization of World Politics: An Introduction to World Politics* (Oxford: Oxford University Press, 2008), p. 29.
6 A. Thomson, *An Introduction to African Politics*, 2nd edn (New York: Routledge, 2009), p. 4.
7 Holsti, *Taming the Sovereigns*, p. 42.
8 United States Department of State, *Independent States in the World* (Washington, DC: Bureau of Intelligence and Research, 2012), accessed at www.state.gov/s/inr/rls/4250.htm on February 25, 2017.
9 J. Hill, 'Beyond the other? A postcolonial critique of the failed states thesis', *African Identities*, 3:2 (2005), 146.
10 R. Jackson, *Quasi-States: Sovereignty, International Relations, and the Third World* (Cambridge: Cambridge University Press, 1990), p. 29.
11 Hill, Beyond the other? 146.
12 Jackson, *Quasi-States*, p. 27.
13 R. Rotberg, 'Failed states, collapsed states, weak states: Causes and indicators', in R. Rotberg (ed.), *State Failure and State Weakness in a Time of Terror* (Washington DC: Brookings Institution Press, 2003), p. 2.
14 Ibid., p. 3.
15 J. Pennock, 'Political development, political systems, and political goods', *World Politics* (XVIII, 1966), 433.
16 Rotberg, 'Failed states, collapsed states, weak states', p. 2.
17 W. Zartman, 'Introduction: Posing the problem of state collapse', in W. Zartman (ed.), *Collapsed States: The Disintegration and Restoration of Legitimate Authority* (Boulder, CO: Lynne Rienner Publishers, 1995), p. 5.
18 Jackson quoted in Hill, 'Beyond the other?' p. 145.
19 J. Gros, 'Towards a taxonomy of failed states in the new world order: Decaying Somalia, Liberia, Rwanda and Haiti', *Third World Quarterly*, 17:13 (1996), 456.
20 Hill, 'Beyond the other?' p. 145.
21 See Call, 'The fallacy of the "failed state"', for a detailed discussion of these points, pp. 1494–1500.
22 Ibid.
23 Rotberg, 'Failed states, collapsed states, weak states', pp. 3–4.
24 Ibid.
25 M. Bøås and K. Jennings, '"Failed states" and "state failure": Threats or opportunities?' *Globalizations*, 4:4 (2007), 478.
26 S. Rice, *Testimony before the US House Committee on International Relations* (November 2001), accessed at http://commdocs.house.gov/committees/intlrel/hfa76191.000/hfa76191_0f.htm on February 25, 2017.
27 The White House, *National Security Strategy of the United States of America* (Washington, DC: The White House, 2002), accessed at www.state.gov/documents/organization/63562.pdf on February 25, 2017.

28 DCI, 'DCI's worldwide threat briefing' (February 11, 2003), accessed at www.cia.gov/news-information/speeches-testimony/2003/dci_speech_02112003.html on February 25, 2017.
29 S. Patrick, 'Are "ungoverned spaces" a threat?' (Council on Foreign Relations, January 11, 2010), accessed at www.cfr.org/somalia/ungoverned-spaces-threat/p21165 on February 25, 2017.
30 Quoted in A. Araoye, 'Hegemonic agendas, intermesticity and conflicts in the post-colonial state', *African Journal on Conflict Resolution*, 12:1 (2012), 15.
31 Quoted in K. Smith, 'Has Africa got anything to say? African contributions to the theoretical development of International Relations', *The Roundtable: The Commonwealth Journal of International Affairs*, 98:402 (2009), 273–4.
32 Zartman, 'Introduction: Posing the problem of state collapse', p. 2.
33 Ibid., p. 3.
34 W. Zartman, 'Life goes on and business as usual: The challenge of failed states', in *The (Un)Making of Failing States: Profits, Risks, and Measures of Failure* (Berlin: Heinrich Böll Foundation, Fall/Winter 2008/9), accessed at www.boell.org/downloads/hbf_failed_states_talk_series_William_Zartman.pdf on February 25, 2017.
35 D. Francis, *Uniting Africa: Building Regional Peace and Security Systems* (Aldershot: Ashgate Publishing Ltd., 2007), p. 56.
36 DCI's worldwide threat briefing.
37 R. Lamb, *Ungoverned Areas and Threats from Safe Havens* (Washington, DC: Office of the Under Secretary of Defense for Policy, January 2008), p. 1.
38 S. Emerson, 'Regional security initiative: Combined task force—Horn of Africa', in *Newport Papers No. 29: Shaping the Environment* (Newport, RI: US Naval War College Press, 2007), p. 78.
39 *NBC News*, 'U.S. aims to root out "ungoverned spaces" as hotbeds of terrorism' (August 23, 2014).
40 *Al Jazeera*, 'Burundi's president threatens to fight AU peacekeepers' (December 30, 2015).
41 *Al Jazeera*, 'Burundi crisis: AU to vote on peacekeeping mission' (January 30, 2016).

5

Terrorism and extremism

Since September 2001, the struggle against international jihadist terrorism all across the globe has become a defining security paradigm of the twenty-first century. Even the most remote and neglected corners of the earth have become caught up in the fight, and the African landscape is now an inescapable—and increasingly critical—part of this new security equation. Without a doubt several areas of the continent have become the new foci of African and international efforts to combat the rising tide of international jihadist and extremist violence. This development presents an enormous political and socio-economic challenge for many African countries and organizations, which are already overburdened trying to cope with a whole host of new and diverse security threats besides terrorism. Moreover, this lack of state and institutional capacity is at times further overshadowed by an African wariness and lack of political will over what some see as an imported problem. Their fear is that the continent is once again becoming a battlefield for an ideological clash of civilizations not of Africa's own making.

Terrorism and extremism, however, are certainly not new to Africa. Jihadist and messianic movements dating back to the early 1800s gave rise to the Sokoto caliphate in what is now northern Nigeria and the rise of the Mahdist movement in Sudan. It has also been an important part of the political and security dynamic of the continent from the de-colonialization struggle to the Cold War and beyond, although it has been primarily driven by distinct domestic political factors and inwardly focused. What has changed in the post-9/11 world for Africa is the apparent melding of domestic and international terrorism in a deadly cocktail of wider regional and even international destabilization. Nor is this something Africans can afford to ignore. Most disturbing of all is the emergence of the continent as an incubator of violent international extremism itself, with the growing possibility that it may become an exporter of international terrorism to the world in the coming decades.

Just as during the Cold War, the success or failure of counterterrorism efforts in Africa will be as much affected by the actions and policies of external forces as on the ability of African countries themselves. Since 2003, when the United States aggressively stepped up its counterterrorism efforts on the continent, Washington has sought to redefine the nature of the terrorist threat from the perspective of the American-led war on terror. Unfortunately, this approach is patently ill-suited to tackling the complex problems that breed terrorism in Africa. The danger here is that "Washington will continue treating Africa as simply another front in the war on terror, thereby neglecting real security needs on the continent."[1] Moreover, many embattled African leaders have sought to exploit the US preoccupation with terrorism to obtain American financial largess, to secure security assistance to shore up their faltering domestic political positions, and to deflect attention away from pressing internal problems.

What is terrorism?

Although rarely acknowledged directly, at the center of the debate over the rising terrorist threat on the continent are profound, yet subtle differences between Africans and the West over the definition of "terrorism" and what it means to be a "terrorist" in Africa. While everyone from scholars and pundits to governments and legal experts has also struggled with the definition of terrorism over the years, the debate in Africa is uniquely grounded in the people's historical experience during the anti-colonial struggle and the accompanying ideological baggage that tended to link African nationalism to terrorism, as well as its use by African governments to quash political opposition. Thus, it is not surprising that many in Africa remain highly suspicious of the motivations behind those pushing the war on terror and question whether this "new terrorist threat" is really fundamentally different from what they have experienced in the past.

While hundreds of definitions of terrorism exist—including differing versions within some countries[‡]—most cite the use of violence to instill

---

[‡] For example within the US government there is no single uniform definition, but variations across departments and agencies: "The calculated use of unlawful violence or threat of unlawful violence to inculcate fear; intended to coerce or to intimidate governments or societies in the pursuit of goals that are generally political, religious, or ideological" (Department of Defense); "Premediated politically-motivated violence perpetrated against non-combatant targets by subnational groups or clandestine agents, usually intended to influence an audience" (Department of State); "Terrorism is the unlawful use of force and violence

fear or intimidate by causing or threatening to cause serious injury or death to civilian populations or symbolic targets to gain wider visibility and coerce political or social change. Terrorism is usually viewed as a form of political violence that, according to Martha Crenshaw, is designed "to influence broader political behavior and advance a set of political or social objectives."[2] Many post-9/11 definitions also include references to religious or ideological goals too. It is a criminal, premeditated act by non-state or sub-state actors. Bruce Hoffman distinguishes terrorism from pure criminality by noting the existence of "an organization with an identifiable chain of command or conspiratorial cell structure."[3]

Despite all this specificity, most definitions blur a number of issues. If one focuses only on non-state or sub-state actors, then the whole concept of "state terrorism" or the use of terror by governments to advance a set of political, social, or ideological objectives is left unaddressed. The use of terror as a tactic by anti-government insurgents is usually specifically excluded, even though these groups would meet most of the above criteria. If one is using an action driven definition, then is the underlying motivation of no consequence? Was anti-apartheid "terrorism" the same as Pakistani suicide bombings? And if it is not, then where does one draw the line? All of this of course matters beyond the academic discourse because how one defines the problem invariably determines the parameters for crafting a solution.

While definitions certainly matter, perceptions, especially in Africa, matter even more. Differing perceptions over what constitutes terrorism highlights not only contrasting historical experiences and notions of security between the West and Africa, but also raises serious questions about the future of the international security agenda and what this means for the continent and its people. These differences can be quite pronounced. The ability to instill fear is seen as a tool of empowerment by the weak to force change and it has been an important weapon in asymmetrical warfare and to gain global recognition of embattled causes.

It was in this context that terrorism, or at least the use of fear and intimidation, played a powerful role in many African anti-colonial struggles. Deep apprehension that African liberation movements could be labelled "terrorist organizations," however, pushed the Organization of African Unity (the predecessor of the modern African Union, AU)

> against persons or property to intimidate or coerce a government, the civilian population, or any segment thereof, in furtherance of political or social objectives" (Department of Justice/FBI).

to explicitly reject this label by accepting the notion that "all struggles undertaken by peoples for their full national independence ..., including armed struggle, are entirely legal."[4] But even after accepting this moral and legal justification, the debate over terror tactics was contentious and divisive. For instance, the African National Congress (ANC) grappled with this issue for decades before embarking on the armed struggle in South Africa.[5] Even afterwards, protocols were put in place (although not always followed[6]) to limit civilian deaths and to target only government security organs and symbols of apartheid power. Also very important to many in Africa is the seeming avoidance of discussing the use of terror by the state against its own people. Although not usually falling within commonly used definitions of terrorism, its relevance is a high priority for those struggling for democratic reform, human rights, and equality.

Further distorting the issue of terrorism in Africa was the politicization of the term "terrorist" as it became intermingled with the Cold War. Western allies like Portugal (a NATO member), as well as would-be defenders of Western interests in Africa (such as Rhodesia and South Africa), sought to make common cause with the United States and the West by portraying nationalist insurgents as communist surrogates and themselves as the last line of defense against a global communist onslaught. Liberation movements' heavy reliance on Soviet, Eastern Bloc, and Chinese military training, weapons, and supplies played directly into this characterization, as did the guerrilla tactics of terror. From the mid-1960s onward communiqués from Lisbon to Pretoria hyped the strategic threat that "communist terrorists" posed to the West in Africa and of the need to stand behind the forces of capitalism and Western civilization—Portugal, Rhodesia, and South Africa.

This linking of communism and terrorism also enabled governments to rationalize draconian anti-terrorism legislation. These types of measures gave sweeping powers to military and security organs to crack down (often with legal impunity) against any threat to the state, including nonviolent political opposition. Civil liberties were suspended or ignored completely; the right to peacefully assemble and protest circumscribed. Courts and legislatures were either rendered impotent or coopted. The power of the executive branch became nearly all encompassing with small, but powerful, groups of so-called securocrats running the show. Ironically, some of the same powers and security legislation is still being used—in places like Zimbabwe, for instance—to crackdown on political opponents by labelling them terrorists.

With the end of the Cold War and the collapse of apartheid in South Africa, Africa and the debate over terrorism on the continent largely fell by the wayside in the 1990s. Even the bombings of the American embassies in Nairobi and Dar es Salaam in 1998 failed to illicit much more than a limited response by the United States, let alone resurrect the issue of terrorism for African countries. While certainly true that parts of the continent were still terrorized by anti-government rebel groups, warlords, and private militias, the issue was highly localized or seen as a relic of the liberation struggles and the Cold War. It appeared to have little relevance to the developing new world order. All this began to change, however, following events of September 11, 2001, and the issue of terrorism in Africa would steadily come to the fore as one of the continent's most pressing security challenges of the new century.

Scope and nature of the problem

The 9/11 attacks clearly redefined the global nature of the terrorist threat and set the stage for a critical reexamination and rethinking of the challenge of terrorism in Africa.

First, though, Africans would have to overcome their strong reticence to sign up for Washington's new crusade—the Global War on Terror—amid concerns that this was a problem not of their making, but one that was being imported into the continent much like the Cold War. This skepticism was well placed given empirical data. From 1989 through 2001 the continent saw a downward trend in the number of terrorist incidents, according to the Global Terrorism Database.[7] By 2001, the annual number of incidents was about one-third of this 13-year period's average and down almost 70 percent from the highs in the early 1990s.[8] Moreover, despite an upward spike in 2005, sub-Saharan Africa was averaging 40 percent fewer incidents per year over the previous five-year period, and the entire continent accounted for just 12 percent of all worldwide incidents from 2001–2005.[9] Hardly the hotbed of terrorism that many claimed it was becoming.

All this began to change dramatically, however, from 2006 onward with the convergence of two key developments—the rise of radical Islamist extremists[§] and the melding of domestic and international terrorism organizations. Globalization has acted to accelerate both the scope

---

[§] Broadly defined by the Washington Institute for Near East Policy as those espousing the ideologies of *takfiri* jihadist groups (like al-Qaeda, Hamas, and Hizballah) as well as so-called "conveyor belt groups" like Hizb al-Tahrir, which do not perpetrate acts of terrorism but help lay the groundwork for jihadist groups' message to take hold. Washington Institute for Near East Policy, 'Rewriting the Narrative: An Integrated Strategy for Counterradicalization', Washington, DC, March 2009, p. 1 footnote.

and degree of the terrorist threat now facing Africa today. Likewise, dramatic changes set in motion during the 2011 Arab Spring will significantly influence the shape of this new threat and counterterrorism policies well beyond North Africa.

The threat redefined
The growth of radical Islamist terrorism since the early 1990s has been one of the most disturbing trends and it now poses one of the biggest, and more direct, threats to African peace and stability. As such, it has been accorded a high priority by African governments, regional and sub-regional organizations, and the international community. The reason for this is clear. As distinct from the African ethno-nationalist terrorism of the liberation struggle with its well defined goals—independence and a transfer of political and economic power—this form of the so-called "new terrorism" seeks a fundamental transformation of the world. Radical Islam epitomizes the new terrorism: driven by an extremist religious ideology that "appeals to a glorious past, places aspects of religious identity above all others, and relies on a distorted interpretation of Islam,"[10] they are more than willing "to use highly lethal methods in order to destroy an impure world and bring about the apocalypse."[11] The underlying ideological narrative for al-Qaeda for instance, charges that the United States, and more broadly the West, are at war with Islam in a clash of civilizations and that the Muslim world must unify to defeat this threat.[12] Thus, for radical Islamists, gaining political power within the existing societal framework is not the objective; only the complete abolishment of the existing order (notably the Western values underpinning it) is an acceptable outcome. In the interim, the perpetuation of international anarchy and creating a global climate of fear goes a long way in undermining Western society and highlighting the impotence of its response.

There are numerous home-grown radical Islamist groups in Africa with varying degrees of organization, structure, and activism that engage in and/or facilitate this type of new terrorism. At one end of the spectrum are a wide variety of Islamist groups (such as national Muslim Brotherhood movements) and Islamic charities that are actively promoting a fundamentalist political agenda, but have generally rejected violence. Although they do not directly engage in terrorist activity, some counterterrorism experts believe some of these groups function as recruiting nodes for some of the more militant, extremist groups mentioned above.[13] These so-called "conveyor belt" organizations are widespread across the continent. Some are home-grown organizations, such as South Africa's Qibla, while others are foreign-based like Pakistan's

Tabligh. Many Islamic charities in Africa also have links to fundamentalist movements in Saudi Arabia and the Gulf States.[14]

At the other end of the spectrum are large, highly visible, and violent groups that are either linked directly to global jihadist movements, like al-Qaeda or the Islamic State, or share their violent extremist agenda. It is these groups that are responsible for the overwhelming majority of the terrorist violence in Africa and the ones that pose the most serious threat to security.

Al-Qaeda in the Islamic Maghreb (AQIM)
Formerly known as the Salafist Group for Preaching and Combat (GSPC), it grew out of the 1990s Algerian civil war and embraced the global jihadist struggle by ultimately rebranding itself in January 2007 as al-Qaeda's North African affiliate: "al-Qaeda in the Lands of the Islamic Maghreb." The group operates in Algeria, Tunisia, southern Libya, and across the pan-Sahel from Mauritania to Chad. Following the outbreak of the Tuareg nationalist rebellion in January 2012, AQIM and its Islamists allies, most notably Ansar Dine, became heavily engaged in fighting against the government of Mali and its Western allies.

Constant leadership infighting, internal divisions, and defections, as well as increased competition for new recruits with other radical Islamist groups, has hindered the group's growth. Moreover, while still espousing a radical fundamentalist ideology, AQIM has also evolved into a quasi-criminal organization. Not surprisingly, this has earned them the moniker of "gangster-jihadists" for their proclivity to engage in smuggling, kidnapping of Westerners for ransom, and drug and arms trafficking.[15] Nonetheless, AQIM's extensive operational reach, its ability to strike high profile targets, and its integration into local communities and alliance building continues to make it a serious security threat. In 2016 there were more than 200 AQIM-linked attacks in North and West Africa, mostly in Mali, but also at least 19 incidents in neighboring states.[16]

Al-Shabaab in Somalia
From its roots as a small Somali faction within the Union of Islamic Courts in 2006, the group and its central leadership have steadily become more violent and radicalized and al-Shabaab is now the preeminent domestic threat in Somalia, as well as the chief terrorist threat in the greater Horn of Africa. Following a factional purge and bloodletting in 2008, the newly reconstituted al-Shabaab squarely aligned itself with al-Qaeda in 2010.[17] Despite military setbacks at the hands of the West and its African allies over the years, the group has shown amazing

resilience at efforts to defeat it and has even expanded its influence with other Islamist elements in the Horn and down the east coast of Africa.

In 2011, with the rise to power of Moktar Ali Zubeyr, aka "Godane," the group abandoned its Islamic nationalist aspirations of creating a "Greater Somalia" in favor of embracing the global jihadist cause with a widening campaign of terror into neighboring countries.[18] It began to adopt al-Qaeda tactics, targeting civilians and increasing reliance on suicide bombings, as well as becoming a magnet for foreign fighters. At one time foreign fighters may have accounted for up to 25 percent of al-Shabaab's strength. Following the death of Godane in an American air strike in September 2014 there have been signs of fractionalization, desertions, and reports of fratricide within al-Shabaab as pro-al-Qaeda and pro-Islamic State elements contend for power and influence.[19]

Nonetheless, al-Shabaab remains the primary challenge to Somalia's internationally recognized government and has repeatedly demonstrated its ability to strike at AU peacekeepers and against African countries supporting the Somali government. From 2006 to 2016, the group launched 364 attacks inside Somalia and dozens of attacks against neighboring countries, according to press reporting.[20] The latter include the deadly, high profile attacks in Kenya on the Westgate Mall in Nairobi in 2013 and on Garissa University College in 2015. These attacks appear designed not only to undermine Kenyan military assistance to the Mogadishu government, but to inflame Muslim–Christian tensions in the northeast of country, which has a large population of ethnic Somalis.

Boko Haram

This group has grown since it was established in northeastern Nigeria by the radical Muslim cleric Mohammed Yusuf in 2002 from an uncoordinated separatist movement relying on primitive weapons to one of the most sophisticated and brutal terrorist insurgencies in Africa. The emergence of Boko Haram, once known locally as the "Nigerian Taliban," is tied directly to the spread of radical Islamist ideologies from Pakistan and Saudi Arabia. Characteristic of such fundamentalist doctrines is the notion that the Nigerian state is *taghut* or evil, unworthy of allegiance on the part of true Muslims.[21] This also provides Boko Haram's religious rationale for targeting police officers, politicians, and other government officials.

Notably Boko Haram has become increasingly internationalized since 2011. There is a building body of evidence of increased coordination with AQIM affiliates and splinter groups in West Africa, as well as reported ties to al-Shabaab in Somalia.[22] Boko Haram too has claimed that its fighters had been sent to Afghanistan, Lebanon, Pakistan, Iraq,

Mauritania, and Algeria for further military training.[23] Moreover, in March 2015 the group pledged its allegiance to the Islamic State and in response an Islamic State spokesman announced "the good news of the expansion of the caliphate to West Africa."[24] Boko Haram's relationship with the wider Islamic State movement, however, continues to evolve and it appears that, at least for now, it desires to maintain a large degree of self-autonomy.

Following the assumption of power by Abubaker Shekau after the death of Mohammed Yusuf in July 2009, Boko Haram embarked on an intensely violent campaign of attacks on government officials and buildings, suicide bombings, kidnappings, and civilian massacres, which left at least 15,000 people dead and a wake of destruction and fear across northeast Nigeria.[25] By February 2015 nearly 1.2 million people had been displaced by fighting, according to relief agencies.[26] With the election of President Muhammadu Buhari in March 2015 the conflict entered a new phase as Buhari vowed to crush Boko Haram once and for all; they will "soon know the strength of our collective will."[27] A multinational offensive by forces from Chad, Niger, and Nigeria was soon underway, which resulted in heavy fighting and loss of lives, especially among the civilian population. Even as major Boko Haram strongholds in Nigeria were overrun during 2015–16, the violence spilled over into neighboring Cameroon, Chad, and Niger. The Chadian capital suffered its first suicide bombings in June and July 2015, and deadly Boko Haram forays into Cameroon, Chad, and Niger have become widespread, forcing thousands to flee the border areas.[28] While the capture of the last Boko Haram stronghold in the Sambisa forest in December 2016 was a major military milestone, the group's ability to continue its campaign of suicide attacks, often using children and women bombers, shows that it is still a force to be reckoned with and is far from being completely defeated.

Libyan Islamist groups
The chaos surrounding the collapse of the Qadhafi regime in 2011 fed the emergence of a diverse collection of Islamist militant groups that "have a legitimacy born out of the position that they played in the struggle."[29] They ranged from the old-line Libyan Islamic Fighting Group and factions of the Muslim Brotherhood to radical militia elements. Libya also quickly became a magnet for international jihadists, following the collapse of the Qadhafi regime. Hundreds of veteran Libyan fighters from Syria began returning home and Islamic militants from other parts of North Africa and the Sahel soon began flowing into the country.[30]

Several existing and newly formed groups, such as the Salafist Ansar al-Sharia (implicated in the 2012 attack on the US Consulate in Benghazi) and the Islamic Youth Shura Council, publicly aligned themselves directly with the Islamic State beginning in 2014.[31] This helped energize the Islamic State's growth in Libya and by early 2015 the group was able to gain control of several key cities, including Derna and Sirte, as well as large parts of the countryside. This in turn triggered fears that Libya had "become the [Islamic State] caliphate's most important colony in North Africa after Egypt."[32] Since then, however, the Islamic State in Libya has suffered major setbacks with the loss of key cities, such as recapture of Sirte in December 2016 by government-allied militia forces, and defections to other Islamist groups, including al-Qaeda aligned groups. There are recent reports that Islamic State militants have regrouped in parts of western and southern Libya, where the group has strong links to smuggling and criminal networks, as it seeks to rebuild itself.[33]

For the most part, Libyan Islamist groups have been more preoccupied with the internal power struggle, competition for influence, and control inside the country than in exporting terrorism. They appear more focused on consolidating or defending their gains and shoring up their financial positions through criminal activities, including lucrative migrant smuggling, than in conducting international jihad against the West and its allies. The longer-term threat is real, however, as the ongoing chaos and instability in Libya serves as an incubator of violence and extremism that will over time spread to neighboring countries. There are already concerns that this is happening in Tunisia.[34]

Why the reason for the growth in Islamic extremism in Africa? A driving factor is the emergence of a favorable political and social environment. In particular, the rising appeal of political Islam—whereby Islamic beliefs form the foundation for all political, economic, social, and legal societal relationships—to Muslim populations is fueling an Islamic revival across the continent. It is seen as offering "a vision for achieving a more moral society in response to endemic African problems,"[35] as well as the widely held belief that the West is at war with Islam. Extremist ideology thus is able to play off this populism to justify political violence and even acts of terrorism. Likewise, the ability of radical Islamists "to frame local grievances in an extremist global narrative" and link their global jihadist agenda to conflict situations in Africa has widened their appeal among the young, poor, and disenfranchised of the continent.[36] Ironically too, the tide of democratic reforms that began to sweep across Africa, beginning in the late 1990s, has created a new openness and political freedom that extremists have sought to exploit. Many African governments have been loath to restrict these

Table 2 Key terrorist groups in Africa

	AQIM	al-Shabaab	Boko Haram	Islamic State (Libya)
Founded	2007	2006	2002	2014
Operational area	Algeria, Tunisia, Libya, Mauritania, Mali, Niger	Somalia, northern Kenya	Northeastern Nigeria, Cameroon, Chad, Niger	Libya, Tunisia, Egypt
Estimated size (2017)	1,000	7,000–9,000	4,000–6,000	4,000–5,000
Affiliation	al-Qaeda	al-Qaeda	al-Qaeda (2010) Islamic State* (2015)	Islamic State
Tactics	Kidnapping, hostage taking, ambushes, bombings	Large-scale attacks, targeted attacks, car bombings	Large-scale attacks, targeted attacks, suicide bombings	Targeted attacks
Major incidents	Algiers UN bombing (2007) Isser police bombing (2008) Kidnapping spate (2009–13) Mali intervention (2012) Bamako hotel attack (2015) Ouagadougou hotel attack (2016) Grand-Bassam resort attack (2016)	Kampala bombing (2010) Westgate Mall (2013) Garissa College (2015) Mogadishu car bombings (2016–17)	Military campaign (2010–14) Chibok school kidnapping (2014) Suicide bombing campaign (2015–17)	Sirte beheadings (2015) Tunis museum attack (2015) Sousse resort attack (2015)

Note: *Although the leadership of Boko Haram swore allegiance to the Islamic State in 2015, there are significant internal divisions within the group and many members still remain loyal to al-Qaeda.

Source: Data derived from: BBC News, CNN, Global Terrorism Database (University of Maryland), and Mapping Militant Organizations (Stanford University).

freedoms for fear of alienating their Muslim communities. Kenya, in particular, has grappled with how best to balance civil liberty concerns with public security in a democratic society following a spate of cross border terrorist attacks on Kenyan soil. Egypt, on the other hand, has opted for a return to draconian security legislation since 2013 in an attempt to suppress any and all forms of Islamist opposition to the el-Sisi regime.

Nonetheless, for the large part this groundswell of Islamic empowerment has not translated into a huge proliferation of radical Islamist extremist groups bent on waging international jihad against their governments and the West. So far, a combination of domestic political and social reforms, along with greater international sensitivities to Muslim perceptions concerning the war on terror, has kept things in check. But the situation is tenuous. Sensational terrorist incidents in North and East Africa in 2014–15, for example, fed a heavy-handed, reactionary backlash that played into the hands of extremist factions and served as a recruiting tool. Ongoing instability in places like Libya, Mali, or Somalia likewise serve as an incubator for rising levels of radicalism and extremist violence as old and new Islamists groups compete for power and influence.

Although still very small in terms of absolute numbers, Islamist extremists—notably those affiliated with al-Qaeda and the Islamic State—have been responsible for unleashing an unprecedented wave of deadly and brutal violence across Africa in the past five years. Nearly all the high-profile terrorist attacks in recent years can be traced to Islamist extremists: the Kampala bombings in July 2010; the hostage taking at the Amenas, Algeria gas plant in January 2013; the September 2013 Westgate Mall attack in Nairobi, Kenya; numerous deadly suicide bombing across northern Nigeria from 2013 onward; the public beheading of Egyptian Christians in Sirte, Libya in February 2015; the April 2015 massacre at Garissa College in northeast Kenya; the attack on foreign tourists in Sousse, Tunisia in June 2015; and the spate of car bombings in Mogadishu in 2016–17.

In 2009, the US Department of State called AQIM and al-Shabaab two of the three "most active affiliates of Al-Qaeda" (the other being al-Qaeda in the Arabian Peninsula)[37] and recognized that they were better led, organized, funded, and structured than other groups. Moreover, their robust operational capability has given them far greater sub-regional reach and more expansive support networks. AQIM commanders now operate across all of North Africa and far into the Sahel, while the al-Shabaab organization is alleged to have active cells in Ethiopia, Kenya, and possibly Tanzania. This not only makes them powerful sub-regional non-state actors, but has allowed them to play significant military and political roles in ongoing conflicts in Libya, Mali, and Somalia.

Even more worrisome has been the meteoric rise of Islamic State affiliates across North Africa in 2014, Boko Haram's pledge of allegiance in 2015, and the mimicking in Africa of brutal IS tactics used in Syria and Iraq. The Islamic State's goal "of expanding its caliphate and its adherence to a strict form of *Shariah* has definitely resonated with a collection of extremists across North Africa," according to a US intelligence official.[38] It has also grown through recruiting "an army of the poor" from impoverished pan-Sahel countries by offering financial incentives, and through defections from other Islamist groups.[39] This growth has often been at the expense of al-Qaeda and its affiliates. Moreover, contrasting strategies for opposing the West and its African allies, competition for new recruits, and leadership rivalries have led to violent clashes between the two groups competing for control of the heart and soul of the African jihadist movement.

The melding of domestic and international terrorism

While terrorism has long been a prominent feature of African domestic conflicts, it has become increasingly internationalized and transformed by the forces of globalization, and in Africa this has blurred the delineation between domestic and international terrorism.

Domestically rooted or sub-state terrorism remains the most prevalent form of African terrorism, yet international terrorism—that threatens the global political and economic order**—on the continent is clearly on the rise and gaining in prominence. From a low of 6 percent of all terrorist attacks in Africa during 1990 to 2002, international terrorism rose to just over 20 percent from 2003 to 2008 and continues its upward trend.[40] Since 2013 there has been a large spike in the number of both incidents and deaths attributed to the spread of Boko Haram and al-Shabaab transnational attacks in neighboring countries.[41]

In trying to explain this upward trend, many observers cite the return to Africa in the late 1980s of some 1,000 battle-hardened Algerian veterans of the mujahedin-lead fight against the Soviets in Afghanistan.

** International terrorism is typically characterized "as the result of actions by individuals or groups operating across an international border," but database methodologies vary considerably in differentiating domestic from international acts of terrorism. In addition, some of the widely used databases, like the Global Terrorism Database, avoid using the labels entirely. In this discussion, however, we find that Jakkie Cilliers' broader conceptualization present here is more useful in uncovering and assessing emerging trends in African terrorism. See J. Cilliers, 'Terrorism and Africa', *African Security Review* 12:4, (2003), pp. 92–3.

These so-called "Afghanis" would form the armed nucleus of a more militant opposition to authoritarian governments in North Africa and their return would be a watershed in the surge of international terrorism on the continent. Moreover, a series of new conflicts called for a wholesale transformation of society. Starting with Algeria in 1989, but quickly spreading to Egypt, Sudan, and other parts of North Africa and the Horn in the 1990s, a new wave of radical Islamist inspired violence would ensue, and a new more deadly pattern of terrorism would begin to take shape.

The onset of the American-led global war on terror, along with the US invasion of Iraq in 2003, would likewise be used by international terrorists in Africa to justify their actions. As Jakkie Cilliers warned at that time, "the reality is that international terrorism in Africa is awakening and that it has links in a number of African countries from South Africa through to Algeria in the north. It is, given the present volatile international context ... only a matter of time before it is fully awake."[42] Spurred on by the events of the 2011 Arab Spring, the ongoing civil war in Syria, and the rise of the Islamic State there, that prediction has now become reality. It is believed that "more than 20,000 foreign fighters have gone to Syria," which is "about twice the number that went to Afghanistan in the 1980s," according to Deputy Assistant Secretary of State Brett McGurk.[43] Almost 30 percent of these jihadist fighters have come from Africa—nearly all from the North African countries, with the bulk coming from Tunisia and Morocco.[44] In a repeat of the "Afghani experience," many of these battle-hardened Islamic State veterans have returned home to continue their fight on African soil.

It is not simply the increase and spread of imported international terrorism in Africa that is potentially frightening, but rather the melding of domestic and international terrorism that is underway in some parts of Africa. Earlier forms of terrorism on the continent, as we have noted, were the outgrowth of domestically driven conflicts by groups seeking to redress perceived injustices or gain access to political and/or economic power. Unlike international terrorism, domestic terror groups are not seeking a fundamental reordering of their societies (let alone the global order), but are pursuing narrowly defined domestic objectives. What is now emerging in Africa, however, is a convergence or "complex mixture and intermingling" of terrorism,[45] either because of shared objectives, a common enemy or the potential for building synergetic relationships.

This convergence now poses the most serious terrorism challenge to key sub-regions of the continent and it shows no signs of abating. It is now the central driver of conflict in Algeria, Tunisia, Libya, northern Nigeria, and Somalia, where domestic terrorist groups have publicly realigned themselves with al-Qaeda's and/or the Islamic State's internationalist agenda. Moreover, AQIM, Boko Haram, and al-Shabaab, along with other smaller affiliates of al-Qaeda and the Islamic State are not only responsible for the majority of terrorist attacks and deaths across the continent, but they also now threaten the continued functioning and stability of national governments. Prior to its military setbacks in 2015, for instance, Boko Haram was on the verge of eviscerating the Nigerian central government's authority in an area the size of Belgium. Likewise, the anarchical situations in Libya and Somalia will most likely never be resolved until the threat to stability from the Islamic State and its affiliates and al-Shabaab is addressed.

This does not, however, mean that all (or even the majority of) domestic terrorist groups will seek to meld their movements with international terrorist organizations. All the critical factors need to align for this to take place: the physical, political, and social environment of the country or region must be conducive to a melding with outside forces; the structural organization of both groups must be compatible; ideological differences may have to be bridged; leadership personalities and styles must mesh; and agreement over strategy and tactics reached. Most of all, both parties need to perceive a win-win situation that advances both their individual and shared political objectives. And this is not always the case in Africa. While one can see how the conditions in Algeria, Libya, parts of Mali, or Somalia might meet most of these requirements, it is difficult to imagine the Lord's Resistance Army in Uganda or Congolese militias in the eastern DRC finding common cause with international terrorist organizations. Even when there is an apparent convergence of interests and a favorable environment, this melding may not take place. Osama bin Laden's 2006 call for jihadists to join the fight in Darfur against the Western crusaders failed to internationalize the conflict there. The repeated failure of al-Qaeda affiliates to form lasting alliances with Tuareg rebels (or even other Islamist movements) in Mali and Niger during multiple rebellions there from 2006 to 2013 also shows the difficulty of making this happen.

Emerging trends
African terrorism over the years has proven itself to be extremely adaptive in the face of a changing world. Whether driven by macro international trends, newly emerging political and socio-economic problems, or simply as a reaction to counterterrorism measures, terrorism in Africa in the twenty-first century is likely to look significantly different from that of the past. Although some characteristics, such as the role of ethno-religious conflict or separatist politics, will admittedly continue to be key

themes of this new narrative, many of these older elements are likely to give way as the scope and nature of African terrorism evolves.

One such transformation already underway is the reconstitution of large, umbrella terrorist organizations into multiple smaller, more tight-knit, and ideologically driven groups. Although smaller in size, these groups are more radicalized, militant, and deadlier than their predecessors. The historical situation in Algeria is emblematic of this pattern. Rising out of the civil war in the 1990s, following the government's voiding of the Islamic Salvation Front's electoral victory, the *Groupe Islamique Arme* or GIA may have numbered up to 10,000 fighters at one time, but the 1999 political reforms, a government amnesty, and military setback greatly reduced its effectiveness and popular appeal. More militant and disaffected members broke off to form the Salafist Group for Preaching and Combat (GSPC) in 1998 and continued the war of terror. Eventually the GSPC too would seek reconciliation with Algiers and fragment, leaving a hard-core element that would become AQIM in 2007, espousing a broader internationalist jihadist agenda. In the decade since, AQIM itself has also become a flatter and less centralized organization with various local commanders assuming greater operational independence and some elements breaking entirely with the central leadership.

Not all African groups will undergo this transformation. Ethnonationalists or separatist movements will likely still seek to maintain large forces and a high degree of centralized control in their operations. This is especially true for organizations that are dependent on personalized or charismatic leadership, such as the Lord's Resistance Army or ethnic militias. The situation in some places also is likely to be mixed. In failing states, such as Libya and Somalia, some old-line terrorist organizations will likely follow the pattern of fragmenting into smaller, hard-core extremists groups, but other organizations will probably seek to maintain themselves as larger, more cohesive nationalist-based movements.

This transformation into smaller, but more militant organizations is likely to be accompanied by a tactical and operational shift toward more high-profile and often more deadly, terrorist attacks over a wider operating area. These attacks are designed to not only garner maximum publicity, but also to highlight the group's capabilities. The recent shift toward suicide bombings (including the use of children and female bombers) in Nigeria and Somalia is one example. While the goal of inflicting the maximum casualties is a key consideration, more important is the objective of instilling fear in the widest possible audience and demonstrating the group's long reach. Thus, kidnappings and public beheadings are likely to become more commonplace, as will transnational Kenya Westgate-style attacks.

Most disturbing, because of its acute long-term implications, is the increasing fluidity with which terrorist groups operate with—and/or become—transnational criminal networks in Africa. Scholars and security experts alike have long warned of this critical nexus and the symbiotic relationships that can emerge to make both sets of actors even more dangerous and capable. Stefan Mair's 2003 work on privatized violence provides a useful framework for exploring this relationship by noting a structural network that motivates cooperation and "makes use of comparative advantages and synergies" across groups, which he also observes is certainly a factor in making differentiation between groups exceedingly difficult these days.[46] In the case of Africa, these organizations "are complex and highly fungible structures that tend to have multiple identities" and "it is often difficult to determine whether a political agenda (for rebels and terrorists) or an economic agenda (for warlords and criminals) is the driving force, because groups tend to disguise and cloud their true motivations."[47] The reasons for this shift are as complicated as they are unique to each organization, but undoubtedly a survival instinct is pushing terrorist groups to diversify their activities and broaden their base of logistical and financial support. This is in keeping with the growing decentralization and independence of African terrorist organizations whereby individual cells or factions need to become increasingly self-reliant and self-supporting.

Criminal activity often is the answer. Since 2009 AQIM cells and battalions operating in the pan-Sahel have increased their kidnapping of Westerners and become heavily involved in the trans-Saharan drug trade, according to press reports.[48] The result has been the inflow of millions of dollars into the organization's coffers, but has led some security experts and locals alike to see AQIM "as more of a criminal gang than a group of ideologically committed terrorists;" "they're not al-Qaeda, they're just a mafia."[49] Libya too, appears to be following this pattern with terrorist and extremist militias now involved in all manner of criminal activity, from extortion and gun running to contraband and human trafficking.[50]

Another trend of less immediate concern, but still with serious implications, is the growing potential in Africa for a new type of very small-scale, locally driven, terrorism that "bubbles up from below."[51] Also known as "micro-terrorism" or "lone wolf terrorism," it marries aspects of globalization—particularly the spread of technology and information access—with individual empowerment. As many Western countries have already experienced, this can take the form of uncoordinated, but ideological sympathy for launching terrorist attacks. Africa may in fact be more susceptible to this micro-terrorism because of a continuing failure to meet the basic needs of its people, rising frustration with the inability of democracy to deliver tangible rewards, loss of faith in national institutions and governments, and corrupt and self-promoting leaders. On a continent already struggling to cope with more conventional forms of terrorism, the prospect of more locally driven lone wolf terrorism is a deeply frightening thought.

Implications for security

Terrorism in Africa is a reality, but it needs to be carefully viewed in the context of the continent's unique historical development and its manifestation as symptomatic of far reaching political and socio-economic problems. This is the real security challenge for the twenty-first century. Too narrow a focus on terrorism alone—and particularly on international terrorism—as the fount of African insecurity would be a serious mistake and one that the international community especially needs to scrupulously avoid. Nonetheless, the face of terrorism in Africa is clearly changing. And this will require Africans to reassess and question their old, long-held beliefs about the nature of terrorism, and to develop new strategies for a continent that is now becoming a part of an increasingly interconnected and globalized world.

How exactly the fight against terrorism plays out in Africa will have significant implications, as the way in which African governments and institutions, as well as the international community, handle this issue will go a long way in shaping and defining the meaning of security. Will the precepts of human security gain sway? Or will a more traditional state-centric view of security come to the fore? There is, indeed, a lot at stake for both the future of African and global security in the decades ahead.

At the heart of the terrorism challenge in Africa is a plethora of other domestic problems, ranging from violent conflict, state failure, endemic poverty, poor governance, and lack of political and socio-economic inclusiveness. Terrorism is more of a symptom of these societal problems than a driver of insecurity itself and unless headway is made against these problems then terrorism will continue to plague the continent. It has become a tool of the weak and disenfranchised to articulate domestic grievances. And while forces outside Africa will undoubtedly continue to try and exploit these local grievances to advance their own objectives, ultimately the solution to African terrorism will be found in promoting broader societal security. To be sure, developing stronger counterterrorism capability is part of the equation, but it must be used judicially and not at the expense—or instead of—other non-military tools that seek first to alter the conditions that breed terrorism and allow it to prosper.

The human security-driven approach to countering terrorism is clearly in keeping with the actual level of the threat in Africa today. As we have seen, the most serious, current terrorist challenges are well-identified and highly concentrated zones of violence. Moreover, the most dangerous groups, those with strong Islamist extremist ties, are largely confined to certain areas of North Africa, the remote reaches of the pan-Sahel, northeastern Nigeria, and in parts of Somalia. Other lower-level terrorist activity related to ethno-nationalist or separatist insurgencies is more widespread and prevalent, but not as highly visible. Although militaries have a role to play in both instances, especially in the fight against international jihadists and their transformational agenda, domestic-fueled terrorism and related insurgencies are best dealt with through a combination of selected military pressure and appropriate political-economic incentives. The goal in these situations, as Africans have learned, is not to try and defeat terrorists militarily, but to remedy the conditions that spawned them.

Africa and its challenges, however, is no longer the isolated and neglected continent that it once was, and handling the challenge of terrorism in Africa (in all its forms) has been complicated by the American-led war on terror and Washington's pursuit of its own international agenda on African soil.

In the aftermath of the 9/11 attacks, the United States dramatically ramped up its military involvement and began aggressively pushing its counterterrorism objectives in Africa: Combined Joint Task Force-Horn of Africa (CJTF-HOA) was established in 2002; Pan Sahel Initiative and East Africa Counterterrorism Initiative was implemented in 2003; and joint military training exercises began as part of Operation Enduring Freedom-Trans Sahara in 2005. Stepped-up US military operations to hunt down terrorists in the Horn, secret military cooperation with Ethiopia, CIA involvement with Somali warlords in counterterrorism efforts, and fears that Somalia might become "another Afghanistan" brought the war on terror to African shores. Heavy lobbying by Washington in regional and international forums for African governments to adopt more aggressive counterterrorism policies and legislation also resurrected fears that the continent was once again in danger of becoming a proxy venue for a global conflict.

Worries that a new Cold War was emerging, with the terrorist threat replacing the communist threat, were all too real, and raised concerns both in and outside Africa. Of serious concern was that hard won political advances would be pushed aside or compromised in the name of fighting terrorism. Blossoming American security relationships after 2001 with authoritarian regimes in Algeria, Chad, Egypt, Ethiopia, and Sudan, as well as an apparent willingness to look the other way on issues of democratic reform and human rights served to reinforce this perception. The 2003 invasion of Iraq and the well-publicized use of "enhanced interrogation techniques" by the United States in the name of fighting terror were seen as signaling a new era in relations. There was a justifiable fear, both on the continent and abroad, that support for the war on terror would become the new litmus test of bilateral relations.

This message was not lost on some African governments, who sought to leverage the new American obsession with counterterrorism to curry political favor with Washington. Algeria was the greatest beneficiary of this new US policy. Once shunned for its poor track record on civil and human rights and its heavy-handed security tactics, the country quickly became a lynchpin of American counterterrorism strategy in North Africa and the pan-Sahel, much to the dismay of many of its neighbors. Likewise, governments from Mauritania to Egypt used the threat of violent extremism to justify the repression and banning of opposition parties. So much so, that veteran Africa diplomat Princeton Lyman warned, "The United States has to be especially careful that we do not become partners in a political process that drives people into the arms of Islamist extremists."[52]

Fortunately for Africa, the United States gradually adopted a more sophisticated and nuanced counterterrorism strategy to allay African fears of a new militarized American foreign policy. Much more attention was given to addressing the underlying factors and conditions that spawn and maintain terrorism, as the Pentagon started to implement a hearts and minds strategy.[53] As part of the Trans-Sahara Counter-Terrorism Partnership program (which replaced the Trans-Sahara Counter-Terrorism Initiative), funding rose to more than $350 million from 2005 to 2008 to support "a wide range of diplomacy, development assistance, and military activities aimed at strengthening partner countries' counterterrorism capacity and inhibiting the spread of extremist ideology" in West and North Africa.[54] Likewise, CJTF-HOA began to focus more on development and humanitarian assistance efforts, such as building schools and clinics, providing direct medical and veterinary assistance, or digging wells, than on hunting down terrorists.[55] Or, as the former task force commander put it, "we feel the best way to counter terrorism is to go after the conditions that foster terrorism."[56] Washington also moved quickly—and publicly—to criticize actions that threaten democratic progress and circumvent civil liberties, such as condemnation of the military coups in Mauritania in 2005 and 2008 or President Tandja's manipulation of Niger's constitution in 2009. All non-humanitarian aid was suspended despite these countries' important role in the pan-Sahel counterterrorism effort. If there was any doubt as to the shift in policy, Washington's willingness to embrace the uncertainty of democratic change following the Arab Spring protests across North Africa appeared to signal that the rules of game had clearly changed.

Over the past several years, however, "the American vision of a more subtle and differentiated long-term approach to counterterrorism [in Africa] has foundered on the rocks of reality" and Washington has reverted to "an increasing reliance on the more aggressive use of military power."[57] Several factors—all with serious implications for African security—appear to account for this change:

- *The persistent imbalance between civilian and military resources.* Despite all the talk of relying more on diplomatic and developmental tools and the use of soft power to advance US counterterrorism objectives in Africa, the American military remains the primary instrument of power. The US military presence on the continent has grown to at least 5,000 personnel. Drone aircraft regularly operate from bases in Djibouti, Ethiopia, and Niger; American Special Forces personnel are engaged in training and operational missions from the Sahel to the Horn of Africa; and the United States conducts regular large-scale training exercises with its African partners.[58] As such, the Department of Defense receives the bulk of security assistance funding. US security assistance to several key countries in the war on terror—Djibouti, Ethiopia, Kenya, and Nigeria—has more than tripled compared to pre-2001 levels, while developmental assistance (outside of humanitarian and health funding) has lagged badly behind.[59]
- *The rising Islamist extremist threat to strategic American allies.* The rapid and unexpected growth of Islamic State affiliates in Egypt, Libya, and Nigeria caught Washington by surprise and pushed it to assume a more aggressive and immediate counterterrorism response at the expense of its long-term hearts and minds strategy. As one former Pentagon adviser noted in 2012, "Drones have become the counterterrorism weapon of choice for the Obama Administration."[60] With Egypt and Nigeria facing growing internal unrest and Kenya becoming an increasing target of high profile al-Shabaab attacks, Washington steadily ramped up its military profile, increased security assistance, and assumed an increasingly pragmatic approach to human rights and democratic reforms.

- *A subconscious acceptance of the Franco-Algerian approach.* The steady erosion of the civilian component of the American counterterrorism strategy, along with pent up frustration over the lack of immediate results, pushed many in Washington into the hands of those advocating more direct action. This "iron fist approach" has long been a mainstay of Algerian counterterrorism philosophy.[61] Immediate results, it was argued, are what mattered most. Following the successful French intervention in Mali against the Islamist jihadists in 2013–14, the Hollande government created a 3,000-man task force in July 2014 as part of Operation Barkhane to "target Islamist extremists in Mali, Chad and Niger."[62] Likewise, the large-scale military success of joint Nigerian-Chadian-Nigerien operations against Boko Haram in 2015–16 is likely to add momentum to increase the level of US military counterterrorism engagement.
- *A mounting reliance on African proxies.* A central theme of US counterterrorism policy has been to keep the American—and especially the military—footprint as small as possible. To accomplish this, Washington has steadily increased its reliance on its local allies to shoulder much of the burden. And while militarily sound, this approach has not been without its political costs; a rising dependence on strong military allies, like Egypt, Ethiopia, Kenya, and Nigeria, also means reduced American political leverage in areas of human rights, civil liberties, and democratic reforms in these countries.

The result of all this is a new phase of the war on terror in Africa, whereby the United States is pursuing an aggressive war of attrition while steadily moving away from a long-term hearts and minds strategy. Counterterrorism is now more about drone strikes and body counts than about building schools and digging wells. Moreover, a dynamic similar to the Cold War is emerging too as both sides escalate and expand the conflict into new areas.

For their part, African countries and organizations too are critically reassessing the changing nature of terrorism and are seeking to strike a balance between the immediate threat posed by terrorism and longer-term need of building prosperous, secure and stable societies.

Kenya in particular has grappled with this issue. Despite the obvious presence of al-Qaeda operational cells and a well-establish support network, as evidenced by the 1998 and 2002 attacks, many in Kenya refused to acknowledge a growing problem with Islamist extremists. Politicians were especially wary of alienating the small, yet influential, Muslim business community (roughly 10 percent of the population) along the coast. Instead terrorism was labeled a "foreign problem," imported into the country or associated with the spillover of violence from neighboring Somalia.[63]

As a growing target of al-Shabaab retaliatory attacks because of its peacekeeping role in Somalia, Kenyans are themselves facing not only an external threat, but a home-grown one as well. The deadly April 2015 Garissa College attack, in particular, underscored once and for all the threat domestic radical Islam poses to Kenya, and that terrorism's roots run deep inside the country. Beyond greater scrutiny of its citizens and organizations with close ties to radical Islamists, the government is also working with mainstream Muslim groups to address concerns over discrimination and lack of economic opportunity, especially among the majority nomadic Muslim population in the north.[64] Nonetheless, Christian–Muslim tensions continue to run high and are exacerbated by the presence of more than 350,000 Somali refugees in the country. This situation provides a convenient divide that al-Shabaab and other Islamist extremist groups will continue to exploit.

Likewise, the ANC government in South Africa, which has traditionally viewed itself as immune to terrorism because of its historical legacy, is attempting to come to terms with the growing use of its territory as a recruiting ground and to support terrorist networks. More so than in any other African country the mention of "anti-terrorism legislation" brings back dark and haunting memories of past abuses under apartheid. Nonetheless, since the late 1990s the specter of domestically grown international terrorist movements operating in South Africa has been a reality. By 1997 both Hizballah and al-Qaeda have established their presence in the country.[65] Although incident free, the threat of terrorism during the 2010 FIFA World Cup re-energized the debate over how best to balance security concerns with individual rights and the country's tainted past.

In the meantime, many believe South Africa has already become an important "base for fundraising and logistics" by terrorist organizations.[66] Media reports indicate that the country may be becoming a significant recruiting ground for the most violent Islamist extremist groups, with one recent estimate putting the number of South Africans fighting for the Islamic State overseas at 140.[67] The fear here is that many of these hardened jihadists will return home in the future to establish sleeper cells in South Africa, and will pose a serious security challenge to the government that it is ill-equipped to handle.

The terrorist threat—both real and imagined—has pushed some countries, like Egypt and Ethiopia, to enact increasingly more draconian security legislation, suspension of civil liberties, and a crackdown on political opponents.[68] Other rulers, like Robert Mugabe of Zimbabwe and Swazi King Mswati III, have long used the pretext of domestic terrorism to suppress popular dissent and quash any opposition. While this approach may have produced some immediate security benefits, it also has pushed legitimate opposition underground, and papers over long-standing problems under the guise of fighting terrorism. Moreover, it is rolling back many of the positive changes accompanying the Arab Spring or other associated democratic reforms by rationalizing a return to more authoritarian rule. Likewise, deadly terrorist incidents in Tunisia and Nigeria since 2014 could also push these governments to backtrack on their democratic transformations.[69] This would be a pity as it plays into the hands of extremists. Just as Western countries need to be wary of an overly militarized and reactive approach, so too must African countries avoid falling into the very same trap—a trap that they have rightly so criticized in the past.

Conclusion

The problem of terrorism is not going away. It is a reality in today's world both for the international community and individual countries—and Africa is no exception. In recent decades the challenge terrorism presents to the world has risen enormously. It has evolved into a more deadly, grassroots, and mobilizing phenomenon that has proven its ability to combine ancient grievances and a lack of empowerment with modern technology through the power of globalization. It is, without a doubt, one of the major threats to global security in the twenty-first century.

As has been noted before, terrorism has been a significant feature of the African landscape since the independence struggle and it is an evolving security challenge for the continent. It is widely recognized as an asymmetric tool of the weak to obtain redress or gain concessions from governments. Moreover, even in predominantly Muslim African countries, international jihadist networks have yet to find a truly universal rallying cry for mass mobilization in Africa and for their acceptance of a transformational vision of a new world order. Ultimately, the majority of Africans remain committed to evolutionary change through democratic reforms and greater socio-economic inclusion rather than through violent, revolutionary transformation.

Pockets of terrorism will undoubtedly continue to exist and some will even expand to become a source of contagion for their neighbors, but for the most part terrorism will be a manageable security challenge. The most dangerous nodes of terrorism are likely to remain confined to specific parts of the continent—the Algerian, Libyan, and Somali epicenters—where they will no doubt continue to fuel violence and instability. This terror challenge, however, is unlikely to threaten vital economic and political centers of power in Africa, although Nigeria remains highly vulnerable, and a return to the situation of 2010–14 could prove the exception. Well thought-out concerns for an increase in terrorism and its consequences for the continent is surely warranted, but for most African countries this concern is unlikely to become the lynchpin of their security agendas. Nor should it be.

A real danger, however, is that of overreacting to the terrorism challenge, not only by African countries themselves but by the United States and the international community. A basic strategy of terrorists is to provoke an excessive government backlash and thereby escalate violence and further strain on existing societal divisions; this process is well underway in several African countries, such as Algeria, Egypt, and Ethiopia. Although an iron-fist approach will yield some positive short-term benefits, letting counterterrorism drive security agendas is more about ensuring regime security for authoritarian governments and preventing their international isolationism. Not surprisingly, Algiers, Cairo, and Addis Ababa have sought to appropriate the terrorism issue in their sub-regions, which may be detrimental to the actual long-term security interests of these regions as a whole. Likewise, from 2002 onward, Washington's aggressive counterterrorism agenda for Africa is doing more harm than good. While some progress has been made in tempering the heavy-handed US counterterrorism approach, the United States continues to play an exaggerated role in shaping the terrorism debate in Africa. And Africans need to be mindful of this reality. Security on the continent is more than simply fighting terrorism, and an Americanized version of security that fails to acknowledge the growth of terrorism as a manifestation of wider societal ills will do little to tackle the underlying causes. External security assistance is surely needed and the flow of billions of dollars into Africa as a result of the war on terror is difficult to resist. But African government and institutions cannot let outsiders steer their agenda without question or determine where terrorism falls on a list of African priorities.

In addition, unless the West, and the United States in particular, become more discerning about the nature of African terrorism and the actual factors driving it, the international community's involvement is more likely to hurt rather than help mitigate the terrorist threat. Broad brush characterizations of "African Islamic terrorists" by outsiders often do more harm than good. Lack of sophistication in disaggregating anti-government movements or internal factions who utilize the tactics of terror from international extremists simply confuse the situation and hinder real progress. One only needs to be reminded of the multiple US policy failures in attempting to resolve the domestic upheaval in Somalia over the past two decades to see the results. Moreover, patience and caution should be the watch words of any international involvement. In the frequent rush to do something to fight terrorism and improve security, the law of unintended consequences comes into play and short-term fixes (which often involve a strong military component) can ultimately lead to longer-term instability. The international mantra for involvement should be: "Do some good, but first do no harm." The situation in North Africa coming out of the 2011 Arab Spring will require special care in the years ahead as new governments there grapple with democratic reforms, political inclusion, and balancing security with civil liberties. It is bound to be a chaotic process. Extremists are seeking to take advantage of the situation, but patience and forbearance by the West in working with governments in these countries will, in the end, produce stronger and safer societies that are better able to resist the siren call of terrorism and extremism.

A nuanced and thoughtful approach to the challenge of terrorism in Africa, however, does not diminish the threat that it can pose to the continent. The continent's fragile governments, extensive poverty, simmering conflicts and chronic instability, plus lack of state capacity and endemic corruption make Africa highly vulnerable to exploitation. Several disturbing global trends, such as the emergence of the Islamic State, are giving rise to a significant increase in more deadly terrorist activity and are facilitating an expanded presence of international terrorist networks. Accordingly, counterterrorism will remain an important agenda item for the foreseeable future.

Ultimately, the solution will be found in Africa. Just as the overwhelming sources of the continent's terrorism problem are local, so too must be found the answers. Improving security against the threat of terrorism will take a bottom-up approach that is more political and developmental oriented than military, and one that takes into account the wide diversity and history of the continent and its people. This will require a good deal of money and resources (both of which are in short supply in Africa), as well as commitment on the part of governments, institutions, and societies. The continent's shortcomings can only really be effectively addressed through African mechanisms, albeit with international community assistance, and some of these are already in place as we shall see, but the political will to use them effectively is too often lacking. For without the political will and leadership to address the true causes of societal insecurity, terrorism will continue to present a lingering threat not only to the people of Africa but to the rest of the world as well.

Notes

1. S. Emerson, 'The battle for Africa's hearts and minds', *World Policy Journal* (Winter, 2008/9), 54.
2. M. Crenshaw, 'The causes of terrorism', in C. Kegley, *The New Global Terrorism: Characteristics, Causes, Controls* (New York: Pearson, 2002), p. 98.
3. B. Hoffman, *Inside terrorism*, 2nd edn (New York: Columbia University Press, 2006), p. 41.
4. R. Friedlander, 'Terrorism and national liberation movements: Can rights derive from wrongs?', *Case Western Reserve Journal of International Law*, 13:2 (1981), 287.
5. See H. Holland, *The Struggle: A History of the African National Congress* (New York: George Braziller, Inc., 1990), pp. 128–47, for a detailed look at the birth of *Umkhonto we Sizwe* or MK, as the armed wing of the ANC.
6. Holland, *The Struggle*, p. 219.
7. Global Terrorism Database (website hosted by the University of Maryland), accessed at www.start.umd.edu/gtd/ on February 26, 2017.
8. Ibid.
9. Ibid.
10. J. Carpenter *et al.*, *Fighting the Ideological Battle: The Missing Link in U.S. Strategy to Counter Violent Extremism* (Washington, DC: The Washington Institute for Near East Policy, July 2010), p. 2.
11. M. Crenshaw, 'The psychology of terrorism: An agenda for the 21st century', *Political Psychology*, 21:2 (June 2000), 411.
12. Carpenter, *et al.*, *Fighting the Ideological Battle*, pp. 7–8.
13. See, for example, ibid.; A. Rabasa, *Radical Islam in East Africa* (Santa Monica, CA: RAND Corporation, 2009); and H. Glickman, 'The threat of Islamism in sub-Saharan Africa: The case of Tanzania', *E-Notes* (Foreign Policy Research Institute, April 2011).
14. Rabasa, *Radical Islam in East Africa*, pp. 41–4.
15. *Reuters*, 'Special report: In the land of gangster-jihadists' (October 25, 2012).
16. C. Weiss, 'AQIM claims two attacks in northern Mali', *Long War Journal* (November 30, 2016), accessed at www.longwarjournal.org/archives/2016/11/aqim-claims-two-attacks-in-northern-mali.php on February 26, 2017.
17. See K. Menkhaus, 'Violent Islamic extremism: Al-Shabaab recruitment in America' (Hearing before the Committee on Homeland Security and Governmental Affairs, United States Senate, Washington, DC, March 11, 2009) for a look at the evolution of the group from Somali nationalists to international terrorists.
18. H. Solomon, *Terrorism and Counter-Terrorism in Africa* (Basingstoke: Palgrave Macmillan, 2015), p. 56.
19. A. Meleagrou-Hitchens, 'Terrorist tug-of-war', *Foreign Affairs.com* (October 8, 2015), accessed at www.foreignaffairs.com/articles/kenya/2015-10-08/terrorist-tug-war on February 26, 2017.

Terrorism and extremism

20 *Al Jazeera*, 'Al-Shabaab attacks in Somalia (2006–2016)' (August 31, 2016).
21 A. Abimbola, 'Between Maitatsane and Boko Haram: Islamic fundamentalism and the response of the Nigerian State', *Africa Today*, 57:4 (2010), 103.
22 T. Johnson, *Boko Haram* (Washington, DC: Council on Foreign Relations, 27 December 2011), pp. 4–5, accessed at www.cfr.org/africa/boko-haram/p.25739 on February 26, 2017.
23 I. Mantzikos, 'The absence of the state in northern Nigeria: The case of Boko Haram', *African Renaissance*, 7:1 (2010), 60.
24 *BBC News*, 'Islamic State "accepts" Boko Haram's allegiance pledge' (March 13, 2015).
25 *Agence France-Presse*, 'Boko Haram kills nearly 200 in 48 hours of Nigeria slaughter' (July 3, 2015).
26 Internal Displacement Monitoring Centre, 'Boko Haram's terror ripples through the region' (April 16, 2015), accessed at www.internal-displacement.org/publications/2015/boko-harams-terror-ripples-through-the-region on February 26, 2017.
27 *BBC News*, 'Nigeria elections: Winner Buhari issues Boko Haram vow' (April 1, 2015).
28 *Agence France-Presse*, 'Boko Haram attacks kill 17 in Chad, Nigeria' (July 11, 2015).
29 A. Pargeter, 'Islamist militant groups in post-Qadhafi Libya' (February 20, 2013), accessed at www.ctc.usma.edu/posts/islamist-militant-groups-in-post-qadhafi-libya on February 26, 2017.
30 *CNN*, 'ISIS comes to Libya' (November 18, 2014), accessed at www.cnn.com/2014/11/18/world/isis-libya/ on February 26, 2017.
31 H. Solomon, 'What to do about Libya?' *Research on Islam and Muslims in Africa* (RIMA Policy Papers, 3:3, June 2015), accessed at https://muslimsinafrica.wordpress.com/2015/06/02/what-to-do-about-libya-professor-hussein-solomon on February 26, 2017.
32 M. Keilberth and C. Reuter, 'A threat to Europe: The Islamic State's dangerous gains in Libya', *Spiegel Online* (February 23, 2015), accessed at www.spiegel.de/international/world/islamic-state-advance-in-libya-could-present-threat-to-europe-a-1010076-druck.html on February 26, 2017.
33 *Washington Post*, 'Islamic State loses its stronghold in Libya, but more chaos could soon follow' (December 7, 2016).
34 *Newsweek*, 'As ISIS flees Sirte in Libya, Tunisia faces greater threat from returning jihadis' (October 27, 2016).
35 A. Le Sage, 'Terrorism threats and vulnerabilities in Africa', in A. Le Sage (ed.), *African Counterterrorism Cooperation* (Washington, DC: National Defense University Press, 2007), p. 32.
36 Carpenter, *et al.*, *Fighting the Ideological Battle*, p. 2.
37 Office of the Coordinator for Counterterrorism, *Patterns of Terrorism 2009* (Washington, DC: US Department of State, August 2010), p. 11.
38 *DailyMail Online*, 'ISIS opens new front in North Africa' (November 28, 2014), accessed at www.dailymail.co.uk/news/article-2853255/ISIS-opens-

new-North-Africa-two-extremist-groups-Libya-Egypt-pledge-allegiance-terror-leader.html on February 26, 2017.
39 *The Telegraph (UK)*, 'Isil recruiting "army of poor" with $1,000 sign-up bonus' (February 1, 2016), accessed at www.telegraph.co.uk/news/worldnews/islamic-state/12134806/Isil-recruiting-migrant-army-of-the-poor-with-1000-sign-up-bonuses.html on February 26, 2017.
40 Emerson, 'The battle for Africa's hearts and minds', p. 55.
41 Global Terrorism Database.
42 Cilliers, 'Terrorism and Africa', p. 99.
43 *CNN*, 'U.S. official calls ISIS a problem "off the charts historically"' (April 13, 2015).
44 *Washington Post*, 'Foreign fighters flow into Syria' (January 27, 2015).
45 Cilliers, 'Terrorism and Africa', p. 101.
46 S. Mair, 'The new world of privatized violence', *International Politik und Gesellschaft* (Bonn, Germany: International Politics and Society, 2:2003), p. 22. Mair identifies the five areas of cooperation and synergy across these non-state actors as arms dealing, drug trafficking, illegal trade in diamonds, smuggling of consumer goods, and money laundering.
47 S. Emerson, 'The metamorphosis of Al Qaeda in the Islamic Maghreb', *Research on Islam and Muslims* (Rima Occasional Papers Series, Pretoria: International Institute of Islamic Studies, No. 03/2010).
48 *The Telegraph* (UK), 'Revealed: how Saharan caravans of cocaine help to fund Al-Qaeda in terrorists' North African domain' (January 26, 2013); *Forbes.com*, 'The secret of Al Qaeda in Islamic Maghreb Inc; *allAfrica.com*, AQIM Partners With Colombian Drug Cartel.
49 Emerson, 'The metamorphosis of Al Qaeda in the Islamic Maghreb'.
50 F. El Kamouni-Janssen, 'Understanding instability in Libya' (Netherland Institute of International Relations, March 17, 2015), accessed at www.clingendael.nl/publication/understanding-instability-libya-will-peace-talks-end-chaos on February 26, 2017; *theguardian.com*, 'How cigarette smuggling fuels Africa's Islamist violence' (January 26, 2013), accessed at www.theguardian.com/world/2013/jan/27/cigarette-smuggling-mokhtar-belmokhtar-terrorism on February 26, 2017.
51 F. Zakaria, 'The year of microterrorism', *Time* (December 17, 2010–January 3, 2011), p. 26.
52 *Washington Times*, 'Analysis: Quiet on terror's "new front"' (May 13, 2005).
53 Emerson, 'The battle for Africa's hearts and minds', p. 57.
54 Government Accounting Office, 'Combating terrorism: Actions needed to enhance implementation of trans-Sahara counterterrorism partnership', *GAO Report-08-860* (Washington, DC: Government Accounting Office, July 31, 2008).
55 *Associated Press*, 'Horn of Africa may be the next terror front' (October 21, 2006).
56 Emerson, 'Regional security initiative', p. 79.

57 S. Emerson, 'Back to the future: The evolution of US counterterrorism policy in Africa', *Insight on Africa*, 6:1 (2014), 6, 10.
58 Ibid., p. 7.
59 See Foreignassistance.gov for more information on funding to Africa. Foreignassistance.gov houses the sites for the United States foreign funding, including the US Department of State, Africa Regional Office (DOS), accessed at http://beta.foreignassistance.gov/agencies/DoS#/search on February 26, 2017.
60 M. Hastings, 'The rise of the killer drones', *Rolling Stone* (April 16, 2012).
61 Emerson, 'Back to the future', p. 11.
62 *BBC News*, 'France sets up anti-Islamic force in Africa's Sahel' (July 14, 2014).
63 US Department of State, *Country Reports on Terrorism 2009* (Kenya), p. 21, accessed at www.state.gov/documents/organization/141114.pdf on February 26, 2017.
64 Rabasa, *Radical Islam in East Africa*, p. 38.
65 *TimesLive* (SA), 'Al-Qaeda at the gates', February 2015, accessed at www.timeslive.co.za/thetimes/2015/02/20/al-qaeda-at-the-gates on February 26, 2017.
66 Ibid.
67 H. Solomon, 'South Africa and the Islamic State', *Research on Islam and Muslims in Africa*, accessed at https://muslimsinafrica.wordpress.com/2015/04/09/south-africa-and-the-islamic-state-professor-hussein-solomon on February 26, 2017.
68 *Reuters*, 'Egypt's Sisi issues decree widening scope of security crackdown' (February 2015); Human Rights Watch, 'Ethiopia: Crackdown on dissent intensifies' (29 January 2015), accessed at www.hrw.org/news/2015/01/29/ethiopia-crackdown-dissent-intensifies on February 26, 2017.
69 *Associated Press*, 'Tunisia pledges tough security measures after Sousse Hotel attack' (June 27, 2015).

6

Trafficking in drugs and small arms

The explosive growth of free trade, global capital, and labor markets, along with the rapid pace of technological innovation and dissemination, has helped fuel massive economic growth and global consumerism since the end of the Cold War. The decade of the 1990s and up to the financial crisis of 2008 saw world growth rates averaging roughly 3 percent per year, with the number of people living in extreme poverty falling by 325 million between 1999 and 2005.[1] During the boom years from 2000 to 2008, low- and middle-income countries averaged an astounding 6.2 percent growth per year.[2] This economic expansion also produced a more integrated and interdependent world economy than ever before. Despite setbacks related to the global economic crisis of 2008–9, the world economy had recovered to reach nearly $80 trillion by 2014 (up from $59 trillion in 2006) with a projected annual growth rate of 2.7 percent in 2017 thanks in large part to a continued expansion of global trade and investment.[3]

Globalization has been at the heart of many of these changes. It has proven to be an unusually powerful phenomenon for better or worse. While globalization clearly has the ability to improve the everyday lives of people around the world and help them achieve new successes, it can also just as easily bring about greater exploitation of the weak and vulnerable and increase human suffering, and too often overlooked is its impact on security in emerging countries.

The dark side of globalization: the global trafficking problem

The carrying on of trade between communities and across great distances spans the ages and has been, and will continue to be, a fundamental aspect of global relationships. While the evolution of international commerce has grown more complex, structured, and institutionalized, the basic objective of linking distant sources of production with more affluent consumers has remained fundamentally the same. Another aspect has remained constant too—the process of attempting to circumvent legal and regulatory restrictions to maximize profits. Modern-day trade trafficking, however, is more than simply a reflection of this age old criminal problem for governments; it is one that increasingly poses a significant threat to both national and human security. This is not so much because the types of activities or methods have fundamentally changed, but that globalization acts as a powerful, new force multiplier that makes trafficking today more far reaching than ever before, more instantaneous, and responsive to changing market demands. Thus, not only can traffickers do more business today, but they can do it much more efficiently and profitably than in the past.

Formidable macro socio-economic trends since the end of the Cold War have altered global trafficking by transforming it from a purely criminal issue into a modern-day security challenge as well. Heretofore neglected or bypassed parts of the world have now become part of the global economy as either new sources of production or new centers of consumption. Increased access to technology that is inexpensive and easy to use, and improved information flows have helped to create a global marketplace. Producers and consumers are more connected than ever before. Thus, increased integration of the developing world into the global economy has intensified the push/pull effect on international flows of capital and labor, thereby creating new or enhanced trafficking opportunities.

The problem is further compounded by state weakness. On the one hand, weak states are increasingly unable to mitigate the negative impact of globalization that helps fuel trafficking and may even provide a facilitating environment for it to flourish. On the other hand, weak states are often unable or incapable of generating the enhanced societal benefits ascribed to a globalized economy and this, in turn, can push people to engage in trafficking to reap the rewards of globalized economy.

The drug trafficking challenge

At the top of these challenges is drug trafficking.[††] In 1998 the international community came together to combat the scourge of drugs that "destroy lives and communities, undermine sustainable human development and generate crime" by proposing a ten-year plan "with a view to eliminating or significantly reducing" the illicit supply and demand

---

[††] Drug trafficking is defined by the UNODC as the "global illicit trade involving the cultivation, manufacture, distribution and sale of substances which are subject to drug prohibition laws." UNODC website: www.unodc.org/unodc/en/drug-trafficking/index.html.

for drugs.[4] Since that time, however, success in the global war on drugs has been fleeting at best; it is now estimated that there are some 250 million annual drug users worldwide, with some 10–12 percent deemed "problem drug users."[5] Although cannabis is "the most widely produced and used drug in the world," according to the United Nations Office on Drugs and Crime (UNODC), it is now more commonly grown within consuming countries.[6] This makes cocaine and heroin the most lucrative global market for trafficking; the global retail market for cocaine and heroin appears to have surpassed $150 billion per year[7]—greater than the combined GDP of 29 sub-Saharan African countries.

The major markets for cocaine and heroin are found in North America and Western Europe respectively. However, production of both these drugs is highly concentrated in the developing world. Almost all of the world supply of cocaine is produced in Colombia, Peru, and Bolivia, and 85 percent of the global opium production comes from Afghanistan with other significant amounts grown in Laos, Mexico, and Myanmar.[8] Shipments follow well-established routes and patterns with cocaine being transported by land, sea, and air via Central America, Mexico, and the Caribbean to the United States, and across the Atlantic Ocean to Europe. The two main routes for heroin are either via southeastern Europe (the so-called "Balkan Route") or via the "Silk Route" using Russia, the Baltic States, and Poland.[9] In Africa, Kenya and Tanzania serve as an important gateway for southwest Asian heroin, supplying the small, but growing domestic African market and for onward delivery to Europe and other regions.[10]

Beyond the direct cost to societies as a result of drug abuse, empowered and flourishing transnational trafficking and criminal networks "undermine state institutions, threaten democratic processes, fuel armed and social conflict in the countryside and foment insecurity and violence."[11] In 1998 the United Nations General Assembly called the global drug problem "a grave threat to the health and well-being of all mankind [and] the stability of nations."[12] The destabilizing influence of trafficking on transit countries and regions that serve as way stations are particularly telling because of the enormous amount of money generated, associated violence, and rising power of drug traffickers. In addition, rising rates of drug addiction are common in transit countries as the availability of cheap drugs filtering into the local market displaces more traditional drugs and creates a new demand for imports. While violence associated with the trafficking of drugs is well-established, a threat to state security, the UNODC notes, can also come in the form of financially strengthening anti-government insurgents or armed groups involved in the drug trade, or indirectly through the high-level corruption of state officials and institutions.[13] Likewise, the emergence of symbiotic relationships between drug trafficking and terrorist organizations threatens state security, as witnessed with the rise of powerful narco-terrorist movements in South America during the 1980s and 1990s.

The illegal arms trade challenge
The global proliferation of weapons that feeds escalating arms races has long been seen as an enabler of conflict and political instability. Although only a very small fraction of the estimated $45 billion in annual worldwide arms transfers,[14] the illegal arms trade plays a significant role in sustaining regional and domestic conflict, fueling human rights violations, and endangering humanitarian relief and development efforts. The trade can not only buttress the position of embattled authoritarian regimes by supplying the tools of domestic repression, but it can also strengthen the power of non-state actors by providing them the means for directly challenging governmental authority. In both instances, the legitimacy of the state is endangered.

The very nature of the illegal arms trade makes estimation extremely difficult, but it may be worth $6 billion to $10 billion per year[15] and consists of everything from major weapons systems and state of the art targeting technology to small arms and light weapons (SALW), as well as ammunition. The five major suppliers of conventional weapons—the United States, Russia, China, Germany, and France—with some three-quarters of global exports, have also historically been the primary source of the illegal trade, either through the black or gray arms market. Unlike the trade in drugs, the trafficking in illegal arms tends to flow from the developed or emerging countries of Western and Eastern Europe, North America and Asia to conflict zones in developing countries.

One element of the illegal arms trade that is disproportionally significant because of its strong correlation with a whole host of security problems is the trafficking in SALW.‡‡ The annual illicit trade in these weapons is now believed to be upwards of $1.5 billion.[16] Most significantly, the direct and indirect cost of this illegal SALW trade is staggering, with the United Nations and others repeatedly pointing out that "most present-day conflicts are fought primarily with small arms and

---

‡‡ Small arms and light weapons are defined by the United Nations as 'revolvers and self-loading pistols, rifles and carbines, assault rifles, submachine guns, and light and heavy machine guns, as well as hand-held under-barrel and mounted grenade launchers, portable anti-tank and anti-aircraft guns, recoilless rifles, portable launchers of anti-tank and anti-aircraft missile systems, and mortars of less than 100mm caliber.' United Nations, 'Annex A: Report of Government Experts on Small Arms', August 27, 1997.

light weapons" and that they "are the weapons of choice in civil wars and for terrorism, organized crime and gang warfare."[17] They fuel and sustain large- and small-scale conflicts around the world.[18] They hinder development, imperil humanitarian relief, threaten personal safety, and facilitate human rights violations. The developing world, and Africa in particular, is forced to shoulder most of this burden.

Scope and nature of the trafficking problem in Africa

With Africa's increasing integration into the global economy, the continent is becoming ever more vulnerable to the dark side of globalization, which drives international trafficking. The challenge that the illicit trade in drugs, people, and small arms brings to the continent is one far beyond the immediate regional impact of rising transnational criminal activity, but one that has broad implications for the future of African governance and long-term stability. Whether it is the global market pull for drugs in the industrialized northern hemisphere or the push of small arms into developing countries in conflict, the heavy costs of trafficking fall disproportionally on some of the weakest and most fragile societies on the continent. It will certainly come as no surprise that the African countries most affected by trafficking are among the poorest, those actively engulfed in violent conflict, struggling with post-conflict situations, or caught up in incessant cycles of political turmoil and instability.

Drug trafficking

The rise of West Africa as a major transit route for drugs—most prominently South American cocaine—into Europe and even the United States beginning in 2004, however, is a more recent and disturbing trend, as is the growing use of the continent as a transshipment point for Asian drug shipments. This led UN Secretary-General Ban Ki-moon to conclude in 2010 that "drug trafficking is ... a rising threat to international peace and security in Africa."[19]

Well known to law enforcement officials throughout the late 1980s and 1990s was the use of commercial flights out of and connecting through major African airports by African and Asian drug mules working for Nigerian and other West African criminal syndicates to move small quantities of heroin and cocaine into European capitals and the United States.[20] All this began to change with the UN narcotics watchdog warning in 2001 that West African syndicates "are actively looking for new connections in Latin America and are bringing cocaine trafficking to all parts of sub-Saharan Africa."[21] And connections they would find.

The rapidity at which this change took place caught Africans and most of the world off guard. The UNODC reported in 2010 that the proportion of cocaine seizures in Europe that had African countries as the point of origin was negligible as late as 2002, but by 2007 this figure may have jumped to as high as one-third of all shipments.[22] Some 40 tons of cocaine worth $1.8 billion at the wholesale level (and at least $10 billion on the street) was entering Europe from West Africa by 2007, according to UNODC estimates.[23]

What accounted for this explosion of cocaine trafficking and West Africa's new role? Three words for each side of the Atlantic: "Colombian drug cartels" and "corrupt African officials." Stepped-up law enforcement efforts in Central America and the Caribbean, as well as a rising demand in Europe in the mid-2000s meshed nicely with a desire by West African criminal syndicates to expand their drug trafficking operations. A large number of West African countries, such as Guinea-Bissau, have long, unprotected coastlines and isolated islands, which made them ideal transit points for Colombian cocaine. But the key factor in the emergence of this new narco-alliance was the ability of South American drug lords to coopt and corrupt the highest levels of governments and their security institutions with massive amounts of cash.[24]

The partnership flourished before peaking in 2007; UNODC seizure data and interception rate estimates indicate that nearly 160 tons of cocaine, with an estimated street value of nearly $45 billion, is likely to have transited West Africa between 2005 and 2010.[25] West Africa's importance has declined markedly since then, leveling off to what we estimated at 15–18 tons annually or just over $1 billion by 2016. The reasons behind the decline are difficult to determine with any certainty, but major disruptions to the trade after 2008 as a result of increased international awareness and crackdowns, major internal political instability in key transit countries, and possible tensions between Colombian suppliers and their African middlemen appear to figure prominently, according to UNODC reporting.[26]

Although lacking the higher profile of West African cocaine trafficking, parts of East and Southern Africa are maturing as hubs for heroin and synthetic drug trafficking from Southwest and Southeast Asia.[27] According to UNODC estimates "as much as 22 tons of pure heroin" (nearly all from Afghanistan) is trafficked annually into East Africa and is worth some $1.4 billion.[28] Only about 10 percent of the heroin imported is believed to be for African domestic consumption in the subregion or elsewhere on the continent; Europe (and to a lesser degree the United States) is the ultimate destination. Many experts, however, believe that more Afghan heroin is flowing into East Africa, which is becoming known as the "Smack Track," based on the record setting value of drugs seized since 2010.[29]

Kenya, Tanzania, and Ethiopia, with their fairly well-developed regional and international transportation infrastructure, have been identified by international drug agencies as key hubs for the trafficking of heroin from Southwest Asia,[30] although South Africa and Nigeria also play important roles in the onward trade as well. East and West African criminal syndicates, along with Asian criminal gangs operating out of Southwest Asia are reportedly heavily engaged in the trafficking. At least ten major international drug trafficking networks, headed mainly by West Africans but including Kenyans too, are thought to be responsible for the bulk of heroin trafficking through Kenya, according to local intelligence sources.[31]

Another disturbing trend is the growing unease that "multiple countries in Africa are being used as hubs for the illicit diversion of chemical precursors [primarily ephedrine and pseudoephedrine] used to manufacture illegal [synthetic] drugs."[32] The first indication of this was uncovered in Guinea back in 2009 with the discovery of chemicals and equipment used in the illicit manufacture of ecstasy. West Africa currently seems to be at the center of the African amphetamine-type stimulants (ATS[§§]) trade with Nigeria as the focal point. Nigeria was the first West African country to officially report illicit methamphetamine manufacture in 2011, and laboratory discoveries and ATS seizures are now a regular occurrence.[33] Besides Nigeria, other West African manufacturing facilities are now thought to be operating in Benin, Cote d'Ivoire, and Ghana, and multiple countries across the sub-region serve as transit points for onward shipments to Asia and Europe.[34]

South Africa has also emerged as both a source of production and transshipment point for ATS that serve a steadily growing domestic and sub-regional market, as well as foreign markets in Europe and South Asia.[35] According to the UNODC, Kenya and Tanzania appear to have become a significant source of precursor chemicals with more than 2.5 tons of pseudoephedrine and ephedrine being stolen between 2009 and 2011.[36] There are also indications of ATS trafficking from West Africa to wealthy Asian countries via Ethiopia that "raises the possibility of a parallel flow of drugs between East and West Africa: heroin going west and amphetamines going east."[37] Egypt has traditionally served a "significant role as a departure country for ATS shipments to the Middle

---

[§§] Amphetamine-type stimulants (ATS) are a group of substances comprised of synthetic stimulants including amphetamine, methamphetamine, methcathinone, and ecstasy-group substances (such as MDMA and its analogues). UNODC, 'West Africa: 2012 ATS Situation Report', June 2012, p. 6.

East" from West Africa,[38] although the chaotic post-Arab Spring situation there may have curtailed much of this activity.

The issue of government corruption is a longstanding one in Africa, but the development of the continent as a major drug transit point in the mid-2000s took it to new and unprecedented heights. By all measures the level of official corruption has certainly worsened in those countries most affected by the drug trade. Since 2009 senior government officials in The Gambia, Guinea, Guinea-Bissau, Senegal, and Sierra Leone, as well as Kenya and South Africa, have either been convicted or implicated for their involvement in drug trafficking.

Case study: the Guinea-Bissau epicenter

No country was more heavily impacted and transformed in such a short period of time by drug trafficking in the mid-2000s than Guinea-Bissau. One of the poorest countries in the world, this impoverished former Portuguese colony on the west coast of Africa quickly became a haven for Colombian drugs traffickers after 2004 and the preferred transshipment route for South American cocaine flowing into Western Europe. The allure of easy money and unprecedented government corruption quickly turned Guinea-Bissau into what has often been called "Africa's first narco-state."

With a long history of post-independence political intrigue and infighting within the ruling party, the country was also buffeted by intense personal rivalries, ethnic patronage politics, and repeated military interventions that undermined democratic development. Corruption was also a way of life. The country's sparsely inhabited coastal line with numerous small and remote islands, plus its close proximity to Western European and major trans-Atlantic shipping routes, however, made it an ideal transshipment point for South American cocaine. Thus, Guinea-Bissau was ripe for the picking when Colombian drug lords showed up in 2004. At the height of the West African drug trade in the mid-2000s some 30–35 tons of cocaine per year was transiting the sub-region—much of it facilitated by those in Guinea-Bissau—according to international law enforcement officials.[a]

The numbers tell an alarming story. The entire GDP of Guinea-Bissau in 2004 was only $523 million or $382 per capita.[b] With Guinea-Bissau

---

[a] UN Office on Drugs and Crime, *World Drug Report 2010*, pp. 84–5; United Nations Office on Drugs and Crime, *Transnational Trafficking and the Rule of Law in West Africa: A Threat Assessment* (New York: United Nations Publication, July 2009), pp. 16–17.

[b] World Bank, *World Development Indicators Database* (April 18, 2006), accessed at www.pdwb.de/archiv/weltbank/gdp04.pdf on February 28, 2017; Indexmundi, 'Guinea-Bissau GDP', accessed at www.indexmundi.com/guinea-bissau/gdp_per_capita_(ppp).html on February 28, 2017.

accounting for the bulk of West African transshipments into Europe at their peak in 2006–7, some $500 million in illegal funds—nearly equal to the entire 2004 GDP of the country—was probably flowing into it. Or to put it another way, the value of just over 8 tons of cocaine sold on the streets in Western Europe was equal to the entire 2004 GDP of Guinea-Bissau.[c] The influx of dozens of big time drug traffickers and money was hard to ignore in such a small country. As the head of the UNODC put it, "Drug money is not only buying real estate and flashy cars: it is buying power."[d] By 2008, multiple high-ranking Guinea-Bissau government and military officials were implicated in cocaine trafficking. These included the country's minister of interior, the head of Judicial Police, the former head of the army, and the air force chief of staff. In early 2010 the US government designated former commander of the navy, Rear Admiral Bubo Na Tchuto, a "drug kingpin" at the center of the trade.[e]

By 2010 increased international awareness and interdiction efforts, along with political turmoil—such as military coups in Guinea, Guinea-Bissau, and Mauritania over the course of two years—reduced traffic through coastal West Africa and Guinea-Bissau in particular.[f] Rather than simply abandon the West African route completely, South American drug traffickers changed their way of operating and shifted operations elsewhere in the sub-region. Large drug seizures in The Gambia and Liberia, and evidence of cocaine being shipped into Mali by air, clearly showed the trade was alive and flourishing as before, but that international traffickers and their local counterparts were now utilizing new and multiple points of entry into West Africa.

The Guinea-Bissau connection, however, was far from dead. With the complicity of military officers and corrupt politicians, the country continued to be an important player in facilitating transit activities. Rear Admiral Na Tchuto's return from exile and the strengthening of Lt. General Antonio Indjai's grip over the trade following the April 2010 coup all but assured that business as

---

[c] Authors' projection based on data from UNDOC estimates of West African drug trade. UN Office on Drugs and Crime, *Transnational Trafficking and the Rule of Law in West Africa*, p. 17; United Nations Office on Drugs and Crime, *World Drug Report 2006: Volume 2. Statistics* (New York: United Nations Publication, 2006), Table 5.2, p. 368.

[d] A.M. Costa, 'ECOWAS high-level conference on drug trafficking as a security threat in West Africa' (Praia, Cape Verde, October 28, 2008).

[e] UN Office on Drugs and Crime, *World Drug Report 2010*, pp. 242–4; L. Vincent, *Guinea-Bissau: Cocaine and Coups Haunt Gagged Nation* (Paris: Reporters Without Borders, November 2007), p. 2.

[f] UN Office on Drugs and Crime, *World Drug Report 2010*, p. 84.

usual would continue, albeit on a smaller scale.[g] Nonetheless, the hay days of the trade were waning because of slowing demand in Europe and stepped up international law enforcement pressure. The arrest and capture of Na Tchuto by US Drug Enforcement Administration officers in April 2013 signaled a major turning point.[h] In early 2014 two of Na Tchuto's key deputies pleaded guilty to narcotics importation charges in the United States; Na Tchuto did the same a few months later.[i] Under domestic and international pressure to reform the military, General Indjai was sacked as head of the armed forces in September 2014 by President Jose Mario Vaz.

Although West Africa continues to serve as a transshipment point for South American cocaine entering Europe (albeit on a much smaller scale than at its peak), Guinea-Bissau is no longer the epicenter of this trade, as distribution networks have become more diversified and fragmented throughout the entire sub-region.

[g] New York Times, 'Former exile holds power in West African nation' (May 25, 2010); UN Office on Drugs and Crime, *Transnational Organized Crime in West Africa*, p. 16.
[h] New York Times, 'U.S. sting that snared African ex-admiral shines light on drug trade' (April 15, 2013).
[i] Reuters, 'Guinea-Bissau's ex-navy chief pleads guilty in U.S. drug case' (June 3, 2014).

Of deep concern too is the development of symbiotic relationships in parts of Africa between drug trafficking criminal organizations and armed groups, including terrorist organizations. Such relationships, according to UN Secretary-General Ban Ki-moon, pose "a rising threat to international peace and security in Africa."[39] Such a lucrative and mutually beneficial arrangement would provide militant elements with new sources of funding to raise recruits and secure new weaponry to continue their separatist and terrorist struggles. Likewise, the drug trade often feeds pre-existing drivers of domestic instability within transshipment countries and thus makes the state increasingly weaker as the trade grows.[40] The growth of trans-Saharan trafficking routes after 2008, in particular, raised fears from UN experts that Tuareg rebels in the north of Mali and neighboring Niger were becoming involved and that other militant groups in West Africa could be revivified by the trade.[41] Even more worrisome was the continuing involvement of AQIM terrorists in criminal activity that raked in tens of millions of dollars in ransom payments and that positioned the organization to become a major force in the trans-Saharan drug trade.

These dire predictions have yet to come true. The trans-Saharan trade, especially in cocaine, has, in point of fact, declined, reflecting larger regional trends. Moreover, armed militant groups and terrorist organizations do not appear to have allied themselves with transnational criminal organizations involved in drug trafficking (although some elements of AQIM and other Islamist groups continue to be deeply involved in other criminal activity, such as kidnapping, smuggling, and gun running). Several factors appear to account for this situation. First and foremost, massive and ongoing political instability plagued much of the region from 2009. From Mauritania to Niger and into parts of North Africa the region has witnessed over half a dozen military coups, destructive civil wars in Mali and Libya, multiple foreign military interventions, and continuing social instability. This chaotic environment is antithetical to the smooth functioning of the drug trade. Second, growing media attention on the West Africa drug trade brought with it increased international law enforcement attention and donor resources to address the threat. In addition, the establishment of a large international peacekeeping and foreign military presence in countries such as Mali presented a significant obstacle to drug trafficking operations in the region. Finally, the growth of regional Islamist extremist groups presents an ideological barrier to engaging in the drug trade, especially where other criminal revenue streams are available as sources of funding.

Africa's role as a significant transit hub in the global drug trade, however, is leading to increased domestic drug use and creating a burgeoning health challenge. While cannabis is still the most widely used drug, the use of opioids, such as heroin, is "increasing significantly" and many countries are reporting greater usage rates of cocaine and ATS as well, according to the UNODC.[42] Many believe this growth is clearly linked to international trafficking, as widely available cheap cocaine and heroin feed demand away from traditional drugs. Or, as an ECOWAS official put it: "A region that trafficks ... becomes a region that consumes."[43]

Several countries, for example, are already experiencing addiction problems: crack cocaine in Guinea-Bissau, "brown-brown" (an alcohol and heroin mix) in Sierra Leone, cocaine use in Cape Verde, and rising opioid use in Nigeria.[44] Several West African countries and Nigeria now appear to have a national amphetamine usage rate higher than South Africa.[45] Meanwhile, several East African countries are witnessing a rise in heroin use because of its greater availability. And while cocaine use in South Africa has remained steady, it is reporting increases in the use of heroin, methamphetamine, and methcathinone.[46]

Small arms: Africa's weapons of mass destruction
The longstanding and widespread illicit trade in SALW comprises the second element of Africa's deadly trafficking cocktail, and in many

aspects this trade is much more pervasive, ingrained, and immediately threatening than either drug or human trafficking. The uncontrolled spread and easy access to these weapons—the AK-47 and its variants is the most widely available assault rifle in Africa, often costing less than $100[47]—is felt by nearly every African country. This makes it a complex and multi-dimensional problem that is deeply intertwined with other broader security and societal issues and, as such, presents a serious threat to domestic and regional security. Nonetheless, numerous regional and international initiatives have failed to stem illicit arms trafficking, causing former UN Secretary-General Kofi Annan to note that "indeed, there is no single tool of conflict so widespread, so easily available and so difficult to restrict, as small arms."[48]

Of the estimated 875 million SALW now in global circulation, approximately 35–40 million are thought to be in Africa, with the overwhelming majority of these believed to be in civilian hands outside the control of governments.[49] Contrary to popular perception, just 2 percent of all African SALW (less than 800,000) are thought to be in the hands of armed groups or insurgents, according to Small Arms Survey data projections.[50] Strikingly, it is this "relatively few number" of weapons that have unleashed such enormous misery and devastation across Africa. Although small arms clearly are not in and of themselves the cause of violent conflict per se, their ready availability and lethality contributes to prolonging and intensifying conflict situations.

Although trafficking in small arms occurs across all parts of the continent and in various ways, it takes place at three very different and distinct levels, which are distinguished by the type of weaponry, nature and sophistication of the distribution network, and source of supply.

International trafficking

Africa as a venue for superpower conflict during the Cold War contributed to massive influxes of conventional weapons—including large numbers of small arms—that were used to equip guerrilla forces fighting proxy wars. While the end of the Cold War resulted in reduced demand for these weapons, it also opened the floodgates to massive amounts of surplus weaponry and ammunition held in former communist inventories. And in doing so it gave rise to a new breed of international arms traffickers, such as Victor Bout, Leonid Minn, and Jacques Monsieur, complete with their own air fleets and holding companies who exploited the post-Cold war chaos to build vast global trafficking networks supplying arms to Africa.[51] From the early 1990s onward they gained increasing prominence and earned hundreds of millions of dollars by becoming equal opportunity weapons suppliers to anyone who could pay, from authoritarian governments to aspiring warlords or insurgent leaders, and thus helped to fuel multiple conflicts across Africa, from Angola and the DRC to Liberia and Sierra Leone.[52]

Over the past decade, international small arms trafficking patterns have undergone multiple transformations in response to supply and demand requirements and international efforts to curb this aspect of the illicit arms trade. As cheap ex-Soviet Bloc surplus stocks began to dry up, and with tighter control enacted on new production after 2001, key sources of supply and new trafficking routes first shifted to parts of the former Yugoslavia and the Balkans, according to Small Arms Survey reporting,[53] although some Eastern European countries like the Ukraine and Bulgaria continued to play a significant role.[54] Since the mid-2000s China, with its relatively inexpensive small arms and ammunition, has come to the fore as "the provider of choice in Africa for small arms and light weapons" and is believed to have delivered a large, but unknown quantity of small arms to at least 27 African countries. From 2001 to 2012 China accounted for 58 percent of reported arms transfers to Sudan, and Chinese military equipment "has become increasingly common" in Sudan and South Sudan.[55] Nevertheless, the overall numbers of—legal and illegal—SALW entering Africa appear to have declined precipitously since their post-Cold War peaks and now new imports to the continent likely account for less than 5 percent of the global small arms trade, in our view.

Sub-regional recirculation

The recirculation of existing weapon stocks already on the continent is now the most pressing arms trafficking challenge in Africa. The problem is enhanced by the continent's highly porous borders, easily exploitable natural resources (to pay for weapons), extensive use of armed proxy groups, and fragmented and uncoordinated approaches to conflict resolution at the national and sub-regional level. All this feeds a pattern of arms trafficking that is more ubiquitous and difficult to overcome than international trafficking.

Huge arms inflows during the Cold War created readily available stockpiles of SALW in some of the continent's most volatile regions. Guinea-Bissau, for example, with its violent anti-colonial past and incessant political turmoil was believed to be host to some 650,000 small arms alone, according to international experts.[56] Not unexpectedly, the highest concentrations of arms are found in Africa's primary conflict zones: West Africa's greater Mano River Basin, Central Africa's Chad-Dafur-CAR region, the greater Horn of Africa, and the Great Lakes District. These conflict zones, we believe, may account for nearly two-thirds to three-quarters of the continent's estimated 35–40 million SALW. In addition, a historical legacy and culture of violence in places like Algeria, Angola, the DRC, Mozambique, Sudan/South Sudan, Somalia, South Africa, and Uganda has left these societies heavily armed. Prior to South Sudan's independence, for example, it was estimated that there were some 2.7 million small arms inside Sudan and in the years since, that number now likely exceeds 3 million.[57] South Africa continues to be one of the most heavily armed societies on the continent with some non-governmental organizations (NGOs) estimating that there are 12 firearms for every 100 people.[58]

More recently the plundering of Qadhafi's extensive arms stockpiles in the aftermath of the 2011 Libyan revolution has unleashed a flood of new and sophisticated weaponry into the hands of armed groups and jihadist organizations across parts of North and West Africa.[59] Prior to the overthrow of the Qadhafi regime, the Libyan government maintained a large arsenal of SALW (estimated at between 250,000 and 700,000 firearms), which was stored along with other heavy weaponry throughout the country in more than 100 arms depots and warehouses.[60] Government stockpiles also were estimated to contain "as many as 20,000" man-portable air defense systems or MANPADS, mainly older Soviet-made Streta-2Ms, according to Western military officials.[61] By mid-2011 anti-Qadhafi forces had captured or looted much of these supplies. The problem worsened after Qadhafi's fall, with British intelligence estimating that more than one million tons of weapons was looted from arms dumps by 2012, and that Libya had "become the 'Tesco' [a multi-billion dollar British grocery and general merchandise chain] of the world's illegal arms trade."[62] To date, many of these weapons have turned up in conflict zones all across the sub-region; Libyan stockpiles—including supplies of MANPADS and heavy weapons—have become an "important source of material" for Tuareg rebels and jihadists in northern Mali, according to a Small Arms Survey assessment.[63] A UN Panel of Experts has linked recovered launch tubes in the CAR, Lebanon, Mali, and Tunisia to previous Libyan inventories.[64]

Post-conflict disarmament, demobilization, and reintegration programs have had some limited success at removing excess weapons from these societies, but the continuing strong demand for weapons and lingering sense of insecurity has complicated small arms abatement efforts. The process in Liberia and Sierra Leone successfully disarmed and demobilized 175,519 ex-combatants yet recovered only 70,644 weapons, according to the United Nations.[65] Some multilateral efforts have proven more effective: Since 1995 Operation Rachel (a joint Mozambican-South African police task force) has destroyed over

50,000 firearms and 31 million rounds of ammunition leftover from the Mozambican civil war,[66] and the Mozambican civil society program, "Tools for Arms," has reportedly destroyed at least another 700,000 more small arms.[67] The price of an AK-47 in South Africa has risen nearly 30 times as a result.[68] Needless to say a lot more needs to be done to reduce the supply of weapons still circulating in post-conflict zones.

Domestic trafficking

Often overlooked in discussions of the small arms trade in Africa are the tens of thousands of weapons that are illegally trafficked within national borders each year. Moreover, unlike other forms of arms trafficking, this trade is geared primarily toward supplying civilians. Handguns, shotguns, and long guns tend to dominate this trade in most countries, although the sale of assault rifles is not uncommon too. There are, however, no reliable estimates as to the number of guns trafficked or the value of this trade in Africa.

Fear over personal and communal security is the primary factor driving demand. As many governments are either incapable or unwilling to safeguard their own citizens, individuals and communities assume this responsibility by arming themselves. This, in turn, can create an escalating race to arm in the name of protecting oneself or one's community. The result is many heavily armed societies; it is estimated that nearly 80 percent of all African small arms—between 28 and 32 million—are thought to be in civilian hands.[69] The percentage of civilian ownership and number of personal weapons, however, varies widely from country to country. Relatively affluent countries like Kenya or South Africa—the country with the highest ratio of firearms to people on the continent—where criminal violence is a serious concern rank high on this list,[70] as do many war-ravaged societies, such as Angola, Somalia, South Sudan, and Sudan.

More so than in other aspects of the African arms trade, the sources of supply for domestic trafficking are among the most varied, but can be loosely grouped into three major categories:

- *Government stockpiles.* The practice of arming civilians from government stockpiles to improve local security at times of civil strife has become a significant source of weapons leakage into the domestic market. Poorly paid, ill-disciplined, and inadequately supervised self-defense militias and civil defense units often end up engaging in banditry, imposing "taxes" or selling their weapons and ammunition for cash.[71] Ironically, the weapons intended to protect individuals and communities often become a tool of increased insecurity.

- *Homemade or craft production.* Another key source of domestic weapon supply is the production of crudely made and assembled pistols, rifles, and shotguns. These homemade firearms (common known as craft guns) can be found throughout large urban centers across the continent, but the majority of this craft production resides in West Africa. Usually purchased for personal protection, they are just as likely to be used by criminals. An official with the Ghana National Commission on Small Arms claimed that "about 80 percent of the locally manufactured arms are used in committing crime."[72]
- *Lost or stolen weapons.* The sale of lost or stolen firearms on the black market is another significant source of supply, especially in high gun ownership societies. For instance, official South African police statistics show more than 230,000 guns were lost or stolen between 1994 and 2007.[73] Moreover, 46 percent of firearms confiscated by the South African police from 2009–12 were once legal firearms that found their way into criminal hands after having been lost or stolen.[74]

While African governments clearly understand the need to curtail both the supply and demand side of the domestic trafficking problem, actually making progress has been exceedingly difficult. Corruption and mistrust in government, the need to protect scarce communal resources, personal security fears, and lucrative financial rewards work to undermine these efforts. Nonetheless, some progress is being made, thanks to civil society groups, NGOs, and government commissions that are at the forefront of legislative reform efforts, civic education, conflict mediation, and disarmament initiatives.

Implications for security

While the illicit global trade in everything from raw commodities and precious metals to rare minerals and people has been a defining feature of Africa's integration into the wider world economy for centuries, the modern-day confluence of trafficking in drugs and small arms poses a particularly worrisome problem for the future of the continent and its security. Beyond the inherent criminal nature of these activities, the mutually reinforcing aspects of this trafficking connection strikes squarely at the very heart of human security by helping to fuel violence and armed conflict, undermine governance, and threaten political stability. Moreover, the full impact of trafficking tends to fall disproportionally on the most vulnerable and weak of society—women and the very young.

The trafficking challenge to security in Africa is twofold. First, there is the immediate problem of escalating criminality and its impact on personal safety. Second, there is the longer-term threat to the functioning of state and the future welfare of the society itself. With good reason trafficking is viewed as a serious criminal problem that reaps billions of dollars for individuals and organized crime syndicates, as well as endangering the lives of individuals and even whole communities. Rarely, however, does African criminal activity alone pose an immediate challenge to the continued existence and security of the state itself. Rather, a weak and corruptible state that provides some institutional structure and norms is preferable to none at all for criminal enterprises. Criminal activity may, as Chabal and Daloz point out, compensate for the dysfunctional state by serving to strengthen the informal economy, bolstering client-patron and informal political relationships, and thus actually "provide some order ... to facilitate the productive domestication of prevailing disorder."[75] Nonetheless, over time trafficking has the capability to seriously damage the state and structure of society. It distorts political and economic development, inculcates a culture of violence and fear, feeds corruption, and undermines human rights and the rule of law. This danger is further amplified by the mutually reinforcing and overlapping nature of the illicit trade in drugs, people, and small arms with their potential linkage to other serious security challenges, like failing states or terrorism. Since the pace of globalization shows no signs of abating, the security challenges posed by trafficking are only likely to rise in the decades ahead.

Fuels violence and armed conflict
By far trafficking's most serious implication for African security is its inordinate capability to inflame, sustain, and worsen the levels of societal violence and armed conflict. On a continent already desperately groping to find effective ways to address these twin evils, this is something Africa can ill afford. Aside from this very direct and immediate threat, trafficking also poses several significant indirect and long-term security challenges in terms of added social costs and weakening development prospects.

For instance, although clearly not the underlying source of armed conflict in Africa, trafficking in SALW plays a critical role not only in fueling and sustaining conflict, but also in escalating the type and level of the violence. The trafficking in new and recirculated SALW creates a readily available supply of easy to use weapons that can be quickly accessed, thereby increasing the likelihood of conflicts turning violent. Moreover, given the high stakes involved—access to power, wealth, or resources—in these types of armed conflicts, it is not unusual for violence to escalate quickly and the level of lethality and brutality to increase. According to the United Nations, "more human rights abuses are committed with them [small arms] than with any other weapon," including killing and maiming, sexual violence against women, torture, and forced recruitment of children by armed groups.[76]

One might naturally expect the level of violence to rise in proportion to the potential rewards gained, but the trafficking of small arms may have its greatest impact at the low end of the conflict spectrum. Longstanding disputes over water or grazing rights, for example, can quickly escalate into bloody clashes once automatic weapons enter the picture. The pastoral communities of Uganda's northeast Karamoja region, where cattle raiding has been a way of life for centuries, have witnessed this impact directly; "serious insecurity ... exacerbated by the pervasive use of illegal weapons and collapse of elaborate social constraints which used to limit bloodshed, present a significant law and order problem in Karamoja."[77] Multiple governmental efforts at disarmament since 2001 have failed to remedy the problem (and in fact have often escalated the level of violence) because of the robust tri-border arms trade between South Sudan, Kenya, and Uganda and personal security fears. As a herdsman in South Sudan put it, "you must have a gun or else you will be robbed of your animals and killed like a dog. We have no choice."[78]

Likewise, criminal violence associated with drug and arms trafficking, including assassinations, turf wars over control of distribution networks, and armed robbery and assaults help to nourish a culture of societal violence and fear. Although major trafficking hubs in Africa have not experienced the extraordinary and extreme levels of violence like those in Colombia or Mexico, there does appear to be a strong correlation between the growth of these hubs and a heightened level of crime and societal violence. Trafficking-related crime in Kenya, Nigeria, and South Africa is certainly one contributing factor in sustaining the overall level of violence in these countries, which have some of the highest murder and violent crime rates on the continent.[79] The Kenyan capital is often jokingly referred to as "Nairobbery." This creates a self-reinforcing culture of violence and fear where people are frightened "not just by the high level of crime but the wanton violence that usually accompanies it."[80] Unfortunately, many defensive responses simply pour more fuel on the fire by attacking the symptoms of trafficking-related crime in terms of adding more firearms into civilian hands or through harsh government security crackdowns that endanger human rights.

Often overlooked in any discussion of trafficking-fueled violence are the indirect costs and second order consequences to African societies. These added social and development costs can be quite specific and immediate or have a wide-ranging and long-term impact. For example, the added financial burden of treating gunshot victims, a new generation of drug addicts or caring for displaced families and war orphans can be staggering for cash strapped governments.[81] In addition, children and adolescents are "specifically and disproportionally affected by many consequences of armed violence whether physiological, psychological, or social," with young men generally becoming direct victims of armed violence, while younger children may suffer through targeted attacks on civilians or be recruited into armed groups.[82] In the longer term, however, violence and armed conflict are likely to inhibit economic development; an NGO study in 2007 estimated that armed conflict cost Africa around $18 billion per year, with an average loss of 15 percent to national GDPs, which has totaled $284 billion from 1990 to 2007.[83] This is an amount greater than all foreign aid to Africa since the start of the new century.

Perhaps most detrimental to the fundamental underpinnings of human security prospects, however, is the ingraining of cultures of violence and lawlessness that accompanies increased trafficking. The result is entire societies living in constant fear. Social and economic development is distorted. Governments and national institutions become increasingly irrelevant in the eyes of their own people. Thus, the creation of a wider sense of community and belonging that is so critical to human security is severely weakened and security comes to be perceived as belonging only to the strongest and most powerful within society.

Undermines governance
The negative impact of trafficking on human security is also strongly felt through its effect on African governance by facilitating corruption and undermining human rights and the rule of law. This is especially true for fragile countries grappling with the transition to democracy and struggling with issues of corruption, accountability and transparency, political and social inclusion, and respect for human rights and the rule of law. Building effective governance lies at the heart of these challenges for many of the continent's nascent democracies. Although multiple definitions abound, the core principles of good governance emphasize: the promotion of legitimacy and popular participation; responsiveness and effectiveness of institutions; personal and institutional accountability and transparency; and fairness, equity, and respect for the rule of law.[84] Likewise, good governance relies heavily on broad and active societal involvement from the bottom up, and anything that hinders this or undermines public confidence in the process is detrimental to developing effective governance mechanisms. The vast sums of money generated by the illicit trade in drugs and small arms create just that hindrance.

While no one disputes the very high levels of corruption across the continent, which place it at the bottom of the scale—five of the bottom ten "highly corrupt" countries are in Africa, according to Transparency International rankings[85]—nor how it has become an integral part of informal political and social relationships, the nature of trafficking-driven corruption is significantly changing established patterns and norms and worsening the problem. Rather than function as a redistribution, patronage or economic mechanism for socially desirable purposes as some have argued,[86] the "new corruption" is more about personal greed and aggrandizement. African societies are increasingly forced to shoulder the social costs (especially in terms of violence) of trafficking, but end up reaping little in the way of the rewards that trickle down.

Even without the impact of trafficking, the challenge of ensuring human rights and the rule of law in Africa is a difficult one. Enshrined in the United Nations *Declaration of Human Rights* is the belief that people everywhere are entitled to life, liberty, and security. The critical emphasis on personal security and freedom is a foundation block of good governance. The use of child soldiers, rape as a weapon of war, and the overall increased levels of societal violence associated with drug and arms trafficking threaten the weakest and most vulnerable elements of society. Likewise the growing power and influence of criminal syndicates engaged in trafficking permit them to corrupt, coopt, or intimidate those involved in the administration of justice, such as court officials, policemen, and politicians. The resulting dysfunctional arrangement serves to weaken the rule of law in the eyes of the people.

Threatens political stability

For many of the continent's countries struggling with issues of political inclusion, national fragmentation or simply making the difficult transition to democracy, trafficking can create problems for political stability. It has, for example, the potential to stimulate the growth of alternative power structures, which may directly and indirectly challenge central government authority. Here again, it is rarely the actual trafficking activities themselves that are politically destabilizing, but the formidable consequences of trafficking that are able to markedly strengthen power-seeking groups who pose a risk to national stability.

The linkage between small arms and drug trafficking, and the flow of weapons and money into the hands of armed insurgents or terrorists, is clearly destabilizing. The traffickers' provision of material and financial resources to these armed groups puts them in a stronger position to challenge the existing power structure. Often in return, armed groups enter into symbiotic relationships with traffickers, whom they afford protection from government interference. While nothing on the order of the insurgent-narco alliances that have emerged in parts of Latin America or Asia, these budding relationships in Africa are nonetheless troubling for governments already teetering on the verge of serious instability. From separatist groups and local political bosses in Mali or Nigeria's Niger Delta to AQIM or Islamic affiliates across North Africa and the Horn of Africa, trafficking undoubtedly plays a major factor in fueling volatility.

Likewise, the powerful role of warlords and criminal organizations in many parts of the continent can be critical to the rise of alternative sources of political power. Through trafficking activities these groups seek to advance, first and foremost, their own economic, rather than political, interests. While warlords are often partially motivated by a desire to achieve some degree of political power, this is more a means to an end—reaping greater economic benefits.[87] By aligning with sympathetic or coopted political groups or leaders, they often can provide an alternative basis of support outside the existing institutionalized political process—more importantly, one that is unaccountable to the society. In doing so, compromised political groups and leaders in return directly or indirectly facilitate ongoing warlord and criminal economic enterprises. The destabilizing impact of the drug trade on Guinea-Bissau politics is perhaps the most extreme example of this phenomenon.

Groups engaged in trafficking pursue their own narrow objectives at the expense of the larger society because they thrive in environments where money, violence, fear, and intimidation are prevalent. Moreover, a study by the World Bank shows that resulting instability from repeated cycles of political and criminal violence complicates development efforts and traps entire populations in dire poverty. It noted that people living in these fragile states "are twice as likely to be undernourished and 50 percent more likely to be impoverished."[88] Thus, the destabilizing impact of trafficking can have significant second and even third order effects on political stability that are not always readily apparent.

Conclusion

Although the illegal trade in goods and services has long been a vibrant component of the international economic system, the massive economic expansion since the end of the Cold War, and the rapid pace of globalization, have significantly altered the nature of global trafficking in both size and scope. And this, in turn, has transformed the problem from a purely criminal issue to a broader security challenge for the international community—and especially for Africa. As the continent increasingly becomes integrated into the global economic and security order of the twenty-first century, so too will it continue to find itself caught up in the dark side of globalization that the trafficking in drugs and small arms represents. Moreover, given the fertile ground and facilitating environment that Africa provides to international traffickers, the problem is only likely to worsen in the decades ahead.

As we have seen, Africa's weak and fragile countries are especially ill-equipped to deal with this rising challenge, given their lack of capacity, already strained resources, and host of competing political, social, and economic priorities. Nevertheless, African governments and organizations cannot afford to ignore the threat to human security that trafficking poses to the safety and well-being of their societies, their ability to govern, and ultimately their long-term political stability. The case of Guinea-Bissau's rapid transformation into the continent's "first narco state" over the span of only a few years clearly demonstrates the vulnerability of the continent and how quickly countries can succumb to the power, influence, and money that accompanies trafficking.

Contrary to popular perception, relatively wealthier African countries may in fact be more at risk to an escalation in trafficking in the decades ahead. Rather than having more high profile Guinea-Bissaus, the future of African trafficking is increasingly likely to be determined by the subtle expansion of facilitating hubs in better off countries. Egypt, Kenya, Nigeria, and South Africa offer access to modern technology, developed or semi-developed transportation and financial infrastructure, political openness and relative stability, and growing economies, but they also manifest significant income disparities. All of these factors help facilitate the expansion of international, sub-regional, and domestic trafficking. Not only will the impact be more strongly felt in these countries, but the repercussions will have much broader security implications for the continent as well. The four countries named above, for example, currently account for more than one-quarter of the continent's population and more than half of its GDP, so any destabilizing impact will undoubtedly ripple across the continent.

To complicate matters further, the trafficking challenge in Africa will undoubtedly become more and more integrated with already existing or newly developing security threats. The current potent mix of drugs and small arms trafficking with terrorism in West Africa is one example of how the combined threat becomes greater than the whole. Other trafficking linkages that are potentially likely to strengthen are associated with identity and resource conflict, failed states, and even the spread of pandemic disease. How African government and organizations react to this situation will be critical. The key will be their willingness to acknowledge and accept these linkages as serious threats to their security (even if they are less immediate) and take the necessary preemptive steps to stem their growth. The active support and involvement of the international community and global organizations will be essential given the globalized nature of the trafficking problem. Competing global priorities, however, may divert badly needed international resources and this will almost certainly put pressure on African countries to do more with the limited resources they have at their disposal. Unfortunately, the most common result given the continent's past track record is that less will be done with less.

Notes

1 World Bank, *World Development Indicators 2010* (Washington, DC: The International Bank for Reconstruction and Development/World Bank, April 2010), Table 4.1: Growth of output, pp. 228 and 217.
2 Ibid.
3 World Bank, *World Development Indicators 2015* (Washington, DC: World Bank Publications, January 2017), Table 1.1 Size of the economy, p. 3 accessed at http://wdi.worldbank.org/tables on February 27, 2017; World Bank, *Global Economic Prospects* (Washington, DC: World Bank Publications, January 2017).
4 United Nations General Assembly, 'Political declaration' (June 8–10, 1998).
5 UN Office on Drugs and Crime, *World Drug Report 2015* (New York: United Nations Publication, 2015), p. ix. Cannabis remains the top drug of choice, accounting for nearly 75 percent of all drug usage (Table one, p. 1).
6 UN Office on Drugs and Crime, *World Drug Report 2010* (New York: United Nations Publication, 2010), pp. 12–13. Cannabis is by far the most widely consumed and trafficked drug within Africa, but only a very small percentage is trafficked outside of the continent and the cannabis trade has fewer security implications than cocaine or heroin trafficking, although it certainly represents a major health and social challenge. UN Office on Drugs and Crime, *World Drug Report 2010*, p. 13, Table 4.2.1.3: Cannabis usage rates, pp. 287–8.
7 The estimated breakdown is $85 billion for cocaine and $65 billion for heroin. *Business Insider*, 'These maps show the hard drug trade in remarkable detail' (February 19, 2015), accessed at www.businessinsider.com/how-drugs-travel-around-the-world-2015-2 on February 27, 2017; M. Chossudovsky, 'The spoils of war: Afghanistan's multibillion dollar heroin trade' (May 25, 2015), accessed at www.globalresearch.ca/the-spoils-of-war-afghanistan-s-multibillion-dollar-heroin-trade/91 on February 27, 2017; UN Office on Drugs and Crime, *World Drug Report 2010*', pp. 37 and 69.

8 UN Office on Drugs and Crime, *World Drug Report 2015'*, pp. 50 and 42.
9 UN Office on Drugs and Crime, *The Illicit Drug Trade through South-Eastern Europe* (New York: United Nations Publication, March 2014), pp. 5, 8–10; European Monitoring Centre for Drugs and Drug Addiction and Europol, *EU Drug Market Report: A Strategic Analysis* (Luxembourg: Publication Office of the European Union, 2013), pp. 31–3.
10 UN Office on Drugs and Crime, *World Drug Report 2015*, pp. 44–5.
11 International Crisis Group, 'Latin American drugs I: Losing the fight', *Latin America Report No. 25* (March 14, 2008), p. i.
12 United Nations General Assembly, 'Political declaration'.
13 UN Office on Drugs and Crime, *World Drug Report 2010*, p. 5.
14 Authors' projection based on data from R. Grimmett and P. Kerr, *Conventional Arms Transfers to Developing Nations, 2004–2011* (Washington, DC: Congressional Research Service, August 24, 2012), p. 4; Stockholm International Peace Research Institute, 'SIPRI fact sheet: Trends in international arms transfers, 2014' (March 2015), and *SIPRI Arms Transfer Database* accessed at www.sipri.org/databases/armstransfers on February 27, 2017. Other estimates are as high as $60 billion per year.
15 Authors' projection based on data from V. Kozyulin, 'Conventional arms transfers, illicit arms trade: An overview and implications for the region' (PRI Center lecture, circa 2004), p. 15, accessed at www.pircenter.org/data/news/kozyulin091104lect.pdf on February 27, 2017.
16 Authors' extrapolation from World Bank estimates, *World Development Report 2011* (Washington, DC: The World Bank, 2011), p. 241. Small Arms Survey, *Small Arms Survey 2014* (Cambridge: Cambridge University Press, 2014), p. 111 for the $8.5 billion total trade estimate.
17 United Nations Security Council, 'Small arms—Report of the Secretary-General, S/2008/258' (April 17, 2008), p. 1, accessed at www.poa-iss.org/DocsUpcomingEvents/S-2008-258.pdf on February 27, 2017.
18 United Nations General Assembly, 'Towards an arms treaty: Establishing common international standards for the import, export and transfer of conventional arms' (Issues at AMUN, First Committee: Disarmament and International Security, 2010), p. 24.
19 Secretary-General Ban Ki-moon, 'An agenda for prosperity and peace' (Remarks to the Summit of the African Union, Addis Ababa, 31 January 2010), accessed at www.un.org/sg/statements/index.asp?nid=4368 on February 27, 2017.
20 For an in-depth look at the roots of the West African drug trade see S. Ellis, 'West Africa's international drug problem', *African Affairs*, 108:431 (April 2009), 171–96.
21 A. Labrousse, 'Sub-Saharan Africa facing the challenge of drugs' (Ottawa, Canada: Parliament of Canada, February 2001), accessed at www.parl.gc.ca/Content/SEN/Committee/371/ille/presentation/labrousse1-e.htm on February 27, 2017.
22 UN Office on Drugs and Crime, *World Drug Report 2010*, p. 169.

23 UN Office on Drugs and Crime, *Cocaine Trafficking in West Africa: The Threat to Stability and Development* (New York: United Nations Publication, December 2007), p. 3.
24 UN Office on Drugs and Crime, *Transnational Organized Crime in West Africa: A Threat Assessment* (New York: United Nations Publication, February 2013), pp. 9–10.
25 Ibid., pp. 17–18.
26 UN Office on Drugs and Crime, *Crime and Instability: Case Studies of Transnational Threats* (New York: United Nations Publication, February 2010), p. 16.
27 UN Office on Drugs and Crime, *World Drug Report 2013* (New York: United Nations Publication, 2013), p. 24.
28 UN Office on Drugs and Crime, 'Twenty-fourth meeting of heads of national drug law enforcement agencies, Africa' (Addis Ababa, September 15–19, 2014), Item 3 of the provisional agenda, UNODC/HONLAF/24/CRP.1 of July 8, 2014, accessed at www.unodc.org/unodc/en/commissions/CND/Subsidary_Bodies/HONLAF_Index.html on February 27, 2017; UN Office on Drugs and Crime, *Transnational Organized Crime in East Africa: A Threat Assessment* (New York: United Nations Publication, September 2013), p. 25.
29 *Guardian*, 'Drug smuggling in Africa: The smack track' (January 17, 2015).
30 UN Office on Drugs and Crime, *World Drug Report 2010*, pp. 146–8; UN Office on Drugs and Crime, *Transnational Organized Crime in East Africa*, pp. 21–4.
31 P. Gastrow, *Termites at Work: Transnational Organized Crime and State Erosion in Kenya* (New York: International Peace Institute, September 2011), p. 3; UN Office on Drugs and Crime, *Transnational Organized Crime in East Africa*, p. 24.
32 L. Wyler and N. Cook, *Illegal Drug Trade in Africa: Trends and U.S. Policy* (Washington, DC: Congressional Research Service, September 30, 2009), p. 2.
33 UN Office on Drugs and Crime, *World Drug Report 2013*, p. 56.
34 UN Office on Drugs and Crime, *West Africa: 2012 ATS Situation Report* (New York: United Nations Publication, June 2012), pp. 22–4.
35 Wyler and Cook, *Illegal Drug Trade in Africa*, p. 2; UN Office on Drugs and Crime, *World Drug Report 2013*, p. 23.
36 UN Office on Drugs and Crime, *Transnational Organized Crime in East Africa*, p. 20.
37 UN Office on Drugs and Crime, *World Drug Report 2013*, pp. 23–4.
38 Ibid., p. 26.
39 Ki-moon, 'An agenda for prosperity and peace'.
40 D. O'Regan and P. Thompson, 'Advancing stability and reconciliation in Guinea-Bissau: Lessons from Africa's first nacro-state', *ACSS Special Report No. 2* (Washington, DC: Africa Center for Strategic Studies, June 2013), p. 32.
41 UN Office on Drugs and Crime, *World Drug Report 2010*, p. 244.

42 UN Office on Drugs and Crime, *World Drug Report 2013*, p. 10.
43 *Reuters*, 'Drugs trafficking triggers abuse in W. Africa' (May 17, 2011).
44 *IRIN News*, 'Guinea-Bissau: Images of a crack cocaine rehabilitation centre' (March 5, 2008); *IRIN News*, 'Sierra Leone: A ballooning drug problem' (April 7, 2010); *IRIN News*, 'Cape Verde: Deported youth offenders face drugs, unemployment' (November 26, 2008); UN Office on Drugs and Crime, *World Drug Report 2013*, pp. 10–11.
45 UN Office on Drugs and Crime, *West Africa: 2012 ATS Situation Report*, p. 29.
46 UN Office on Drugs and Crime, *World Drug Report 2013*, p. 11.
47 Havocscope, 'AK and other guns on the black market', accessed at www.havocscope.com/black-market-prices/ak-47/ on February 27, 2017.
48 United Nations, 'Addressing the Security Council, Secretary-General says international community must revere global proliferation of small arms', SG/SM/7145, SC/6733 (September 24, 1999).
49 Small Arms Survey, 'Stockpiles', accessed at www.smallarmssurvey.org/weapons-and-markets/stockpiles.html on February 27, 2017; Figures for Africa are extrapolated from Small Arms Survey baseline estimates, Small Arms Survey, *Small Arms Survey 2003* (Oxford: Oxford University Press, 2003), pp. 80–6.
50 Estimate extrapolated from Small Arms Survey baseline data, Small Arms Survey, *Small Arms Survey 2003*; Small Arms Survey, *Small Arms Survey 2010* (Cambridge: Cambridge University Press, 2010), pp. 101–3.
51 G. Curtis and T. Karacan, *The Nexus Among Terrorists, Narcotics Traffickers, Weapons Proliferators, and Organized Crime Networks in Western Europe* (Washington, DC: Library of Congress Federal Research Division, December 2002), pp. 15–17.
52 M. Naim, *Illicit: How Smugglers, Traffickers, and Copycats are Hijacking the Global Economy* (New York: Anchor Books, 2006), pp. 46–50. For an in-depth look at the life and times of Victor Bout, see D. Farah and S. Braun, *Merchant of Death: Money, Guns, Planes, and the Man Who Makes War Possible* (Hoboken, NJ: Wiley & Sons, 2007).
53 Small Arms Survey, *Small Arms Survey 2003*, pp. 118–19.
54 P. Holtom, 'Ukrainian arms supplies to sub-Saharan Africa', *SIPRI Background Paper* (Stockholm: Stockholm International Peace Research Institute, February 2011); Small Arms Survey, *Small Arms Survey 2015* (Cambridge: Cambridge University Press, 2015), p. 170.
55 Small Arms Survey, *Small Arms Survey 2014*, p. 225.
56 *IRIN News*, 'Guinea-Bissau: Lowering the light weapon load' (May 22, 2009).
57 Small Arms Survey, 'Supply and demand: Arms flow and holdings in Sudan', *Sudan Issue Brief*, 15 (December 2009), p. 8.
58 *Mail & Guardian*, 'Ten things about guns in South Africa' (February 22, 2013), accessed at http://mg.co.za/article/2013-02-22-00-ten-things-about-guns-in-south-africa on February 27, 2017.

59 See, for example, the case of Mali in Small Arms Survey, 'Expanding arsenals: Insurgent arms in northern Mali' *Small Arms Survey 2015*, pp. 157–85.
60 Small Arms Survey, *Small Arms Survey 2015*, p. 175.
61 Small Arms Survey, 'Missing missiles: The proliferation of man-portable air defense systems in North Africa', *Issue Brief 2* (June 2015), pp. 4–5.
62 *DailyMail Online*, 'Don't turn Syria into a "Tesco for terrorists" like Libya, generals tell Cameron' (June 17, 2013), accessed at www.dailymail.co.uk/news/article-2342917/Dont-turn-Syria-Tesco-terrorists-like-Libya-generals-tell-Cameron.html on February 27, 2017.
63 Small Arms Survey, *Small Arms Survey 2015*, pp. 174–6.
64 Small Arms Survey, Missing missiles, p. 6.
65 U.N. figures as cited in Human Rights Watch, 'Youth, poverty and blood: The legacy of West Africa's regional warriors', *Human Rights Watch*, 17:5A (March 2005), accessed at www.hrw.org/reports/2005/westafrica0405/7.htm on February 27, 2017.
66 *Sunday Times* (South Africa), 'Declaring war on the arms trade' (September 1, 2009).
67 *allAfrica.com*, 'Mozambique: Christian project collects 700,000 guns'.
68 A. Leao, 'Weapons in Mozambique: Reducing arms availability and demand', *ISS Monograph*, 94 (Pretoria: Institute for Security Studies, January 3, 2004), p. 17; *GM Media Online*, 'Operation—Isuzu continues support for arms clearing operation' (September 27, 2009), accessed at http://media.gm.com/media/za/en/isuzu/news.detail.html/content/Pages/news/za/en/2005/Isuzu/09_27_Operation_Isuzu_support.html on February 27, 2017.
69 Authors' estimate extrapolated from figures presented in Small Arms Survey, *Small Arms Survey 2003*, pp. 80–1; *Small Arms Survey 2007* (Cambridge: Cambridge University Press, 2007), pp. 39–40.
70 Small Arms Survey, *Small Arms Survey 2003*, p. 85.
71 Small Arms Survey, *Small Arms Survey 2006* (Oxford: Oxford University Press, 2006), p. 288.
72 *Ghana News Agency*, 'Tamale blacksmiths to end manufacturing of small arms' (November 3, 2011), accessed at www.ghanaweb.com/GhanaHomePage/NewsArchive/Tamale-Blacksmiths-To-End-Manufacturing-Of-Small-Arms-222866 on February 27, 2017.
73 As cited in G. Lamb, '"Under the gun": An assessment of firearm crime and violence in South Africa' (Report complied for the Office of the President, Pretoria, March 2008), p. 8.
74 Institute for Security Studies, 'South Africa's efforts to collect and destroy firearms', *ISS Today* (April 29, 2013), accessed at www.issafrica.org/iss-today/south-africas-efforts-to-collect-and-destroy-firearms-losing-the-battle-but-winning-the-war on February 27, 2017.
75 Chabal and Daloz, *Africa Works*, pp. 89–91.
76 United Nations Security Council, Small Arms, pp. 2–3.

77 D. Akabwai and P. Ateyo, 'The scramble for cattle, power and guns in Karamojo' (Medford, MA: Feinstein International Center at Tufts University, December 2007), p. 3.
78 *Independent.co.uk*, 'Global arms trade: Africa and the curse of the AK-47' (April 6, 2006), accessed at www.independent.co.uk/news/world/africa/global-arms-trade-and-the-curse-of-the-ak47–472975.html on February 27, 2017.
79 S. Harrendorf, M. Heiskanen and S. Malby (eds), *International Statistics on Crime and Justice* (Helsinki: European Institute for Crime Prevention and Control, 2010).
80 *The Economist*, 'Crime in South Africa: It won't go away' (October 1, 2009), accessed at www.economist.com/node/14564621 on February 27, 2017.
81 In Burundi, a country with per capita government spending of $5, each firearm injury costs the health care system $163. Oxfam International, 'Shooting down the MDGs: How irresponsible arms transfers undermine development goals' (2008), p. 2, accessed at www.oxfam.org/en/research/shooting-down-mdgs on February 27, 2017.
82 Small Arms Survey, *Small Arms Survey 2009* (Cambridge: Cambridge University Press, 2009), p. 212.
83 Hillier, 'Africa's missing billions', p. 3.
84 See, for example, J. Graham, B. Amos, and T. Plumptre, 'Principles for good governance in the 21st Century', *Policy Brief*, 15 (Ottawa: Institute on Governance, August 2003), accessed at http://iog.ca/wp-content/uploads/2012/12/2003_August_policybrief15.pdf on February 27, 2017.
85 Transparency International, 'Corruption perception index 2014: Results', *Corruption Perception Index*, accessed at www.transparency.org/cpi2014/results on February 27, 2017.
86 Chabal and Daloz, *Africa Works*, pp. 101–9.
87 As Stefan Mair points out, insurgent, warlord, terrorist, and criminal organizations are complex and highly fungible structures that tend to have multiple identities that are quite fluid, shifting their primary motivations as they reinvent themselves over time. Mair, 'The new world of privatized violence'.
88 *Agence France-Presse*, 'World Bank highlights conflict as key to poverty' (April 11, 2011).

7

Health and disease

Traditionally viewed as a developmental or a humanitarian challenge, addressing Africa's pressing public health problems has increasingly come to be seen as a critical human security challenge for the twenty-first century. While many have criticized the securitization of health issues, the cross-cutting linkages to other political, social, and economic issues are real, and so too are the implications for security. For ultimately, if enhancing the safety and well-being of individuals and communities lies at the heart of the human security construct, then promoting human survival through better health care and combating disease is surely an integral part of the security equation. And just because many of the linkages between health and security are indirect or even of second and third order consequences, they nonetheless have serious repercussions for the way in which societies seek to enhance their vision of a secure and peaceful future.

The globalization of security, and Africa's steady integration into the international security system, is driving this trend. The modern-day forces of globalization and the interconnectivity of people around the world not only exponentially amplifies both the nature and seriousness of health threats, but creates new opportunities for solutions too. Whereas most health challenges were previously seen as localized problems threatening only the well-being of specific populations, in today's globalized world they can have profound negative implications far removed from the original source of the problem. While many international public health threats, such as disease pandemics, are nothing new (one has only to recall the global 1918–19 influenza pandemic, which claimed as many as 50 million lives worldwide), the ability of new disease epidemics to transcend international borders and continents at a speed and breadth is heretofore unknown in human history. The 2014–15 West African Ebola scare certainly underscored that point.

More so, even basic African health challenges like inadequate health care infrastructure or the provision of clean water can now have far reaching security implications, as they have the capacity to complicate efforts to reduce poverty, resolve conflict, promote political stability, and lessen the impact of humanitarian crises. In the twenty-first century, improving African health and combating disease has moved beyond an issue of simple humanitarianism to one of regional and international security self-interest. In a world where borders mean less, where today's health challenge is truly a transnational reality, an enlightened collective security approach is vital.

As repeatedly noted, the issue of conflict and overall level of violence in Africa is one of the most pressing security problems facing the continent. Hence, its ties to health challenges should come as little shock. From full-scale war to personal violence, conflict acts as a vector for the spread of disease and can overburden fragile health care systems. While the focus of African conflict is typically on war, the direct casualties of war pale in comparison to: the indirect suffering of people displaced, increased malnutrition and hunger, the spread of contagious diseases, and the collapse of health delivery services in those areas affected by widespread violence. Moreover, the extent of interpersonal violence—whether physical, sexual, or psychological—is alarming in Africa, and more so because of the dearth of human and financial health resources to even begin to address the problem effectively in terms of treatment and prevention.

The global health challenge

The goal of improving global health has long been a central component of the development challenge and a longstanding priority of non-governmental organizations (NGOs) and humanitarian groups. Moreover, the potent linkages between poverty, development, and health are well-established, with the World Health Organization (WHO) declaring that "good health is essential to human welfare and to sustained economic and social development."[1] In fact, six of the Millennium Development Goals (MDG) targets for 2015 are directly related to health: improving child nutrition; reducing child mortality; improving maternal health; combating infectious diseases; increasing access to safe drinking water and basic sanitation; and expanding access to affordable medicines in developing countries.[2] Implicit in this international public commitment is the reduction of global poverty through significant improvements to the health of the poorest and most vulnerable populations of the world.

Increasingly, many have also come to recognize the global health challenge as a critical human rights and security issue as well. The inclusion of health care and health delivery services as a means of ensuring human dignity and advancing social justice has come to be seen as part of a fundamental human rights obligation to respect, protect, and ensure that critical human needs are met. This "human right to health" is both a state and international obligation, according to proponents.[3] The 2003 Commission on Human Security also provided a powerful intellectual catalyst in this shift by inextricably linking health and human security. It stated that "Good health is both essential and instrumental to achieving human security ... because the very heart of security is protecting human lives" and thus "health security is at the vial core of human security—and illness, disability and avoidable death are 'critical pervasive threats' to human security."[4]

The good news: decades of progress
The second half of the twentieth century witnessed unprecedented gains in global public health, or what former WHO Director Gro Harlem Brundtland called "a health revolution."[5] These advances have extended life expectancy, successfully combatted communicable diseases, and reduced child and maternal mortality. Thanks to sweeping advancements in the development of powerful new drug treatments and medical techniques, to increased health education and health care delivery systems and preventative medicine, the quality of life for even the poorest of the poor has improved markedly. Significant strides in producing generic medicines have also greatly reduced the cost of medication, making life-saving drugs available to millions more people. A perfect storm of robust global economic growth, tremendous medical innovations and technical progress, and heightened focus on preventative medicine and health education has helped to spur decades of progress in advancing global health care.

The results of this health revolution are impressive:

- Life expectancy at birth rose worldwide from 57 to 72 years between 1960 and 2002 thanks to dramatic increases in China (from 36 to 71 years), Latin America (from 56 to 71 years), and the Middle East and North Africa (from 47 to 69).[6] Sub-Saharan Africa saw an increase of 10 years until the 1990s when the impact of the HIV/AIDS epidemic began to undercut some of these gains, but it has since shown steady improvement with life expectancy reaching 58 in 2013.[7] Significant regional and national differences still persist, but the life expectancy gap between rich and poor is narrowing in nearly all parts of the world, with the notable exception of Africa, which continues to lag noticeably behind.

- Epidemics of infectious diseases like cholera, typhus, yellow fever, and measles, which were once deadly, are now increasingly rare, and smallpox was declared eradicated by the WHO in 1977. The twentieth-century scourge of polio is also on the verge of being completely eliminated.
- Child and maternal mortality is declining, with deaths among children under five years of age falling to less than half of 1990 levels to 5.9 million in 2015—the first year they have dropped below the 6 million mark.[8] Similar reductions in maternal deaths resulting from complications during pregnancy and childbirth have also occurred.[9] Even in sub-Saharan Africa and south Asia, which experienced the highest death rates, noticeable progress has been made in reducing child and maternal mortality rates.

From groundbreaking medical research and the development of new diagnostics tools to the introduction of new, more effective drug treatments and innovative and less invasive surgical techniques, medicine has been on the cutting edge of the transformation of global health. The development of a vast range of powerful antibiotic drugs since the first introduction of mass produced penicillin in 1945 has provided doctors with increasingly effective tools to combat infections and contain the spread of communicable diseases, thereby saving millions of lives each year. Even the gloomiest predictions of an ever escalating death toll as a result of the HIV/AIDS pandemic have been stymied in part by the widespread use of new drug therapies (such as anti-retroviral drug cocktails). Worldwide, the number of AIDS-related deaths per year fell from a peak of 2.4 million in 2005 to 1.1 million in 2015; almost three-quarters of these were in Africa.[10] Increased availability of antiretroviral therapy, better care and support for people living with HIV, and decreasing infection rates starting in the late 1990s are largely responsible for this downward trend. This is especially true in sub-Saharan Africa, where the number of AIDS-related deaths fell by 39 percent between 2005 and 2013, according to UN data.[11]

Likewise, millions more lives have been saved as a result of improved early detection of life-threatening genetic conditions, as well as in cancer diagnosis and early treatment. The first sustained decline in death rates in the United States for breast and prostate cancer—the number two and three killers—which began in the early 1990s, were associated with increased routine screening and testing procedures, according to a major 1998 cancer research study.[12] Likewise, an intensified focus on preventative medicine and an expansion of public health education are saving lives. Better understanding of behavior risk factors for non-communicable diseases—now responsible for two-thirds of worldwide deaths[13]—has fueled global health awareness campaigns that encourage preemptive and early intervention in the form of specialized medications, better nutrition, and life style changes. As a result, mortality rates for several prominent non-communicable diseases, notably lung cancer and heart disease, have fallen significantly in many countries.

While the most significant gains in non-communicable diseases have occurred in advanced industrialized societies, health education to reduce high-risk sexual behavior and promote condom usage in developing countries has been a critical factor in limiting the spread of HIV/AIDS. Improved nutritional knowledge and food preparation safety education for young mothers have undoubtedly been a key factor in combating diarrheal diseases, thereby greatly reducing infant mortality in developing countries as well. More and better trained medical professionals (notably mid-wives and paramedical personnel), who are often supported by advanced communications capability, have also helped extend the reach and quality of primary health care to the most remote regions of the developing world.

As the world entered the first decade of the twenty-first century the future looked bright for improving global health. Deadly infectious diseases that once killed millions were on the verge of complete eradication and even the AIDS pandemic was waning thanks to new drug treatments and the promise of a cure on the horizon. New progress into controlling age-old insect-borne diseases, like malaria and yellow fever, was being fueled by new private–government partnerships. Improved prenatal care, primary health care delivery, and public education were eliminating millions of needless deaths annually. The new bio-green revolution in agriculture was continuing to make headway in ending famine and advancing global nutrition. Unprecedented global economic growth and continuing technological advancements held the potential for further improvement in the lives of millions of the poorest of the poor. The future appeared limitless.

The bad news: a troubling array of old and new problems
Lurking in the background of this optimistic picture of global health, however, were a number of rising challenges that became exacerbated with the global economic collapse of 2008. While it is undeniable that there have been massive improvements in global health over the past five decades, some old problems continue to dog large numbers of people. Moreover, these problems have been further supplemented by a whole new set of health challenges as a result of globalization and the developing world's—particularly African countries—integration into the

international community. As WHO Director-General Margaret Chan warned in 2007, "These threats have become a much larger menace in a world characterized by high mobility, economic interdependence and electronic interconnectedness. Shocks to health reverberate as shocks to economies and business continuity in areas well beyond the affected site. Vulnerability is universal."[14]

Three central themes now appear to define the twenty-first-century global health challenge: 1) controlling and/or eliminating old infectious diseases, while combating the rise of new ones; 2) addressing more effectively the changing global disease profile; and 3) reducing health inequities fed by extreme poverty and underdevelopment.

Controlling old and new infectious diseases

As noted previously, medical advances—especially the widespread use of antibiotics—have sharply curtailed the pandemic threat posed by old-line deadly infectious diseases like smallpox, cholera, yellow fever, and tuberculosis. But the battle is far from won and control remains problematic. Most troubling is the increase in drug-resistant forms of several infectious diseases. In 2006, the WHO noted the emergence of especially virulent drug-resistant strains of tuberculosis—Extensive Drug Resistant TB (XDR-TB)—that is resistant to three or more classes of drugs.[15] In one outbreak of XDR-TB in HIV positive patients, a shocking 98 percent of those infected died in less than one month of contracting the disease.[16] Likewise, further progress in cutting malaria cases is threatened by a developing resistance to artemisinins (a vital component of current treatment therapy), as well as to pyrethroid-based insecticides used in treating mosquito nets and in indoor spraying, according to the 2011 World Malaria Report.[17] A new virulent strain of cholera from Asia was introduced into the Western Hemisphere for the first time by Nepalese UN peacekeepers sent to earthquake stricken Haiti (which was previously free of the disease) in late 2010, killing at least 7,000 and sickening hundreds of thousands more. One senior health professional has since noted that cholera will now be a serious health problem in Haiti for the foreseeable future.[18]

Complacency or failure to maintain existing immunization can also quickly lead to reemergence of diseases under control or even those on the verge of eradication. Polio is a case in point. In August 2003, ongoing polio vaccination programs in northern Nigeria were suspended or vastly reduced over completely unsubstantiated, local fears that the oral polio vaccine was unsafe and could sterilize children.[19] The result was a large outbreak of the disease across the north of the country and even into previously polio-free areas in the south. Thousands of young Nigerian children were left paralyzed. Moreover, by the end of 2006 the WHO linked the Nigerian virus to outbreaks in 19 previously polio-free countries in Africa, Asia, and the Middle East.[20] By 2012 Nigeria accounted for more than half of all worldwide polio cases.[21] Efforts since then, however, have brought the country to the verge of eradication, with the WHO declaring in September 2015 that polio is no longer endemic in that country.

The lack of resources to support successful disease control programs, as well as major social disruptions as a result of conflict, has periodically lead to significant outbreaks in previously disease-free or controlled areas. In 1998, a dengue fever epidemic spread to 56 countries affecting over 1 million people, and the number of cases has continued to grow across Latin America and South East Asia, nearly doubling in each of the past four decades, according to the WHO.[22] The initial handling of the West African Ebola outbreak in early 2014 was severely criticized for its inadequate response because of bureaucratic fumbling and lack of supplies.[23] Outbreaks of the highly deadly Marburg hemorrhagic fever (an infectious disease related to Ebola) in war-torn regions of the eastern DRC in 1998–99 and in Angola in 2004–5 were directly tied to the collapse of health care systems, leading to 85–90 percent fatality rate in those infected.[24] Likewise, a cholera epidemic among hundreds of thousands of refugees fleeing the violence in Rwanda in 1994 left close to 50,000 dead in overcrowded and ill-equipped camps in the eastern DRC.[25]

In tandem with the continuing fight against well-known infectious diseases is the disturbing rise of new and more powerful ones that increasingly adapt as organisms evolve.[26] According to WHO Director-General Chan, there are now nearly 40 diseases that were unknown a generation ago, and new diseases are emerging at the unprecedented rate of one per year.[27] Moreover, many of these are antibiotic-resistant pathogens, new mutant strains that have adapted to changing ecological conditions. MRSA (methicillin-resistant *Staphylococcus aureus*), for example, is responsible for more than 80,000 life-threatening infections each year in the United States alone, with about the same number of Americans dying each year from it as from AIDS, according to US Centers for Disease Control.[28] Newer strains of MRSA are now believed to be five times more lethal and also resistant to even the most powerful antibiotics.[29] Other new mutant diseases like, H5N1 (avian) influenza or the Nipah virus have moved from animal to human hosts; the WHO reports that nearly 75 percent of all new human pathogens have their origins in domestic or wild animals.[30]

Not only is the international community now faced with this twofold disease challenge, but also by the increasingly rapid pace and speed of transmission. Seemingly localized outbreaks can quickly blossom into global pandemics in the blink of an eye. In one five-year reporting period the WHO verified more than 1,100 epidemic events worldwide,[31] indicating that "the world is ill-prepared for a severe pandemic or any similarly global, sustained and threatening public health emergency."[32]

Addressing the changing global disease profile

Up until recently there was a pronounced dichotomy between the disease burden in the wealthier, developed countries of the northern hemisphere and the poorer, developing countries of the southern hemisphere. The most significant health challenge for the former was stemming the rise of non-communicable and often preventable diseases, whereas in the latter combating the spread of deadly infectious diseases was the key challenge. European men, for instance, are 13 times more likely to die from non-communicable diseases, such as cardiovascular disease, cancer, or diabetics, than any other cause.[33] While in developing countries, fighting infectious disease outbreaks and reducing child and maternal mortality rates were the priorities.

Recently, health professionals have begun to notice a significant change in this global disease profile, with the marked rise of non-communicable disease deaths in the developing world. The combined impact of globalization and increased economic growth has now brought the "diseases of affluence" to some of the poorest countries on the planet. Non-communicable diseases are projected by the WHO to grow by 15 percent between 2010 and 2020 with "the greatest increases ... in Africa, South-East Asia and the Eastern Mediterranean, where they will increase by over 20 percent."[34] Already facing the difficult challenge of maintaining progress in the fight against infectious diseases and simple childhood illnesses, developing countries now face the increased burden of rising non-communicable diseases, which threatens to overwhelm their underfunded and ill-equipped health care systems.

Reducing health inequities

The third leg of the global health challenge is driven by the positive correlation between rates of poverty and underdevelopment on the one hand, and poor quality of life and lack of health care on the other. This means it is impossible to advance the global health agenda without directly addressing not only the underlying implications of poverty and underdevelopment, but also the impact of the equity health gap between rich and poor. In light of the disproportional health burden increasingly being carried by the poorest and least capable countries, global health is not likely to improve without redressing serious inequities over resources and their allocation.

Reflecting similar global socio-economic inequities, most of the world's health resources and capability are to be found in the wealthiest and most developed countries of the northern hemisphere. With greater wealth comes better health care and life expectancy; people in the world's richest countries on average live 17 years longer than those in the poorest (life expectancy of 79 years versus 62 years),[35] and health expenditures as a percentage of GDP in the wealthiest countries are more than twice that of the poorest countries (11.6 versus 5.1 percent).[36] Poverty and underdevelopment do not just limit the ability of governments to respond, but are also directly responsible for a number of key health problems in the first place. For instance, diarrheal diseases account for more than 2,000 young children around the world dying each day—more deaths than from AIDS, malaria, and measles combined[37]—usually as a result of inadequate access to clean drinking water and poor sanitation. According to the WHO and UNICEF, 783 million people (mainly from developing countries) lacked access to clean water in 2012.[38]

Scope and nature of the problem

The twenty-first-century challenge of improving global health and quality of life is one facing every country and continent, but nowhere is this problem more daunting than in Africa and Asia. And while Asia—fueled by decades of unprecedented economic growth—is making significant progress at tackling its problems, Africa remains largely mired in a struggle to secure past gains, let alone position itself to address looming new health challenges effectively. For Africa, the continent's increasing integration into the international public health structure offers both opportunities to redress this situation, and new complications for an already vulnerable continent and its people. Despite decades of progress, Africa still faces an enormous health burden, with some 12 million men, women, and children projected to die annually from disease, malnutrition, inadequate care, and non-war related injuries.[39]

The infectious disease threat
Africa is home to a whole host of highly infectious, deadly diseases that kill an estimated 2.2–2.5 million Africans each year—many of them vulnerable women and young children. The leading cause of death among Africans is complications arising from AIDS, and the continent remains at the epicenter of the crisis. Though the HIV/AIDS pandemic peaked in

2005, sub-Saharan Africa is still struggling with its impact and remains the most severely affected region in the world.

As John Iliffe points out in his comprehensive retrospective look at the evolution of AIDS in Africa,[40] a number of socio-economic factors that facilitate the germination and spread of the disease—urbanization, economic growth patterns, increased mobility of populations, poverty, and gender inequalities—continue to hinder the fight against HIV/AIDS well after the epidemiological peak. In 2004, for example, southern Africa contained 2 percent of the world's population, yet it accounted for "nearly 30 percent of the global HIV cases, *with no evidence of overall decline in any national prevalence*, which in several countries exceeded 30 percent of the sexually active population."[41] In 2015, sub-Saharan Africa accounted for two-thirds of all new infections worldwide and 73 percent of the global 1.1 million AIDS-related deaths.[42] The nine countries of southern Africa that experienced the latter stages of the pandemic continue to bear the greatest burden, as all of them have an adult HIV prevalence greater than 10 percent, according to UNAIDS figures.[43] (Swaziland continues to have the highest HIV prevalence rate of any country in the world at over 25 percent and South Africa had more than 6 million people living with HIV in 2015.[44]) Moreover, past successes in reducing new HIV infections through educational outreach and preventative testing have faltered in some countries because of the lack of program sustainability and the complacency of a new post-AIDS generation. Not surprisingly UNAIDS reports that of the nearly 37 million people infected with the disease worldwide by 2014, nearly 26 million (70 percent) were found in sub-Saharan Africa.[45]

While lacking the high public profile of HIV/AIDS until recently, malaria and tuberculosis are responsible for killing as many people in Africa—an estimated 844,680 in 2015.[46] More critical is that these deaths are disproportionally among women and young children. Sixty-five percent of all malaria cases are in sub-Saharan Africa and concentrated in 18 countries, according to the WHO,[47] and the continent continues to account for more than 90 percent of all global malaria deaths; an estimated 394,680 African deaths in 2015, of which 292,000 were children under the age of five.[48] Africa also is home to more than a quarter of all new global tuberculosis cases, which left an estimated 450,000 dead in 2015.[49] Noteworthy for Africa is that 82 percent of HIV-positive individuals were also co-infected with tuberculosis.[50]

Even further below the radar are a whole host of infectious tropical diseases ranging from life-threatening cholera, dengue fever, meningitis, and hemorrhagic fever to severely debilitating ones—known as neglected

Figure 1 The African health challenge.
Source: AVERT, UNAIDS, WHO, UNICEF

- people living with HIV in sub-Saharan Africa, accounting for almost 70% of people living with HIV worldwide¹
- 5.9 million young children died in 2015 mainly from diarrheal disease, pneumonia and respiratory infections, and malaria
- 1 in 12 African children will die before their fifth birthday
- Progress has been made in the fight against HIV. The number of AIDS-related deaths fell by from 2.4 million to 800,000

tropical diseases by the WHO—like *dracunculiasis* (guinea worm), *lymphatic filariasis* (elephantiasis), *schistosomiasis* (snail fever or bilharzia), Human African *trypanosomiasis* (sleeping sickness), and *onchocerciasis* (river blindness). All are highly preventable given advances in medicines and new treatments over the past 30 years, but remain endemic to Africa; 90 percent of the infectious tropical disease burden is in Africa.[51] Some tropical disease specialists believe, however, that several of these diseases could be on the verge of eradication in the next 5 to 10 years with a modest effort.

Although daunting, real progress is being made. The past decade has witnessed a significant, though uneven, decline in deaths from AIDS, malaria, and tuberculosis. Nonetheless, much of this progress could be fleeting without the sustained (or even enhanced) commitment of national, regional, and international resources.

UNAIDS reports that new HIV infections in sub-Saharan Africa dropped overall by 33 percent between 2005 and 2013 and the number of new infections "is falling in every country in the region except Angola and Uganda."[52] South Africa recorded the largest decline in absolute numbers with 98,000 fewer cases.[53] More important, because of increased access to, and the use of, antiretroviral therapies an estimated

4.8 million fewer people in sub-Saharan Africa have died from AIDS-related causes since 1995. From its peak of 2 million in 2005, when Africans were dying at the rate of four each minute,[54] the number of AIDS-related deaths in Africa has dropped below 1 million.

Likewise, great strides have been made in reducing malaria and tuberculosis deaths. Thanks in large part to steadily rising international funding—more than $2.5 billion annually for malaria control efforts alone—there have been some 30 million fewer cases of malaria in Africa since 2005 and the mortality rate for African children under five years of age has fallen by more than half since 2000.[55] While the number of tuberculosis cases is rising, largely due to increasing populations, more people are now being successfully treated. Comprehensive screening for HIV-related tuberculosis also appears to hold the promise of further reducing the tuberculosis death rate by some 5 to 6 percent, according to the WHO.[56]

The rising non-communicable disease threat
The often myopic public focus on combating infectious disease in Africa has overshadowed the new health threat posed by rising rates of non-communicable diseases, such as cardiovascular and chronic respiratory disease, cancer, and diabetes. In 2004, non-communicable diseases accounted for less than a quarter of the continent's disease burden (in contrast to more than 40 percent for infectious and parasitic diseases).[57] But by 2008, Africa had achieved the highest non-communicable disease mortality rates for both men and women across all regions, according to the WHO.[58] Clearly a fundamental change is taking place. This was confirmed in 2011 when a WHO study noted that "non-communicable diseases are [now] the leading cause of death worldwide, killing ever more people each year" and that "nearly 80 percent of these deaths [now] occur in low and middle-income countries."[59]

The increase in four common behavioral risk factors associated with non-communicable diseases—tobacco use; harmful use of alcohol; unhealthy diet; and insufficient physical activity that can lead to obesity, high blood pressure, and raised blood sugar and cholesterol—are all contributing to the growing problem in Africa, which is now responsible for some 3.5 million deaths annually.[60] With a projected growth rate of 20 percent over this decade, the WHO predicts that these diseases will cause nearly 4 million deaths annually in Africa by 2020 and are on track to replace communicable, maternal, prenatal, and nutritional diseases as the leading cause of death for Africans by 2030.[61]

Poverty-fueled health challenges

Abject poverty is more than just a socio-economic challenge for Africa. It is the critical link in the self-perpetuating cycle of poverty, poor health, and underdevelopment that results in further impoverishment and hopelessness. While poverty is certainly a catalyst in facilitating the spread of both infectious and non-communicable diseases, it also has a more direct bearing in Africa on neonatal and maternal mortality rates, children's health, malnutrition, and rising drug resistance.

The negative health consequences of poverty in Africa are felt disproportionally among women and young children. According to UNICEF, Africa has the highest rate of child mortality in the world, with 1 in 12 children dying before their fifth birthday. This is 12 times higher than the 1 in 147 average in industrialized countries.[62] The DRC and Nigeria accounted for at least one-third of all under-five African deaths (1.05 million) in 2015.[63] Two leading causes of death among African children are pneumonia/respiratory infections and dehydration from diarrheal diseases, which is often brought on by poor living conditions and contaminated water. Hundreds of thousands, however, could be saved annually by a simple course of antibiotics, basic childhood vaccinations, access to safe drinking water, and improved living conditions. Likewise, maternal mortality is still the highest in the world in about 25 African countries, with the sub-Saharan region accounting for 62 percent of global maternal deaths in 2013.[64]

These needless deaths can clearly be linked to the impoverished socio-economic conditions and the accompanying health inequities that make people more susceptible to disease and illness. Lower economic status, living in marginal areas, and having little education can be major determining factors for one's health. One UNICEF study, for instance, showed that children in rural areas were about 1.7 times as likely to die as those in urban areas before the age of five, and children from the poorest 20 percent of households were nearly twice as likely to die before their fifth birthday as those in the richest 20 percent.[65]

The impact of poverty on health is readily apparent in the area of meeting basic nutritional needs. Some believe that hunger and malnutrition "are in fact the number one risk to health worldwide—greater than AIDS, malaria and tuberculosis."[66] With some 415 million Africans scraping by on less than $1.25 per day and often struggling just to find adequate food to survive, it is no wonder that Africa, along with South Asia (which together account for 80 percent of the "extremely poor"), also has some of the highest rates of chronic hunger, malnutrition, and under nutrition in the world.[67] Although exact numbers are difficult to determine, an estimated 225–270 million people in Africa suffer from some form of malnourishment.⁶⁸ One international NGO working on the problem estimates that: 25 percent of Africans currently suffer from malnutrition: 25 percent of children are suffering from chronic hunger; and 40 percent of all African children have stunted growth as a result of long-term under nutrition.⁶⁹

The health consequences manifest themselves, especially among young children, not only in higher mortality rates, but also in terms of acute protein energy malnutrition. This can result in kwashiorkor or chronic anemia from iron deficiencies, brain damage or hindered cognitive development from iodine deficiencies, and impaired sight or even blindness from a lack of sufficient Vitamin A.⁷⁰ It is also believed that over half of all pregnant women in Africa are anemic, raising increased health risk during pregnancy and child birth.

All of these conditions are easily preventable at minimal cost. As one NGO official noted, "We know solutions exist to reduce malnutrition through a number of simple, targeted and cost-effective interventions. Fortified staples, the promotion of breastfeeding, [and] complementary foods after 6 months of age are some of those interventions available to help break the cycle of malnutrition."⁷¹ Although the United Nations periodically reports on the progress made toward addressing malnutrition and the underlying problem of poverty in Africa,⁷² more needs to be done in terms of resources, prioritization, and economic development integration.

Absolutely critical to alleviating poverty and reducing disease and illness in the future is the necessity of providing safe drinking water and proper sanitation to hundreds of millions of Africans who currently lack these essential services. Despite steady progress since 1990, sub-Saharan Africa still accounts for about half of the global population (330–358 million people) that lacks access to improved sources of drinking water, and 70 percent (or nearly 600 million) that lacks access to proper sanitation facilities.⁷³ Contaminated water is directly responsible for causing life-threatening diseases, such as acute diarrhea, dysentery, or cholera, which kill hundreds of thousands annually in Africa. It also facilitates the spread of water-borne illnesses that sicken or incapacitate many more. In the DRC, Ethiopia, Kenya, Nigeria, and Tanzania alone, 181 million people do not have access to clean water.⁷⁴ Periodic outbreaks of deadly cholera epidemics are not uncommon and can usually be traced to severe overcrowding (often in makeshift refugee camps) or failing sanitation infrastructure as a result of prolonged economic crises, as was the case in Zimbabwe in 2008–9. This was the worst African cholera epidemic in 15 years, which swept across Zimbabwe and into neighboring Botswana and South Africa before it was finally controlled, leaving 4,287 dead and nearly 100,000 sickened in its wake.⁷⁵

One commonly overlooked challenge facing the continent's poor is not just the costs of basic medicines themselves, but the degree by which the poor seek to safeguard their short-term financial situation at the expense of their long-term medical health. While the financial burden of most widely used medicines and nutritional supplements in Africa would not appear to be especially cost prohibitive—iodized salt, for instance, costs only 5 cents per person annually—for those in extreme poverty it involves difficult trade-offs. Of greater concern, however, is what the WHO terms the "underuse of medicines" (especially of antibiotics) among the poor.[76] Patients will often limit their purchases of medicines to addressing their most pressing and immediate needs and will then stop treatment as soon as they feel better, rather than complete the full course of treatment. Although this behavior saves the patient and their family money it can unintentionally contribute to growing drug resistance that poses the greatest long-term challenge to their health. Even with government-provided free medicines, it is not at all uncommon for people to sell off their "surplus meds" for an immediate economic benefit at the expense of their future medical well-being.

Implications for security

Fear of death is the ultimate threat to one's personal security. When this fear spreads across entire communities or national populations it rises to the level of having significant security implications because it threatens the well-being of the collective society itself. As such, the health challenge of combating deadly and debilitating diseases, chronic illness, the health-related problems of poverty, and lack of adequate delivery services fosters a climate of fear and insecurity that needs to be seen as an important human security priority in Africa. Not only is improving health in Africa central to human security in and of itself, but it also has a significant role to play in addressing other political, social, and economic problems.

Moreover, the security threat presented by the African health challenge extends well beyond the continent and its people. Just as the power of globalization is fueling a global economic and social transformation, so too is it driving the integration and internationalization of the continent's public health challenges. No longer can the outside world afford to view African health threats in blissful detachment, hoping that these threats and their future implications will remain confined and isolated from the rest of the world. The spread of HIV/AIDS, polio outbreaks, or the West African Ebola crisis all contain the clear message that this is not possible in today's world. New diseases can, and do, spread quickly. Not to be overlooked are the wider consequences of health-related poverty on not only the security and stability of African states themselves, but on the greater regional and even international community. Thus, African health issues have certainly moved beyond one of simple humanitarianism to a key element of the new global security agenda.

Unlike a number of the other security issues discussed elsewhere in this book, the health challenge for twenty-first-century Africa is one more associated with second and third order, longer-term implications (with the notable exception of the immediate and deadly consequences of uncontrolled disease epidemics) and their impact and interconnectivity across a broad spectrum of other human security challenges.

The most far reaching of these security implications are from the impact of communicable infectious diseases and they absorb the lion's share of government health spending. Even with the noticeable increase in African public health expenditures and enormous international developmental assistance for health—$11.8 billion or 35.7 percent of the global amount in 2012[77]—to address the continent's health challenge, 2.2–2.5 million Africans still die each year. While often labeled a security threat simply because of the global pandemic potential of communicable diseases, the terrible human toll these diseases exact everyday across Africa and the fear they instill in individuals and communities is all too real.

Beyond this immediate high human cost, the longer-term impact of these diseases on economic development, society, and state institutions is profound, and contributes directly to reinforcing the cycles of poverty, societal fragmentation, and government weaknesses. While malaria has a disproportional impact on child mortality, HIV/AIDS and tuberculosis tend to strike down large numbers of economically active adults, which negatively impacts economic growth. According to various cost projection analyses, HIV/AID, tuberculosis, and malaria probably cost Africa up to $25 billion per year in lost GDP; in the worst affected countries the loss may be as much as 10 percent of GDP.[78] Fighting these diseases also creates a serious strain on fragile national budgets—as much as 40 percent of public health expenditures and 30–50 percent of in-patient admissions in endemic African malaria areas alone, according to one estimate.[79]

The social costs may be even more telling: AIDS orphans, lingering social stigma (particularly from HIV infection), collapse of family structure, and loss of the traditional safety nets for the elderly when their adult children die. Families or even entire communities living on the margins can quickly find themselves pushed into a state of poverty that they have little chance of escaping. Moreover, the inability of leaders and governments to provide significant relief in the face of this seemingly unending disease onslaught can undermine the creditability and legitimacy of already fragile political institutions. While unlikely to result in any popular rebellion, health challenges such as these can help fertilize the seeds of disaffection and alienation rooted in other problems.

For most of the past few decades, much has been made of the impact of the HIV/AIDS pandemic on African militaries and how this validates the critical linkages between health and security issues. "Armed forces are a critical part of any state's security, but are often worst affected by this disease [HIV/AIDS] as it impacts directly on their operational effectiveness" and through "high infection rates, it renders them less capable" by undercutting their "ability to provide humanitarian and peace support to those in need."[80] African militaries have also historically been key political actors within African political systems, as both a source of stability and one of instability. The impact of HIV/AIDS on them has certainly been substantial over the years: In the mid-2000s African militaries were reporting infection rates of 20–40 percent,[81] with the problem even more pronounced among southern African militaries.

Nonetheless, dire predictions of the demise of African militaries' powerful role, let alone their implosion as a result of the pandemic, were in retrospect overblown and based on worst-case scenarios. The most recent health trends indicate that large-scale international assistance, aggressive government actions, extensive indoctrination and preventative education, as well as widespread treatment programs have gone a long way in arresting the HIV/AIDS problems within the most badly affected militaries. Although much more needs to be done, African militaries now appear to be mimicking downward trends in HIV transmission and mortality that their general populations are undergoing.

The more problematic African security challenge arises from the very broad spectrum of multiple and diverse linkages between health issues and other societal challenges. Topping this list of linkages are conflict and the overall problem of societal violence, conflict-induced humanitarian crises, and poverty-related problems that can fuel political instability. These types of linkages often serve to complicate efforts to improve public health, and underscore the essential need not to view health issues in a vacuum, but have them form part of a more holistic approach to security.

Violent conflict acts as a vector for the spread of diseases, increases the likelihood of malnutrition and hunger, disrupts the delivery of essential health services, and can trigger severe humanitarian crises. Moreover, the death toll from the indirect health-related causes of violence frequently exceeds those killed in the actual violence. For example, people displaced by conflict and living in marginal areas or refugee camps are especially vulnerable to health challenges because of overcrowding, the lack of sanitation, prevalence of food and water-borne illness, and food shortages. The resulting destabilizing situation can present a serious security problem that may last for many years. The lingering effects of the 1994 Rwanda genocide are still being felt in the chaos of the eastern DRC today, and the ongoing chaos in Somalia continues to generate a massive humanitarian and security challenge for neighboring Kenya—home to the world's largest refugee camp—and Ethiopia.

The interdependent links between poverty, ill-health, and underdevelopment also have significant implications for political instability and government legitimacy. An inability to break free of the poverty trap means that the poorest Africans are likely to be consigned to a life of impoverishment, chronic illness, and shorter life expectancy with little hope of a better future. This resulting marginalization can create a sizeable pool of politically alienated and disaffected populations that are extremely vulnerable to exploitation and incitement to violence. When combined with other existing historical, social, or communal grievances and vocal leadership, the outcome can produce an explosive mix of everything from spontaneous riots to outright rebellion. While peasant rebellions against government authority are not typically common in Africa, the urban and neglected poor often form a core segment of political opposition movements; the past success of the Movement for Democratic Change in Zimbabwe was based in part on its ability to tap into disenfranchised and disillusioned urban dwellers, for example.

Conclusion

For much of the past century and into the new one, crisis care and humanitarian assistance have been at the center of the African health security challenge. Health security, however, is now more than the absence of disease, a reduction of chronic illness, or increased longevity. It is about developing a comprehensive approach to improving the quality of life, especially for the poorest of Africans, by addressing the related issues that undermine efforts to accomplish this goal. The nature of the health challenge in Africa is changing. It now has a growing importance in the security equation, not just for Africa but for the international community as well. Hence, old approaches and tools must be adapted to more effectively meet the health needs of the continent in a globalized world.

Addressing the continent's immediate threats posed by poverty, infectious disease, chronic illness, and inadequate care delivery have been defining features of the continent's health challenges for more than half a century. This is where the bulk of human and financial resources have historically been committed because these problems are the chief causes of death and incapacitation among Africans. There is good news however. Substantial, steady progress has been made in reducing the number of annual deaths through the fight against communicable diseases like HIV/AIDS and malaria; child and maternal mortality rates have declined; and more people have access to some form of rudimentary health care than ever before. African spending on health and international health assistance has reached record levels. Immunization and supplemental nutritional programs are showing positive results and many longstanding tropical diseases are now on the verge of eradication.

Nonetheless, much of this progress has come at the expense of addressing other lower profile poverty-related problems like clean water and improved sanitation given the narrow focus on specific diseases. This long accepted crisis management strategy all too often diverts attention—and more importantly scarce resources—away from a more comprehensive approach to African health care as set out in the MDG. Moreover, numerous studies have shown that the long-term economic returns to addressing broader MDG health concerns often outweigh their costs;[82] universal access to water and sanitation, for instance, would bring a projected economic benefit of $22 billion a year to Africa.[83] Likewise, the ability and willingness of the international community to respond rapidly in the form of humanitarian health assistance has undoubtedly saved hundreds of thousands of African lives over the years. While this is certainly a good thing, humanitarian health assistance is, by its very nature, reactive. It is also expensive and provides only a short-term fix. Most of all it continues to categorize health assistance as an international moral obligation rather than a global security requirement that requires a long-term perspective and preemptive response.

Further complicating the health security challenge in the future is the increase in non-communicable diseases, which will require resources to be reallocated and more preventive strategies to be implemented. Health education and behavior modification can go a long way in limiting the spread of many of these problems before they become serious health issues. This, however, will require major rethinking and an overhaul of existing approaches to improving African health. If little is done and current forecasts are correct, non-communicable diseases such as cardiovascular disease and cancer will surpass AIDS, malaria, tuberculosis, and diarrheal disease as the primary killers of Africans by 2030.[84] Moreover, this "health double whammy" will present African governments, NGOs, and foreign donors with the thorny challenge of addressing both crisis care and non-communicable disease with resources and infrastructure that are already stretched to the limit.

There have never been enough national, regional, or international resources available to address the daunting health challenges facing the continent. Unfortunately, this situation is unlikely to change. The use of existing resources to combat the most threatening infectious diseases or to address specific issue areas, such as child malnutrition for instance, has clearly shown positive results, but the cost has been very high too. A quarter of all international health assistance is now directed at fighting HIV/AIDS. The United States has provided over $39 billion through the President's Emergency Program for AIDS Relief (PEPFAR) since 2003,[85] but less than 2 percent has been directed at non-communicable diseases over the same period.[86] (A more detailed discussion of PEPFAR follows in Chapter 10: The international response.)

Future progress in many of these areas will remain dependent not only on continued funding, but on an expansion of services necessary to secure the gains that have already been realized. This of course will require more funding that is unlikely to come from within Africa. And with many donors already stretched to the limit with competing national and international priorities, prospects for even maintaining existing levels of health assistance funding in the years ahead are fleeting. Talk of widespread cutbacks in foreign aid, including health assistance, by the new Trump administration indicates that many of the most successful US health initiatives may already be on the chopping block.[87] But as difficult as it may be for foreign governments in the face of their own pressing economic situations, a failure to adequately fund ongoing programs risks serious setbacks to a decade of progress.

Globalization is helping to redefine the nature of health challenges in Africa. Just as the importance of health as a security issue has grown in Africa, so too has it become an increasing part of the global security agenda as well. Accordingly, issues of health have moved beyond simple humanitarianism or moral obligation to ones that have significant human security implications—on political stability, development, and social relationships—at the regional and global level that cannot be ignored. It would be a serious mistake, however, to view the globalization of health as a one-way street whereby Africa is merely seen as an exporter of threats to the rest of the world rather than part of international solutions to common problems. While the gap between rich and poor regions is unlikely to narrow anytime in the near future, the common challenges of improving the health and quality of life of the most vulnerable and poorest of societies transcends regions. Africa and its people never could afford to live in isolation, but today neither can the rest of the world.

Notes

1 World Health Organization, *World Health Report 2010* (Geneva: World Health Organization, 2010), p. 13.
2 World Health Organization, 'Millennium Development Goals: Progress towards the health-related Millennium Development Goals' *Fact Sheet*, 290 (May 2011), accessed at www.who.int/mediacentre/factsheets/fs290/en/index.html on February 28, 2017.
3 L. Gostin, *et al.*, 'The joint action and learning initiative on national and global responsibilities for health', *World Health Report (2010) Background Paper*, 53 (Geneva: World Health Organization, 2010), p. i.
4 Commission on Human Security, *Human Security Now*, p. 96.
5 G. Brundtland, 'The future of the world's health', in C. Everett Koop, Clarence Pearson, and M. Roy Schwarz (eds), *Critical Issues in Global Health* (San Francisco, CA: Jossey-Bass, 2002), p. 3.
6 D. Jamison, *et al.*, *Priorities in Health* (Washington, DC: The World Bank, 2006), p. 6.
7 World Health Organization, *World Health Statistics 2015* (Geneva: World Health Organization, 2015), Table 1: Life expectancy and mortality, p. 52.
8 World Health Organization Media Centre, 'Child mortality rates plunge by more than half since 1990 but global MDG target missed by wide margin' (September 9, 2015), accessed at www.who.int/mediacentre/news/releases/2015/child-mortality-report/en/# on February 28, 2017; World Health Organization Media Centre, 'Three-year study identifies key interventions to reduce maternal, newborn and child deaths' (December 15, 2011), accessed at www.who.int/mediacentre/news/releases/2011/reduce_maternal_deaths_20111215/en/ on February 28, 2017.
9 World Health Organization Media Center, Child mortality rates plunge; World Health Organization Media Center, Three-year study identifies key interventions.
10 UNAIDS, 'Global AIDS update' (January 2016), accessed at www.unaids.org/sites/default/files/media_asset/global-AIDS-update-2016_en.pdf on February 28, 2017.
11 UNAIDS, 'Fact Sheet 2014: Global statistics', accessed at www.unaids.org/sites/default/files/en/media/unaids/contentassets/documents/factsheet/2014/20140716_FactSheet_en.pdf on February 28, 2017.
12 Centers for Disease Control and Prevention, 'New report on declining cancer incidence and death rates; report shows progress in controlling cancer' (March 12, 1998), accessed at www.cdc.gov/nchs/pressroom/98news/cancer.htm on February 28, 2017.
13 The World Health Organization estimates that 38 million (68 percent) of all deaths in 2012 were the result of non-communicable diseases. World

Health and disease   165

Health Organization, 'Noncommunicable diseases (NCD)', *Global Health Observatory data*, accessed at www.who.int/gho/ncd/en/index.html on February 28, 2017.
14 World Health Organization, *World Health Report 2007* (Geneva: World Health Organization, 2007), p. vi.
15 World Health Organization Media Centre, 'Emergence of XDR-TB' (September 5, 2006).
16 Ibid.
17 World Health Organization, *World Malaria Report 2011* (Geneva: World Health Organization, 2011), p. viii.
18 *ABC News*, 'Scientists: UN soldiers brought deadly superbug to Americas' (January 12, 2012), accessed at http://news.yahoo.com/scientists-un-soldiers-brought-deadly-superbug-americas-194141189--abc-news.html on February 28, 2017.
19 World Health Organization, *World Health Report 2007*, p. 20.
20 Ibid.
21 World Health Organization Media Centre, 'WHO remove Nigeria from polio-endemic list' (September 25, 2015), accessed at www.who.int/mediacentre/news/releases/2015/nigeria-polio/en/# on February 28, 2017.
22 World Health Organization, *World Health Report 2007*, p. 12.
23 *Associated Press*, 'Bungling by UN agency hurt Ebola response' (September 21, 2015).
24 World Health Organization, *World Health Report 2007*, p. 21.
25 Ibid.
26 W. Foege, 'Infectious diseases', in Koop, Pearson, and Schwarz (eds) *Critical Issues in Global Health*, p. 115.
27 World Health Organization, *World Health Report 2007*, p. vi.
28 *CNN*, 'MERSA fast facts' (updated June 11, 2015), accessed at www.cnn.com/2013/06/28/us/mrsa-fast-facts/ on February 28, 2017; Centers for Disease Control and Prevention, 'HIV statistics', accessed at www.cdc.gov/hiv/statistics/basics/ataglance.html on February 28, 2017.
29 *ScienceDaily*, 'MRSA strain linked to high death rates' (October 31, 2009), accessed at www.sciencedaily.com/releases/2009/10/0091031222347.htm on February 28, 2017.
30 M. Chan, 'Keynote address at the global health security initiative ministerial meeting in Paris, France' (December 9, 2011), accessed at www.who.int/dg/speeches/2011/health_security_20111209/en/index.html on February 28, 2017.
31 World Health Organization, *World Health Report 2007*, p. 6.
32 Chan, Keynote address.
33 World Health Organization, 'Deaths from NCDs', *Global Health Observatory data*, accessed at www.who.int/gho/ncd/mortality_morbidity/ncd_total_text/en/ on February 28, 2017.
34 World Health Organization, 'Global status report on noncommunicable disease 2010' (Geneva: World Health Organization, 2011), p. 9.

35 World Health Organization, *World Health Statistics 2015*, Table 1: Life expectancy and mortality, p. 52.
36 Ibid., Table 7: Health expenditure, p. 134.
37 Centers for Disease Control and Prevention, 'Global diarrhea burden', accessed at www.cdc.gov/healthywater/global/diarrhea-burden.html on February 28, 2017.
38 World Health Organization-UNICEF press release, 'Millennium development goal drinking water target met' (March 6, 2012), accessed at www.who.int/mediacentre/news/releases/2012/drinking_water_20120306/en/index.html on February 28, 2017.
39 Authors' projection based on UN data: *World Mortality 2009*; UN Department of Economic and Social Affairs, Population Division, *World Population Prospects: The 2010 Revision* (New York: United Nations, 2010).
40 J. Iliffe, *The African AIDS Epidemic: A History* (Oxford: James Currey Ltd., 2006).
41 Ibid., p. 33, emphasis added.
42 UNAIDS, 'Global AIDS update' (January 2016), accessed at www.unaids.org/sites/default/files/media_asset/global-AIDS-update-2016_en.pdf on February 28, 2017.
43 Avert, 'HIV and AIDS in sub-Saharan Africa', accessed at www.avert.org/hiv-aids-sub-saharan-africa.htm on February 28, 2017.
44 Ibid.; *BBC News*, 'South Africa to spend $2.2 bn on HIV/AIDS drugs' (November 18, 2014).
45 J. Cohen, 'New report card on global HIV/AIDS epidemic', *Science Magazine* (July 14, 2015), accessed at http://news.sciencemag.org/funding/2015/07/new-report-card-global-hivaids-epidemic on February 28, 2017.
46 The breakdown is 394,680 deaths from malaria and 450,000 deaths from tuberculosis. World Health Organization, 'Factsheet on the World Malaria Report 2016' (December 2016), accessed at www.who.int/malaria/media/world_malaria_report_2016/en/ on February 28, 2017; *TB Facts.org*, 'TB statistics/global, regional, age & high burden', accessed at www.tbfacts.org/tb-statistics/ on February 28, 2017.
47 World Health Organization, *World Malaria Report 2014* (Geneva: World Health Organization, 2014), pp. 34, 36.
48 World Health Organization, 'Factsheet on the World Malaria Report 2016'.
49 *TB Facts.org*, 'TB statistics/global, regional, age & high burden'.
50 World Health Organization, *Global Tuberculosis Control 2011* (Geneva: World Health Organization, 2011), p. 10.
51 Imperial College London, 'Schistosomiasis control initiative', accessed at www3.imperial.ac.uk/schisto/whatwedo/whatarentds on February 28, 2017.
52 UNAIDS, 'The Gap Report' (September 2014), p. 30, accessed at www.unaids.org/sites/default/files/media_asset/UNAIDS_Gap_report_en.pdf on February 28, 2017.
53 Ibid.

54 Iliffe, *The African AIDS Epidemic*, p. 113.
55 World Health Organization, *World Malaria Report 2014*, pp. xiii, 36, and Table 8.3.
56 World Health Organization, Millennium Development Goals progress: 'World AIDS day report 2011' (Geneva: UNAIDS, 2011) p. 23.
57 World Health Organization, 'Health situation analysis in the Africa region: Atlas of health statistics, 2011' (Brazzaville, Republic of Congo: Regional Office for Africa, 2011), Figure 25: Distribution of burden of disease as percentage of total DALYs by group in the African Region, 2004, p. 11.
58 World Health Organization, 'Global status report on noncommunicable disease 2010', p. 9.
59 World Health Organization Media Centre, 'New WHO study details low-cost solutions to help curb the tide on noncommunicable diseases' (September 18, 2011), accessed at www.who.int/mediacentre/news/releases/2011/NCDs_solutions_20110918/en/ on February 28, 2017.
60 Authors' projection based on UN data: *World Mortality 2009*.
61 World Health Organization, 'Global status report on noncommunicable disease 2010', p. 9.
62 United Nations Inter-agency Group for Child Mortality Estimation, *Levels & Trends in Child Mortality, Report 2015* (New York: UN Children's Fund, 2015), p. 6.
63 Ibid., Statistical Table: Country, regional and global estimates of under-five, infant and neonatal mortality, pp. 18–27.
64 World Health Organization, 'Executive summary', *Trends in Maternal Mortality: 1990 to 2013* (Geneva: World Health Organization, 2014), p. 2.
65 United Nations Inter-agency Group for Child Mortality Estimation, *Levels & Trends in Child Mortality, Report 2011* (New York: UN Children's Fund, 2011), pp. 10–11.
66 World Food Programme, 'Hunger', accessed at www.wfp.org/hunger on February 28, 2017.
67 World Bank, 'Poverty' accessed at www.worldbank.org/en/topic/poverty/overview on February 28, 2017.
68 WorldHunger.org, '2015 world hunger and poverty facts and statistics', accessed at www.worldhunger.org/articles/Learn/world%20hunger%20facts%202002.htm on February 28, 2017; *UN News Center*, 'UN official shines spotlight on hunger and malnutrition in Africa' (May 6, 2010), accessed at www.un.org/apps/news/story.asp?NewsID=34616&Cr=fao&Cr1=africa# on February 28, 2017.
69 *AfricaNews*, 'Malnutrition and Africa: Is there a way out?' (January 26, 2011).
70 World Health Organization, 'Nutrition', accessed at www.who.int/nutrition/topics/en/ on February 28, 2017.
71 *AfricaNews*, Malnutrition and Africa.
72 See, for example, World Health Organization, 'Millennium Development Goals fact sheet no. 290' (updated May 2015), accessed at www.who.int/mediacentre/factsheets/fs290/en/ on 28 February 2017; United Nations

Economic Commission for Africa, *MDG Report 2015: Assessing Progress Toward the Millennium Development Goals* (Addis Ababa: Economic Commission for Africa, 2015).
73 UN Economic Commission for Africa *MDG Report 2015*, pp. 58–9; ONE, 'Water & sanitation', accessed at www.one.org/international/issues/water-and-sanitation on February 28, 2017.
74 UNICEF, 'Water, sanitation and hygiene (WASH)', accessed at www.unicef.org/media/media_45481.html on February 28, 2017.
75 Z. Mukandavire, *et al.*, 'Estimating the reproductive numbers in the 2008–2009 cholera outbreaks in Zimbabwe', *Proceedings of the National Academy of Sciences*, 108:21 (May 24, 2011), 8767–72.
76 M. Chan, 'Antimicrobial resistance: No action today, no cure tomorrow' (Remarks of Dr Margaret Chan at World Health Day 2011, Geneva, Switzerland, April 6, 2011), accessed at www.who.int/dg/speeches/2011/WHD_20110407/en/ on February 28, 2017.
77 Institute for Health Metrics and Evaluation, *Financing Global Health 2014: Shifts in Funding as the MDG Era Closes* (Seattle: Institute for Health Metrics and Evaluation, 2015), p. 11.
78 UNICEF, 'MD goal: Combat HIV/AIDS, malaria and other diseases', accessed at www.unicef.org/mdg/disease.html on February 28, 2017; C. Akukwe, *Don't Let Them Die* (London: Adonis & Abbey Publishers, 2006), p. 88; F. Grimard and G. Harling, 'Impact of tuberculosis on economic growth' (Montreal: McGill University, no date), p. 34.
79 Roll Back Malaria, 'Economic costs of malaria', accessed at www.rollbackmalaria.org/files/files/toolbox/RBM%20Economic%20Costs%20of%20Malaria.pdf on February 28, 2017.
80 L. Heinecken, 'Living in terror: The looming security threat to Southern Africa', *African Security Review*, 10:4 (2001), p. 7.
81 R. Molatole and S. Thaga, 'Interventions against HIV/AIDS in the Botswana Defence Force', in M. Rupiya (ed.), *The Enemy Within: Southern African Militaries' Quarter-Century Battle with HIV/AIDS* (Pretoria: Institute for Security Studies, 2006), p. 40.
82 See, for example, UN Commission for Africa, *MDG Report 2015*.
83 *ONE*, Water & sanitation.
84 World Health Organization, 'Global status report on noncommunicable disease 2010', p. 9.
85 PEPFAR, 'PEPFAR funding: Investments that save lives and promote security' (June 2011), accessed at www.pepfar.gov/press/80064.htm on February 23, 2017.
86 Institute for Health Metrics and Evaluation, *Financing Global Health 2014: Shifts in Funding as the MDG Era Closes* (Seattle: Institute for Health Metrics and Evaluation, 2015), p. 73.
87 *CNN*, 'Alarm bells ring for charities as Trump pledges to slash foreign aid budget' (March 1, 2017).

8

Resource conflict and the environment

Resource conflict and environmental degradation are in reality two-sides of the same security challenge coin. Both address the issue of natural resource abundance and scarcity and how societies deal with these problems and their implications, but from vastly different perspectives. While the first addresses access and control of existing natural resources, the second addresses the environmental impact of the misuse of or declining resources. Regardless of the perspective, both present a serious threat to African peace and stability and make these questions increasingly relevant in today's world.

Conflict arising over the control or access to valued natural resources has been central to the story of mankind, the rise and fall of empires, and the evolution of the modern global economy. Whether it is a struggle over basic necessities (like water and land), precious metals and stones, or raw materials, the historical exploitation of natural resources has often been accompanied by great violence and human suffering.

Nowhere is this truer than in Africa. Powerful pre-colonial African states and empires often owed their preeminence to their ability to control the source and/or the trade in gold, ivory, slaves, and salt. Bloody wars of conquest were fought over natural resource control. The colonial period witnessed the expansion of this competition as European powers vied among themselves to gain control over African gold, diamonds, and ivory. And many of the continent's most violent modern-day conflicts have been fueled directly or indirectly by the desire to reap the economic benefits of national resource exploitation. From Angolan and Nigerian oil to the conflict diamonds of Sierra Leone and the mineral wealth of the DRC, natural resources have been integral elements of these political struggles.

UN environmental experts believe that 40 percent of all intrastate conflicts around the world in the last 60 years have links to natural resources, and "that this link doubles the risk of a conflict relapse in the first five years."[1] Furthermore, over the past two decades some 18 violent conflicts have been fueled by the exploitation of natural resources.[2] But what exactly is the nature of this relationship? Does the mere presence or absence of valued natural resources actually drive conflict or are there fundamental societal flaws in the exploitation and use of these resources that breed conflict? In short, are Africa's vast natural resources a blessing or a curse when it comes to security? While there is a clear lack of scholarly agreement on these questions, there are indeed strong—although not necessarily causal—direct and indirect linkages between resource exploitation, conflict, and human security that are worthy of examination.

Although the notion of environmental security is a relatively new dimension of international relations and of politics in general, it would be inane to assume that problems of environmental change are in any way novel.[3] The 1960s saw a significant rise in the prominence of environmental issues in North America and Western Europe and the decades since have witnessed a steady appreciation of a number of challenges posed by environmental change to conventional interstate relations. Environmental security, however, is a phenomenon that is distinctively associated with the end of the Cold War. The idea of linking the environment with insecurity was one of the first major attempts at the securitization of a non-military security issue by promoting a security agenda which moved away from the Cold War's fixation on military state-centered security.[4]

In recent years much attention has focused on the linkages between environmental degradation and conflict and the implications for a whole host of third order security issues. One of the most powerful environmental images put forth by this school is that of mankind being on the threshold of an environmental crisis, where continued unrestrained human exploitation of resources will inevitably lead to a severe deterioration of the environment with disastrous implications for human welfare.[5] A more realistic and immediate concern, however, is that environmental degradation presents a highly diverse range of security challenges from interstate conflict (over water rights for instance) and population dislocation resulting from drought and famine on the one hand, to domestic conflicts over the exploitation of national resources or localized strife over basic access to land, water, and grazing rights on the other. While these types of challenges are certainly not unique to Africa, the continent, with its limited financial and already overstretched security resources, is particularly vulnerable.

The political economy of conflict

Since the end of the Cold War greater attention has been paid to economic factors as a critical—if not the critical—driver of conflict in much of the developing world. Global conflicts once dominated by ideological, nationalist, or geopolitical concerns were being replaced by clashes over competing economic interests and in particular the competition over resources. From oil and natural gas competition in the Middle East and Asia, to the fight over water rights in the Middle East and Africa, to the struggle over controlling minerals and timber across the global south, "conflict over valuable resources—and the power and wealth they confer—has become an increasingly prominent feature of the global landscape," wrote Michael Klare in 2002.[6]

Much of the underlying premise for this prediction is rooted in the global economics of supply and demand spurred by the world's escalating population and economic growth. Klare cites the rising worldwide demand for energy, the Chinese economic boom, and the unrelenting net resource consumption by the United States and Western Europe colliding with limited or even declining supplies of key natural resources and materials.[7] The resulting disequilibrium vastly increases the likelihood of conflict, according to Klare. In particular, he believes that the incidence of inter-state competition over control or access to supplies of vital materials is likely to increase.[8] Klare also saw rising instability and violence in many developing countries as a result of the rich–poor divide whereby the privileged few secure resource wealth at the expense of the disenfranchised masses.

Building on this latter theme, others, like Paul Collier and Anke Hoeffler, began to assess resource exploitation as a motivational driver of domestic conflict, most notably civil war, in their examination of "greed versus grievance."[9] They ultimately put forth an economic model of civil war from an empirical examination of African conflicts that argued "it is not political or social grievance per se that leads to civil war, but rather, for given levels of grievance, it is the opportunity to organize and finance a rebellion that determines if a civil war will occur or not." Thus, the determinants are primarily economic in nature, according to the Collier-Hoeffler model.[10] Natural resources play a critical role in this equation because they generate economic returns that are much higher than the minimum level needed to sustain these conflicts. In addition, an abundance of resource wealth can distort economic development and fuel social instability through the uneven distribution of the generated revenue, the creation of dependent enclave economies, or by fostering of political separatism. This led Collier to surmise that civil war "is heavily concentrated in countries with low income, in economic decline, and dependent on natural resources."[11]

While the struggle to control oil, diamonds, and rare mineral wealth often captures the most public attention, it is at the other extreme of the political economy spectrum—the micro-economic impact of resource competition—where the stakes may indeed be the highest. For people and communities living in environmentally marginal areas the contest for control and access to basic resource necessities, like arable land and water, may produce some of the highest levels of social violence. Indeed, it may literally be a life-and-death struggle. This is especially true in Africa, as rising population growth places an increasing burden on the carrying capacity of the land. The natural habitat's limited ability to support human life in these areas means that competition is a zero-sum situation. Loss of land for farming or grazing, or lack of water for crops, animals, and people can be a death sentence, thus competition over these resources can easily devolve into violence. This aspect of resource conflict is readily apparent, for example, across the pan-Sahel and in Darfur, South Sudan, Uganda's Karamoja district, and northwestern Kenya.[12]

Rather than focus on the economics driving resource conflict, some scholars view political dysfunction within societies and not the resources themselves as the driving source of conflict. Abiodun Alao, for example, points to a failure of governance in how resources are exploited and utilized within the society.[13] Accordingly, it is the political manipulation of resources in elite and interest politics that can trigger or sustain conflict. Likewise, Paul Williams sees poor governance and weak leadership as crucial in determining whether resources are a blessing or a curse. And although Williams is skeptical that an abundance or scarcity of resources (other than land) is directly responsible for driving conflict, he acknowledges that these factors are "sometimes important for understanding how certain conflicts endured and why they assumed the forms they did."[14] A more useful approach, he believes, is to view them as enablers of conflict; as means to a political end. Thus, the relationship between resources and conflict may be a more complex and indirect one, which is based on the perceptions of those competing for political power and not on the actual economic value of the resources themselves. In this case, it is more about the process that encourages violence rather than the perceived economic return from the competition.

Digging even further, a wide number of organizations and institutions have identified tertiary resource-conflict linkages—ranging from the proliferation of small arms and human rights abuses to peacekeeping and lack of transparency—that have far reaching security implications. Some of these linkages, such as the proliferation of small arms or human rights abuses, are more broadly tied to all types of conflict, while others involving issues of transparency, corruption, and good governance are distinctly rooted in resource exploitation. Much of the focus here is on finding ways to prevent the onset of, or reoccurrence of, violence through more effective and accountable political mechanisms.

Global politics and the rise of environmentalism

The 1960s are typically understood to mark the birth of the modern international environmental movement as a widespread and persistent social movement.[15] This period witnessed increased energy and resource consumption, new and rising sources of pollution, the rapid erosion of the Earth's biodiversity, and rising population pressures on the environment. The failure, however, of established political parties in states to embrace and respond effectively to these issues encouraged the birth of several new NGOs—Friends of the Earth, Greenpeace, and the World Wildlife Fund for instance—alongside more established environmental pressure groups.[16] It is noteworthy that the interest in environmental action at the international level and, indeed, most of the NGOs exerting pressure to this end was an almost exclusively developed states phenomenon.

The emergence of the international environmental movement popularized the idea that there was an imminent and looming "environmental crisis" presenting itself, linked to unrestrained population growth and growing resource scarcities, exacerbated by the weakness of existing social and political institutions.[17] Pollution, like wildlife, does not respect international boundaries and states realized that action to alleviate or conserve the environment sometimes had to involve more than one state. While this resulted in the proliferation of a wide array of international agreements, these new agreements remained the domain of new UN specialized agencies (like the Food and Agriculture Organization) and were hardly central to diplomacy at the United Nations. But by 1972, heightened concern about the negative human health effects of pollution and other forms of environmental change at the global level initiated the convening of the United Nations Conference on the Human Environment (UNCHE) in Stockholm.[18]

The UNCHE had a catalytic effect in initiating some key principles which challenged the conventions of state sovereignty, and in putting environmental change permanently on the agenda of international politics.[19] Principle 21 of the UNCHE notably confirmed that states retain full sovereign authority over resources located in their own territory, but equally emphasized that it is their responsibility to exploit these resources with regard to the effect of this on the environment of other states.[20] The parties to the UNCHE also agreed to acknowledge the concept of a "common heritage of mankind," whereby resources located outside of territorial borders (such as minerals on the deep sea bed, in water, and air) should be considered as belonging to the international community collectively. Apart from providing the first formal recognition of the international importance of environmental issues, the conference also resulted in the establishment of the United Nations Environment Programme and prompted many governments to create new departments of the environment. Moreover, the increased environmental awareness would spark rising demands in the years ahead for a rethinking of traditional understandings of security in the modern age.[21]

Prior to the era of globalization, according to Volger, the international agenda was dominated almost exclusively by the need to mitigate the impact of pollution and to conserve natural resources,[22] but this quickly changed with a growing appreciation in the 1980s of the challenges posed by environmental change that "elevated this realm of international politics to a higher diplomatic level and securitized some of the issues."[23]

The first challenge relates to the fact that localized environmental problems can become global problems. It is argued that although transboundary pollution and the management of the global commons were firmly on the international political agenda by the mid-1980s, most of the harmful effects of environmental change seemed only to be felt locally and thus were of little concern to the international community. But growing evidence that seemingly remote problems—experienced most notably in developing states—had wider repercussions, brought a number of new environmental issues to the attention of international policymakers. Deforestation, traditionally viewed as a problem for forest-dwelling wildlife and humans, suddenly gained prominence by the discovery of the "carbon-sink effect" (trees absorbing atmospheric carbon dioxide and converting it to oxygen by the process of photosynthesis). The realization that the loss of tropical rainforests in Brazil, for instance, could pose a threat to the urban residents in North America and Europe helped to bring the issue to the global political agenda. Likewise, the issue of desertification poses repercussions beyond the immediately affected people, since the removal of once-fertile land will decrease the production of the entire world's food supply.

The second challenge relates to the recognition that some environmental problems are global in scale. The securitization of certain environmental issues in international politics has only tended to occur when states recognized that the problem is truly global in its scale.[24] It can be argued that deforestation and desertification have not been securitized due to the fact that they are ultimately still seen as localized problems with some wider rippling implications. On the other hand, it is widely accepted that ozone depletion and climate change are not challenges that states can protect their citizens from by domestic legislation or by regional political cooperation with like-minded neighboring states. While local and regional air pollution can be reversed with relative ease where the political will to do so exist, the challenge is much more difficult to resolve when the damage is being inflicted on the atmosphere as a whole.[25]

The last challenge is the recognition that environmental issues are inseparable from global economic issues. The vast majority of environmental problems are related in some way to the processes of economic development and growth, which have dominated how governments frame their policies both domestically and in the global marketplace. Industrialization and urbanization, the classic ingredients of development, have put enormous strain on states' resources, while changing the pattern of land use and altering nature's own balance of power.[26] Although most developing states have not yet reached such a devastating level of industrial development as developed states have, the industrialization processes in the vast majority of these states are also showing signs of failure to implement environmental safeguards against the rationale that these developing states could not afford such safeguards.[27]

The international community has come a long way in its understanding of the importance in addressing environmental issues on a global scale. Climate change, carbon offsets, rainforest preservation, and habitat destruction are now part of the lexicon of international politics. And despite sharp differences that continue to divide north and south, developed and developing nations, and producers and consumers, the need for global action is abundantly clear. This coming together of international public opinion was seen during the December 2015 Paris Summit on climate change when 197 parties, including those from the global north and south, signed onto the agreement.

Scope and nature of the problem

Resource challenges, whether fueled by scarcity, abundance, or struggles over control, along with environmental change, have become a defining characteristic of the twenty-first-century security environment—challenges that are only likely to increase significantly as global population pressures and economic demands fuel the potential for violent conflict within societies and across international borders. And while this situation is a far cry from Kaplan's portrait of global anarchy and pervasiveness of war,[28] these types of cross-cutting linkages clearly produce an increased level of complexity that can exacerbate tensions, feed fanaticism, and fuel violence, which makes mitigation exceedingly difficult. Resources in and of themselves are not the source of conflict, as we have noted, but as Philippe Le Billon points out, they do have "specific historic, geographic, and social qualities participating in the shaping of the patterns of conflicts and violence."[29] Moreover, it is often the critical interplay with existing societal political and economic vulnerabilities, such as poor governance and corruption, that determine the nature and degree of resource conflict.

Manifestations abound in Africa. Geopolitics often centers heavily around a country's ability to control and exploit oil and natural gas reserves. Separatists and rebel groups seek to fund their activities through illicit mineral and timber sales. Africa's "First World War" in the eastern Democratic Republic of the Congo from the late 1990s to 2003 was sustained largely by the belligerents' ability to exploit the country's vast mineral wealth. Conflict minerals continue to fuel the ongoing violence and instability there. While the water wars of the new millennium have yet to come to fruition, tensions are indeed rising in parts of the continent as new and proposed water diversion projects threaten to undermine longstanding riparian agreements.

Following the end of the Cold War and the loss of external funding from superpower rivalries to their African proxies, many belligerents turned inward to find new sources of income in the form of natural resources. At the same time some previously simmering conflicts in West and Central Africa reignited violently, fanned in part by exploiting natural resource revenue. The role of conflict diamonds in funding anti-government rebels in Angola and Sierra Leone, illicit timber revenues propping up Charles Taylor in Liberia, warlord mining of tantalum (coltan) in the eastern DRC, and oil bunkering by separatists in the Niger Delta soon captured international headlines (and even the interest of Hollywood movie producers). But now more than two decades later, we have a greater appreciation for the sheer size of the problem—approximately 35 percent of all conflicts in sub-Saharan Africa are resource related, according to one study[30]—and the complex nature of resource competition extends well beyond its simple role in funding purveyors of violence.

What is also clear, however, is that Africa is now home to an entire range of interconnected political, socio-economic, and security challenges posed by resource competition and environmental stress at the local, national, regional, and international levels—challenges that are not only taxing the limits of African abilities to address, but of the international community too.

An area of rising concern, and one that is frequently overlooked by outsider observers, is African scarcity conflict fueled by heightened competition over basic livelihood resources, such as land, water, and pasture. Recent data indicate that localized violence over access to these basic resources is on the increase across the continent.[31] Further compounding the problem, detrimental environmental changes and rising populations are placing an additional burden on the carrying capacity in some of Africa's most vulnerable and poorest regions.

Climate change can act as an accelerator of violence and instability in these instances; the occurrence of conflict in sub-Saharan Africa is more likely after years of poor rainfall, according to a World Bank study.[32] The loss of arable land through desertification, drought, or human misuse (such as overgrazing or urbanization) across the Sahel, the greater Horn of Africa, or even parts of southern Africa, for instance, is pushing already marginal communities into increasingly desperate survival situations, as food supplies, water, and incomes decline further. So much so that the US National Intelligence Council views fragile states in Africa (along with those in the Middle East) as at most risk for food and water shortages in the coming decades.[33]

While rarely capturing the headlines, these types of scarcity conflicts are a regular feature of the African landscape and are increasingly, in our view, becoming a significant factor in sustaining the ongoing low levels of societal violence. Impoverished and desolate regions, such as the Karamoja district of northeast Uganda and the Turkana region of northwest Kenya, where desperately poor, cattle-herding nomads eke out a meager existence, are the most vulnerable to this type of conflict. Traditional resource competition over cattle and water here is compounded by a culture of cattle raiding and fierce independence, as well as the introduction in recent years of automatic weapons, which has produced a deadly cycle of violence. Likewise, competition between farmers and herdsmen over access to limited land and water resources is a major factor in fueling internal strife across much of the Sahel; this certainly was the case in Darfur in 2003–5. Competition for land has also been a key component of the deadly communal violence afflicting Nigeria's Plateau State since 2001.

As a result of African population growth and environmental stress (both natural and man-made) scarcity conflicts over basic livelihood resources almost certainly will increase in the decades ahead. Nonetheless, they are likely to remain highly localized in nature and generate low, yet sustained, levels of violence. The real danger, however, lies in the ability of these types of conflicts to function as facilitators for generating more intense and widespread forms of violence by reinforcing existing societal divisions and thus having the potential to produce much wider domestic and even regional security problems.

As discussed previously, the "resource curse"—and specifically the challenge of effectively managing national resource wealth—makes weak and fragile resource-dependent states highly susceptible to domestic conflict. These states are often characterized by enclave economies, weak institutions, poor governance, and lack of legitimacy and thus, the issue of translating resource exploitation into political stability and economic development is a central challenge for entire regions in the developing world.[34] Unfortunately, all too many African states have become poster children for this problem. It is a sad fact that the overwhelming majority of the continent's richest, resource endowed countries are also some of the most divided and poorly governed (if not outright corrupt) societies in Africa and, with some notable exceptions such as Botswana, are home to high levels of endemic violence over access to or exploitation of natural resources. Moreover, the mismanagement of domestic resource wealth tends to act as a conflict catalyst for already existing political and socio-economic divisions.

Nowhere is this more evident than in the case of oil production—Africa's blessing and curse. In what Nicholas Shaxson called the "dirty politics of oil,"[35] governing elites from the greater Gulf of Guinea to North Africa, who are abetted by shady politicians, manipulative businessmen, and multinational oil companies, have used oil revenues to enrich themselves and bolster their grip on power at the expense of their own people. By some estimates Nigeria is believed to have squandered, through corruption and mismanagement, over half the $600 billion it had earned from 1956 to 2007.[36] Accordingly, few ordinary citizens are able to enjoy the benefits of this wealth; major oil producers Nigeria, Angola, and Sudan rank in the bottom fifth of the UN Development Index.[37] Moreover, the resulting alienation has often been a significant factor in driving separatism conflicts in places like Nigeria's Niger Delta, Angola's Cabinda enclave, and southern Sudan prior to South Sudan's independence. And there is growing evidence that oil dependence can be linked to the initiation of civil wars in Africa.[38] Likewise, oil and natural gas discoveries off the coasts of northern Mozambique and southern Tanzanian in the past several years have sparked new concerns that parts of these countries may seek greater political autonomy from their central governments, which could further inflame existing political tensions.

Beyond facilitating separatism and greater political autonomy, national resource wealth can also facilitate a climate of low-level, yet persistent violence and civil strife. For example, what Le Billon calls "lootable commodities"[39] (such as oil, diamonds, gold, and rare minerals) can create a dependable funding stream for warlords, paramilitary militias, and criminal elements to build or further strengthen their organizations. These types of groups rely heavily on violence and fear to maintain their grip on power and over local communities, but as Stefan Mair points out, they have little interest in overthrowing established central government authority. Rather they seek to create an environment favorable for their continued—and expanding—economic enrichment.[40] Thus, chronic instability is good for business, but not full-scale insurgency.

Another serious challenge is that some domestic conflicts can morph into much more widespread and violent transnational ones that engulf and destabilize entire regions. Although resources themselves are rarely at the center of these conflicts, the revenue generated from their exploitation is often critical to empowering and sustaining the warring factions and increasing the duration of the conflict. Moreover, some recent research indicates that the mere presence of lootable resources "provides a powerful incentive for third-party intervention, even after controlling for political and strategic factors, thus underscoring the importance of economic motives."[41] This was clearly the case with Sierra Leone in the 1990s, as well as with the DRC from 1998–2003 that saw interventions from Uganda, Rwanda, Burundi, Angola, Namibia, and Zimbabwe. Even today, despite the large presence of UN peacekeepers for more than decade, conflict minerals continue to fuel violence in the eastern DRC with armed groups "earning hundreds of millions of dollars each year" through the illicit trade in tin, tantalum (coltan), and tungsten, according to NGO sources.[42] Likewise, the continuing presence of large, semi-permanent internally displaced or refugee populations dislodged by the violence further serves to destabilize the Great Lakes region.

Large-scale population dislocation as a result of man-made or natural environmental degradation is also an increasing source of conflict and regional instability across much of Africa, but particularly in the Sahelian countries of West Africa and much of the Horn of Africa. Already facing numerous economic and security challenges, these often weak and fragile countries are ill-equipped to cope with the added stress of tens of thousands of refugees. Violence against refugees in Chad, Mauritania, and Kenya has become commonplace as local communities in these countries seek to safeguard their own often scarce livelihood resources against increased competition. The dangerous mix of scarcity competition and xenophobia in these situations can easily result in the situation spiraling out of control.

As we have noted previously, direct inter-state conflict is atypical in today's Africa. Rather most conflicts—including resource and environmental stress ones—now arise within states and are fueled by multiple cross-cutting linkages to an array of transnational and non-traditional security challenges. Inter-state competition over access to water, however, may change this in the coming decades. While most of the continent has access to significant water reserves, there are some notable exceptions. The most vulnerable to this type of future conflict are the countries heavily reliant on water from the Nile River Basin—Egypt, Ethiopia, Sudan, and South Sudan. Ambitious hydroelectric development along Ethiopia's Blue Nile, combined with longstanding environmental obstacles along South Sudan's White Nile, will almost certainly reduce the current flow of water downstream to Egypt and Sudan. Painstakingly negotiated water agreements will be jeopardized. Moreover, demographic pressures in all of these countries—estimated to rise by more than 30 percent, adding another 100 million people by 2035[43]—will increase demand for water and thus raise the political and economic stakes for all of these governments. The end result could be the onset of a round of water wars that would further destabilize an already volatile region.

Although a highly complex relationship, resources, the environment, and conflict are intrinsically intertwined. Natural resource revenues, in particular, have become a central feature of African conflict and we expect this will continue, if not grow in importance as global economic growth feeds demand for the continent's bounty. Likewise, environmental degradation will place additional pressure on African governments to make wiser use of their resources and hopefully defuse tensions before they result in violence. In both these areas the role of the international community will be essential in making progress in what are truly globalized challenges.

The future of the Nile River: regional confrontation or cooperation?

The Nile River, with a length of over 4,225 miles (6,800 kilometers) is a very important international river of regional importance, and the control of the river is increasingly becoming contentious as water demands in the region increase drastically. The Nile, which is actually composed of three major tributaries—the White Nile with its principal source in Uganda's Lake Victoria, the Blue Nile originating from Ethiopia's Lake Tana, and the Atbara River with headwaters in the Ethiopian Highlands—flows through some of the most arid regions of northern Africa, and is vital to agricultural production in Egypt and the Sudans. Egypt relies on the Nile for 97 percent of its fresh water, and more than 95 percent of the river's runoff originates outside of Egypt in the other nine riparian states of the basin that include Sudan, South Sudan, Ethiopia, Eritrea, Kenya, Rwanda, Burundi, Uganda, Tanzania, and the DRC.

The Nile, moreover, is nearly synonymous with Egypt and was it not for the river and its sediments, Egypt would have been a mere desert and its great ancient civilizations, as well as the present population, cities, and economy, would never have existed.[a] Although Egypt is the furthest downstream Nile riparian, it effectively controls the majority of the water by possessing greater military and economic power than its upstream neighbors. Given that Egypt's existence largely depends on the river, it comes as no surprise that Egypt has jealously guarded its claim to the Nile waters, threatening military action against upstream Sudan and Ethiopia whenever they have announced water projects on the river.

Apart from the fact that Egypt is very dependent on the waters of the Nile as basically its only source of freshwater, both the Sudans receive 77 percent of their freshwater from the Nile.[b] And while all the Nile Basin riparian states rely to a certain extent on the river for freshwater, Egypt and Sudan have few other options (especially the former) for agriculture and domestic and industry use. Agriculture consumes the majority of the freshwater in the Nile Basin; Egypt spends 86 percent of its freshwater on agriculture; Sudan is thought to apply 99 percent of its freshwater in the same way. Old and inefficient traditional irrigation techniques have wasted substantial amounts of crop-designated water through evaporation in the past, but modern projects are implementing more suitable methods for minimizing water losses.

The strategic importance of the Nile waters to Egypt and the Sudan is self-evident; it can be argued that the river is necessary for the sustainment and support of life in these two countries specifically and, as such, water degradation and tampering with the flow by riparian states can be viewed as a national environmental security threat. As a result of regional population growth, industrialization, and pollution, as well as water diversion by dams and canals, both the quantity and quality of available freshwater from the Nile to riparian states has declined over time. For the most part this has resulted in internal strife, rather than regional conflict, as domestic food production declines and forced population relocations take place. The notable exception is the construction—or even proposed construction—of new dams upstream from Egypt that historically has raised regional tensions to boiling point.

Friction between Cairo and Khartoum over the White Nile flow and between Cairo and Addis Ababa over Blue Nile and Atbara waters increase to new heights whenever Sudan or Ethiopia propose new water development projects. Ethiopia, for instance, proposed a dam on Lake Tana to

---

[a] K. Wiebe, 'The Nile River: Potential for conflict and cooperation in the face of water degradation', *Natural Resources Journal*, 41:3 (2001), 731.
[b] Ibid., p. 734.

preserve headwaters for itself in 1970, and the then Egyptian President Anwar Sadat threatened to declare war if they should pursue their plans.[c] Most recently, in June 2013, Ethiopia announced its intention to construct the Grand Renaissance Dam on the Blue Nile, a $4.7 billion project that the Ethiopian government said will eventually provide 6,000 megawatts of power.[d] Deposed Egyptian President Mohamed Morsi responded by saying that Egypt would defend "each drop of Nile water with our blood if necessary" if the project threatened the water security of his country.[e] Ethiopia responded by saying that the Blue Nile would only be slightly diverted and then allowed to follow its natural course and that Egyptian industry would benefit immensely from the power generated by the dam once it was completed in 2017.

Despite this tension, the historical and contemporary record regarding the potential for conflict arising from the renewable resource of river water suggests that conflict and turmoil occur more often on the internal rather than the international level.[f] The huge dams in Africa that are built to deal with general water scarcity or to generate hydroelectric power appear especially disruptive within their own societies. Landmark projects such as the Aswan Dam and the Kariba Dam, for instance, resulted in the forced relocation of large numbers of people, and generated turmoil as the displaced clashed with local groups in the areas where they were resettled. Moreover, those relocated are often members of ethnic minority groups outside the power hierarchy of the society, who may feel they have little recourse other than to turn to violence to express their grievances.

This is indeed evident in the case of the Nile River Basin where international diplomacy has successfully defused tension for more than a century. Understanding that Nile waters held great economic and political importance for a successful occupation, the British, on behalf of Egypt, concluded an agreement with Ethiopia in 1902 to guard Egypt's claim to the Nile.[g] Likewise, the British acting on behalf of the Sudanese concluded the 1929 Nile Waters Agreement with the Egyptian government. But after gaining independence in 1953, Sudan demanded that the existing agreement be amended and the two states finally settled on a new division of water in the 1959 Nile Waters Agreement.[h]

[c] Ibid., p. 743.
[d] *BBC News*, 'Egyptian warning over Ethiopia Nile dam' (June 10, 2013).
[e] *CNN*, 'Ethiopia's $5bn project that could turn it into Africa's powerhouse' (March 6, 2015).
[f] T.F. Homer-Dixon, 'Environmental scarcities and violent conflict', *International Security*, 19:1 (1994), 20.
[g] Wiebe, 'The Nile River', p. 746.
[h] Ibid., p. 746.

More recently, all the Nile Basin states united in 1992 for the first time to pursue a joint dialogue on sustainable development and management of the Nile waters.[i] Out of shared interest and need, water affairs ministers from the Nile Basin states gathered a group of scientific professionals from all the riparian states for discussion that culminated in the 1997 Nile Basin Initiative (NBI). Even today, the 1999 strategic action program continues to define the NBI's primary guiding principles and formed the basis for the launching of the initiative's Strategic Plan 2012–16.[j] This latest phase provides a clear division of roles and responsibilities, to ensure delivery and increase of tangible benefits by supporting cooperation amongst the Nile Basin countries to promote timely and efficient joint action, by managing and safeguarding water resources through more effective development planning and assessment, and by facilitating investment in trans-boundary water development projects and programs.[k]

Global climatic change and environmental and demographic stress will undoubtedly increase the demand for Nile water by all basin countries in the future. Some countries, such as Egypt and Sudan, are highly vulnerable to these changes, as well as to intentional acts perpetrated by upstream riparian neighbors, yet this need not result in violent conflict, as history has shown. For despite the high stakes, the riparian states of the Nile basin have shown a proven willingness—sometimes reluctantly and amid much verbal blustering—to work together through political and regional mechanisms to resolve their differences and achieve compromise. Ethiopia's Grand Renaissance Dam and other hydroelectric projects will certainly test the limits of this framework and see if the cooperative vision can indeed deliver the tangible economic and social returns all desire.

[i] Ibid., p. 751.
[j] The Nile Basin Initiative, accessed at: www.nilebasin.org/newsite/index.php?option=com_content&view=article&id=139%3Aabout-the-nbi&catid=34%3Anbi-background-facts&Itemid=74&lang=en&limitstart=2 on February 28, 2017.
[k] Ibid.

Implications for security

For the better part of two decades after the end of the Cold War, resource conflict in Africa was viewed almost exclusively through the lens of separatism and civil war. Natural resources were the currency of violence. Resources were cursed. An abundance of resource wealth was an inevitable predictor of domestic strife, insecurity, and instability for African countries. This conceptual perspective dovetailed well with the facts on the ground in the new post-Cold War era—wars were smaller, conducted by factionalized and decentralized groups, fought on the peripheries of countries with cross-border dimensions, and self-funded through illicit activities.[44] Thus, addressing the motivating factors driving separatism and civil war would, by logical extension, address the challenge of resource conflict too.

This simplistic view thankfully has given way to a much more nuanced appreciation of the nature and multi-layered complexity of more broadly defined resource competition and its implication for peace and security in modern-day Africa. We now know that resource competition and exploitation can be linked to a number of political, socio-economic, and environmental conflicts, from the local to the national level, that present serious challenges to building stability and economic development. Moreover, the role of environment degradation in intensifying these conflicts is now seen as an integral part of the resource equation. The human security framework thus allows one to move beyond traditional notions of security thinking to ones that reflect a broader vision of security.

This approach is especially important when addressing implications for environmental security because it moves beyond a state-centric architecture by arguing that any viable solution to global environmental problems must, at least in some sense, transcend the context and category of the nation-state as the only referent object by going beyond simply deepening the content of security studies to include new threats to national security; rather the scope of security must also be broadened to include entities qualitatively different from states as the referent objects.[45] In addition, one of the practical consequences of using a human security approach, as opposed to a more traditional view of national security, is that it becomes possible to identify threats to security at the sub-national, national, and transnational levels, while reinforcing the broadening of the security agenda to include non-military threats such as the environment.[46]

At the same time, this greatly complicates things. How to reconcile economic security with environmental concerns for instance? And what are the implications for sustainable development ("development that meets the needs of the present without compromising the ability of future generations to meet their needs"[47]), which is essential for the economic well-being of developing countries in an increasingly globalized world. Difficult challenges indeed. But rather than ignore them by simply focusing on the well-being of the state, the human security construct seeks to find the appropriate balance between the interests of the state and multiple levels of society.

As an intensifier of violence
Blood diamonds, conflict minerals, scarcity conflicts, and oil wars are all part of the common lexicon of modern-day conflicts involving natural resources, but there is no solid evidence of a causal link between resources and the outbreak of conflict. What the evidence has shown, however, is that natural resources and environmental degradation can be powerful intensifiers of violence, making conflicts more deadly and prolonged once they begin. Likewise, resource competition need not necessarily lead to conflict, but in countries with poor governance, weak institutions, and inadequate conflict prevention mechanisms, avoiding violence is often difficult. This makes African countries particularly susceptible to these types of conflicts.

As long as the economics of war dictate that the immediate benefits of continued fighting outstrip the long-term potential benefits of peace, combatants will be less inclined to end the conflict. Long after the superpower proxy war in Angola had ended, the violence continued, as both the government and Union for the Total Independence of Angola rebels sought the spoils of war—the country's vast oil and mineral wealth. Moreover, the resource revenue allowed both sides to continually re-arm and re-equip their forces. The long-running conflict in the eastern DRC is similarly prolonged by the ability of the combatants to continually fund their war machines with resource revenue, as well as by neighboring countries seeking to manipulate the ongoing chaos to exploit the region's vast natural resource wealth for their own economic gain. The end result is the same. The duration and intensify of African conflicts is increased, with countries and even entire regions plunged into long-term instability that undermines both domestic and transnational security.

Likewise, this prolonged violence places individuals and entire communities at risk for victimization. Mass killings of civilians caught in the cross-fire of warring factions are commonplace, but the overwhelming majority of deaths in these situations are from indirect conflict-related causes. The majority of deaths are a result of malnutrition and disease. Children under five years of age, for example, accounted for nearly half the deaths in the DRC, according to a 2007 study by the International Rescue Committee.[48] Women and children are also vulnerable to massive human rights abuses, including kidnappings, rape, child soldier recruitment, and forced labor. The accompanying dislocations associated with those fleeing the violence not only disrupts subsistence food production and compromises health care delivery, but creates an entire class of vulnerable people dependent on governmental and/or international assistance and protection. There were about 16 million internally displaced people and refugees in Africa at the end of 2015, according to the UN High Commissioner for Refugees,[49] and these people often become targets for further victimization, including crime and sexual and gender-based violence.

As discussed earlier, livelihood conflicts involving local competition over access to land, water, and food are some of the most violent and difficult to solve given their zero-sum nature. Access to these basic resources is thus often a daily challenge for survival that produces clear winners and losers. Accordingly, resource depletion and/or environmental degradation are likely to increase the level of lethality in these conflicts, often reinforced by easy access to automatic weapons and overlapping identity, class, or political divisions. Climate change, in particular, has been cited as a deepening concern because it "will inevitably affect competition over livelihood resources, and will act as an accelerator and, in extreme events, a direct cause of violence and instability."[50] The harm to subsistence agriculture production could be especially devastating for people already living in fragile ecosystems and who often reside in countries with the least adaptive capacity to cope. Although usually low-level and small in scale, daily resource conflicts impact much of the world's population on any given day and have the serious potential to escalate quickly into wider national and transnational problems.[51]

Resource-fueled conflicts are also difficult to end, resulting in zones of chronic violence and insecurity that makes peacebuilding a serious challenge. Multiple, and even transnational, actors with competing agendas can make peace hard to achieve. Even when the fighting has abated, violence can easily flare up again given the ease with which various disgruntled factions can obtain funding from the exploitation and illicit trade of local resources to re-arm and re-equip themselves. This helps create a perpetual climate of fear and insecurity. In addition, past economic disruption, extensive damage to infrastructure, and outward population flows create major challenges to economic development that last well beyond the end of hostilities. Parts of West and Central Africa, such as the Mano River Basin, northern Cote d'Ivoire, or along the Darfur–Chad border, are still trying to recover from pervious prolonged periods of resource-related violence.

Cross-cutting security linkages
Beyond their impact on African conflict and the obvious direct links to food, economic, health, and environmental security issues, resource conflict and environmental degradation can also be indirectly linked to other pressing human security challenges on the continent. These include issues of governance and corruption, poverty, transnational

criminal activity, and migration. While these issues are always relevant to any discussion of human security in Africa, the increasing power and intensity of globalization in recent years has further raised the importance of these linkages when it comes to addressing resource conflict and environmental degradation.

Globalization means more and more state and non-state actors are now playing a direct or indirect role in determining the future of African security. Not only does their involvement increase the level of complexity, but also introduces more potentially competing—and conflicting—agendas that hinder problem solving. This is particularly troublesome when it comes to addressing the security implications of international resource competition in Africa, whereby narrow, individual interests are likely to be the chief consideration. Effective long-term solutions are often sacrificed as foreign governments try to secure access to supplies to fuel their economic growth; multinational corporations pursue ways to maximize their profits; and African governments seek to maximize their revenues. Thus, finding the sweet spot of compromise is often elusive, even when all acknowledge the need for action.

The consequences are now more immediate and far reaching too. Manufacturing and technology decisions made in California's Silicon Valley or Helsinki, Finland, for example, have very real and immediate consequences for everyone from child miners, tantalite brokers, and warlords in the eastern DRC. The so-called global periphery is diminishing across the political, economic, and social spectrum. Interconnectivity and the speed of information transfer are rapidly melding the core and the periphery into one global system through globalization. This is especially true for the challenge of environment degradation, where the scale and rate of ecological change in Africa is not only threatening near-term stability and security on the continent, but creating longer-term political and socio-economic shifts that are already being felt well outside Africa.

All of the above underscores the need for a holistic approach when addressing resource conflict and environmental degradation challenges in a globalized world—one that looks beyond single issue problems and rather focuses on the relevant nature of relationships and of the linkages between them, such as:

- *Governance and corruption.* Poor governance, along with the lack of transparency and public accountability, are at the heart of the most critical challenges facing African countries today. Weak institutional structures, ineffective leadership, and the absence of inclusionary mechanisms undermine good political governance. When combined with an apparent lack of transparency and public accountability the very legitimacy of governments can be called into question. The very nature of resource exploitation and distribution of resource revenue, however, creates expansive opportunities for corruption and political manipulation to flourish. This, in turn, weakens governance by reinforcing internal divisions and increasing popular alienation that sets the stage for rising violence and even separatist conflict.

- *Poverty.* The issue of poverty poses a major obstacle to human security in Africa, and the continent's poorest countries are some of the most vulnerable to scarcity or livelihood conflicts, as well as the impact of environmental degradation, because they lack the basic capacity to redress their problems. This type of bio-poverty can produce long-term instability that in turn fuels more widespread conflict and compromise development. Without adequate development, countries can find themselves caught up in a reinforcing cycle of poverty and conflict.
- *Transnational criminal activity.* We have already seen how the illicit trade in natural resources fuels warlordism, paramilitaries, and separatist violence, which prolong domestic conflicts and regional instability. This trade is also a sizable source of income for criminal syndicates and a factor feeding criminal violence. Oil bunkering in West Africa is the most lucrative activity. However, everything from diamonds, gold, and other rare minerals, to timber and ivory are part of this black market economy that fuels political and police corruption, increases domestic violence, and creates a climate of community fear. In addition, the illicit trade in resources is stimulating the trafficking in small arms (particularly automatic weapons) and thereby increasing the lethality of societal violence.
- *Migration.* Beyond being directly linked to internal population displacement and refugee flows, resource conflict and environmental degradation are also tied indirectly to broader macro migration patterns in Africa. For instance, although minor declines in livelihood resources may not be enough to ignite conflict they can provide the necessary incentive to spur outward migration. The southward expansion of the Sahara Desert and the resulting loss of arable land over the past 35 years, for instance, have forced tens of thousands in Mauritania, Mali, Niger, and Chad to relocate. Even more telling is the shrinking of Lake Chad, which has lost 90 percent of its water mass since 1963 as a result of climate change and increased demands for water.[52] Likewise, the economic pull of better work opportunities often drives significant regional and international migration patterns. Thus, voluntary migration becomes an effective coping mechanism

for deflecting the adverse impact of resource and environmental stress for some countries, while at the same time posing difficult challenges for receiving countries in Africa and Europe.

The challenge of how best to effectively manage natural resources and the environment for the benefit of individuals, communities, and countries is quickly rising to the top of the African human security agenda. It is a highly complex and multi-layered challenge that needs to address security from the local to the international level. While much has been revealed about the nature of the relationship between natural resources, the environment, and conflict, there is still much more that has yet to be discovered concerning linkages to other security challenges.

Conclusion

Growing public concern and rising awareness has increasingly focused attention on an age-old problem—the struggle over control and exploitation of natural resources—and the modern-day challenge of coping with the impact of environmental change on society. The first is a story as old as mankind. Conflict over the control or access to precious natural resources, be it the wealth of gold, silver, or gems, or the life sustaining necessities of food and water, is a key theme throughout world history. While the list of valued resources has expanded exponentially in response to modern economic requirements, the fundamental nature of resource competition has not. What has changed, however, is the rising importance of environmental stress and demographic pressure in shaping many of these local challenges. Local challenges, moreover, that are increasingly being transformed into more far-reaching globalized challenges with global implications. And the Africa of today features prominently in this new equation.

While Kaplan's and Klare's dire predictions fortunately have not come true, they were right in identifying a looming challenge. Today many believe that unless more is done to address the problems arising from the unprecedented global demand for land, energy, food, water, and minerals, "severe market disruptions are likely to occur, as are increased chances of violent conflict" in many "hot spots" in the developing world.[53] For poor, resource-dependent countries "resources are likely to remain the economic focus of most belligerents in years to come."[54] To this we would add that the chief threat for the most vulnerable people will be their inability to adapt and mitigate detrimental environmental changes. Given this forecast, the implication for the future of African security and stability is troubling to say the least.

Several dominant trends are expected to drive the resource and environment debate in Africa over the coming decades—trends that will not only tax the limits of African capabilities to address, but also the willingness of the international community to engage. First and foremost, conflict across the entire spectrum of resource competition will almost certainly rise, with livelihood or scarcity violence showing the largest increase, in our view. Environmental stress, including a combination of adverse climate change and demographic pressure, will exacerbate the problem and complicate conflict prevention and violence mitigation efforts. Second, the aggregation and the layering of challenges associated with resources, the environment, and other aspects of security and political stability will only increase the level of complexity and the degree of difficulty in problem solving. Likewise, the expanding number of actors—both state and non-state—along with their competing interests and agendas will further complicate African and international efforts at consensus building and the development of effective solutions. Finally, climate change will boost the rising importance of environmental security in Africa and its inclusion as an integral component of the human security framework.

As with a number of other security challenges, African societies and their leaders will invariably struggle to balance the political economic challenge of development against the adverse impacts of resource competition and environmental degradation. Short-term needs must be balanced against long-term requirements. This, however, will require a stronger governance and broad-based political regime that utilizes national assets for sustainable development. This will be an enormous undertaking—not only in Africa, but globally too. Here the role of developed countries and their active support for sustainable development will be crucial.

Beyond this role, the involvement of the broader international community of state and non-state actors is likely to be pivotal to the future of African resource conflict and environmental degradation. Will powerful international geo-political or global security interests be the litmus test for supporting reform? Is China's increasing demand for raw materials to fuel economic growth compatible with fostering good governance and democratic accountability? Can multinational corporations see greater value in promoting long-term stability over the ability to collect more short-term revenue? This does not mean that Africans are hapless pawns here. As history has shown, African countries have the proven ability to play off competing external interests to their own benefit. This will, however, require strong political will and a determination to set aside narrow and self-serving interests for the betterment of society.

The resource wealth of Africa has certainly been both a blessing and a curse. Yet it needn't be that way. Just as the forces of globalization helped fuel the frenzied exploitation of the continent's natural resources in a negative way, so too can it spur innovative approaches to better manage this wealth and reduce violent competition for present and future generations. Human security is ultimately about empowering individuals and communities, and globalization provides an effective tool to accomplish this, but only time will tell if African societies will take advantage of it.

Notes

1 United Nations Department of Peacekeeping Operations, 'Conflict and resources', accessed at www.un.org/en/peacekeeping/issues/environment/resources.shtml on February 28, 2017.
2 United Nations Environment Programme, 'From conflict to peacebuilding: The role of natural resources and environment' (Nairobi: UN Environment Programme, February 2009), p. 5.
3 P. Hough, *Understanding Global Security* (Abingdon: Routledge, 2004), pp. 134-5.
4 R. Dannreuther, *International Security: The Contemporary Agenda* (Cambridge: Polity Press, 2007), p. 59.
5 G. Hardin, 'The tragedy of the commons', *Science*, 162:3859 (December 13, 1968), 1243-8.
6 M. Klare, *Resource Wars* (New York: Henry Holt and Co., 2001), p. ix.
7 Ibid., pp. 16-18.
8 Ibid., p. 21.
9 P. Collier and A. Hoeffler, 'Greed and grievance in civil war', *Oxford Economic Papers 56* (2004), 563-95.
10 P. Collier and N. Sambanis (eds), *Volume 1: Africa, Understanding Civil War: Evidence and Analysis* (Washington, DC: The World Bank, 2005), p. xiii. For a detailed explanation of the model see pp. 2-18.
11 P. Collier, 'Natural resources and conflict in Africa', October 2004, accessed at www.crimesofwar.org on February 28, 2017.
12 See L. Young and K. Sing' Oei, 'Land, livelihoods and identities: Inter-community conflicts in East Africa' (Minority Rights Group International, 2011) for a detailed look at the issue in East Africa, accessed at www.minorityrights.org/download.php@id=1076 on February 28, 2017.
13 A. Alao, *Natural Resources and Conflict in Africa: The Tragedy of Endowment* (Rochester, NY: University of Rochester Press, 2007).
14 P. Williams, *War & Conflict in Africa* (Cambridge: Polity Press, 2011), p. 93.
15 R. Eckersley, 'Green theory', in R. Jackson and G. Sørensen (eds), *Introduction to International Relations: Theories and Approaches*, 3rd edn (Oxford: Oxford University Press, 2007), p. 259.

16 J. Vogler, 'Environmental issues', in J. Baylis, S. Smith, and P. Owens (eds), *The Globalization of World Politics: An Introduction to World Politics* (Oxford: Oxford University Press, 2008), p. 355.
17 Dannreuther, *International Security*, p. 59.
18 Hough, *Understanding Global Security*, p. 135.
19 Ibid.
20 United Nations Environment Programme, *Declaration of the United Nations Conference on the Human Environment* (21st plenary meeting, 16 June 1972), accessed at www.unep.org/Documents.Multilingual/Default.asp?DocumentID=97&ArticleID=1503 on February 28, 2017.
21 Dannreuther, *International Security*, p. 59.
22 Vogler, 'Environmental issues', p. 352.
23 Hough, *Understanding Global Security*, p. 140.
24 Ibid., p. 139.
25 Dannreuther, *International Security*, p. 67.
26 D. Kingsbury, 'Environment and development', in D. Kingsbury, *et al.* (eds), *International Development: Issues and Challenges*, 2nd edn (Basingstoke: Palgrave Macmillan, 2012), pp. 321–2.
27 Ibid., p. 303.
28 R. Kaplan, 'The Coming Anarchy', *The Atlantic Monthly* (February 1994).
29 P. Le Billon (ed.), *The Geopolitics of Resource Wars: Resource Dependence, Governance and Violence* (Abingdon: Frank Cass, 2005), p. 2.
30 B. Preiss and C. Brunner (eds), *Democracy in Crisis* (Munster, Germany: LIT Verlag, 2013), p. 382.
31 J. Cilliers and J. Schunemann, 'The future of intrastate conflict in Africa', *ISS Paper 246* (Pretoria: Institute for Security Studies, 23 May 2013), p. 4.
32 World Bank, *World Development Report 2011*, p. 6.
33 National Intelligence Council, *Global Trend 2030: Alternative Worlds* (2012), accessed at www.dni.gov/nic/globaltrends on February 28, 2017.
34 Le Billon, *The Geopolitics of Resource Wars*, p. 22.
35 N. Shaxson, *Poisoned Wells: The Dirty Politics of African Oil* (New York: Palgrave Macmillian, 2007).
36 *National Public Radio*, 'Documenting the paradox of oil, poverty in Nigeria'.
37 *UN Development Index 2015*, accessed at http://hdr.undp.org/en/countries on February 28, 2017.
38 See the findings of Michael Ross, 'What do we know about natural resources and civil war?' *Journal of Peace Research*, 41:3 (2004), 337–56, as an example.
39 Le Billon, *The Geopolitics of Resource Wars*, pp. 561–84.
40 S. Mair, The new world of privatized violence, p. 11–28.
41 M. Findley and A. Mitchel, 'Lootable resources and third-party intervention into civil wars' (Working paper, Brigham Young University, June 23, 2011), p. 21, accessed at https://politicalscience.byu.edu/mfindley/assets/resources_civil-war-intervention_24june2011.pdf on February 28, 2017.

42 Enough Project, 'Conflict minerals', accessed at www.enoughproject.org/conflicts/eastern_congo/conflict-minerals on February 28, 2017.
43 United Nations Department of Economic and Social Affairs; Population Division, Population Estimates and Projection Section, accessed at http://esa.un.org/unpd/wpp/unpp/panel_population.htm on February 28, 2017.
44 S. Straus, 'Wars do end: Why conflict in Africa is falling', *africanarguments.org* (January 28, 2013), accessed at http://africanarguments.org/2013/01/28/wars-do-end-why-conflict-in-africa-is-falling-by-scott-straus/ on February 28, 2017.
45 E. Page, 'What's the point of environmental security?' (Paper presented for the SGIR at the 7th Pan-European International Relations Conference, Stockholm, September 10, 2010), p. 11, accessed at www.academia.edu/2745855/What_s_the_Point_of_Environmental_Security on February 28, 2017.
46 S. Ngubane and H. Solomon, 'Southern Africa's new security agenda', *Africa Insights*, 32:1 (2002), 60.
47 World Commission on Environment and Development, *Our Common Future* (Oxford: Oxford University Press, 1987), p. 43.
48 International Rescue Committee, 'Measuring mortality in the Democratic Republic of Congo' (2007), accessed at www.rescue.org/sites/default/files/resource-file/IRC_DRCMortalityFacts.pdf on February 28, 2017.
49 *DW*, 'UNHCR report: Worsening refugee situation in Africa' (June 20, 2016), accessed at www.dw.com/en/unhcr-report-worsening-refugee-situation-in-africa/a-19338619 on February 28, 2017.
50 Cilliers and Schunemann, 'The future of intrastate conflict in Africa', p. 4.
51 P. Andrews-Speed, *et al.*, 'The global resource nexus: The struggles for land, energy, food, water, and minerals' (Berlin: Transatlantic Academy, May 2012), p. 68.
52 The Brookings Institution, 'Figure of the week: The shrinking of Lake Chad' (February 9, 2017), accessed at https://www.brookings.edu/blog/africa-in-focus/2017/02/09/figure-of-the-week-the-shrinking-lake-chad/ on February 28, 2017.
53 Ibid., p. vii.
54 Le Billon, *The Geopolitics of Resource Wars*, p. 23.

9

The African response

Africa today is a dynamic continent, characterized by a volatile mix of conflict, instability, and state weakness; and one that is testing the limits and capabilities of its societies to build a peaceful and secure future. In as much as Africa and its current problems are often rooted in the past, the continent today finds itself squarely at the forefront of new security thinking and an emerging regional and international security consciousness and activism that is bringing new approaches and ideas to fore. The success or failure of these efforts has serious implications beyond the continent, as Africa becomes increasingly integrated into the global security architecture.

Although the international community historically has played a critical role in shaping the African security debate, true security—and solutions—begin at home. The often misappropriated mantra of "African solutions for African problems" has taken on real and significant meaning in recent years with the development and implementation of new national, sub-regional, and regional approaches. While still a work in progress, these efforts clearly acknowledge past shortcomings of the modern African state and its limitations by seeking to cultivate a cooperative security culture through the African Union (AU), NGOs, and civil society to fashion an African security architecture for the twenty-first century. Without doubt many obstacles and challenges still remain, but these efforts are already proving useful in recasting the continent's security priorities and, moreover, in establishing a direction for future engagement by Africans and non-Africans alike.

The failure of the state-centric approach

The modern-day African state has been the central, if not the preeminent, security actor since the advent of independence, but it has also lurched from crisis to crisis. The state has often served as an unwitting catalyst for fueling insecurity and instability throughout much of the post-independence era. Post-colonial Africa has experienced 85 military coups d'état and this figure surpasses 100 if one takes into consideration the various failed attempts.[1] Since 1945 there have been some 95 conflicts on the continent, nearly half of which were extremely violent, bloody civil wars.[2] To compound matters further, Africa has hosted (and continues to host) some of the longest running conflicts in recent times. Clearly the state has not done a very good job of securing itself or its people.

Despite being a fundamental source of instability and insecurity, the African state still remains the primary actor for implementing solutions and the focal point for engagement. The inherited legacy of centralized control and preserving the status quo continues to foster the deeply held belief that only the state and its traditional security organs—particularly the military—are capable of ensuring real security, despite evidence to the contrary. Thus, a severely flawed top-down approach to security continues to be a defining characteristic of the African approach to security solutions even in the new century.

Nonetheless, things are indeed changing. The rising acceptance of the human security framework has forced African (and non-African) governments and institutions to rethink their state-centric approach to building security and their need for greater societal involvement from the bottom up. The dramatic growth since the turn of the century in the number of African civil society groups, domestic and international NGOs, international governmental organizations (IGOs), and private organizations tackling the continent's pressing security challenges is evidence of the new face of African security engagement.

Most of this change is being driven by pure necessity. Despite the overall decline in violence and conflict since the end of the Cold War, African countries and leaders, by and large, have yet to mitigate the root causes of domestic conflict and insecurity. In addition, they are ill-prepared to deal with the dramatic growth of non-traditional and transnational security threats. The resulting erosion of African state power and its inability to safeguard its citizenry is not the cause of this situation, but indicative of the symptomatic failure of the state itself and its discredited approach to building security. This vacuum has in turn propelled the entry of an increasing and diverse number of non-state actors into the security sector and is forcing a critically needed reassessment of the role of the state. Despite its flaws and inefficiencies, the African state is here to stay and will undoubtedly continue to be the dominant actor within any new framework. However, it will need to do so by reinventing itself to these new realities and to a multipolar approach that more effectively aligns its ways and means with that of society's broader security objectives.

The recasting of the role of the state in security has several significant implications for international security engagement as well. First, the structure of the global nation-state system means that the African state and its central government will continue to be the primary conduit for interaction with other states and bilateral and multilateral security relationships. This status quo, however, will likely be tempered by the rise of non-state actor-state security relationships. This will be especially true in the areas of health, food, and environmental security with African and international NGOs, along with IGOs and private foundations benefiting most from this trend.

Second, along with an increased role for non-state actors, Africa has witnessed the growth in importance of sub-regional and regional security organizations. Originally created as economic integration structures in the 1970s and 1980s, sub-regional economic communities, such as Economic Community of West African States or the Southern African Development Community, now play an essential role in the continent's security architecture. Likewise, the AU's charter and security mechanism have dramatically evolved since the days of the old Organization of Africa Unity (OAU) to assume a more proactive and cooperative peace and security role. The result of all these changes signals a decline in state unilateralism and less control by individual governments over security issues.

And finally, the declining utility of a state-centric approach will force Africa's international security partners to rethink their longstanding pattern of engagement and the provision of security assistance. Heretofore military-to-military engagement has been the lynchpin of Western engagement on the continent and has worked to shore up African regimes and maintain the status quo while also advancing Western security priorities. The heavy focus on counterterrorism programs since 2001 is a prime example of this quid pro quo. Yet the shift toward a human security approach will require international donors, like the United States and France, to shift gears away from their militaries as the primary tools of engagement toward a greater focus on development and diplomatic tools. And this will be exceedingly difficult. Decades of relying on military-to-military relationships as the foundation of bilateral assistance will be hard to change; vested African and non-African interests, bureaucratic momentum, and a psychological reluctance to commit fully to the human security construct will undoubtedly hinder progress even as the power of the state continues to wane.

Since the onset of independence the state-centric approach has been the chief driver of African security priorities. It continues to linger despite its declining usefulness in tackling the continent's current problems because it produces a short-term benefit of ensuring the status quo and reinforces the self-fulfilling prophecy that there are no other viable alternatives. As we have seen, this outmoded approach is proving ineffective at addressing the challenges of a new century, which require a broad range of actors and a more multi-faceted, decentralized approach to building African security. Human security appears to offer the best solution, but even if it does not, the role of the state will never be the same.

The roots of African cooperative security

Regionalism and cooperative security are now at the heart of the continent's approach to its security challenges. "Regionalism" implies cooperation among states in geographically proximate areas for the pursuit of mutual gain, while "cooperative security" attempts to broaden security beyond traditional military concerns to change state behavior from one of competition to cooperation with other states. Not surprisingly, this mix of regionalism and cooperative security has produced some of the "most effective regional security structures in the post-Cold War era."[3] The adoption of this strategy was spurred by a growing sense of regional awareness and collective identity to the extent that Africa became what Emanuel Adler calls a "cognitive region."[4] That is to say that following independence, African leaders and elites perceived themselves to be members of an "African" international society based on a degree of shared historical experiences and cultural ties. At the core of this notion was the ideology of African nationalism that paved the way to today's cooperative security framework.

Early discourses about African nationalism and identity were based on the concept of Pan-Africanism, which referred to the idea "that all Africans have a spiritual affinity with each other and that, having suffered together in the past, they must march together into a new and brighter future."[5] Apart from encouraging the campaign against apartheid in South Africa, Pan-Africanism, however, made little practical headway and failed to instigate the formation of a pluralist society of sovereign states in Africa.[6] Nevertheless, this shared cognitive consciousness would lay the groundwork for a common African security culture reflective of core assumptions, leaders' beliefs and values, and the efficacy of specific approaches. An articulation of this can be found in the documents and statements of the AU and its officials, its predecessor the OAU, as well as in foreign policy pronouncements of its member states, particularly expressions of collective identity, solidarity and what counts as appropriate and legitimate conduct.[7]

From the OAU ...

The establishment of the OAU was a crucial moment in the process of norm socialization in Africa.[8] The OAU was established in 1963 out of what Colin Legum described as "historic necessity and a welter of conflicting political ideas and interests."[9] Haile Selassie noted at the time that the idea behind the establishment of the OAU was to "create a single institution to which we will all belong, based on principles to which we all subscribe."[10] This, however, was easier said than done.

The eventual formation of the OAU reflected a rather fragile compromise between three distinct—and often competing—geopolitical currents that ran through the continent at the time: namely, Francophone, Anglophone, and Arab.[11] By the time of the OAU negotiations this had created two competing visions of African unity. One was dubbed the "United States of Africa" where Kwame Nkrumah and Julius Nyerere argued for the future formation of a single continental government. The other vision of African unity envisioned a "United Nations of Africa," which eventually won the day and was exemplified by the creation of an organization of newly independent, sovereign African states.

Four of the OAU's subsequent articles of faith as set out in its founding charter provided the foundation for the organization's security culture.[12] First, imperialism was identified as the principle obstacle to achieving African unity, which meant that African disputes had to be quarantined from external, non-African influences. The second principle was that of sovereign equality and, as Legum observed, "consensus politics is, in fact, a crucial aspect of the 'African way of doing things'."[13] The third principle relates to the institutionalization of the norm of non-intervention in line with the United Nations Charter and the principle of sovereign equality. As Nyerere stated, this norm meant that "we must avoid judging each other's internal policies, recognizing that each country has special problems."[14] The final principle that contributed to the OAU's security culture was that of *uti possidetis* or the legal doctrine asserting that existing colonial boundaries would become international boundaries of the new countries upon achieving independence.[15]

At a Council of Ministers meeting in 1979, the OAU decided to divide Africa up into five sub-regions corresponding to the number of regional economic communities (RECs) in existence at the time, while also promoting the establishment of other new RECs.[16] The 1991 Abuja Treaty, which sought to rationalize the Pan-African and regional agendas, established that the RECs would henceforth form part of the constitutive elements of a Pan-African integration agenda. (The AU has retained this organizational structure, which as we shall see has become the building blocks of its security engagement.)

The OAU did not fare very well in the field of direct security-related activities.[17] Although the organization managed to institutionalize a number of norms and standards, the OAU was never able to effectively enforce them on its member states. Arguably the most poignant example in this regard was the outlawing of the use of mercenaries with the 1985 Convention for the Elimination of Mercenarism in Africa, which failed miserably to prevent the use of mercenaries and private military companies by states, such as Sierra Leone, during its protracted civil war.

Besides the setting of standards and norms, in addition the OAU took steps to upgrade its conflict prevention and management capacity.[18] The AU, for example, incorporated the OAU's 1993 *Declaration on the Establishment of the OAU of a Mechanism for Conflict Prevention, Management and Resolution* into its enforcement mechanism under the AU Peace and Security Council (AUPSC).[19] The OAU also ventured ineffectively into the field of peace support operations in Chad (1981–82), Rwanda (1990–93), Burundi (1993–96), and the Comoros (1997–99). Nonetheless these early efforts set the stage for the growth and development of future conflict prevention and peacekeeping mechanisms.

... to the AU

The ambitious design of the African Union as the successor of the OAU, as set out in its 2000 Constitutive Act, was already taking shape at a remarkable pace in 2004.[20] Less than two years after the AU's inauguration in Durban, South Africa, member states were already busy moving from the paper and ratification process to the launch of two key organs of the organization: the Peace and Security Council and the Pan-African Parliament. The new institutions were intended to ensure a greater degree of enforcement and oversight of the AU's decisions. The perceived weakness of the OAU was that it lacked both the will and the means to enforce its decisions, given that public commitments made by heads of states and governments to ensure peace and security, respect for democracy, the safeguarding human rights and the rule of law were often broken with impunity. So much so, that the OAU was often seen as "a dictators' club," where personal relationships and self-serving interests trumped the interests of the African people.

The Constitutive Act underlined the need to "promote peace, security and stability as a prerequisite for the implementation of our development and integration agenda" and expressed the determination "to promote and protect human and peoples' rights," consolidate democratic institutions and culture, and to ensure good governance and the rule of law.[21] One could argue that there are seven norms contained in the Act that the AU adopted and institutionalized which constitute the

AU's central tenets of its security culture: 1) sovereign equality of its members; 2) non-intervention by member states; 3) anti-imperialism; African solutions first; 4) *uti possidetis*; 5) non-use of force; peaceful settlement of disputes; 6) condemnation of unconstitutional changes of governments; and 7) the Union's right to intervene in a member state in instances of grave circumstances or threats to regional security.[22]

What is of particular interest is the decision to establish the continent's first continent-wide, regional, collective security system, the AUPSC. It was agreed at the Addis Ababa Summit in July 2002 to establish the AUPSC, intended as "an operations structure for the effective implementations of the decisions taken in the areas of conflict prevention, peace-making, peace support operations and intervention, as well as peace-building and post-conflict reconstruction."[23] Following ratification by 27 of the AU's 53 member states the AUPSC protocol entered into force in December 2003. Thus, the AUPSC joined the ranks of the Economic Community of West African States (ECOWAS) Mechanism on Conflict Prevention, Management and Resolution, Peace-Keeping and Security and the South African Development Community (SADC) Organ of Politics, Defence and Security Cooperation as one of the three African mechanisms established to manage conflict on the continent through inter alia military intervention and diplomacy.[24] Moreover, the objectives of the AUPSC were not new to the African political landscape, rather they complemented the principles enshrined in the Constitutive Act and echoed earlier attempts at building a collective security framework.[25]

More than ever before, it was realized that there was an urgent need for a strong and robust response to the challenges of peace and security on the continent, which spurred the creation of the Panel of the Wise, The Continental Early Warning System, and the African Standby Force (ASF). While all three of these organs form part of the AU's strategic response mechanism, the ASF has become "one of the most important—and probably the most ambitious—institutional tools" of the AUPSC.[26] Should preventive diplomacy through either the chairman of the Commission or the Panel of the Wise fail in conflict resolution attempts, the AUPSC system should trigger the rapid deployment of a standby force of peacekeepers to prevent or reduce bloodletting.[27]

The ASF was meant to be the centerpiece of African efforts to bridge the gap between international foot dragging or lack of effective involvement in restoring peace and the deployment of peacekeepers on the ground. Organized into five sub-regional brigades of 5,000 men each, every ASF brigade was envisioned as a light, flexible, and mobile force that was capable of rapid deployment. Specific brigades were to be co-located within each of the existing five sub-RECs to reinforce a common sub-regional identity, speed reaction, and enhance situational awareness. Overlapping sub-regional memberships and/or divergent ASF organizational boundaries, however, have created problems. Likewise, the lack of clarity as to where the AU lines of authority end and those of the economic communities begin has created more confusion. Not surprisingly, the actual stand up date for the ASF kept being delayed. More recently, the AU is considering establishing yet another immediate response force called the African Capacity for Immediate Response to Conflict but this, too, is far from being implemented.

Nonetheless, African peacekeepers from individual countries or as part of a multinational force are often the first to arrive in the conflict zone, paving the way for a more vigorous follow on global response and increasingly effective African-international cooperation. Lacking a formal, established peacekeeping structure, however, these interventions are usually ad hoc affairs and fraught with problems. The initial AU Mission in Somalia (AMISOM) was very much a hybrid force consisting of several extra-sub-regional forces rather than emanating from elements of the East African ASF brigade. Moreover AMISOM would never have been operational had it not been for funding, logistics, and intelligence provided by a variety of Western countries. Similarly, in terms of the 2012 Malian intervention, it was the French military taking a primary role and then working on a bilateral basis with West African states to stabilize the country. In the case of CAR, the South Africans were already present as part of a bilateral training mission. This mission was then converted to a peace enforcement mission in 2013, although the South Africans were not equipped for such a task and as a result had to be extricated.

Still the AU has achieved new levels of regional cooperative security and activism beyond anything accomplished by its predecessor. Far from being "an old boys' club" or "talk shop," the AU has demonstrated its willingness to address threats to African peace and security through interventionist policies. The track record of the nearly decade-long peacekeeping mission in Somalia is a case in point. Originally conceived as a bridgehead to UN intervention, AMISOM has persevered in the face of significant military and logistical challenges. Likewise, al-Shabaab's escalating campaign of cross-border terrorist violence into Kenya and Uganda (two of AMISOM's key troop contributors) has failed to undermine political support for the mission. But the AUPSC is still very much a work in progress. Controversial long-term challenges to stability (especially those surrounding human rights, the rule of law, and democratic transparency) are often sidestepped by the AU when politically expedient. Serious shortfalls in funding, logistics, and administrative support have rendered the ASF a stillborn dream. As Cilliers and Sturman warn, "a failed intervention can do as much damage as failing to intervene at all" and "an inappropriate response to a complex emergency situation ... [may take] the situation from bad to worse."[28]

The AU's workhorse: the sub-regional security mechanisms

While strategic guidance and administration is the purview of the AU, the conflict response mechanisms of its sub-regional bodies (also known as the regional economic communities or RECs), such as ECOWAS, the SADC, and the Intergovernmental Authority on Development (IGAD), form the essence of the AU's overall security architecture and it is the area that has seen the most significant expansion. In this context, the AU commits itself to "harmonize and coordinate" with sub-regional mechanisms to achieve peace, security, and stability on the continent "through the exchange of information and analyses" and the establishment of liaison offices.[29] The RECs for their part are seen not only as implementing organs of the AUPSC, but also as assuming greater responsibility for independently addressing challenges to peace and stability within their own respective regions. Thus, the RECs have increasingly come to be seen as the leading edge of African security engagement.

The intervention by ECOWAS in Liberia in 1990 brought the organization to international attention, and marked a watershed for the emerging security role of the RECs, because it showed the world that sub-regional structures will not stand idly by whilst massive crimes are perpetrated during factional conflict. It also clearly showed that the conceptual and empirical sanctity of the norms of sovereignty and non-intervention in a state's affairs would not serve as a barrier for collective action. Despite its near disastrous beginning with the Nigerian-led monitoring group in Liberia in 1990, ECOWAS follow on intervention in Liberia is largely regarded as a success. Likewise, the assistance of a large ECOWAS military force led to the successful restoration of Ahmad Tejan Kabbah as president of Sierra Leone in 1998.

In both cases, ECOWAS established its Cease-fire Monitoring Group that ultimately helped in restoring peace and stability to both countries and established a template for successful peacekeeping operations. The ECOWAS deployments prepared the way for more robust UN missions using African peacekeepers—the United Nations Mission in Liberia, the United Nations Observer Mission in Sierra Leone, and later the United Nations Mission in Sierra Leone. Moreover, it demonstrated that sub-regional organizations (even ones suffering from structural, financial, or logistic problems) were capable of reacting to conflict situations in their regions much quicker and with expert local knowledge not available to other international organizations, even if only as a stopgap until these operations can be supported and/or supplemented by a more robust AU or UN presence.

Despite being the centerpiece of the AU's enhanced peace and security efforts, as well as a focal point for international engagement and collective sub-regional security, progress toward building stronger and more capable conflict mitigation mechanisms and peacekeeping capacity has been mixed and very uneven across the RECs. Persistent problems with a lack of resources, inadequate (or unrealistic) planning and support, operational and logistical challenges, and political infighting and mistrust have hindered their institutional development. Even more challenging is overcoming what Soderbaum and Tavares call "the African paradox"—asking governments to cede sovereignty to regional organizations in the name of security even as that sovereignty eludes them because they lack the ability to govern parts of their own countries.[30]

Nonetheless, the picture is not as bleak as the naysayers would have one believe. The ECOWAS and SADC have made great strides in developing their peacekeeping and crisis intervention capability over the years, both in terms of organizations and among individual member states. Now with regularized and specialized training, better equipment, and the establishment of fusion centers, permanent secretariats, and early warning mechanisms ECOWAS and SADC have participated in dozens of successful missions within their own regions and across the continent. Moreover, in contrast to the past where large countries such as Nigeria and South Africa dominated these operations, smaller countries like Botswana, Ghana, Niger, Mozambique, and Rwanda are now more effectively sharing much of the organizational and manpower burden. ECOWAS's partnership and engagement with the international community at the bilateral, multilateral, and IGO level in particular is now increasingly being seen as a template for successful development.

Likewise, thanks to the efforts of the Kenyan and Ugandan governments IGAD is also growing its capacity and has shown amazing resilience in the face of decades of persistent regional turmoil. Well known for its activist role in regional mediation—successfully in Sudan's north-south conflict and unsuccessfully in Somali reconciliation efforts—IGAD has steadily expanded its military intervention capability and both Kenya and Uganda have played prominent bilateral roles as well in supporting AU and UN operations in Somalia since 2007.

At the other end of the spectrum, significant obstacles to the development of regional security in Central Africa remain hampered by the lack of a clear lead country, inadequate funding, the existence of multiple overlapping sub-regional bodies (the Economic Community of Central African States, the Central African Monetary and Economic Community (CEMAC), and the Economic Community of the Great Lakes Countries), and the acceptance of a fragmented approach to security issues.[31] The latter is indicative of "regionalism a la carte" that avoids compromising members' autonomy, requires few commitments and contributions, and allows members to pursue their own self-interests, which allows individual states to "demonstrate their authority and artificially boost their power without fear [of being] ... pushed into directions that may compromise their interests."[32]

Despite these major obstacles, intense domestic turmoil in the CAR precipitated the deployment of a *Force Multinationale en Centrafrique* by CEMAC in 2002 and although ultimately unsuccessful at stemming the unrest, the action was a watershed moment in the organization's history.[33] Other post-2002 interventions by CEMAC and the Economic Community of Central African States have also proven largely ineffective, but many of the security problems of Central Africa have taxed the resources of much larger and capable organizations too; the UN effort in the eastern DRC has lasted more than 15 years, required the presence of some 20,000 peacekeepers, and cost nearly $15 billion and yet peace and stability are as elusive as ever. Even as member states grapple with institutionalizing a regional security response, several countries, such as Burundi, Chad, and Rwanda, are unilaterally boosting their capabilities by partnering with Western governments (particularly France) and serving directly in AU and UN peacekeeping missions.

The outlook is even bleaker in North Africa where efforts at building a regional security consciousness, let alone security structure, remain stillborn. The member states are not only facing many of the same obstacles as their Central African brethren, but long-running bilateral animosities (like those between Morocco and Algeria over the Western Sahara), Morocco's strained relationship with the AU, and disintegration of the Libyan state have stifled any progress. The Arab Maghreb Union—of which Egypt is not even a member—remains an empty shell, both economically and as a security mechanism. The North Africa Regional Standby Brigade exists only on paper, so North African countries have largely opted for a go it alone or an ad hoc approach to sub-regional threats.

Despite all the challenges facing the development of the REC's sub-regional security mechanisms, they have come a remarkable way. Overall they are stronger organizations, more focused, and with improved capabilities to support their security mission. Yes, much more needs to be done and some regions lag badly behind, but the progress to date in building cooperative security has been substantial. The prominent role that the AU has assigned to its sub-regional organizations will allow the AU to build further on the REC's comparative advantage, experience and established frameworks and mechanisms for conflict prevention, management and resolution.[34] The REC's proximity to regional conflicts provides them with a better understanding of its dynamics, key players, and context-specific management and resolution options. Moreover, sub-regional leaders and organizations may be more accountable and vested in their pursuits than Pan-African and international organizations, and therefore give them a greater stake in finding a peaceful solution to the conflict. While certainly not a panacea to the continent's security challenges, the current framework provides a useful way forward that promotes African independence while concurrently building international security partnerships.

Thinking locally: grassroots security initiatives

As a consequence of colonial governance, the post-independence emphasis on national unity and nation building, and Western engagement predilections (which will be addressed in the following chapter), African

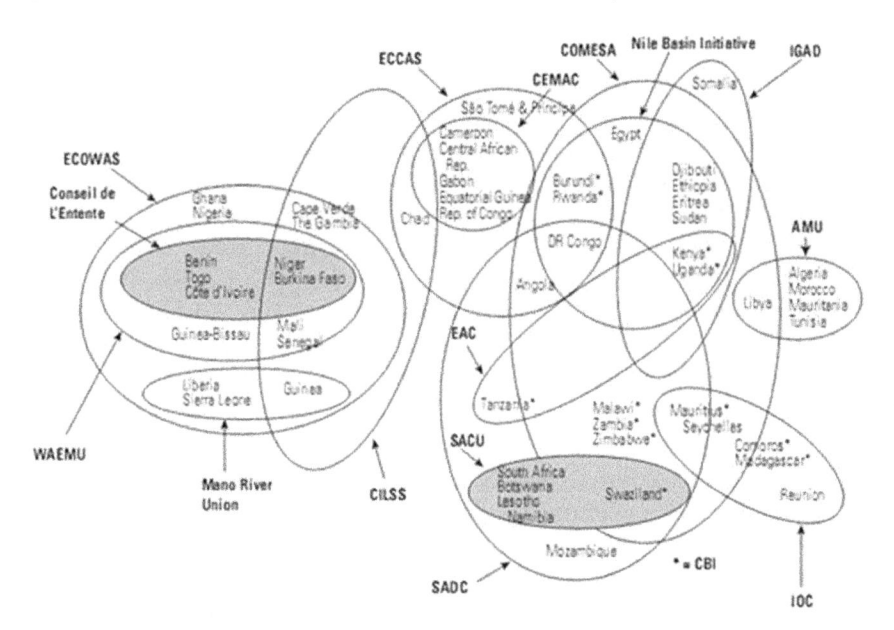

Figure 2 Regional economic community diagram
Source: World Bank staff

security solutions have typically been state-centric, highly centralized, and government-driven from the top down, reflecting a very traditional approach to enhancing security. The growing acceptance of the human security paradigm in Africa, however, has highlighted the often ineffectual and inappropriateness of this approach. As has been highlighted throughout this book, security today is more about improving the lives and welfare of people than about preserving and protecting the institution of the nation-state. Without the former, the latter is nothing more than a hollow shell detached from society that will eventually implode and collapse.

Although the focus on grassroots initiatives that promote the advancement of human security is a relatively recent post-Cold War phenomenon, the concept of home-grown or community-based security is not new to Africa or African societies. Challenges regarding food security, health and welfare, environmental degradation, and most of all conflict were typically handled at the local level prior to the onset of European colonialism. Even within larger more cohesive African empires, power tended to be much more decentralized and problems handled within existing customary societal structures. As we noted in Chapter 1, it was the advent of European colonial rule that sought to reinvent African societies into sharply defined "tribal" identities with rigid hierarchical structures of governance, and to build strong, centralized state security mechanisms. The ultimate goal was the continuation of the status quo and the maintenance of colonial power. It was this top-down approach to security that African leaders inherited at independence and embraced as the most effective way to ensure national unity and, moreover, safeguard their grip on power. The effect of the Cold War in Africa only further served to reinforce the twin tenets of regime security and status quo stability.

Now, however, with African societies facing a more diverse and increasingly complex set of security challenges, this approach is outmoded and increasingly ineffective at boosting security, and Africans are coming full cycle to once again embrace grassroots, bottom-up solutions to their security problems.

Often overlooked or minimized, grassroots security initiatives provide some of the most effective and least resource demanding security solutions. The latter point is particularly important given the scarcity of national resources in most countries and the often limited reach of central government authority. In often sharp contrast to widely touted large-scale national or international initiatives, home-grown grassroots programs tend to show a very high degree of ownership and commitment that makes them more sustainable. Most important, these programs address actual local security priorities, not externally imposed ones and avoid the all too common 'if you fund it, we will do it' model of priority setting.

The driving force behind these initiatives is an expansive, yet very loose, collection of individual activists, civil society groups, domestic NGOs, and local leaders, who heretofore have been largely excluded from the security debate or marginalized. While many of these groups have long been active in socio-economic, education, and health issues, they remained largely on the fringes of the security debate. The one notable exception is the highly visible and activist role of women's groups in post-conflict peacebuilding and community reconciliation efforts. Grassroots efforts by newly formed civil society groups in the mid-1990s in Rwanda (such as *Pro-Femmes Twese Hamwe*) proved critical in advancing post-conflict reconstruction and reconciliation, as they also have in other war-torn parts of the continent. One such example is The Mano River Women's Peace Network created in 2000.[35]

This type of activism, along with the growing acceptance of the human security paradigm, has fueled the growth—and moreover, the acknowledgement—of civil society's inclusion as developing and implementing security solutions. These groups bring a completely different set of tools, skills, and perspectives to the table. With their local knowledge and networks they have the ability to more effectively mobilize community support and create buy-in for new programs. This is particularly important in that it avoids the often heavy hand of central government intervention and a reliance on the military instrument of power.

Moreover, in many instances local initiatives are better suited for dealing with many of the non-traditional and transnational challenges facing African governments today. Addressing the challenges of small arms proliferation, drug trafficking, the spread of pandemic disease, and dealing with environmental degradation, demand holistic solutions that fundamentally require broad-based societal participation and support. Activists, civil society groups, domestic NGOs, and local leaders are all part of the equation, and many are at the cutting edge of new approaches. Although focused primarily on seeking ways to enhance individual and community security, the nature of many of these challenges often lends itself to the development of broader, cross-cutting solutions to national and regional problems as well. For example, community efforts to ensure a reliable supply of clean water and wood for fuel have direct implications for protecting the local eco-system, but also address the larger security issues of land degradation and livelihood conflict, natural resource exploitation and competition, health (waterborne diseases), and climate change.

Greatly facilitating the effectiveness and reach of these groups have been global advancements in technology and communications, which reduce organizational cost while expanding membership, providing new opportunities for social mobilization, building regional and international partnerships, and opening new doors for funding. While usually created to address a very specific local problem, many of these groups have now blossomed into fully fledged transnational organizations with continental reach—and influence. The Coalition for Grassroots Women Organization was formed in 1996 to help defuse clan conflict in Somalia, but has now become a national umbrella organization for some 26 Somali NGOs doing everything from peacebuilding and agrarian reform to health care delivery and education initiatives.[36] Likewise, the Kenyan-based Agency for Cooperation and Research in Development now works with 2,000 partners and community groups in 17 countries across the continent to promote peacebuilding, women's rights, community health care, and food security.[37] Many other groups, however, continue to focus on their core mission, often with a high degree of success; Gun Free South Africa worked to build a powerful gun control alliance that was influential in passing the Firearms Control Bill of 2000, which is believed to have cut gun deaths by half from 1998–2009.[38]

While African civil society has more than justified its relevance and inclusion in helping to craft security solutions, not all of the continent's security challenges are conducive to this type of engagement at the grassroots level. The bottom-up approach works best in tackling issues that require extensive social mobilization and community buy-in, produce immediate and recognizable security benefits, contain an educational component, and result in simple and easy to replicate solutions. This is where the comparative advantage of grassroots security initiatives lies; it can best be applied to:

- *Conflict mediation and peacebuilding.* The tradition of grassroots involvement by religious leaders, community activists, civil society groups (especially women's groups), and local NGOs is a proven model of conflict mitigation in both the pre- and post-conflict stages. It has been successfully applied to some of Africa's most divided societies—Angola, Nigeria, Rwanda, and South Africa—where a volatile mix of identity and resource/political conflict has yielded much human suffering. So much so, that the participation of local groups is now widely accepted as a core component of post-conflict reconstruction and is fully integrated into peacekeeping planning. While there certainly have been setbacks (eastern DRC or Somalia) and local

activism does have its limits, the way forward toward greater, not less, engagement is clear.
- *Small arms proliferation.* This is another area where longstanding grassroots security initiatives have been highly successful at building a constituency, raising local, national, and even regional awareness, and producing concrete programs of action. Once not even on the radar of policymakers and security planners, the issue of small arms proliferation and its important linkages to other security challenges (such as failing states, identity and resource conflict, crime, and domestic violence) has gained enormous traction across the continent. West Africa leads the way with its vast and robust network of national and sub-regional organizations, but no part of the continent is excluded. Not only have these groups put pressure on national governments to enact local legislation, the UN Programme of Action on Small Arms and Light Weapons, and other sub-regional protocols (such as ECOWAS Convention on SALW or the SADC Protocol on the Control of Firearms, Ammunition and Related Materials), but they have become a significant force on the global stage too by partnering with international IGOs and NGOs. The success of this grassroots-government partnership, however, has been tempered by the inability of this model to address the flow of weaponry coming from chronic lawless and unstable states, such as Libya and Somalia.
- *Health care.* Community involvement in improving health care delivery, health education, and general quality of life has long been a critical prerequisite for advancing health security in Africa. However, many well-intentioned initiatives are externally driven—either dictated from the central government or enacted as part of international aid packages. Thus, these beneficial programs often lack essential community support, are frequently misunderstood or viewed with suspicion, and are difficult to sustain once external assistance wanes. To redress this situation, grassroots health initiatives have become one of the fastest growing components of engagement in the African health sector. Often in partnership with IGOs and international NGOs, local health education programs are making a real difference in terms of improving nutrition, disease prevention, better sanitation and access to clean water, and ameliorating women and child mortality rates. As the 2014–15 West African Ebola outbreak demonstrated, community-based efforts were an essential ingredient in containing and ultimately stopping the spread of the virus, thanks to a combination of training for community health volunteers, preventative education, and the implementation of screening and detection programs.

- *Food security and the environment.* The historic African attachment to the land is one that transcends political, socio-economic, and cultural differences, and forms a powerful spiritual connection that long predates the modern environmental movement. Likewise, the competition to control fertile land and water resources has also been a perennial source of conflict for much of African history. And it was often a life-and-death struggle. Community-based organizations recognize the importance of their environment as a sustainable source of food and its prominent role in conflict resolution. Accordingly, they have strived in recent years to advance land reform, secure individual and communal property rights, limit development-related environmental damage, and address climate change. However, it has been an uphill struggle that often pits local communities against much more powerful and entrenched corporate and government interests; interests that frequently equate unbridled economic development with increased security and stability. Nonetheless, African environmental challenges are likely to evolve and become an increasing part of the security debate in the decades ahead, moving well beyond social concerns to become an essential component of the broader human security construct.

Popular participation from the bottom up, and inclusionary solutions, are fundamental building blocks of human security, and are critical when it comes to addressing the challenging African security environment. Fortunately, African civil society and community-based groups have a long and strong tradition of engagement and mobilization across various political, social, economic issues. Thus, increasing their role and involvement in the security arena should be seen as part of a natural evolution. An increasingly globalized world and advancements in technology and communications will undoubtedly facilitate this transformation and create new roles for these groups. It remains to be seen, however, how accepting security traditionalists and those in power will be of this new dynamic and, moreover, how willing they are to work with these new partners to enhance security for all.

Prospects for the future

Although not yet anachronistic, the African state is steadily losing its position as the pre-eminent security actor. A legacy of colonialism, inherited security mechanisms and thinking, and the creation of a patchwork of fragile independent African states have produced entities plagued by widespread corruption, with questionable legitimacy, and frequently lacking a monopoly of coercive force. The result is a state structure that relies on a multiplicity of formal and informal power relations and is ill-equipped to deal with the challenges that it now faces.

Thus, the failure of the state-centric approach to security, and the rising tide of non-traditional security threats, have mandated change. While not completely abandoning the state's role, Africans have adopted a cooperative security model through the African Union and sub-regional organizations as the most effective approach to solving the continent's security challenges. The evolution of regional and sub-regional security mechanisms since 2000 reflects a changed security culture that places collective security and the interests of continental peace over the narrow self-interests of state security. Although far from perfect in implementation, this growing pan-African vision of security means Africans are increasingly taking responsibility for their problems, and are holding their leaders and governments more accountable. The rise of civil society's engagement in the security sector is also further broadening the level of national participation, and thus strengthening not only the legitimacy of the state, but of the human security construct.

The path ahead, however, will be a difficult one. The AU's ambitious security architecture mechanisms are still in their embryonic stages, and while regional and sub-regional security engagement, particularly in the area of peacekeeping operations, has been encouraging there are still noticeable shortcomings.[39] No matter how popular the phrase "African solutions to African problems" may be, the fact of the matter is that African states, and regional and sub-regional organizations are currently not able to conduct any sustained or long-term peace support operations on the continent without the requisite financial, logistical, and technological capacity of external donors. In addition, the same level of commitment has not fully been translated to other security challenges, such as public health, food security, climate change, and migration. These non-traditional security issues often require long-term commitments, but due to the nature of Africa's many impoverished states and their lack of resources, they have often ceded responsibility to international organizations, aid agencies, and development partners.

While chronic state weakness, poor governance, and lack of resources will continue to hinder the development of centrally controlled African security mechanisms, civil society and community-based groups are playing a growing—and independent—role through the development of their response capability. Given their specialized local knowledge and presence, these groups have been able to work at the grassroots level in areas where central governments and international organizations are often reluctant or unable to venture, making them an attractive alternative for engagement. Moreover, many international NGOs and foreign organizations are now channeling financial resources directly to grassroots organizations and thus bypassing corrupt and ineffective institutional mechanisms.

Beyond the immediate security benefits, these local initiatives are also advancing the democratization processes and hopefully spurring governmental reform. Their mobilization efforts, mass campaigns, and educational awareness efforts on specific issues have the added long-term benefit of engaging people and making governmental institutions more accountable. This undoubtedly reinforces the positive links between human security and democratic inclusion.

With a strong and cohesive vision of African peace and security, African leaders, governments, institutions, and communities are stepping up to the challenge of implementation and indeed moving forward. The forceful stance taken by ECOWAS in supporting the electoral outcome in The Gambia that ousted strongman Yahya Jammeh as president in 2017 is but one such recent example. However, there are no quick fixes and it will be difficult. There will be pitfalls and backsliding, as we have seen on the process of democratization and a return to the regime security paradigm in places like Egypt, Ethiopia, and Uganda. The engagement and support of the international community will be essential, both in terms of resource commitment and perseverance. A lot has been accomplished over the past few decades with Africans bringing at least relative peace to some areas of the conflict-ridden continent and making inroads against other emerging challenges. This is important because in an increasingly globalized and interconnected world their success is the world's success too.

Notes

1 Araoye, 'Hegemonic agendas, intermesticity and conflicts in the post-colonial state', *African Journal on Conflict Resolution*, 12:1 (2012), 10.
2 Ibid.
3 C. Snyder, 'Regional security structures', in C. Snyder (ed.), *Contemporary Security and Strategy* (Basingstoke: Macmillan, 1999), pp. 102–19.
4 E. Adler, 'Imagined (security) communities: Cognitive regions in international relations', *Millennium: Journal of International Studies*, 26:2 (1997), 249–77.
5 R. Emerson, 'Pan-Africanism', *International Organization*, 16:2 (1962), 280.
6 Ibid., 288.
7 P. Williams, 'From non-intervention to non-indifference: The origins of development of the African Union's security culture', *African Affairs* 106:423 (2007), 257.
8 Ibid., pp. 253–79.

9 C. Legum, 'The organisation of African unity—success or failure?' *International Affairs*, 51:2 (1975), 208.
10 H. Selassie, 'Towards African unity', *Journal of Modern African Studies*, 1:3 (1963), 285.
11 Legum, 'The organisation of African unity', p. 209.
12 Selassie, 'Towards African unity', p. 287.
13 Legum, 'The organisation of African unity', p. 214.
14 J. Nyerere, 'A United States of Africa', *Journal of Modern African Studies*, 1:1 (1963), 5.
15 Williams, 'From non-intervention to non-indifference', pp. 253–79.
16 K. Powell, 'The African Union and the regional mechanisms for conflict prevention, management and resolution', in K. Powell, *The African Union's Emerging Peace and Security Regime* (ISS Monograph Series No. 119, May 2005), p. 19.
17 B. Møller, 'The African Union as security actor: African solutions to African problems?' *Crisis States* (Working Papers Series 2:57, London: Crisis States Research Centre, August 2009), p. 6.
18 Ibid., p. 7.
19 J. Levitt, 'The Peace and Security Council of the African Union: The known unknowns', *Transnational Law and Contemporary Problems*, 13:109 (Summer 2003), 109–37.
20 J. Cilliers and K. Sturman, 'Challenges facing the AU's Peace and Security Council', *African Security Review*, 13:1 (2004), 97–104.
21 African Union, *Constitutive Act of the African Union* (Adopted July 11, 2000), accessed at www.au.int/en/sites/default/files/Constitutive_Act_en_0.htm on February 28, 2017.
22 Ibid.
23 Assembly of the African Union, First Ordinary Session, *Protocol Relating to the Establishment of the Peace and Security Council of the African Union* (July 9, 2002), accessed at www.au.int/en/sites/default/files/Protocol_peace_and_security.pdf on February 28, 2017.
24 Levitt, 'The Peace and Security Council of the African Union', pp. 109–37.
25 Ibid.
26 H. Solomon, 'The role and place of the African Standby Force within the African Peace and Security Architecture', *ISS Paper 209* (Institute for Security Studies, January 2010), p. 1.
27 Cilliers and Sturman, 'Challenges facing the AU's Peace and Security Council', 97–104.
28 J. Cilliers and K. Sturman, 'The right intervention: Enforcement challenge for the African Union', *African Security Review*, 11:3 (2002).
29 Assembly of the African Union, First Ordinary Session.
30 F. Soderbaum and R. Tavares, *Regional Organizations in African Security* (New York: Routledge, 2011), p. 146.
31 A. Meyer, *Regional Integration and Security in Central Africa—Assessment and Perspectives 10 Years After the Revival* (Brussels, Belgium: Egmont—The

Royal Institute for International Relations, December 2008), p. 27; A. Meyer, *Peace and Security Cooperation in Central Africa* (Uppsala, Sweden: Nordiska Afrikainstitutet, 2011), p. 10.

32 Meyer, *Regional Integration and Security in Central Africa*, p. 26-7.
33 See Meyer, *Peace and Security Cooperation in Central Africa*, pp. 26-8 for a detailed assessment of the CAR intervention.
34 Powell, *The African Union's Emerging Peace and Security Regime*, p. 19.
35 K. Hussein, D. Gnisci, and J. Wanjiru, 'Security and human security: An overview of concepts and initiatives. What implications for West Africa?' (Paris, December 2004), p. 21, accessed at www.oecd.org/swac/publications/38826090.pdf on February 28, 2017.
36 Coalition for Grassroots Women Organization, 'Report of COGWO board election' (February 21, 2013), accessed at http://cogwosomali.org/documents/COGWO-Election-2013.pdf on February 28, 2017.
37 Agency for Cooperation and Research in Development, 'Partners', accessed at www.acordinternational.org/acord/en/about-us/about-us/partners/ on February 28, 2017.
38 Gun Free South Africa, 'Annual report 2012–2013', accessed at www.gfsa.org.za/wp-content/uploads/2012/12/GFSA-AR_12_13_FINAL.pdf on February 28, 2017.
39 K. Aning, 'Africa: Confronting complex threats' (The International Peace Academy, February 2007), p. 11, accessed at http://africacenter.org/wp-content/uploads/2007/07/Africa-Confronting-Complex-Threats.pdf on February 28, 2017.

10

The international response

While candidly acknowledging that African governments, institutions, and societies need to take more responsibility and ought to do more to address their security, they just cannot do it alone. Given the increasingly interdependent nature of African security, the continent simply lacks the resources and capacity to tackle current and future problems. Thus, the active involvement and constructive participation of the wider global community is essential if any real—and sustainable—progress is to be made.

Simply throwing more money and resources at its problems will not work. This has been tried and it has failed. The security landscape of the continent is littered with the debris of well-intentioned, but misguided international programs that failed miserably to mitigate (much less solve) old threats or address new challenges. Their legacy is one of hundreds of billions of dollars wasted, frustrated donors, and an atmosphere of eternal pessimism for the future of Africa and its people.

International involvement must be intelligently focused, prudently implemented and done in partnership with Africans. It requires listening to African concerns. Moreover, it must, out of necessity, be geared to addressing African needs rather than a set of externally imposed security concerns and priorities. Imposing an agenda on Africans will not work. The dominant global security players who desire to make a tangible difference in the lives of Africans need to understand—and accept—that pursuing an African-driven security agenda will ultimately improve their security as well. It will, however, be a long and tedious road and one that will require great perseverance in the face of numerous setbacks and mistakes. No one said it would be easy.

What ultimately is needed is a security paradigm shift backed up with actions and not simply words. The international community and its global leadership need to move beyond just talking the talk of human security and actually begin to walk the walk. This will require an across the board overhaul of programs, tools, and strategic vision. It also means a vastly reduced role for militaries and short-term fixes, with a greater emphasis on finding the ways and means that empower people and societies through political, social, and economic development and build long-term security for all.

The changing (and changeless) face of engagement

Foreign powers, international organizations, and individuals have been drawn to Africa for centuries. From the colonial period to independence and throughout the Cold War and beyond, external actors have been instrumental in defining not only the nature of African security, but also in determining the continent's security agenda. Security during the colonial period, as we have seen, was frequently defined in terms of maintaining the power and status quo of those in authority—foreign governments, companies, or people. Even in post-independent Africa, political stability and security became synonymous with maintaining the existing order. Moreover, the continued involvement of former colonial powers and the superpowers in security matters reinforced African cynicism about their inability to determine their own future. This legacy has created lasting tension between the sensitive issue of retaining national sovereignty and the conflicting modern-day need to not only build, but enhance, international engagement.

Nonetheless, international actors have—and will continue to have—vested and legitimate security, geopolitical, economic, and humanitarian interests in Africa. This is a reality that Africans have come to accept, but the ways in which the international community engages will ultimately determine how supportive African governments and societies are of this engagement. The word "partnership" is often bandied about by outsiders, yet all too often external factors and perceptions of what is best for Africa drive the agenda. Real partnership requires listening. It means responding to African concerns and sensitivities. For this is the only effective way to solve common problems, but it will require an unprecedented level of international commitment and a transformed view of the meaning of African security.

There has been a dramatic sea change in not only the meaning of security, but also in the transformation of relations between African governments, institutions, and people and the wider international community, as well as a growing international acceptance of the human security construct and of Africa's place in today's globalized security environment.

Action by the international community, however, has not always kept pace with its rhetoric, especially for the United States. Old habits and perceptions about the nature of security in Africa die hard. Despite numerous successful examples, such as the British security sector reform effort in Sierra Leone, the US President's Emergency Plan for AIDS Relief (PEPFAR), or European community developmental assistance for health and educational infrastructure, military and hierarchical government-led programs continue to dominate Western security engagement. Fueled by more than a decade of counterterrorism initiatives, American military and security assistance to Africa has seen a steady rise to over $400 million annually, although this number is dwarfed 20:1 by non-military assistance.[1] Total American aid to all of Africa is likely to have reached more than $8 billion in 2016 with PEPFAR the largest aid component, accounting for more than 40 percent of the total.[2]

Historically a small, but very influential handful of countries led by the United States have dictated the cooperative international response to Africa's security challenges. The United States, the United Kingdom, France, and Germany not only underwrite the bulk of security assistance going to the continent, but provide critical expertise and support for a vast array of African security initiatives and programs. More important, this security engagement has increasingly become part of a holistic approach to achieving broader economic and development assistance objectives.

What has changed, however, is the nature of international engagement by the global community. It is more diverse, complex, and multifaceted than ever. Moreover, the recent entry of an entirely new set of actors—most notably China—into the African security arena is complicating coordination because of suspicions by the United States and its allies as to these countries' ultimate objectives and the potentially destabilizing effects of their actions. For even in the new era of globalized security, competing national agendas will continue to take precedence over international cooperation and hinder a truly unified response to the continent's security challenges.

While nation-states will continue to play a powerful role in African security issues, the role of international government organizations (IGOs) and quasi-governmental groups are expanding and their influence increasing at an even greater pace. This involvement goes beyond those high profile organizations with longstanding engagement in Africa, such as the United Nations and its affiliates or the European Union. This growth is not just part of these organizations' natural evolution, but reflects the rising importance of multilateralism and inter-agency collaboration that is a hallmark of the human security construct. In doing so, it broadens the pool of resources and expertise available, but it can also complicate coordination and implementation by creating unnecessary duplication, fueling infighting over priorities and objectives, and adding additional layers of bureaucracy to the mix. Nonetheless, this should be seen as a positive development because greater inclusion, a diversity of perspectives, and multiple constituencies open up new avenues and opportunities for tackling the security challenges.

Parallel to this growth in IGO engagement has been an explosion in the number of non-governmental organizations (NGOs) actively involved in some aspect of human security outreach. No longer are these international NGOs and their domestic counterparts and civil society allies willing to sit idly on the sidelines in the national and regional security debate. For their part, governments and their militaries now recognize that NGOs bring a whole new set of tools and expertise. Rather than being viewed as obstacles, NGOs are now seen as part of the solution to the continent's problems. Long-established humanitarian organizations working in Africa, like CARE, Save the Children, or Doctors without Borders, as well as newer sector- or issued-oriented groups (The Bill and Melinda Gates Foundation, Water Aid, or Women and Children First (UK) for instance) are becoming an integral—and indispensable—part of the human security equation.

Putting theory into practice, however, has not been easy for international proponents of the human security approach. Even with the best intentions, coordinating and aligning ends, ways, and means across this vast array of national governments, international organizations, and NGOs presents a monumental task. And thus, rarely is the full capability of the international community brought to bear against any single challenge. More often than not, conflicting priorities, agendas or approaches, as well as clashing institutional cultures, can make international coordination and implementation all but impossible. Likewise, the frustration "to do something" and a desire for more immediate results can spur a return to the use of hard power and over reliance on the military tool of international engagement. This is particularly true when it comes to dealing with the terrorism challenge, where the military instrument of power has once again become the centerpiece of American counterterrorism in Africa and provides a false sense of confidence, which is ultimately likely to fail.[3]

Real change in how the international community thinks about security and engages in Africa, however, is taking place. Not only is there widespread international acceptance of the human security paradigm as the cornerstone for addressing the continent's challenges, but also a recognition of the role Africa plays in building globalized peace and security. This partnership is essential, as the task transcends regional and continental boundaries with the international community finally acknowledging that there are indeed African solutions to not just African problems, but to global ones too.

Addressing Africa's security challenges

Not only will the age-old challenges of addressing ethnic, religious, and resource-fueled conflict and endemic poverty continue to plague the continent, but multiple new and unforeseen threats are likely to arise, which will stretch both African and international security resources and capabilities to breaking point. Thus, more—not less—international engagement will be required. Fortunately, there are positive signs that the international community and Africans can work together to chart a new course and build new and innovation solutions. The way forward, however, will be long and there will be many setbacks and recriminations, but the cost of failing to work together is one that neither side can afford to risk.

The old boys' club

Since the end of the Cold War, four countries—the United States, the United Kingdom, France, and Germany—have been at the forefront of international security engagement in Africa. Collectively known as the "P3+1," these governments have traditionally provided the bulk of bilateral and multilateral security assistance and have been a powerful force behind shaping the security agenda through this assistance. Hard security concerns, such as terrorism, peacekeeping, military training and readiness, and maritime security, tend to dominate their security assistance programs. Moreover, their traditionally state-centric approach to security engagement is heavily reliant on strengthening the African state and its institutions, which in turn undercuts the ability of civil society and non-state actors to play a significant role in enhancing security.

The dominant role of the P3+1 has facilitated coordination across the group, making for a more effective division of labor, and maximizing resource allocation. For example, the group has sought to enhance Economic Community of West African States (ECOWAS) peacekeeping capability, with the Americans focusing on strategic planning, the British on operational capability, the French addressing tactical training, and the Germans providing funding support. Wherever possible, the P3+1 governments try to provide strong security leadership through existing multilateral structures like the United Nations, European Union, NATO, or the Organization for Economic Cooperation and Development (OECD). To address the rising threat of piracy off Somalia, for instance, a multinational naval task force was created under UN authorization in 2009 to safeguard maritime traffic off the Horn of Africa; some 16 nations have participated since that time.[4]

Official American policy objectives as outlined in the 2012 *U.S. Strategy Toward Sub-Saharan Africa* call for the United States to partner with African countries to pursue interdependent and mutually reinforcing goals of strengthening democratic institution; spurring economic growth, trade and investment; advancing peace and security; and promoting opportunity and development.[5] The emphasis is clearly on a whole of government approach, as Washington works with Africans to address the challenges of sustainable growth, poverty alleviation, food security, climate change, and health threats.[6] Advancing hard security priorities are just as evident in the peace and security guidance. The number one priority remains counterterrorism, with a focus on "disrupting, dismantling, and eventually defeating al-Qa'ida and its affiliates and adherents" in Africa.[7] Regional security cooperation is being advanced by deepening US security partnerships with African countries, as well as with regional organizations and sub-regional stand-by forces to build African military capabilities.

Essential to implementing this strategy since 2008 is US Africa Command (AFRICOM),[***] which has become the de facto face of American security engagement. Though envisioned as "a different kind of command," designed to address twenty-first-century realities by relying on a whole of government, inter-agency approach to engagement, which utilizes military, diplomatic, and development tools, it has failed to live up to its promise. Budget shortfalls, frustration at the slow pace of progress, and the need to show immediate results has caused AFRICOM to revert to its more traditional military roots and focus on its counterterrorism role. This, in turn, has undercut longer-term US developmental assistance programs that advance human security objectives. For example, US security assistance to several key African countries in the war on terror, such as Ethiopia, Djibouti, Kenya and Nigeria, more than tripled from 2000 to 2013, while developmental assistance (outside of humanitarian and health funding) lagged far behind.[8]

Not surprisingly, critics of American engagement see an increasingly militarized policy as other soft power tools of engagement are

---

[***] Created as a new unified combatant command in February 2007, and operating as a stand-alone command since October 2008, AFRICOM is responsible for coordinating all US military security assistance to the continent (less Egypt, which falls under Central Command's area of responsibility) and for conducting military operations in Africa as directed by national command authorities. It is headquartered in Stuttgart, Germany.

increasingly discarded. Moreover, US policymakers may be creating for themselves a self-fulfilling prophecy that sees the American military as the sole effective tool for building security in Africa. Those in Washington would thus be wise to remember the old Russian adage: "When all you have is a hammer, every problem begins to look like a nail." And, as we have seen, many of Africa's security challenges are not amenable to the military hammer.

For their part, British and French security engagement in Africa remains largely rooted in each's respective longstanding and extensive historical, cultural, political, and economic ties to the continent. Although they lack the extensive resource base and power projection capability of the United States, they still have the formidable ability to leverage their political and economic influence in key regions. This, combined with their leadership and activism, provides an enormous advantage for Western engagement.

While both countries are heavily involved in efforts to enhance African security, their styles of engagement are vastly different. The French, for their part, have never shied away from their self-declared obligation to act as the ultimate guardian of security and stability in their former African territories. With three major military bases and some 7,000 troops (peaking at nearly 9,000 in 2014) in Africa,[9] Paris has shown little reluctance to put boots on the ground when French or its African allies' interests are threatened. In contrast, British activism has been more tempered and one that recognizes the limits of its power. While not averse to direct action when necessary (the military intervention in Sierra Leone in 2000–3 or support for the NATO action in Libya in 2011, for instance), Whitehall clearly prefers an economy of power approach that relies heavily on a coordinated British inter-agency soft power response, supplemented by selective military engagement.[10]

The new comer to this old boys' club is Germany. Long hampered by domestic and constitutional obstacles to its overseas military engagement, Berlin has steadily been increasing its involvement and, more importantly, the nature of its role in Africa. With Chancellor Angela Merkel proclaiming "a new path for Germany in Africa," the German government in May 2014 released new guidelines for engagement, which recognized that its "African partners and the international community as a whole are expecting more of Germany."[11] This means moving beyond simply funding humanitarian, developmental, and security assistance programs, toward a more robust role for the German military. The deployment of a small contingent of German troops and equipment to Mali in 2013, as well as Berlin's contributions to the European Union's stabilization force in the Central African Republic (CAR), and the announcement in January 2017 of a "Marshal Plan for Africa" is a clear indicator that German engagement in Africa is indeed entering a new era.

Despite this new found political willingness by the P3+1 to more actively engage, resource limitations and fears of operational overreach have driven the United States and its allies to concentrate on helping Africans address three critical challenges: 1) combating terrorism; 2) building peacekeeping capacity and boosting stability; and 3) curbing the proliferation of deadly infectious diseases and improving the general health of Africans.

Combating terrorism
The number one priority of US security engagement in Africa is countering the threat of terrorism fueled by ideological extremism, political and social alienation, and state failure. It is here that Washington commits the bulk of its efforts and resources. Washington and its allies have focused their attention on three areas that they see as most severely threatened by terrorism: the Horn of Africa, coastal East Africa, and the greater trans-Sahara (including Libya since 2015). It is on these battlefields that they believe the war on terror in Africa will ultimately be won or lost.

Growing concern over the Horn of Africa, and of Somalia in particular, becoming the "next Afghanistan" led US Central Command to create the Combined Joint Task Force-Horn of Africa (CJTF-HOA) in 2002. With some 1,500–2,000 military and non-military personnel based primarily out of Camp Lemonier in Djibouti, and an annual budget of nearly $320 million, the task force is has the job of: conducting capacity building operations and civic-action "hearts and minds" programs, designed to prevent conflict; promoting regional stability; and undermining support for violent extremists in the region.[12] Djibouti also serves as the long-standing hub for the French military presence in the region, housing 1,400 ground troops at Camp Monclar, as well as air and naval assets, many of which are involved in counterterrorism and anti-piracy operations.[13] In recent years, however, CJTF-HOA and its allies have increasingly moved away from exercising soft power and now rely more on the use of surgical air and ground strikes using drones and American Special Forces against al-Shabaab militants in Somalia. It also provides essential logistical support and pre-deployment training to the 22,000-man African Union (AU) peacekeeping force in Somalia.

To stem the larger regional terror threat to East Africa beyond the immediate Horn of Africa, the US Department of State created the East Africa Counter-Terrorism Initiative in 2003. Now known as the Partnership for Regional East Africa Counter-Terrorism, Washington is working with 12 countries from Djibouti to the Comoros Islands "to build counterterrorism capacity and capability of member countries to thwart short-term terrorist threats, counter violent extremism and address longer-term vulnerabilities" by improving regional cooperation on border and aviation security, cracking down on terrorist financing mechanisms, training local police forces, and developing youth programs.[14] The US Department of State spends approximately $50 million per year on these programs.[15] Likewise, the United Kingdom has sought to build on its established military-to-military relationship with Kenya and has played a growing role in training and equipping that country's Anti-Terror Police Unit. Unfortunately, the Unit has also been accused by Western and local human rights groups in recent years of engaging in torture, arbitrary detentions, and suspect disappearances.[16]

On the other side of the continent, Washington moved to counter the rising tide of jihadist-inspired terrorism coming out of Algeria by creating the Pan Sahel Initiative in late 2002. Originally a five-year program to assist Mali, Mauritania, Niger, and Chad in strengthening their border security and counterterrorism capabilities, the US Department of State program (now known as the Trans-Sahara Counter-Terrorism Partnership) and its Department of Defense counterpart—Operation Enduring Freedom-Trans Sahara—has since morphed into a more than $100 million dollar a year program with annual joint military exercises that encompass 10 countries from Morocco to Nigeria.[17] It seeks not only to enhance the security capabilities of these partners, but also to implement educational and developmental initiatives to counter violent extremism. According to a senior US defense official, "It becomes a broader package approach [than just security assistance]. You're not just developing one muscle in the body, you're developing the whole body."[18]

The situation in the trans-Sahara grew increasingly dangerous following the overthrow and death of Muammar Qadhafi in 2011, which unleashed long suppressed jihadist forces and gave rise to a multitude of powerful local Islamist militias. Not only has this left Libya in constant turmoil, but it opened the door for inroads by the Islamic State starting in 2014 and a new front in the war on terror. Thanks to the combined efforts of militias allied with the recognized Libyan government and US-led air strikes, Islamic State fighters were finally pushed out of their stronghold in Sirte in December 2016. Nonetheless, the group is far from being defeated and is reportedly regrouping in remote parts of southern Libya.[19]

The Libyan chaos also unleashed a flood of expatriate trained fighters, military equipment, and small arms—including sophisticated surface-to-air missiles—flowing southward into conflict zones in Algeria, Mali, Mauritania, Niger, and Chad. A simmering nationalist Tuareg rebellion in northeast Mali became reinvigorated in 2012 following a military coup that allowed the rise of the fundamentalist Ansar Dine movement and the strengthening of al-Qaeda affiliates in the country. Only timely Western military intervention, spearheaded by 2,500 French combat troops, prevented the government from collapsing under the weight of the Islamist threat. Since April 2015, a 15,000-man UN peacekeeping force, the United Nations Multidimensional Integrated Stabilization Mission in Mali, with American and European logistical support has been responsible for securing the volatile northern region of the country.

More than 1,500 miles away, the security situation in northeast Nigeria spun out of control, beginning in 2011 as Boko Haram fundamentalists gained ground and launched ever more aggressive attacks on Nigerian civilians, government offices, and military and police facilities in their effort to carve out an Islamic state. Bombings, assassinations, and mass abductions (including the April 2014 kidnapping of more than 200 Chibok schoolgirls, which gained global attention) became the norm. Although the United States designated Boko Haram a terrorist organization in 2010,[20] it was only after the group became a growing threat to Nigerian stability, and with its public alignment first with al-Qaeda and the Islamic State, that it really captured Washington's full attention. President Muhammadu Buhari's successful military offensive against Boko Haram in 2015–16 was welcomed by the United States, but serious concerns over large-scale human rights violations during the campaign have complicated US efforts to enhance counterterrorism cooperation with the Buhari government and supply it with military equipment.

None of these initiatives have worked, and after more than 15 years and spending billions of dollars the United States and its allies are no closer to victory in the war on terror. Moreover, despite publicly declaring that this effort will be a generational struggle of not just arms but of ideas, impatience and the need to show results has caused international counterterrorism efforts to vacillate sharply between a soft power approach to capture hearts and minds and a more militarized iron fist approach aimed at killing jihadists. The result has been a mish-mash between ends, ways, and means and rising frustration.

With the French decision in early 2014 to establish a 3,000-man expeditionary force permanently deployed to the pan-Sahel, and British Prime Minister David Cameron's earlier call for Britain to form a strategic partnership on policing, defense, counterterrorism, and intelligence with Algiers,[21] the United States finds itself under pressure to pursue an even more hardline counterterrorism approach. While likely to produce some short-term successes, this strategy is also pushing Washington and its allies into the arms of authoritarian governments in Algeria, Egypt, Ethiopia, and Uganda, whose commitment to democracy, civil liberties, and human rights is questionable at best. The increasingly aggressive and high profile nature of terrorist attacks in recent years undoubtedly warrants the need for a strong military response, but the West cannot simply bomb its way to victory. Washington needs to be mindful that "too heavy a reliance on the sharp edge of military power is likely to be counterproductive" in the battle for African hearts and minds.[22] To be successful, the American military tool of engagement needs to be tempered and more effectively incorporated, and subordinated to, diplomatic and developmental engagement efforts that foster long-term human security objectives. For in the end, this approach is more likely to turn the tide in the war on terror. Unfortunately, the March 2017 decision by the new Trump administration to declare parts of Somalia "war zones" and open the floodgates to more aggressive American military action against al-Shabaab is a move in the wrong direction[23]—one that is likely to drive more vulnerable Somalis into the arms of extremists and exacerbate the growing humanitarian crisis in the sub-region.

Building peacekeeping capability and boosting stability
Large-scale conflict across the continent has historically been trending downward since the 1990s and significantly so since 2002, according to Human Security Centre reporting.[24] The significant levels of violence that do exist are heavily concentrated in specific zones of conflict—the CAR, northeastern Nigeria and its neighbors, the Somali epicenter in the Horn of Africa, and Sudan and South Sudan[25]—and highlight the critical need for peacekeepers. By working directly with national governments, sub-regional and regional African organizations, and also indirectly through the United Nations, the P3+1 countries have sought to help Africans build their capacity, increase their effectiveness, and improve coordination and cooperation. Since 2000, we conservatively estimate that the United States alone has committed at least $14 billion to these bilateral and multilateral peacekeeping efforts in Africa.

The continent was home to more than half of all the United Nations' peacekeeping operations in 2016 and of the 117,306 personnel deployed on peacekeeping missions, 83 percent were to Africa and five out of the six missions with more than 10,000 personnel are also on the continent.[26] The United Nations currently spends $5.87 billion annually in support of these African operations.[27] In addition, the Africa Union has authorized the deployment of more than 40,000 peacekeepers to six countries, including major ongoing missions to Somalia, Darfur, Mali, and the CAR.[28] As a result, the demand for well-trained and well-equipped peacekeepers is unrelenting.

In 2004 the United States and other G-8 nations undertook several initiatives to build "more effective means to stabilize regions in turmoil, and to halt religious violence and ethnic cleansing" through the creation of "permanent capabilities to respond to future crises" in part through the creation of a global cadre of peacekeepers. The American component of this effort was the Global Peace Operations Initiative (GPOI) by which Washington agreed to spend $660 million to train 75,000 troops worldwide by 2013, with an emphasis on training African peacekeepers.[29] Implementation in Africa was handled through the Department of State's existing African Contingency Operations Training and Assistance program (ACOTA[†††]), which was absorbed into GPOI at the end of 2004. Between 2005 and the end of 2014 Washington spent $914 million on GPOI, with more than $500 million committed to African training and assistance, according to the US Department of State.[30] Thanks to these efforts, the ACOTA program and its predecessors have provided training and non-lethal equipment to more than 250,000 peacekeepers from 25 African nations, including Burundi, Ethiopia, Ghana, Kenya, Nigeria, Rwanda, Senegal, South Africa, and Uganda.[31]

These American efforts at increasing African peacekeeping capacity are supplemented by British and French programs. Since ECOWAS's ill-fated cease-fire monitoring operation in Liberia in the early 1990s, Washington, London and Paris, for example, have successfully assisted the organization in developing a more robust and effective peacekeeping structure that has allowed ECOWAS to provide more timely and effective intervention, not only within the sub-region, but across the continent. Thousands of West African peacekeepers now serve in African and UN peacekeeping missions across the continent. Elsewhere in Africa, British advisers have provided extensive pre-deployment training for Kenyan and Ugandan troops heading to Somalia as part of the AU's

---

[†††] ACOTA training is conducted by civil contractors working through the Office of Regional and Security Affairs, Bureau of African Affairs at the Department of State. It began as the Africa Crisis Response Initiative in 1997 to enhance the capacity of African partner countries to participate in worldwide peacekeeping operations. It was restructured as ACOTA in 2002 and is now the African component of GPOI. US Department of State Fact Sheet, 'African Contingency Operations Training and Assistance (ACOTA) Program', Washington, DC, February 6, 2013. Found at: www.state.gov/r/pa/prs/ps/2013/02/203841.htm.

Table 3 UN/AU peacekeeping missions in Africa

	Misson name	Designation	Date established	Authorizing authority	2017 strength	Key contributors	Budget*	Fatalities
Central African Republic	UN Multidimensional Integrated Stabilization Mission in the Central African Republic	MINUSCA	2014 March	UN	10,750	Bangladesh, Burundi, Egypt, Pakistan, Rwanda	$921 million	25
Cote d'Ivoire	UN Operation in Cote d'Ivoire	UNOCI	2004 April	UN	3,656	Burundi, Senegal	$153 million	144
Darfur, Sudan	AU-UN Hybrid Mission in Darfur	UNAMID	2007 July	AU UN	20,645	Ethiopia, Nigeria, Pakistan, Rwanda, Senegal	$1,040 million	237
Democratic Republic of the Congo	UN Organization Stabilization Mission in the Democratic Republic of the Congo	MONUSCO	2010 July	UN	22,590	Bangladesh, India, Pakistan, South Africa, Tanzania, Uruguay	$1,235 million	102
Liberia	UN Mission in Liberia	UNMIL	2003 September	UN	3,018	Nigeria	$187 million	197

Table 3 (*Continued*)

	Misson name	Designation	Date established	Authorizing authority	2017 strength	Key contributors	Budget*	Fatalities
Mali	UN Multidimensional Integrated Stabilization Mission in Mali	MINUSMA	2013 April	UN	13,456	Bangladesh, Burkina Faso, Chad	$933 million	110
Somalia	African Mission in Somalia	AMISOM	2007 January	AU UN	22,126	Burundi, Ethiopia, Kenya, Uganda	$1,200 million**	1,200 to 3,000**
South Sudan	UN Mission in South Sudan	UNMISS	2011 July	UN	15,171	China, Ethiopia, Ghana, India, Nepal, Rwanda	$1,082 million	47
Sudan (Abyei)	UN Interim Security Force for Abyei	UNISFA	2011 June	UN	4,719	Ethiopia	$269 million	21
Western Sahara	UN Mission for the Referendum in Western Sahara	MINURSO	1991 April	UN	467	Bangladesh, Egypt, Russia	$56 million	15

* 7/2016 to 6/2017 funding ** Estimated

African Mission in Somalia peacekeeping force. Meanwhile, through its biannual RECAMP (*Renforcement des Capacités Africaines de Maintien de la Paix* or Reinforcement of African Peacekeeping Capabilities) cycles, the French military conducts extensive large-scale African peacekeeping exercises.

In addition to this direct peacekeeping assistance, and in light of American political reluctance to put boots on the ground in Africa, both France and the United Kingdom have used their militaries to help stabilize African partner countries in crisis. Paris, in particular, has increasingly come to recognize a special role for the continent in France's national defense and security strategy, highlighting the Sahel, the Gulf of Guinea, and the Maghreb as priority regions in an April 2013 White Paper on defense policy.[32] Moreover, in contrast with past French interventions in the 1970s, 1980s, and 1990s, recent stability operations, such as in Mali (Operation Serval), have been more positively received across Africa. This likely explains President Hollande's 2014 decision to base a permanent 3,000-man reaction force in the Sahel as part of Operation Barkhan.[33] The Hollande government has also been a strong advocate of greater EU involvement—such as its engagement in Mali with the European Union Training Mission—to support the development of more effective security structures. Germany's expanded, yet minor, military role in these types of operations is a good indicator of a growing acceptance of a larger multinational EU role in the future.

Combating infectious diseases and improving health
This third major area of attention has powerful implications for human security. As we saw earlier, rampant virulent disease, malnutrition, limited access to clean water, and poor sanitation pose enormous challenges to African countries given their limited health care capacity and overburdened health delivery infrastructure. In addition, the spread of highly deadly communicable diseases resulting from African pandemics pose an increasingly serious threat to global health security, as the 2014–15 Ebola outbreak in West Africa clearly highlighted. Accordingly, the public health sector is an area where the United States and many of its allies have committed significant resources. It is one of the fastest growing areas of international engagement with tens of thousands of bilateral, multilateral, and public–private partnership initiatives having been created.

Addressing the challenge of reducing deaths from infectious diseases—particularly HIV/AIDS, tuberculosis, and malaria—has been a common priority of the United States and its partners for more than a decade. A critical Millennium Development Goal benchmark was to: "Have halted by 2015 and begun to reverse the spread of HIV/AIDS; achieve, by 2010, universal access to antiretroviral therapy for all those who need it; and have halted by 2015 and begin to reverse the incidence of malaria and other major diseases."[34] Thanks to the efforts of the United States and many of its Western partners significant progress on these goals has been achieved and African deaths from HIV/AIDS and other diseases have all fallen sharply since the mid-2000s. While there certainly has been valid criticism at home and abroad over the overly narrow focus of this effort, one cannot argue with the powerful overall results of saving the lives of millions of African men, women, and children, who otherwise would have succumbed to these diseases.

The most prominent of these programs for the United States is the President's Emergency Plan for AIDS Relief, better known as PEPFAR. Created in 2003 by President George W. Bush to address the global HIV/AIDS pandemic, PEPFAR "holds a place in history as the largest effort by any nation to combat a single disease," according to the US Department of State.[35] Since its inception PEPFAR has spent more than $70 billion dollars—with nearly $50 billion dedicated to Africa— to provide prevention, care, and treatment programs.[36] Currently 95 percent of babies born to African women testing positive for HIV are now born HIV-free thanks to PEPFAR intervention; care and support assistance is being given to over 11 million people across the continent; and approximately 5 million African men, women, and children are receiving antiretroviral treatment annually.[37] In 2016, Washington will have spent some $3.3 billion on PEPFAR programs in Africa alone.[38]

Washington's allies have heavily invested in this effort too, largely through their assistance to Global Fund to Fight AIDS, Tuberculosis and Malaria and other multilateral initiatives. A December 2013 donors' conference for the Global Fund raised $12 billion in funding for the next three years with Canada, France, Germany, Japan, and the United Kingdom pledging 45 percent of the new aid. These pledges, along with that of the United States, accounted for $9.38 billion in new funding through 2016.[39] Importantly, the Global Fund has come to be viewed as a highly effective public–private partnership for bringing together national governments, international organizations, private foundations, corporations, and faith-based organizations.

Beyond the success in combating these big three infectious diseases, additional progress is also being made to address neglected tropical diseases in Africa, thanks to numerous bilateral and multilateral initiatives. These include African sleeping sickness, river blindness, and guinea-worm disease and while these types of disease do not kill large numbers of people, they inflict enormous misery and disability on those afflicted. Stemming these and other less lethal infections is seen as critical to meeting Millennium Development Goal health targets, and many health professionals believe several of these disease could be eradicated completely within a few years if progress continues.[40]

More generally, international health policies—aimed at improving overall societal health (especially for women and children), care delivery systems, and basic health infrastructure—have become an indispensable component of foreign policy for the United States and its allies, strengthening the linkage between security and development. The US Global Health Initiative expands American health assistance by partnering with countries to improve health outcomes in reproductive, maternal, newborn, and child health and to strengthen local health systems and their workforce.[41] Likewise, the British and Canadian governments identified improving maternal and child health, access to clean water and sanitation, and improved nutrition as key objectives of their international health engagement.[42] Japan has also pledged to use some of its $32 billion in aid and investment to "promote health care that everyone [in Africa] can access—in other words, 'universal health coverage'."[43]

New kids on the block

The globalization of the African security environment has led to the rising international engagement of not just established powers in North America and Europe, but also among emerging new powers of Asia and the global South.

China

Nowhere is this more evident than with China's new role in Africa and its impact for better or worse on the continent's security challenges. The highly publicized explosion of Chinese trade, investment, and developmental aid in Africa since the turn of the new century has been popularized as a struggle between East and West to control not only the riches of the continent, but Africa's political future as well. Quite naturally this burgeoning Sino-American rivalry elicits historical comparisons to the Cold War, which we will not try to replicate here.[44] Rather, we will explore the narrower topic of how current Chinese engagement in Africa is—or is not—helping Africans to solve their pressing security challenges. It is critical to bear in mind that China's role on the global stage has been undergoing significant changes, which are making its foreign and security policy increasingly complex, nuanced, and even contradictory. This is especially true for Beijing's African engagement, as it seeks to reconcile its national economic and political interests with a desire to be seen as the patron of the developing world and global leader.

China's engagement in Africa is nothing new. Chinese diplomats often take great pride in reminding both Africans and Westerns alike of Admiral Zheng He's historic voyages to the east coast of Africa in the early fifteenth century, long before the voyages of discovery by Columbus and de Gama. Or of the central role of China in providing political support, educational training, and military assistance to Africans engaged in the liberation struggle. Or of its willingness to assist newly independent African countries in the 1960s and 1970s with developmental projects that Western governments and businesses refused to invest in.

Be that as it may, this historical legacy has clearly been eclipsed by China's modern-day economic engagement in Africa and its multilateral Forum on China-Africa Cooperation, designed to strengthen political ties and forge new commitments. The numbers are telling. Sino-African trade mushroomed from just $4 billion in 1995 to nearly $60 billion in 2006, to nearly $200 billion in 2012—twice the US-Africa trade volume.[45] China-Africa trade shows no sign of slowing; it approached $300 billion in 2015 and a senior Chinese official predicted it would eventually rise to $400 billion by 2020.[46] Chinese direct foreign investment also reached $12 billion in 2012 (a thirty fold increase in ten years) and Beijing has provided at least $75 billion in foreign aid since 2003 and recently pledged another $32 billion in loans to support African infrastructure development.[47]

Beyond this well-reported economic and financial involvement, Beijing also has been seeking to increase its efforts to help Africans address their pressing challenges while burnishing its international political image. Success, however, has been mixed. Much of this difficulty can be found in China's need to reconcile its new global responsibilities with its long-standing national economic and foreign policy objectives in Africa: for example, by promoting peace and stability through conflict prevention while still continuing to arm and finance repressive regimes. Can it balance its fervent quest for raw materials against the destructive cost to the environment? Moreover, is it possible to maintain adherence to the guiding principle of non-interference while still pursuing greater Chinese security engagement on the continent?

China's impact on security in Africa continues to evolve, and while undoubtedly positive and in tune with the global norms in some areas, it continues to reinforce negative trends and complicate international and African efforts at fostering human security.

Once highly skeptical of multilateral engagement, China increasingly sees advantages in working with other countries and international organizations to bring about peace and security in Africa. It has played a largely positive role within the United Nations Security Council in politically supporting peacekeeping missions, although it has sought to temper international—especially Western—interventionism. Beijing maintains that military intervention is only legitimate if both the UNSC and host state consent, and has frequently argued that many internal African crises fall outside the United Nations' mandate.[48] Nonetheless, since 2000 China has committed police and military personnel to some of Africa's most challenging conflicts, from Darfur to the Democratic Republic of the Congo (DRC). With some 2,630 personnel serving in seven peacekeeping missions in Africa in 2016, China is the largest contributor among the permanent five members.[49] Since 2009 the Chinese navy has also actively been cooperating with multinational naval forces to counter piracy off the Horn of Africa, and Beijing's July 2017 opening of its new military base in Djibouti will further enhance its maritime security, as well as its peacekeeping role, in the sub-region.

Despite this new-found respect for multilateralism, much of China's engagement on peacekeeping and conflict mediation challenges continues to be done through bilateral mechanisms. This is clearly reflected through its use of the Forum on China-Africa Cooperation to strengthen ties with the AU and individual African countries by implementing the Initiative on China-Africa Cooperative Partnership for Peace and Security. In a May 2014 speech at the AU headquarters in Addis Ababa, Premier Li Keqiang pledged Chinese help to develop the African Standby Force and the African Capacity for Immediate Response to Crises, as well as assistance for other African collective security mechanisms, and to expand bilateral training, intelligence sharing, and joint exercises with the ultimate goal of enhancing African peacekeeping, counterterrorism, and anti-piracy capacity.[50] Unsurprisingly, this approach has ruffled American and Western feathers and hindered closer cooperation and coordination that "would make the delivery of outside [international] support more effective, both practically on the ground and politically in capitals."[51]

Beijing is also charting its own independent course in the African health and environment sector. While political and ideological factors drove China to send medical teams to Africa during the Cold War, improving overall African health care delivery has now become a central feature of Beijing's health sector engagement. Although it is difficult to estimate the total extent of this assistance, some numbers are compelling. Since 1963 more than 15,000 Chinese health workers have treated an estimated 170 million patients.[52] And Premier Li has further pledged even greater future assistance in providing safe drinking water, preventing infectious diseases, and enhanced bilateral health care cooperation as part of China's poverty alleviation efforts on the continent.[53]

Despite seeking common health care objectives, however, Beijing largely eschews the use of multilateral health mechanisms, such as the Global Fund, in favor of its own initiatives. For example, in 2006 China announced its intentions to establish 30 malaria treatment centers across the continent with state-of-the-art equipment and donated medicine. However, lack of training and follow-up support meant much of this material remains underutilized or unused, according to press reports.[54] Likewise, from 2002–14 China provided only $3.5 million annually to the Global Fund (and has marginally increased this to $5 million annually through 2016). In contrast, the Canadian government has provided some $125 million annually or more than $1.5 billion over the same period.[55] The same independent approach holds true for the environmental sector, where Beijing has provided modest grants in support of closer technical cooperation between China and African countries and has agreed to work toward the creation of its own China-Africa joint research center in Kenya.[56]

Chinese unilateralism, however, has also frequently complicated international efforts to address security challenges in such areas as: resource and identity conflict; trafficking in small arms, drugs, and people; and government accountability with respect to human rights and civil liberties. Despite some signs of flexibility within international forums with respect to peacekeeping and conflict mediation, as noted above, Beijing's longstanding deference to issues of national sovereignty and non-interference remains a major driving force behind its African foreign policy. Moreover, these engagement principles allow it to rationalize its pursuit of short-term national interests at the expense of longer-term peace and security objectives. These actions have fueled popular charges of China shirking its global responsibility and thwarting the will of the African people by supporting repressive, non-democratic regimes, although a similar argument can realistically be made about American and Western engagement as well.

China's willingness to ignore, or at least look the other way, enforcement of international sanctions or multinational control mechanisms when its national interests are at stake is probably the most telling measure of Chinese foreign policy priorities. The challenge of stemming small arms and light weapons proliferation in Africa is a case in point. As we noted previously, small arms proliferation plays a powerful role in fueling and sustaining multiple type of conflicts; it makes these conflicts more deadly, and peace more difficult to achieve. Despite the lack of reliable data and of Chinese transparency with respect to arms sales, trafficking experts believe the vast majority of Chinese arms exports go to the developing world and Beijing is the largest supplier of small arms and light weapons to Africa.[57] From 2000–6, for instance, China is believed to have delivered small arms to at least half of Africa's 54 countries.[58] Not only is Africa an attractive market for low-cost Chinese weapon exports, but Beijing's willingness to supply ostracized African governments in return for economic and political concessions means it is often the supplier of choice. And without a doubt, many of these weapons and ammunition have inflamed conflict and increased insecurity; Chinese weaponry has been used in Sudan, the DRC, and Zimbabwe to commit human rights violations and suppress opposition groups, according to human rights experts.[59] China has also repeatedly flaunted UN and other international arms embargos, especially in its dealings with the Khartoum government.

Brazil and India
Often overshadowed by the rise of China is the emergence of Brazil onto the African stage, along with an expansion of India's traditional role. For more than a decade they have been successfully leveraging their longstanding historic and cultural links to the continent to expand economic and commercial ties with their African brethren. Since the end of the Cold War, trade between Brazil and Africa has registered growth of 16 percent per year; from 2000 to 2011 it increased more than six-fold, rising from $4.2 billion to $27.6, according to Chatham House analysis.[60] It now probably exceeds $30 billion annually. Although small by global standards, Brazil's foreign direct investment may be upwards of $20 billion and the continent is reportedly gaining greater interest among Brazilian corporations.[61] Large Brazilian multinational companies are increasingly becoming key players in the construction, mining, and energy sectors for not just Lusophone countries, but across the entire continent.

Likewise, the volume of India-Africa trade has been on a steady rise too. Despite some large-scale investment in mining, energy, and telecommunications, much of India's commercial activity continues to be conducted by small and mid-size businesses long integrated into local African economies. Putting this economic activity in perspective, the combined Brazil-India trade relationship with Africa is only exceeded by that of China and the United States.

Unfortunately, this robust economic engagement has yet to be matched by an increased activism in the African security sector for either Brazil or India, but there are positive signs that this may be changing. Brazil, in particular, under the former administration of President Luiz Lula da Silva went to great lengths to expand non-economic ties through a series of diplomatic and developmental initiatives. During his time in office Brazil doubled the number of embassies in Africa from 17 to 37 from 2003.[62] Brazilian presidents now regularly visit the continent "to maintain a special relationship with Africa [that] is strategic for Brazil's foreign policy" and the country recently announced the cancelation or restructuring of nearly $900 million of African debt.[63] Moreover, Brazil has moved from an aid recipient to an aid donor as it seeks to help African governments address the challenges of healthcare and poverty alleviation through its small, but growing, developmental assistance efforts.

And several of these initiatives are having a direct impact on Africa's security challenges. Through the work of the Brazilian Cooperation Agency, ABC, the equivalent of USAID, Brazil is providing education and training to African health professionals and leveraging its public health experience to increase African capacity in healthcare delivery. A centerpiece of this assistance is the Afro-Brazilian cooperative effort to combat HIV/AIDS, whereby the ABC and the Oswaldo Cruz Foundation are working to establish clinical and epidemiological facilities in Africa with trained local staff, as well as constructing a large pharmaceutical factory in Mozambique capable of producing anti-retro-viral drugs.[64] In the area of food security and poverty alleviation, the Brazilian Ministry of Agriculture's research arm, EMBRAPA, has been working in 11 African countries since 2010 to improve agricultural production in both food and cash crops. Although its largest project is in Mozambique, EMBRAPA is also working in Francophone West Africa to upgrade cotton and rice production, genetic diversity, and quality.[65] While generally well received, some of these efforts have come under criticism for promoting large-scale commercial agriculture methods at the expense of the environment and the livelihood of peasant farmers.

In the more traditional security realm, however, Brasilia has yet to make great strides. While it has long been involved in various African UN peacekeeping operations, it continues to have only a nominal presence in these missions.[66] Its closest security relationship is with Angola, with whom it has signed numerous defense cooperation and training agreements and in 2012 the two governments agreed to expand training of Angolan military personnel in Brazil.[67] Brazil is a significant supplier of military equipment to the Luanda government as well. There are some indications that Brazil may be exploring an expanded African security role. One possible area under review is multilateral maritime cooperation in the south Atlantic and Gulf of Guinea with Angola, Nigeria, and

South Africa to address the problems of piracy, human trafficking, drug and small arms smuggling, and illegal fishing.

Despite India's long-standing cultural and commercial ties to eastern and southern Africa and the presence of a large Indian diaspora across the continent, New Delhi pursues a low-key and minimalist approach to its African engagement. This is somewhat surprising at first glance given the five-fold increase in Indo-African trade from 2006 to 2013, which topped $65 billion in 2013 (more than double Brazil's volume), and this trade was estimated to have reached $100 billion in 2015.[68] On closer inspection, however, the Indian approach is actually in keeping with its well-established decentralized and grassroots commercial philosophy in Africa, which emphasizes small to mid-size business engagement and a reliance on private–government investment partnerships.

This does not mean, however, that India has completely eschewed an enhanced security role in its African foreign policy. India is highly supportive of African peacekeeping efforts, where it continues its legacy of contributing to UN missions in Africa; over 6,000 Indian troops and police are currently serving in the DRC and South Sudan alone.[69] Likewise, the Indian Navy plays an active role in the multinational effort to stem piracy in the Gulf of Aden and the Horn of Africa. Diplomatically, New Delhi remains highly supportive of non-traditional African security concerns in global forums, including trafficking in people, drugs, and small arms, as well as the threat of environmental degradation and the spread of pandemic disease.

It is in the area of enhancing health security, for example, that New Delhi is quietly upping its engagement on the continent. Reportedly, several African governments are seeking Indian assistance in improving healthcare delivery and the supply of affordable medicines to their citizens.[70] Making greater use of technology and Indian tertiary delivery methods, along with a massive training program—nearly 5 million primary healthcare workers in 10 years—are being explored. Likewise, new Indian pharmaceutical investment on the continent is seen as a potential way to reduce the rising burden of treating non-communicable diseases such as cancer, diabetes and hypertension through greater access to low-cost drugs.

The Russian wild card

Despite Moscow's waning influence in Africa since the end of the Cold War, a brief note concerning the nature and the future of Russian security engagement in Africa is clearly warranted here. This is especially salient given the increasingly aggressive nature of Russian foreign policy under President Vladimir Putin since the 2014 annexation of Ukraine's Crimean peninsula. While Africa clearly does not rank at the top of Putin's priorities, he could likely seize unexpected opportunities to burnish Russia's image and security role on the continent in the years ahead.

Following the collapse of the old Soviet Union, Moscow largely abandoned Africa politically, economically, and diplomatically, as it turned inward and ceded the international security agenda to Western leadership. As a result Russia plays an increasingly minor role and runs the risk of being further displaced by the entry of China, Brazil, and India. Nonetheless, Russia's prominent position on the United Nations Security Council and other international bodies, as well as its critical global importance in combating terrorism, small arms proliferation, human and drug trafficking, and transnational crime means that it cannot be ignored. Active Russian engagement is not indispensable in tackling pressing African security challenges, but Moscow's assistance would undoubtedly accelerate progress toward solving them.

The recent entry of Gazprom into the African energy market, however, may spur Moscow to reassess its future security role. Russia could easily improve its investment prospects and revitalize its image within Africa by working alongside the international community to address the continent's pressing transnational security challenges. But more robust Russian engagement could come at a price and prove detrimental for Africa too. Moscow may seek to advance its own foreign policy agenda, placing its global geopolitical calculations above African needs. For instance, Foreign Minister Sergey Lavrov's high-profile visit to Zimbabwe in September 2014 to announce Russia's $3 billion platinum mining investment was as much, if not more, about foreign policy as international business.[71] The visit came on the heels of heightened tensions between the West and Moscow over eastern Ukraine and talk of increased international economic sanctions against Russia. Unsurprisingly, President Mugabe took the opportunity to lambaste the West over this unacceptable use of sanctions.[72] Thus, the new East–West competition in Africa many not be about China and the West after all, but about an older ghost of the Cold War—Moscow.

Institutionalized multilateralism

The growing importance of IGOs, along with the exponential growth of NGOs, civil society groups, and public–private partnerships, is transforming the face of security engagement by creating new opportunities for innovative solutions, providing new sources of independent funding, and shifting priorities away from short-term external foreign policy goals toward more macro long-term African security objectives.

Long seen as the leading actor in African peacekeeping and conflict prevention and mediation, the United Nations is, without a doubt, the preeminent international organization in Africa. While its role as a peacekeeper and mediator will continue to characterize much of its engagement, the United Nations now finds itself increasingly active in addressing many of the continent's non-traditional and transnational security challenges as well. From countering human, drug, and small arms trafficking and protecting the environment, to fighting the spread of pandemic disease and improving food security, the United Nations and its affiliate organizations are at the forefront of intergovernmental multilateralism.

Part of this stems from its well-established structure, as well as local acceptance of UN involvement, but it also reflects the willingness of UN leadership going back to Secretary-General Kofi Annan to tackle non-traditional security issues of interest to Africans that were being overlooked or neglected by the United States and other global powers.

All has not been smooth sailing though. The United Nations too has struggled with resource limitations, poor communication and coordination, inadequate prioritization, and bureaucratic politics. Nonetheless, the United Nations has been successful in laying the foundation for broader international multilateral engagement, improving cooperation and coordination between state and institutional actors, and furthering a security agenda that is more in keeping with the needs of African governments and societies.

Other IGOs have stepped up to the plate as well. Once purely confined by geo-strategic constraints, the EU, NATO, and the OECD are now actively engaging in Africa. EU and NATO involvement, from Libya, Mali, and the CAR, to the Horn of Africa, is reflective of this growing—and increasingly proactive—security engagement. Working through the AU's Africa Peace Facility, for example, the European Union committed more than $1 billion in assistance from 2014–16 in support of the prevention, management, and resolution of conflicts in Africa.[73] While still largely confined to more traditional security missions, such as peacekeeping, stability operations, and counter-piracy, some of these organizations like the OECD are becoming increasingly adept at working with non-military multinational partners. The OECD's annual Africa Partnership Forum, for instance, brings policymakers, private sector representatives, academics, and civil society leaders together to address the performance of African economies and the challenges ahead. Thus, the nexus of development, aid, and stability has progressively blurred the traditional distinctions over the nature of IGO security engagement on the continent. And rightly so, for just as Western governments have learned to adapt, so too are IGOs recognizing the need for a more holistic approach to engagement.

Accordingly, IGO involvement has expanded rapidly to new areas and programs heretofore on the sidelines of international security engagement. For example:

- The International Criminal Police Organization or INTERPOL is not only facilitating greater African access to national and criminal databases,[74] but is working with the European Union to develop Libyan policing capacity to address transnational crimes, such as drug, small arms, and human trafficking that "generate violence and threaten to destabilize the country and region."[75] Moreover, in 2014 INTERPOL established a dedicated unit in Nairobi to assist African countries to better tackle the problem of wildlife crime (especially illegal ivory trafficking) and other environmental crimes.[76]
- The International Organization for Migration has expanded its traditional mission of prevention, awareness raising, and humanitarian assistance to migrants to now include migration health issues. Monitoring, controlling, and preventing the spread of communicable diseases, such as HIV/AIDS, malaria, and tuberculosis among migrant communities in now a major feature of its work with African governments and their sub-regional organizations.[77] As if any reminder is needed, the recent West African Ebola outbreak dramatically highlights the powerful links between migration and health security on a global level.
- The World Food Programme and its UN affiliates—the Food and Agricultural Organization and the International Fund for Agricultural Development—are committing substantial human and financial resources to ensuring long-term food security in Africa. While emergency food assistance remains at the heart of the its mission, its 2014–17 Strategic Plan emphasizes risk reduction by enabling people "to meet their own food and nutrition needs' and 'break the intergenerational cycle of hunger."[78] Moreover, promoting more effective agricultural and social development among the most vulnerable in African societies has the potential for undercutting resource conflict over land and water.
- On a macro level the OECD is expanding its brief in Africa beyond economic and fiscal reform to now include sustainable growth, green growth, food security, and gender equality.[79] In particular, the organization's Fragile States Report seeks to address the issue of failing states by identifying 31 fragile states in Africa that are facing extreme poverty, aid funding shortfalls, and developmental challenges so

serious that their ability to function as states and ensure peace and stability is severely compromised.[80]

Complementing the growth of this IGO engagement has been a dramatic rise in the number and type of international NGOs and civil society groups addressing some of Africa's most pressing challenges. And while many of these have a long and impressive history of humanitarian engagement, old-line organizations and groups are expanding their activities into fresh areas, and new international NGOs and civil society groups are springing up almost daily. A driving force behind this explosive growth is their desire to play a more active and relevant role in the continent's security. This has been both a blessing and a curse. On the one hand, this heightened level of engagement has brought increased global visibility to neglected issues, badly needed expertise, and additional sources of funding. On the other hand, it has complicated coordination, produced redundancy, and often distorted African priorities to better reflect the international donor agenda.

Many of the largest and most well-established NGOs in Africa have their roots in humanitarian assistance and disaster relief operations and not security engagement. But all this began to change after the Cold War and the rise of non-traditional security challenges that international governments and organizations were ill-equipped or politically reluctant to address. Into this void stepped many old-line international NGOs and civil society groups, which were driven by a changing view of security and of their new roles and missions. It was within the nascent human security construct that they found a solid conceptual framework for underpinning and expanding their engagement into new areas. For instance, NGOs such as CARE, Doctors Without Borders, and Save the Children—long known for their humanitarian and disaster relief operations—are now heavily engaged in health security activities. These programs include field and research work to stem the spread of pandemic diseases, including clean water and sanitation efforts, and community health and nutrition. Other engagement activities by these organizations now include women's empowerment, education, and economic development, which are also designed to prompt the long-term peace and security of African societies.[81] Likewise, Salvation Army International's southern African branch has been heavily involved in efforts to counter human trafficking across the sub-region.[82]

At the same time, a host of newer international NGOs and civil society groups have sought to carve out unique engagement niches. Many of these organizations and groups focus on a specialized aspect of human security. Advocacy groups such as the International Crisis

Group or International Alert engage in monitoring and creating early warning mechanisms for countries in crisis and/or in conflict mediation efforts. While the NGO Working Group on Women, Peace and Security seeks to ensure "the equal and full participation of women in issues relating to peace and security,"[83] other groupings have more narrowly defined agendas. The International Action Network on Small Arms, for example, is an umbrella organization that "links civil society organizations [in Africa and elsewhere] working to stop the proliferation and misuse of small arms and light weapons."[84]

By far, the largest collection of these newer and specialized NGOs and civil society groups can be found working in the health security sector. They range from very large and highly visible organizations with billions of dollars in funding to small, under-the-radar groups with miniscule staff and budgets. For example, the Bill & Melinda Gates Foundation provides nearly $2 billion in health security grants annually,[85] while PureMadi, a small University of Virginia student-faculty NGO, is working to provide clean water to communities in South Africa's Limpopo valley.[86] Although engaged in a wide variety of issues within this sector, from Vitamin A and iodine deficiencies to providing clean water and reducing gun violence, stemming the spread of pandemic disease has been central for many of these post-Cold War organizations and groups. Not surprisingly, HIV/AIDS sits atop this sector.

Nonetheless, despite all the useful work and good intentions of IGOs, NGOs, and international civil society community over the years, institutionalized multilateralism has, at times, complicated rather than advanced international security engagement efforts, and has funneled tens of billions of dollars into marginal engagement activities often at the expense of actual African security priorities. The field is as crowded as ever and African governments and regional organizations are ill-equipped to keep tabs on, let alone try to coordinate, cooperation across this huge number of actors. Many a minister has candidly acknowledged that they have no idea on how many groups are actually operating within their borders or what specific activities these groups are engaged in.

Likewise, African countries and regional organizations can find themselves in the difficult position of either refusing donor assistance (often quite substantial) or accepting an external donor-driven security agenda. This has long been the case with the war on terror, whereby international actors are the driving force, and long-term socio-economic prevention strategies often fall victim to externally driven short-term, militarized responses. This distortion of African priorities extends broadly across all areas of security engagement and Africans certainly need to do a better job of avoiding the old maxim, "if they fund it, we will do it" mentality.

The future of international engagement

From the early days of colonialism through the height of nineteenth-century European imperialism to the superpower rivalry of the Cold War, Africans have been an integral—albeit an underappreciated—part of the global security equation. Africa mattered to the world then. And it matters to the world now more than ever, as globalization and transnational threats have accelerated the continent's integration into the twenty-first century's international security structure. Importantly, this integration is a two-way street and Africa can no longer be viewed simply as a source of international security threats, but also as a target of external threats as well. Thus, the peace and stability of Africa is as much about global challenges as it is about African challenges. Acceptance of this reality will be essential if solutions are to be found.

Africans, however, cannot do it alone. Given the increasingly complex and interdependent nature of the African security environment the continent must look to the international community for assistance. Thus, more and not less international engagement will be the key to address these challenges and it will come at a cost. Not only requiring more financial and human resources, but more importantly strong Africa-centric leadership that is willing to set national agendas aside to help build a more peaceful and stable continent that has long-term benefits for all. The task will indeed be daunting as more countries, international organizations, and groups enter onto the scene. National interests will undoubtedly clash. There will undoubtedly be problems in setting priorities, coordinating responses, and in effectively utilizing donor resources. These obstacles can be overcome if both international and African leaders are truly committed, but no one said it would be easy.

Most important, African leaders and institutions must take ownership of their own security agenda and not let the international community (no matter how well intended) drive the agenda. International engagement is a supporting mechanism; a way for outsiders to assist Africans to address what they see as their most pressing human security challenges and top priorities. While the international perspective and expertise can be invaluable, at the end of the day effective solutions are ones that are locally sustainable and produce positive change at the ground level. Moreover, this approach shifts accountability for the success or failure of these initiatives to where it belongs—on African leaders and their societies.

On a positive note, the growing widespread acceptance in Africa and abroad of a human security approach to engagement is exactly what is needed. It is reflective of African concerns. It provides donor countries with a holistic approach to engagement. It allows for the full integration of all instruments of power across the defense, diplomatic, and development spectrum. Likewise, the traditional bilateral model of international engagement is being supplemented by more multilateral and diverse engagement models that reflect the rising role and power of international organizations, public–private partnerships, and civil society.

Unfortunately, there are dark clouds on the horizon that may very well undermine this progress in the years ahead. The 2016 election of Donald Trump and the rise to prominence of neo-isolationist and extreme nationalist agendas in the United States and parts of Western Europe will certainly complicate—if not reverse—international efforts to advance human security objectives on the continent. Some of this rollback already appears to be underway with Trump administration proposed large-scale cuts to US Department of State and USAID assistance programs. How badly human security efforts are affected still remains to be seen, but these cuts and a rejection of the cooperative security engagement model will certainly be felt in Africa, as will the potential American leadership vacuum that it creates. Africa may very well return to the strategic backwater of the 1990s for the United States as Trump pursues his "America first" policies. Alas, this shortsightedness is likely to allow old security threats to fester and new ones to evolve, which threatens not only African, but international, security as well.

Notes

1. K. Opalo, 'The consequences of the U.S. war on terrorism in Africa', *Al Jazeera America* (June 2, 2014), accessed at http://america.aljazeera.com/opinions/2014/6/africom-u-s-war-onterrorisminafricaalshabaabbokoharam.html on March 1, 2017.
2. President's Emergency Plan for AIDS Relief, 'Budget information', accessed at www.pepfar.gov/funding/budget/index.htm on March 1, 2017.
3. Emerson, Back to the future, p. 54.
4. Combined Maritime Forces, 'CTF-151: Counter-piracy', accessed at http://combinedmaritimeforces.com/ctf-151-counter-piracy/ on March 1, 2017.
5. United States Government, 'US strategy toward sub-Saharan Africa' (Washington: DC, The White House, June 2012), p. 2.
6. Ibid., pp. i–ii.
7. Ibid., p. 4.
8. Emerson, Back to the future, p. 50.

9 P. Melly and V. Darracq, *A New Way to Engage? French Policy in Africa from Sarkozy to Hollande* (London: Chatham House, May 2013), p. 4. The additional commitment of some 2,000 men to the Central African Republic in early 2014 to help quell the violence as part of Operation Sangaris pushed this number to over 9,000.
10 Africa All Party Parliamentary Group, 'Security and Africa: An update' (London, November 2012), p. 8, accessed at www.royalafricansociety.org/sites/default/files/reports/AAPPG_securityreport_nov2012.pdf on March 1, 2017.
11 *The Local*, 'Germany wants key role in Africa security' (April 3, 2014), accessed at www.thelocal.de/20140601/germany-will-be-a-motor-in-un-africa-plan_on March 1, 2017; German Information Centre Africa, 'Germany's new Africa policy recognises continent's changing position in the world' (May 23, 2014), accessed at www.gicafrica.diplo.de/Vertretung/suedaafrika-dz/en/_pr/2014/05/05-New-Africa-pol on March 1, 2017.
12 Emerson, 'Regional security initiative', p. 78. Budget figures, which do not include the $70 million lease fee paid to the Djiboutian government, are from a 2010 General Accountability Office report, 'Defense management: DOD needs to determine the future of its Horn of Africa task force', *GAO-10–504* (Washington, DC: US General Accountability Office April 2010), accessed at www.gao.gov/products/GAO-10–504 on March 1, 2017.
13 D. Styan, *Djibouti: Changing Influence in the Horn's Strategic Hub* (London: Chatham House, April 2013), pp. 11–12.
14 United States Department of State, 'Counterterrorism programs and initiatives', accessed at www.state.gov/j/ct/programs/index.htm on March 1, 2017.
15 L. Ploch, *Countering Terrorism in East Africa: The U.S. Response* (Washington, DC: Congressional Research Service, November 3, 2010).
16 *BBC News*, 'Kenya police accused of counter-terror abuses' (November 20, 2013).
17 Emerson, Back to the future, p. 51.
18 Deputy Assistant Secretary of Defense for African Affairs Theresa Whelan, as quoted in *American Forces Press Service*, 'New counterterrorism initiative to focus on Saharan Africa' (May 16, 2005), accessed at www.defense.gov/news/newsarticle.aspx?id=31643 on March 1, 2017.
19 *Washington Post*, Islamic State loses its stronghold in Libya.
20 *BBC News*, 'Who are Nigeria's Boko Haram Islamists?' (May 20, 2014).
21 *France24*, 'France revises counter-terrorism strategy in Africa' (January 29, 2014). *Guardian*, 'Britain to work with Algeria on counter-terrorism, says David Cameron' (January 30, 2013).
22 Emerson, 'Regional security initiative', p. 81.
23 *Newsweek*, 'Trump Expands U.S. Military Campaign in Africa with Somalia Offensive' (March 31, 2017) access at www.newsweek. com/trump-expand-military-campaign-africa-somalia-offensive-577347 on March 31, 2017.

24 Human Security Report Project, *Human Security Report 2005*, Figure 1.2: Number of armed conflicts, 1946–2003: Global and regional breakdowns, p. 24.
25 *AfricaCheck* Factsheet.
26 United Nations Department of Peace Keeping Operations, 'United Nations Peacekeeping Operations Factsheet (as of December 31, 2015)', accessed at www.un.org/en/peacekeeping/resources/statistics/factsheet.shtml on March 1, 2017.
27 Ibid.
28 P. Williams, 'Peace operations in Africa: Lessons learned since 2000', *Africa Security Brief*, 25 (Washington, DC: Africa Center for Strategic Studies, July 2013), p. 2.
29 N. Serafino, *The Global Peace Operations Initiative: Background and Issues for Congress* (Washington, DC: Congressional Research Service, Updated October 3, 2006), p. 1.
30 Author's email correspondence with Global Peace Operations Initiative, Bureau of Political-Military Affairs, US Department of State, September 2014.
31 US Department of State, 'African Contingency Operations Training and Assistance (ACOTA) Program', *Fact Sheet* (Washington, DC, February 6, 2013), accessed at www.state.gov/r/pa/prs/ps/2013/02/203841.htm on March 1, 2017.
32 Melly and Darracq, 'A New Way to Engage? French Policy in Africa from Sarkozy to Hollande' (London: Chatham House, May 2013), pp. 12–13.
33 Melly and Darracq, A New Way to Engage?, p. 13; *France 24*, France revises counterterrorism strategy; *Agence France-Presse*, 'France ends Mali offensive, redeploys troops to restive Sahel' (July 13, 2014).
34 United Nations, 'Millennium Development Goals, Goal 6: Combat HIV/AIDS, malaria, and other disease', accessed at www.un.org/millenniumgoals/aids.shtml on March 1, 2017.
35 President's Emergency Plan for AIDS Relief, 'Executive summary of PEPFAR's strategy', accessed at www.pepfar.gov/about/strategy/document/133244.htm on March 1, 2017.
36 PEPFAR, 'PEPFAR funding', accessed at http://pepfar.gov/documents/organization/252516.pdf on February 23, 2017.
37 President's Emergency Plan for AIDS Relief, '2014 PEPFAR latest results – fact sheet', accessed at www.pepfar.gov/documents/organization/234738.pdf on March 1, 2017.
38 PEPFAR, Budget information.
39 The Global Fund, 'Government donors', accessed at www.theglobalfund.org/en/government/ on March 1, 2017.
40 *Guardian*, 'Guinea worm disease poised to be eradicated within a few years' (September 12, 2012).
41 The White House, 'President Obama's global development policy and global health initiative', accessed at www.whitehouse.gov/sites/default/files/Global_Health_Fact_Sheet.pdf on March 1, 2017.

42 See, for example, HM Government, *Health is global: An outcomes framework for global health 2011–2015* (London: Department of Health, March 31, 2011), accessed at www.gov.uk/government/publications/health-is-global-an-outcomes-framework-for-global-health-2011-15-2 on March 1, 2017.
43 Speeches and Statements by the Prime Minister, 'The Africa that joins in partnership with Japan is brighter still' (Opening Session of the Fifth Tokyo International Conference on African Development, June 1, 2013), accessed at http://japan.kantei.go.jp/96_abe/statement/201306/01speech_e.html on March 1, 2017.
44 See, for example, *USA Today*, 'How China is taking over Africa' (May 19, 2014); *Al Jazeera*, 'China in Africa: Investment or exploitation?' (May 4, 2014); *The New Yorker*, 'China in Africa: The new imperialist?' (June 12, 2013); D. Shinn and J. Eisenman, *China and Africa: A Study of Engagement* (Philadelphia: University of Pennsylvania Press, 2012); I. Taylor, *China's New Role in Africa* (Boulder, CO: Lynne Rienner, 2010); M. van Dijk (ed.), *The New Presence of China in Africa* (Amsterdam: Amsterdam University Press, 2009); S. Michel, M. Beuret and P. Woods, *China Safari: On the Trail of Beijing's Expansion in Africa* (New York: Nation Books, 2009).
45 A. Vines, 'China in Africa: A mixed blessing?' *Current History* 106:700 (May 2007), p. 213; *Reuters*, 'In Africa: U.S. promotes security, China does business' (May 30, 2014).
46 *China Daily.com*, 'China-Africa trade approaches $300 billion in 2015' (November 10, 2015).
47 *Al Jazeera*, China in Africa; *Guardian*, 'Soft power, hard cash' (April 29, 2013).
48 Saferworld, *China's Growing Role in African Peace and Security* (London: Saferworld January 2011), p. 62, accessed at www.saferworld.org.uk/resources/view-resource/500-chinas-growing-role-in-african-peace-and-security on March 1, 2017.
49 United Nations Department of Peacekeeping Operations, 'Troop and police contributors', accessed at www.un.org/en/peacekeeping/resources/statistics/contributors.shtml_on March 1, 2017.
50 Premier L. Keqiang, 'Bring about a better future for China-Africa cooperation' (Speech at the AU Conference Center, Addis Ababa, 5 May 2014), accessed at www.fmprc.gov.cn/mfa_eng/wjdt_665385/zyjh_665391/t1154397.shtml on March 1, 2017.
51 Saferworld, China's growing role, p. 69.
52 D. Shinn, 'China in Africa Symposium' (Indiana University at Bloomington, March 6–7, 2009).
53 Premier L. Keqiang, China-Africa Cooperation.
54 *Guardian*, 'Reality check cast doubts on Chinese health aid to Africa' (June 10, 2013).
55 The Global Fund, 'Canada and the Global Fund', accessed at www.theglobalfund.org on March 1, 2017. (Replenishment_2013CanadaDonorSheet_ReportReplenishment_2013CanadaDonorSheet_Report).

56 Premier L. Keqiang, China-Africa Cooperation.
57 Saferworld, China's growing role in African peace and security, p. iv.
58 D. Shinn, 'Chinese Involvement in Africa Conflict Zones', *China Brief*, 9 (The Jamestown Foundation, April 2, 2009), p. 7.
59 Saferworld, China's growing role in African peace and security, pp. 51–4.
60 C. Stolte, *Brazil in Africa: Just Another BRICS Country Seeking Resources?* (London: Chatham House, November 2012), p. 3.
61 Ibid., p. 5.
62 Stolte, *Brazil in Africa*, p. 5.
63 *BBC News*, 'Brazil 'to write off' almost $900m of African debt' (May 25, 2013).
64 BRICS Policy Center, 'Solidarity among brothers? Brazil in Africa: trade, investment and cooperation', *PBC Policy Brief*, 4:65 (February 2014), p. 13.
65 Ibid., p. 14.
66 UN Department of Peacekeeping Operations, 'Troops and police contributors'.
67 *The New York Times*, 'Brazil gains business and influence as it offers aid and loans in Africa' (August 7, 2012).
68 *IndiaAfrica Connect*, 'Five-fold increase in India-Africa trade: Minister' (9th CII-EXIM Bank India-Africa Project Partnership, March 6, 2013), accessed at www.indiaafricaconnect.in/index.php?param=news/5806/india-africaconclave/120 on March 1, 2017; *Washington Post*, 'How Other Countries Are Scrambling for Africa Alongside the U.S.' (August 5, 2014).
69 UN Department of Peacekeeping Operations, 'Troops and police contributors'.
70 *IndiaAfrica Connect* 'Africa seeks Indian investment in healthcare' (9th CII-EXIM Bank India-Africa Project Partnership, March 6, 2013), accessed at www.indiaafricaconnect.in/index.php?param=news/5811/india-africaconclave/120 on March 1, 2017.
71 *Independent Online*, 'Russians start $3bn mine in Zimbabwe' (September 17, 2014), accessed at www.iol.co.za/business/news/russians-start-3bn-mine-in-zimbabwe-1.1751935#.VCA4kfldVg0 on March 1, 2017.
72 Ibid.
73 The Africa-EU Partnership, 'Assessing achievements and perspectives for peace and security in Africa' (June 4, 2014), accessed at www.africa-eu-partnership.org/newsroom/all-news/assessing-achievements-and-perspectives-peace-and-security-africa on March 1, 2017.
74 *INTERPOL News*, 'Annual Report 2012', p. 19, accessed at www.interpol.int/News-and-media/Publications#n627 on March 1, 2017.
75 Ibid., p. 7.
76 *INTERPOL News*, 'INTERPOL announces formation of dedicated environmental crime team in Africa' (October 7, 2014), accessed at www.interpol.int/News-and-media/News/2014/N2014-196 on March 1, 2017.
77 International Organization for Migration, *Migration Health, Annual Review 2012* (Geneva: International Organization for Migration, 2013).

78 World Food Programme, 'Strategic Plan', accessed at www.wfp.org/about/strategic-plan on March 1, 2017.
79 OECD, 'Sub-Saharan Africa and the OECD', accessed at www.oecd.org/africa/africa-focusedbodies.htm on March 1, 2017.
80 OECD, 'Fragile States 2014', accessed at www.oecd.org/dac/incaf/FSR-2014.pdf on March 1, 2017.
81 See CARE, www.care.org/work, for instance.
82 Salvation Army International, 'Our work', accessed at www.salvationarmy.org/ihq/ourwork on March 1, 2017.
83 NGO Working Group for Women, Peace and Security, 'About us', accessed at www.womenpeacesecurity.org/about/ on March 1, 2017.
84 IANSA, 'About us', accessed at www.iansa.org/aboutus on March 1, 2017.
85 Bill and Melinda Gates Foundation, '2012 Bill & Melinda Gates Foundation Annual Report', p. 6, accessed at www.gatesfoundation.org/Who-We-Are/Resources-and-Media/Annual-Reports on March 1, 2017.
86 PureMadi, accessed at www.puremadi.org/ on March 1, 2017.

11
The future of African security

The African security environment of the twenty-first century is an exceedingly dynamic and fluid one. It is composed of highly complex and interconnected problems, which present immense challenges, not only across all levels of African society, but to global institutions and leadership as well. It can be said to be a microcosm of a new world disorder of traditional, non-traditional, and transnational threats that test the limits of old definitions of security and necessitate the use of new methods and tools to achieve lasting solutions. What is also equally clear is that the African Union's state-centric security architecture provides an ill fit to current security realities. As such, the Africa of the future will be a place that is more about people and less about states; more about innovation and communication from the bottom up rather than the unbridled exercise of power from the top down. This makes it fraught with many obstacles, but also presents great opportunities for addressing the most pressing global—and not just African—challenges of the twenty-first century.

With more than its share of fragile, unstable states and impoverished societies, the continent was once seen almost exclusively as an incubator of instability and insecurity; a venue for addressing rising challenges and an exporter of global security threats. But this is no longer the case. Africa, like everywhere else in the world, is becoming increasingly integrated into a globalized security system, whereby Africans are just as vulnerable to threats emanating from outside the continent as they are from home-grown ones. Globalization, more so than any other factor, has facilitated this process. It will continue to propel the continent's security integration, for better or worse, by magnifying challenges, but also at the same time increasing the opportunities for solutions.

Thus, Africa—and what happens there—matters more than ever. Simply ignoring it and hoping for the best is not an option in an increasingly globalized world; containment and isolation is not an effective strategic response. Moreover, the cost of failure is also growing. Inability, or unwillingness, to nip problems in the bud has allowed many localized threats in Africa to morph into larger regional or even global security threats. Clearly, the lack of African government resources, capabilities, political will, and overburdened security agendas are a huge obstacle to progress and admittedly Africans should and must do more. Nonetheless, the harsh reality is that they cannot do it alone. Nor should they have to because, as we have seen, Africa's twenty-first-century challenges are the world's challenges too. Not only should the international community move more proactively to assist Africans to fill the resource and technical expertise gap, but it needs to work smarter and more efficiently. And this will mean more than simply paying lip service to the human security framework, but rather making concrete changes to better align their ends, ways, and means of African engagement.

Emerging trends: opportunities and pitfalls

While Africa is certainly facing daunting challenges that will severely strain its capabilities to provide a more peaceful and secure future for its citizens, there is room for optimism that tomorrow will be better than today. The legacies of colonialism and the Cold War are steadily fading into the background. The rise of new generations, each calling for greater inclusion and government accountability, are maintaining the momentum—albeit uneven at times—for greater democratization and political reform across the continent. Economies are growing, and the middle class in Africa is expanding. The rapid pace of technological advancements and global integration are facilitating communication and the exchange of ideas between Africans, as well as non-Africans, as never before. The continent and its people are increasingly being accepted as part of the global community and steadily acknowledged as playing a role in developing global solutions. All of this will lead to the emergence of greater opportunities for tackling the continent's most pressing security challenges in the decades ahead. Serious obstacles and pitfalls still will need to be overcome, but this harsh reality should not dissuade one from trying.

The evolving nature of African conflict

Violent conflict is at the center of African security challenges. It results in immense human suffering, disrupts economic development, divides societies, and destabilizes countries and even entire sub-regions. It has a very direct negative impact on human security on multiple levels. However, the overall intensity of violent conflict worldwide—and in Africa in particular—has been declining since the end of the Cold War; overall conflicts have fallen by 40 percent and the deadliest conflicts (those that kill at least 1,000 per year) have declined by more than half.[1] Even more significantly, "there are now compelling reasons," according to the Human Security Research Group, "for believing that the historical decline in violence is both real and remarkably large—and also that the future may well be less violent than in the past."[2] This means fewer Africans are likely to die as a direct result of violent conflict over the next decade than died in the previous one.

It also highlights the changing scope and nature of African violence that is both advantageous and detrimental to the future of human security. On the one hand, large-scale inter-state or intra-state violence across the continent is likely to continue to decline, which means fewer deaths and less destructive violence (although undoubtedly there will be periodic episodes of extreme violence). On the other hand, low-level violence is likely to become more widespread and persistent than ever. Moreover, many of these low-level conflicts have the potential to quickly burst into more intense domestic or sub-regional violence and instability if allowed to persist. In addition, we are likely to see an expanded role by external actors (both state and non-state) in shaping the course of future African conflicts.

Likewise, mutually reinforcing and cross-cutting linkages of identity, resource competition, weapons availability or poor governance and political alienation can provide further tinder to fan the flames of these conflicts. Identity and resource-based conflicts are especially vulnerable to political manipulation and are particularly difficult to resolve. Without improved governance and enhanced democratic inclusion across the continent's most divided societies these types of conflicts will likely continue to plague African societies for years to come. In extreme instances this may even result in future outbreaks of genocidal-like warfare. At the end of 2016, outgoing UN Secretary-General Ban Ki-moon warned that South Sudan was "on a trajectory toward mass atrocities" as the extreme ethnic violence there showed no sign of abating.[3] Sadly, it seems that the Rwandas and Darfurs have yet to be relegated to the dustbins of history.

This mixed picture provides both opportunities and obstacles.

The good news in all of this is that many of these smaller, lower intensity conflicts are more manageable and susceptible to conflict mitigation and resolution efforts. Greater awareness of cross-cutting linkages to other security challenges means that multiple strategies can be employed and various partnerships developed to address the problem of conflict. For example, the challenge of livelihood conflicts could be mitigated by also addressing environmental degradation, reducing the influx of weaponry into an area or increasing minority participation in local governance mechanisms. Including civil society groups and international developmental or environmental NGOs into the process would also bring additional resources to bear.

The bad news is that the rising number and interconnected complexity of these conflicts will make it impossible for African countries—even with extensive international assistance—to address all of these conflict situations effectively. While a holistic approach certainly brings more stakeholders and resources to bear on the problem, it also severely complicates planning and coordination among the participants, which can result in the inefficient use of resources and unnecessary duplication of efforts. Likewise, the dark side of globalization means that external actors—particularly non-state actors—are now able to exercise considerable capability to fuel or sustain violence as part of their own agendas. This can result in the original source of a conflict becoming subsumed by other outside interests and thereby increase the difficulty in bringing about a peaceful resolution.

Finally, the growing involvement and importance of non-state actors in African conflicts also raises another distressing trend that in some ways mimics the Cold War—the return of proxy forces and the fostering of international alliances among groups. While not comparable by any measure to the type and level of military support rendered by the superpowers to their African clients during the Cold War in Africa, the psychological and propaganda value of these alliances is significant. It allows African groups to raise their global profile, burnish their domestic credentials, and increase the potential pool of recruits while opening doors to new sources of financial and technical assistance through the development of affiliate networks. This is especially true for African extremist and Islamist jihadist groups, who rely on terrorist tactics to advance their causes. The most visible of these are Islamic State-affiliated groups in Libya, as well as al-Qaeda in the Islamic Maghreb in North-West Africa and al-Shabaab in the Horn of Africa with their self-proclaimed alliances with al-Qaeda, and Nigeria's Boko Haram with its pledge of allegiance and loyalty to the Islamic State.

The rise of globalized non-traditional challenges
As we have highlighted throughout this book, a highly diverse set of non-traditional and transnational threats now pose some of the most pressing and serious challenges to African security—challenges that African societies today are least able and equipped to address. Next to endemic conflict, these challenges will most likely become the greatest danger to human security in the decades ahead and will be the most

difficult to mitigate unless new strategies and alliances are vigorously implemented. For it is here, within the non-traditional security arena, that either the success or failure of the human security construct in Africa will likely result.

Although the challenges from combating terrorism and the trafficking in drugs, people, and small arms to tackling pandemic disease, improving health care, and countering environmental degradation are enormous, so too are opportunities for making a real difference in advancing human security. Even small advancements in disease prevention, child nutrition, and health care delivery, for example, would improve the well-being of many of the poorest individuals and communities across the continent. Without freedom from want in meeting the basic needs of individuals and communities, personal security cannot be achieved. Moreover, it effectively redefines poverty alleviation and development as being an integral part of the security equation. Likewise, addressing illicit trafficking and the criminal networks behind these activities would go a long way in improving public safety. By tackling these types of personal and community security needs, societies can then begin to build a stronger security foundation from the bottom up, which is ultimately at the heart of the human security construct.

Non-traditional and transnational challenges also provide an effective entry point for establishing and/or reinforcing international security partnerships because, by their very nature, they present globalized security challenges. These types of challenges cannot be addressed by a single country or even region, but require the mobilization of the international community and the development of a comprehensive global response. While large countries like the United States and its Western allies or powerful international institutions (such as the United Nations) often drive this agenda given their ability to bring significant financial resources and expertise to bear, smaller countries and specialized international organizations have sought—often with success—a greater role in partnering with African countries and organizations. Canada, Japan, and many of the Scandinavian countries are now heavily engaged in human security initiatives, as are specialized IGOs like INTERPOL, the International Organization for Migration, the Wassenaar Arrangement, and the Nordic Development Fund. Also the expanding role and mission of both the international and African NGO community is an encouraging one because they bring not only badly needed additional resources and technical expertise to the fight, but also the ability to generate greater public awareness and build international support for issues like combating human trafficking, reducing gun violence, improving children's health, or protecting the environment.

Just as, if not more, important than the actual expansion in the sheer number of international stakeholders with an interest in African security is their heightened emphasis on utilizing non-traditional security approaches and tools in their engagement. Their focus is more on development, rather than military, assistance and on addressing the root causes of problems rather than simply reacting to the symptoms of a problem. This means redirecting resources and efforts toward increasing micro-financing and infrastructure development instead of providing weaponry and other high tech military equipment, and adding more health professionals, agronomists, and community activists, instead of military advisers and trainers.

These efforts, however, pale in comparison to the current level of traditional security provided by the United States and its Western allies. And while able to "talk the talk" of human security, these governments have yet to restructure their engagement methods and tools or reprioritize their budgets to reflect the reality on the ground. As we have noted earlier, many African security partners—and especially the United States—remain too deeply rooted in a traditional view of national security and are still too military-centric in their approaches, so that other options have yet to be fully explored. This will be a difficult obstacle to overcome in the years ahead.

In addition to these differing engagement approaches to tackling non-traditional security challenges, the growing number of stakeholders in itself is likely to complicate implementation efforts, even when and where there is widespread agreement. Lack of cooperation, difficulty in coordinating and prioritizing multinational and multi-organizational activities, mutual distrust and suspicion between military and civilian organizations, and competing leadership roles will need to be overcome. Likewise, the issue of China's role (or even Beijing's willingness to participate) in this global security partnership has yet to be answered and presents a major stumbling block to success. The end result of all this could be a severe weakening of the overall desire for greater international engagement in Africa, a return to fragmented programs and policies, countries and organizations working at cross purposes, and rising frustration and donor fatigue—none of which would be good for the future of African security.

The declining role of the state
With the growth of a multitude of new actors and non-state interests, the role and importance of the state in African security has clearly diminished from what it once was. The once omnipresent vision of the inseparability of regime and state security is a thing of the past and the

strength of African governments are no longer viewed as the sole determinants of stable and secure societies. This narrow view of security, as we have seen, has now been replaced by a much more diverse and complex one that encompasses a vast array of stakeholders. Moreover, external forces and non-state interests have become such key factors in shaping the African security agenda that the emerging challenges of the continent are becoming just another facet of the wider global security agenda. This is not to say that the African state has become irrelevant. The state is here to stay. For all its defects, it remains the single most powerful and influential actor is shaping security. Nonetheless, its preeminent role and dominance has changed and will almost certainly continue to diminish in the future.

This changed reality opens the door for multiple additional opportunities to advance human security and to address some of the continent's most pressing security problems, although it also will most likely complicate the traditional engagement efforts of some of Africa's most influential international partners. The declining dominance of the state has spurred the growing security participation of many heretofore neglected sectors of African society. Civil society organizations (especially women's groups), issue-specific NGOs, human rights advocates, and local communities and their leaders now have an active voice in the security debate. Moreover, many of these new stakeholders have formed strong international partnerships to further leverage their positions. Thus, greater attention is now being paid to challenges at the individual and community levels, there is a sense of broader societal inclusion that enhances government legitimacy, and this environment facilitates the development of a bottom-up security framework that better reflects human security priorities. Ideally, over time, this also would mean less money and resources spent on building stronger and more effective militaries and more directed toward development and poverty alleviation programs as ways and means are better aligned with human security goals.

Despite all its flaws, the state is still the dominant power within African societies and is likely to remain the central focal point for international security engagement. Any reduction in its role, no matter how well intended, has the potential to negatively impact the future of African security. While the increased participation of multiple new actors in the security debate is a good thing, it also severely complicates efforts to develop and implement a comprehensive national security strategy. There will never be enough money and resources to address all societal concerns and this leads to winners and losers. The state's ability to function as the final arbiter is critical in overriding parochial concerns (no matter how valid) to achieve what is best for the nation overall and for ensuring national cohesion. As we have seen, historically the politics of division has been a central characteristic in undermining African peace and security. Thus, finding the right balance of state power and meeting the needs of social inclusion when it comes to advancing human security will be essential. Some countries will get it right, but more are likely to get it wrong.

One of the central themes of this book has been the notion of collective global security and of international participation in working jointly with African governments, institutions, and societies to address Africa's security challenges. Although the international NGO community is more involved than ever on the continent, the bulk of this assistance to Africa will almost certainly continue to come from donor governments and IGOs. States and international organizations know how to engage with other states; the state structure inherently provides the mechanism for funneling assistance and coordinating engagement efforts. Governments are comfortable dealing with other governments and it is often the path of least resistance. Moreover, many of Africa's key partners (especially the United States) are still struggling with adapting their engagement models and tools to reflect the changing requirements of human security engagement. For these countries, state-to-state relationships and strengthening traditional security structures, such as the military, police, and intelligence organizations, are a higher priority than development or poverty alleviation.

Clearly the declining role of the state is a mixed blessing and for the foreseeable future the state will no doubt continue to function as the primary building block in the African security framework, but how it reinvents itself to better reflect the fundamental security needs of its people will be the ultimate determining factor in its success or failure.

Some final thoughts

The twenty-first-century African security environment is not only one of the most complex in terms of the array and depth of the challenges facing it, but also one of the most demanding given the dearth of available resources needed to advance peace and stability. While the Africa of today and many of its problems are certainly rooted in the legacy of colonialism, the Cold War, and outside interference, much of the failure to deal effectively with these problems falls squarely on the shoulders of African leaders, who are more concerned with burnishing regime security and furthering their own narrow, parochial self-interests than in safeguarding their own people. In many respects, Africans were dealt a bad hand. But, for far too long they have also failed to step up and take ownership of their problems and undertake the difficult task of self-introspection. All this may be changing, however, with a new generation that views poor governance, lack of societal inclusion, and insufficient development as key stumbling blocks to the evolution of a successful and secure Africa. They know it will not be an easy task as they confront entrenched authoritarian leaders and those who seek to usurp the democratic process and will of the people to maintain their grip on power at whatever the cost.

The human security paradigm, and its widespread acceptance across the continent, echoes this new thinking. It puts people first and develops security from within societies, and it is through this principle that the future of African security will be determined. To be effective the traditional state-centric approach needs to give way to the mobilizing power of individuals and local communities to develop a well-grounded security foundation at the grassroots level. Moreover, security strategies need to better reflect this shift by focusing more on the non-traditional and transnational challenges that affect the daily lives of people rather than on securing the state and its institutions of power from external attack. The most serious threats now arise from within rather than outside the state. Thus, the future is more about addressing livelihood and identity conflict, improving public health, limiting environmental degradation, and tackling demographic challenges than fighting international terrorism, strengthening military prowess or countering the rise of global powers' proxies.

This is not to say that Africans should ignore very real and pressing global challenges or developments outside the continent, because they do impact African security. As repeatedly noted, Africa—and its challenges—has become integrated into the global security architecture; just as many of the world's challenges have become the continent's too. This globalization of security, however, does not mean that African leaders and countries need to see every emerging global challenge as their own, or more importantly, as a security priority. The African security agenda needs to be *the African security agenda* and not one dictated from outside. This will require a more nuanced and sophisticated approach to examining global challenges. How do they really impact the safety and security of Africans? Are they the source of a problem or merely exploiting an existing one? And where do they rank as priorities for Africans? These are tough questions and ones that will likely require a steadfast adherence to the human security framework in the face of considerable external pressure.

Which brings us to the role of the international community in assisting (or hindering) this security transformation. The harsh reality is that African governments and institutions simply lack the resources, technical expertise, and mechanisms to cope with all the challenges facing them. And this situation is unlikely to change. There will never be enough African resources. Thus, the participation of the foreign governments, international institutions, and the global NGO community is critical in bridging the resource and capability gap. However, this does not mean that Africans must accept lock, stock, and barrel *any international security assistance*, especially those reflecting non-African priorities. Unfortunately, the continent is littered with tens of thousands of examples of programs and initiatives (most well intended) that simply collapsed once the funding ended. The fault lies with both donors and recipients. Each side could and must do better in offering and accepting security assistance that supports established human security strategies and objectives. In some instances, this will require donor countries to reassess their own engagement approach to better align ends, ways, and means—not simply talking the talk of human security, but employing the proper tools to achieve it.

The human security construct is not a panacea for all the continent's ills. It is, however, a solid starting point for focusing the security debate on concerns that matter to Africans and that will make a difference in advancing actual peace and stability. The road ahead will be difficult, especially in light of an apparent rising tide of neo-nationalism and protectionism in the United States and parts of Western Europe. Thus, it will be filled with many obstacles and setbacks as these new leaders likely pursue policies that are antithetical to human security principles. But not all is lost, for resilience, perseverance, and optimism for a better future are defining hallmarks of the African character and so too should they be for its global security partners.

Notes

1 Human Security Report Project press release, 'The decline in global violence: Reality or myth?' (March 3, 2014), accessed at www.hsrgroup.org/docs/Publications/HSR2013/HSR_2013_Press_Release.pdf on 28 February 2017.
2 Human Security Report Project, *Human Security Report 2013*, p. 11.
3 C. Vinograd, 'The revenge of Salva Kiir', *Foreign Policy.com* (January 2, 2017) accessed at http://foreignpolicy.com/2017/01/02/the-revenge-of-salva-kiir-south-sudan-genocide-ethnic-cleansing/ on February 28, 2017.

Bibliography

ABC News, 'Scientists: UN soldiers brought deadly superbug to Americas' (January 12, 2012), accessed at http://news.yahoo.com/scientists-un-soldiers-brought-deadly-superbug-americas-194141189-abc-news.html on February 28, 2017.

Abimbola, Adesoji, 'Between Maitatsane and Boko Haram: Islamic fundamentalism and the response of the Nigerian State', *Africa Today*, 57:4 (Summer 2011).

Adam, H., 'Somalia: A troubled beauty being born', in W. Zartman (ed.), *Collapsed States: The Disintegration and Restoration of Legitimate Authority* (Boulder, CO: Lynne Rienner Publishers, 1995).

Adler, Emanuel, 'Imagined (security) communities: Cognitive regions in international relations', *Millennium: Journal of International Studies*, 26:2 (1997).

Africa All Party Parliamentary Group, 'Security and Africa: An update' (London, November 2012), p. 8, accessed at www.royalafricansociety.org/sites/default/files/reports/AAPPG_securityreport_nov2012.pdf on March 1, 2017.

AfricaCheck, 'Factsheet: Conflict-related deaths in sub-Saharan Africa', Factsheets and Guides, accessed at https://africacheck.org/factsheets/conflict-related-deaths-in-sub-saharan-africa/ on February 24, 2017.

The Africa-EU Partnership, 'Assessing achievements and perspectives for peace and security in Africa' (June 4, 2014), accessed at www.africa-eu-partnership.org/newsroom/all-news/assessing-achievements-and-perspectives-peace-and-security-africa on March 1, 2017.

AfricaNews, 'Malnutrition and Africa: Is there a way out?' (January 26, 2011).

African Union, *Constitutive Act of the African Union* (Adopted July 11, 2000), accessed at www.au.int/en/sites/default/files/Constitutive_Act_en_0.htm on February 28, 2017.

Agence France-Presse, 'World Bank highlights conflict as key to poverty' (April 11, 2011).

— 'France ends Mali offensive, redeploys troops to restive Sahel' (July 13, 2014).

— 'Boko Haram kills nearly 200 in 48 hours of Nigeria slaughter' (July 3, 2015).

— 'Boko Haram attacks kill 17 in Chad, Nigeria' (July 11, 2015).

Bibliography

Agency for Cooperation and Research in Development, 'Partners', accessed at www.acordinternational.org/acord/en/about-us/about-us/partners/ on February 28, 2017.

Akabwai, Darlington and Priscillar Ateyo, 'The scramble for cattle, power and guns in Karamojo' (Medford, MA: Feinstein International Center, December 2007).

Akukwe, Chinua, *Don't Let Them Die* (London: Adonis & Abbey Publishers, 2006).

Alao, Abiodun, *Natural Resources and Conflict in Africa: The Tragedy of Endowment* (Rochester, NY: University of Rochester Press, 2007).

Al Jazeera, 'Al Shabaab "Joins Ranks" With Al-Qaeda' (February 10, 2012).

— 'China in Africa: Investment or exploitation?' (May 4, 2014).

— 'Burundi's president threatens to fight AU peacekeepers' (December 30, 2015).

— 'Burundi crisis: AU to vote on peacekeeping mission' (January 30, 2016).

— 'Al-Shabaab attacks in Somalia (2006–2016)' (August 31, 2016).

allAfrica.com, 'Mozambique: Christian project collects 700,000 guns' (January 26, 2010).

— 'East Africa: Illicit small arms and light weapons pose serious security threat to region' (April 16, 2011).

— 'South Africa: 11,935 SAPS firearms "disappear" over five years' (September 11, 2011).

— 'North Africa: AQIM partners with Colombian drug cartel' (December 5, 2014) accessed at http://allafrica.com/stories/201412060088.html on February 22, 2017.

— 'Boko Haram attacks kill 17 in Chad, Nigeria' (July 11, 2015).

— 'Somalia: Election heralds unexpected fresh start' (February 13, 2017), accessed at http://allafrica.com/stories/201702130819.html on February 28, 2017.

American Forces Press Service, 'New counterterrorism initiative to focus on Saharan Africa' (May 16, 2005), accessed at www.defense.gov/news/newsarticle.aspx?id=31643 on March 1, 2017.

Andrews-Speed, Phillip, Raimund Bleischwitz, Tim Boersma, *et al.*, 'The global resource nexus: The struggles for land, energy, food, water, and minerals' (Berlin: Transatlantic Academy, May 2012) accessed at www.transatlanticacademy.org/sites/default/files/publications/TA%202012%20report_web_version.pdf.

Aning, Kwesi, 'Africa: Confronting complex threats' (The International Peace Academy, February 2007), accessed at http://africacenter.org/wp-content/uploads/2007/07/Africa-Confronting-Complex-Threats.pdf on February 28, 2017.

Araoye, Ademola, 'Hegemonic agendas, intermesticity and conflicts in the postcolonial state', *African Journal on Conflict Resolution* 12:1 (2012).

Armstrong, David, 'The evolution of international society', in John Baylis, Steve Smith, and Patricia Owens (eds), *The Globalization of World*

Politics: An Introduction to World Politics (Oxford: Oxford University Press, 2008).

Assembly of the African Union, First Ordinary Session, *Protocol Relating to the Establishment of the Peace and Security Council of the African Union* (July 9, 2002), accessed at www.au.int/en/sites/default/files/Protocol_peace_and_security.pdf on February 28, 2017.

Associated Press, 'Horn of Africa may be the next terror front' (October 21, 2006).

— 'Tunisia pledges tough security measures after Sousse Hotel attack' (June 27, 2015).

— 'Bungling by UN agency hurt Ebola response' (September 21, 2015).

AVERT, 'History of HIV/AIDS in South Africa', accessed at http://hivsa.com/?q=content/hiv-aids-south-africa on February 23, 2017.

— 'HIV and AIDS in sub-Saharan Africa', accessed at www.avert.org/hiv-aids-sub-saharan-africa.htm on February 28, 2017.

Bates, Robert H., 'Ethnic competition and modernization in contemporary Africa', *Comparative Political Studies*, 6:4 (1974).

BBC News, 'Nigeria clashes: 50,000 killed' (October 7, 2004).

— 'Nigeria violence in Jos: Q & A' (March 8, 2010).

— 'Q&A: Who are Somalia's Al Shabaab?' (October 5, 2012), accessed at www.bbc.co.uk/news/world-africa-15336689 on February 28, 2017.

— 'Brazil "to write off" almost $900m of African debt' (May 25, 2013).

— 'Egyptian warning over Ethiopia Nile dam' (June 10, 2013).

— 'Kenya police accused of counter-terror abuses' (November 20, 2013).

— 'Who are Nigeria's Boko Haram Islamists?' (May 20, 2014).

— 'France sets up anti-Islamic force in Africa's Sahel' (July 14, 2014).

— 'South Africa to spend $2.2 bn on HIV/AIDS drugs' (November 18, 2014).

— 'Islamic State "accepts" Boko Haram's allegiance pledge' (March 13, 2015).

— 'Nigeria elections: Winner Buhari issues Boko Haram vow' (April 1, 2015).

— 'Making sense of Nigeria's Fulani-farmer conflict' (May 5, 2016).

Bekker, S., M. Dodd, and M. Khosa, *Shifting African Identities* (Pretoria: Human Sciences Research Council, 2001).

Belloc, Hilaire, *The Modern Traveller*, cited in *The Oxford Essential Quotations Dictionary—American Edition* (New York: Berkley Books, 1998).

Berman, Bruce, Dickson Eyoh, and Will Kymlicka, 'Ethnicity and the politics of democratic nation-building in Africa', in Bruce Berman, Dickson Eyoh, and Will Kymlicka (eds), *Ethnicity and Democracy in Africa* (Oxford: James Currey Publishers, 2004).

Bill and Melinda Gates Foundation, '2012 Bill & Melinda Gates Foundation Annual Report', accessed at www.gatesfoundation.org/Who-We-Are/Resources-and-Media/Annual-Reports on March 1, 2017.

Bøås, Morten and Kathleen Jennings, '"Failed states" and "state failure": Threats or opportunities?' *Globalizations*, 4:4 (2007).

BRICS Policy Center 'Solidarity among brothers? Brazil in Africa: trade, investment and cooperation', *PBC Policy Brief* 4:65 (February 2014).

Brooke-Smith, Robin, *The Scramble for Africa* (Basingstoke: Macmillan Education, 1987).

Brundtland, Gro Harlem, 'The future of the world's health', in C. Everett Koop, Clarence Pearson, and M. Roy Schwarz (eds), *Critical Issues in Global Health* (SanFrancisco: Jossey-Bass, 2002).

Burke, Peter and J. Stets, *Identity Theory* (New York: Oxford University Press, 2009).

Business Insider, 'These maps show the hard drug trade in remarkable detail' (February 19, 2015), accessed at www.businessinsider.com/how-drugs-travel-around-the-world-2015-2 on February 27, 2017.

Call, Charles, 'The fallacy of the "failed state"', *Third World Quarterly* 29:8 (2008).

Campbell, John, 'This is Africa's new biggest city: Lagos, Nigeria, population 21 million', *The Atlantic* (July 10, 2012), accessed at www.theatlantic.com/international/archive/2012/07/this-is-africas-new-biggest-city-lagos-nigeria-population-21-million/259611/ on February 22, 2017.

CARE, www.care.org/work.

Carpenter, J. Scott, Matthew Levitt, Steven Simon, and Juan Zarate, *Fighting the Ideological Battle: The Missing Link in U.S. Strategy to Counter Violent Extremism* (Washington, DC: The Washington Institute for Near East Policy, July 2010).

Centers for Disease Control and Prevention, 'HIV statistics', accessed at www.cdc.gov/hiv/statistics/basics/ataglance.html on February 28, 2017.

— 'Global diarrhea burden', accessed at www.cdc.gov/healthywater/global/diarrhea-burden.html on February 28, 2017.

— 'New report on declining cancer incidence and death rates; report shows progress in controlling cancer' (March 12, 1998), accessed at www.cdc.gov/nchs/pressroom/98news/cancer.htm on February 28, 2017.

Chabal, Patrick and Jean-Pascal Daloz, *Africa Works: Disorder as Political Instrument* (Oxford: James Currey Publishers, 1999).

Chan, Margaret, 'Antimicrobial resistance: no action today, no cure tomorrow' (Remarks of Dr Margaret Chan at World Health Day 2011, Geneva, Switzerland, April 6, 2011), accessed at www.who.int/dg/speeches/2011/WHD_20110407/en/ on February 28, 2017.

— 'Keynote address at the global health security initiative ministerial meeting in Paris, France' (December 9, 2011), accessed at www.who.int/dg/speeches/2011/health_security_20111209/en/index.html on February 28, 2017.

China Daily.com, 'China-Africa trade approaches $300 billion in 2015' (November 10, 2015), accessed at www.chinadaily.com.cn/business/2015-11/10/content_22417707.htm on March 1, 2017.

Chitiyo, Knox and Anna Rader, *Somalia 2012: Ending the Transition?* (Johannesburg: The Brenthurst Foundation, Discussion Paper 4, 2012), accessed at www.thebrenthurstfoundation.org/files/brenthurst_commisioned_

reports/Brenthurst-paper-201204-Somalia-2012-Ending-the-Transition.pdf on February 28, 2017.

Chogugudza, Crisford, 'Ethnicity main cause of instability, civil conflict and poverty in Africa', *AfricaResource* (January 8, 2008), accessed at www.africaresource.com/essays-a-reviews/politics/478-ethnicity-main-cause-of-instability-civil-conflict-and-poverty-in-africa on February 24, 2017.

Chossudovsky, Michael, 'The spoils of war: Afghanistan's multibillion dollar heroin trade' (May 25, 2015), accessed at www.globalresearch.ca/the-spoils-of-war-afghanistan-s-multibillion-dollar-heroin-trade/91 on February 27, 2017.

Christie, Ryerson, 'Critical voices and human security', *Security Dialogue* 41:2 (April 2010).

CIA, *The World Factbook* (Washington, DC: Central Intelligence Agency), accessed at www.cia.gov/library/publications/the-world-factbook/rankorder, accessed February 22, 2017.

Cilliers, Jakkie, 'Terrorism and Africa', *African Security Review* 12:4 (2003).

— *Human Security in Africa: A Conceptual Framework for Review* (Pretoria: African Human Security Initiative, 2004).

— *Conflict Trends in Africa: A Turn for the Better in 2015?* (Institute for Security Studies, November 4, 2015), accessed at www.issafrica.org/iss-today/conflict-trends-in-africa-a-turn-for-the-better-in-2015 on February 22, 2017.

— and Julia Schunemann, 'The future of intrastate conflict in Africa', *ISS Paper 246* (Pretoria: Institute for Security Studies, May 23, 2013).

— and Kathryn Sturman, 'The right intervention: Enforcement challenge for the African Union', *African Security Review*, 11:3 (2002).

— and Kathryn Sturman, 'Challenges facing the AU's Peace and Security Council', *African Security Review*, 13:1 (2004).

CNN, 'ISIS comes to Libya' (November 18, 2014), accessed at www.cnn.com/2014/11/18/world/isis-libya/ on February 26, 2017.

— 'Ethiopia's $5bn project could turn it into Africa's powerhouse' (March 6, 2015).

— 'U.S. official calls ISIS a problem "off the charts historically"' (April 13, 2015).

— 'MERSA fast facts' (updated June 11, 2015), accessed at www.cnn.com/2013/06/28/us/mrsa-fast-facts/ on February 28, 2017.

___ 'Alarm bells ring for charities as Trump pledges to slash foreign aid budget' (March 1, 2017).

Coalition for Grassroots Women Organization, 'Report of COGWO board election' (February 21, 2013), accessed at http://cogwosomali.org/documents/COGWO-Election-2013.pdf on February 28, 2017.

Cohen, Jon, 'New report card on global HIV/AIDS epidemic', *Science Magazine* (July 14, 2015), accessed at http://news.sciencemag.org/funding/2015/07/new-report-card-global-hivaids-epidemic on February 28, 2017.

Collier, Paul and Anke Hoeffler, 'Greed and grievance in civil war', *Oxford Economic Papers 56* (2004).

— 'Natural resources and conflict in Africa' (October 2004), accessed at www.crimesofwar.org on February 28, 2017.

— and Nicholas Sambanis (eds), *Volume 1: Africa, Understanding Civil War: Evidence and Analysis* (Washington, DC: The World Bank, 2005).

Combined Maritime Forces, 'CTF-151: Counter-piracy', accessed at http://combinedmaritimeforces.com/ctf-151-counter-piracy/ on March 1, 2017.

Commission on Human Security, *Human Security Now* (New York: Commission on Human Security, 2003).

Costa, Antonio Maria, 'ECOWAS high-level conference on drug trafficking as a security threat in West Africa' (Praia, Cape Verde, October 28, 2008).

Crawford-Browne, T., *ECAAR-SA Annual Report* (November 17, 2011), accessed at http://accountabilitynow.org.za/ecaar-sa-annual-report-terry-crawford-browne/ on February 23, 2017.

Crenshaw, Martha, 'The psychology of terrorism: An agenda for the 21st century', *Political Psychology*, 21:2 (June 2000).

— 'The causes of terrorism', in Charles Kegley, *The New Global Terrorism: Characteristics, Causes, Controls* (New York: Pearson, 2002).

Curtis, Glenn and Tara Karacan, *The Nexus Among Terrorists, Narcotics Traffickers, Weapons Proliferators, and Organized Crime Networks in Western Europe* (Washington, DC: Library of Congress Federal Research Division, December 2002).

Dagne, Ted, *Somalia: Current Conditions and Prospects for a Lasting Peace* (Washington, DC: Congressional Research Service, October 2010).

— and Amanda Smith, 'Somalia: Prospect for peace and U.S. involvement', in Nina Fitzgerald (ed.), *Somalia: Issues, History and Bibliography* (New York: Nova Science Publishers, 2002).

DailyMail Online, 'Don't turn Syria into a "Tesco for terrorists" like Libya, generals tell Cameron' (June 17, 2013), accessed at www.dailymail.co.uk/news/article-2342917/Dont-turn-Syria-Tesco-terrorists-like-Libya-generals-tell-Cameron.html on February 27, 2017.

— 'ISIS opens new front in North Africa' (November 28, 2014), accessed at www.dailymail.co.uk/news/article-2853255/ISIS-opens-new-North-Africa-two-extremist-groups-Libya-Egypt-pledge-allegiance-terror-leader.html on February 26, 2017.

Daily Trust, 'Nigeria: The presidential panel report on Jos crises' (September 2, 2010).

Dannreuther, Roland, *International Security: The Contemporary Agenda* (Cambridge: Polity Press, 2007).

DCI, 'DCI's worldwide threat briefing' (February 11, 2003), accessed at www.cia.gov/news-information/speeches-testimony/2003/dci_speech_02112003.html on February 25, 2017.

Dorn, Walter, 'Human security: An overview' (Paper prepared for the Pearson Peacekeeping Centre, undated), accessed at http://walterdorn.net/23-human-security-an-overview on February 23, 2017.

DW, 'UNHCR report: Worsening refugee situation in Africa' (June 20, 2016), accessed at www.dw.com/en/unhcr-report-worsening-refugee-situation-in-africa/a-19338619 on February 28, 2017.

Eckersley, Robyn, 'Green theory', in R. Jackson and G. Sørensen (eds), *Introduction to International Relations: Theories and Approaches*, 3rd edn (Oxford: Oxford University Press, 2007).
The Economist, 'Crime in South Africa: It won't go away' (October 1, 2009), accessed at www.economist.com/node/14564621 on February 27, 2017.
— 'Arms and the African' (November 22, 2014).
Ekeh, Peter, 'Individuals' basic security needs and the limits of democracy in Africa', in Bruce Berman, Dickson Eyoh, and Will Kymlicka (eds), *Ethnicity and Democracy in Africa* (Oxford: James Currey Publishers, 2004).
El Kamouni-Janssen, 'Understanding instability in Libya' (Netherlands Institute of International Relations, March 17, 2015), accessed at www.clingendael.nl/publication/understanding-instability-libya-will-peace-talks-end-chaos on February 26, 2017.
Ellis, Stephen, 'West Africa's international drug problem', *African Affairs*, 108:431 (April 2009).
Emerson, Rupert, 'Pan-Africanism', *International Organization*, 16:2 (1962).
Emerson, Stephen, 'Regional security initiative: Combined task force—Horn of Africa', *Newport Papers No. 29: Shaping the Environment* (Newport, RI: US Naval War College Press, 2007).
— 'The battle for Africa's hearts and minds', *World Policy Journal* (Winter, 2008/9).
— 'The metamorphosis of Al-Qaeda in the Islamic Maghreb', *Research on Islam and Muslims in Africa*. RIMA Occasional Papers 1:3 (2010).
— 'Back to the future: The evolution of US counterterrorism policy in Africa', *Insight on Africa* 6:1 (2014).
Enough Project, 'Conflict minerals', accessed at www.enoughproject.org/conflicts/eastern_congo/conflict-minerals on February 28, 2017.
European Monitoring Centre for Drugs and Drug Addiction and Europol, *EU Drug Markets Report: A Strategic Analysis* (Luxembourg: Publication Office of the European Union, 2013).
Farah, Douglas and Stephen Braun, *Merchant of Death: Money, Guns, Planes, and the Man Who Makes War Possible* (Hoboken, NJ: Wiley & Sons, 2007).
Findley, Michael and Ashley Mitchel, 'Lootable resources and third-party intervention into civil wars' (Working paper, Brigham Young University. June 23, 2011), accessed at https://politicalscience.byu.edu/mfindley/assets/resources_civil-war-intervention_24june2011.pdf on February 28, 2017.
Foege, William, 'Infectious diseases', in C. Everett Koop, Clarence Pearson, and M. Roy Schwarz (eds), *Critical Issues in Global Health* (SanFrancisco: Jossey-Bass, 2002).
Forbes.com, 'The secret of Al Qaeda in Islamic Maghreb Inc.: A resilient (and highly illegal) business model' (December 12, 2013), accessed at www.forbes.com/sites/kerryadolan/2013/12/16/the-secret-of-al-qaeda-in-islamic-maghreb-inc-a-resilient-and-highly-illegal-business-model/ on February 22, 2017.

Foreignassistance.gov, accessed at http://beta.foreignassistance.gov/agencies/DoS#/search on February 26, 2017.

France24, 'France revises counter-terrorism strategy in Africa' (January 29, 2014).

Francis, David, *Uniting Africa: Building Regional Peace and Security Systems* (Aldershot: Ashgate Publishing Ltd., 2007).

Freedom House, *Freedom in the World 2006*, accessed at https://freedomhouse.org/report/freedom-world/freedom-world-2006 on February 23, 2017.

— 'Progress in south Asia', *Freedom in the World 2009*, accessed at www.freedomhouse.org/report/freedom-world/freedom-world-2009 on February 23, 2017.

— 'Global erosion of freedom', *Freedom in the World 2010*, accessed at www.freedomhouse.org/report/freedom-world/freedom-world-2010 on February 23, 2017.

— 'Anxious dictators, wavering democracies: Global freedom under pressure' *Freedom in the World 2016*, accessed at www.freedomhouse.org/report/freedom-world/freedom-world-2016 on February 23, 2017.

Friedlander, Robert, 'Terrorism and national liberation movements: Can rights derive from wrongs?', *Case Western Reserve Journal of International Law*, 13:2 (1981).

Fukuda-Parr, Sakiko and Carol Messineo, 'Human security: A critical review of the literature', *CRPD Working Paper No. 11* (January 2012), accessed at https://soc.kuleuven.be/web/files/12/80/wp11.pdf on February 23, 2017.

Fund for Peace, *The Failed States Index 2006*, accessed at http://fsi.fundforpeace.org/rankings-2006-sortable on 22 February 2017.

— *Fragile State Index 2015*, accessed at http://fsi.fundforpeace.org/rankings-2015 on February 22, 2017.

— *Fragile State Index 2016*, accessed at http://fsi.fundforpeace.org/rankings-2016 on February 22, 2017.

Gastrow, Peter, *Termites at Work: Transnational Organized Crime and State Erosion in Kenya* (New York: International Peace Institute, September 2011).

General Accountability Office, 'Defense management: DOD needs to determine the future of its Horn of Africa task force', *GAO-10-504* (Washington, DC: US General Accountability Office April 2010), accessed at www.gao.gov/products/GAO-10-504 on March 1, 2017.

German Information Centre Africa, 'Germany's new Africa policy recognises continent's changing position in the world' (May 23, 2014), accessed at www.gicafrica.diplo.de/Vertretung/suedaafrika-dz/en/_pr/2014/05/05-New-Africa-pol on March 1, 2017.

Ghana News Agency, 'Tamale blacksmiths to end manufacturing of small arms' (November 3, 2011), accessed at www.ghanaweb.com/GhanaHomePage/NewsArchive/Tamale-Blacksmiths-To-End-Manufacturing-Of-Small-Arms-222866 on February 27, 2017.

Glickman, Harvey, 'The threat of Islamism in sub-Saharan Africa: The case of Tanzania', *E-Notes* (Foreign Policy Research Institute, April 2011).

The Global Fund, 'Canada and the Global Fund', accessed at www.the globalfund.org on March 1, 2017.
— 'Government donors', accessed at www.theglobalfund.org/en/government/ on March 1, 2017.
Global Terrorism Database (website hosted by the University of Maryland), accessed at www.start.umd.edu/gtd/ on February 26, 2017.
GM Media Online, 'Operation Rachel—Isuzu continues support for arms clearing operation' (September 27, 2009), accessed at http://media.gm.com/media/za/en/isuzu/news.detail.html/content/Pages/news/za/en/2005/Isuzu/09_27_Operation_Isuzu_support.html on February 27, 2017.
Gostin, Lawrence, Gorik Ooms, Just Haffeld, and Sigrun Mogedal, 'The joint action and learning initiative on national and global responsibilities for health', *World Health Report Background Paper*, 53 (Geneva: World Health Organization, 2010).
Graham, John, Bruce Amos, and Tim Plumptre, 'Principles for good governance in the 21st Century', *Policy Brief*, 15 (Ottawa: Institute on Governance, August 2003), accessed at http://iog.ca/wp-content/uploads/2012/12/2003_August_policybrief15.pdf on February 27, 2017.
Grimard, Franque and Guy Harling, 'Impact of tuberculosis on economic growth' (Montreal: McGill University, no date).
Grimmett, Richard and Paul Kerr, *Conventional Arms Transfers to Developing Nations, 2004–2011* (Washington, DC: Congressional Research Service, August 24, 2012).
Gros, Jean-Germain, 'Towards a taxonomy of failed states in the new world order: Decaying Somalia, Liberia, Rwanda and Haiti', *Third World Quarterly*, 17:13 (1996).
Guardian, 'Guinea worm disease poised to be eradicated within a few years' (September 12, 2012).
— 'Britain to work with Algeria on counter-terrorism, says David Cameron' (January 30, 2013).
— 'Soft power, hard cash' (April 29, 2013).
— 'Reality check cast doubts on Chinese health aid to Africa' (June 10, 2013).
— 'Drug smuggling in Africa: The smack track' (January 17, 2015).
Guardian.com, 'How cigarette smuggling fuels Africa's Islamist violence' (January 26, 2013), accessed at www.theguardian.com/world/2013/jan/27/cigarette-smuggling-mokhtar-belmokhtar-terrorism on February 26, 2017.
Gun Free South Africa, 'Annual report 2012–2013', accessed at www.gfsa.org.za/wp-content/uploads/2012/12/GFSA-AR_12_13_FINAL.pdf on February 28, 2017.
Gurr, Ted, *Minorities at Risk: A Global View of Ethnopolitical Conflict* (Washington, DC: US Institute of Peace, 1993).
Hardin, Garrett, 'The tragedy of the commons', *Science* 162:3859 (December 13, 1968).

Harrendorf, Stefan, Markkus Heiskanen, and Steven Malby (eds), *International Statistics on Crime and Justice* (Helsinki: European Institute for Crime Prevention and Control, 2010).

Hastings, Michael 'The rise of the killer drones', *Rolling Stone* (April 16, 2012).

Havocscope, 'AK and other guns on the black market', accessed at www.havocscope.com/black-market-prices/ak-47/ on February 27, 2017.

Heinecken, Lindy, 'Living in terror: The looming security threat to Southern Africa', *African Security Review*, 10:4 (2001).

Hesse, Brian, 'The myth of "Somalia"', *Journal of Contemporary African Studies*, 28:3 (2010).

Hill, Jonathan, 'Beyond the other? A postcolonial critique of the failed states thesis', *African Identities* 3:2 (2005).

Hillier, Debbie, 'Africa's missing billions: International arms flows and the cost of conflict', O*xfam.org Briefing Paper* (International Action Network on Small Arms, Oxfam International and SaferWorld, October 11, 2007), accessed at www.oxfam.org/sites/www.oxfam.org/files/africas%20missing%20bils.pdf on February 22, 2017.

H.M. Government, *Health is Global: An Outcomes Framework for Global Health 2011–2015* (London: Department of Health, March 31, 2011), accessed at www.gov.uk/government/publications/health-is-global-an-outcomes-framework-for-global-health-2011-15-2 on March 1, 2017.

Hoffman, Bruce, *Inside terrorism*, 2nd edn (New York: Columbia University Press, 2006).

Holland, Heidi, *The Struggle: A History of the African National Congress* (New York: George Braziller Inc., 1990).

Holsti, Kalevi, *Taming the Sovereigns: Institutional Change in International Politics* (Cambridge: Cambridge University Press, 2004).

Holtom, Paul, 'Ukrainian arms supplies to sub-Saharan Africa', *SIPRI Background Paper* (Stockholm: Stockholm International Peace Research Institute, February 2011).

Homer-Dixon, Thomas 'Environmental scarcities and violent conflict', *International Security* 19:1 (1994).

Horowitz, Donald, *Ethnic Groups in Conflict*, 2nd edn (Berkeley, CA: University of California Press, 2000).

Hough, Peter, *Understanding Global Security* (Abingdon: Routledge, 2004).

Human Rights Watch, 'Jos: A city torn apart', *Human Rights Watch*, 13:9A (December 18, 2001), accessed at www.hrw.org/report/2001/12/18/jos-city-torn-apart on February 24, 2017.

— 'Youth, poverty and blood: The legacy of West Africa's regional warriors', *Human Rights Watch*, 17:5A (March 2005), accessed at www.hrw.org/reports/2005/westafrica0405/7.htm on February 27, 2017.

— 'Ethiopia: Crackdown on dissent intensifies' (January 29, 2015), accessed at www.hrw.org/news/2015/01/29/ethiopia-crackdown-dissent-intensifies on February 26, 2017.

Human Security Report Project, *Human Security Report 2005: War and Peace in the 21st Century* (Oxford: Oxford University Press, 2005).

— *Human Security Brief 2007* (Vancouver: Human Security Research Group, 2008).

— *Human Security Report 2013* (Vancouver: Human Security Research Group, 2013), accessed at www.hsrgroup.org/human-security-reports/2013/text.aspx on February 23, 2017.

— 'The decline in global violence: Reality or myth?' (Press release, March 3, 2014), accessed at www.hsrgroup.org/docs/Publications/HSR2013/HSR_2013_Press_Release.pdf on February 28, 2017.

Human Security Resource Centre, *Human Security Report 2005* (New York: Oxford University Press, 2005).

Human Security Unit, *Human Security in Theory and Practice* (New York: United Nations Trust Fund for Human Security, 2009).

Hussein, Karim, Donata Gnisci, and Julia Wanjiru, 'Security and human security: An overview of concepts and initiatives. What implications for West Africa?' (Paris, France, December 2004), accessed at www.oecd.org/swac/publications/38826090.pdf on February 28, 2017.

IANSA, 'About us', accessed at www.iansa.org/aboutus on March 1, 2017.

Ibrahim, Mohamed, 'Somalia and global terrorism: A growing connection?' *Journal of Contemporary African Studies*, 28:3 (2010).

Iliffe, John, *The African AIDS Epidemic: A History* (Oxford: James Currey Ltd., 2006).

Imperial College London, 'Schistosomiasis control initiative', accessed at www3.imperial.ac.uk/schisto/whatwedo/whatarentds on February 28, 2017.

Independent.co.uk, 'Global arms trade: Africa and the curse of the AK-47' (April 6, 2006), accessed at www.independent.co.uk/news/world/africa/global-arms-trade-and-the-curse-of-the-ak47-472975.html on February 27, 2017.

Independent Online, 'Russians start $3bn mine in Zimbabwe' (September 17, 2014), accessed at www.iol.co.za/business/news/russians-start-3bn-mine-in-zimbabwe-1.1751935#.VCA4kfldVg0 on March 1, 2017.

Indexmundi, 'Guinea-Bissau GDP', accessed at www.indexmundi.com/guinea-bissau/gdp_per_capita_(ppp).html on February 28, 2017.

IndiaAfrica Connect, 'Five-fold increase in India-Africa trade: Minister' (9th CII-EXIM Bank India-Africa Project Partnership, March 6, 2013), accessed at www.indiaafricaconnect.in/index.php?param=news/5806/india-africaconclave/120 on March 1, 2017.

— 'Africa seeks Indian investment in healthcare' (9th CII-EXIM Bank India-Africa Project Partnership, March 6, 2013), accessed at www.indiaafricaconnect.in/index.php?param=news/5811/india-africaconclave/120 on March 1, 2017.

Institute for Health Metrics and Evaluation, *Financing Global Health 2014: Shifts in Funding as the MDG Era Closes* (Seattle: Institute for Health Metrics and Evaluation, 2015).

Institute for Security Studies, 'South Africa's efforts to collect and destroy firearms', *ISS Today* (April 29, 2013), accessed at www.issafrica.org/iss-today/

south-africas-efforts-to-collect-and-destroy-firearms-losing-the-battle-but-winning-the-war on February 27, 2017.

Internal Displacement Monitoring Centre 'Boko Haram's terror ripples through the region' (April 16, 2015), accessed at www.internal-displacement.org/publications/2015/boko-harams-terror-ripples-through-the-region on February 26, 2017.

International Crisis Group, 'Latin American drugs I: Losing the fight', *Latin America Report 25* (March 14, 2008).

— 'Somalia's divided Islamists', *Africa Briefing No. 74* (Policy Brief, May 2010).

International Monetary Fund, 'Debt relief under the heavily indebted poor countries (HIPC) initiative', *International Monetary Fund Factsheet* (February 2010), accessed at www.imf.org/external/np/exr/facts/hipc.htm on 22 February 2017.

International Organization for Migration, *Migration Health, Annual Review 2012* (Geneva: International Organization for Migration, 2013).

International Rescue Committee, 'Measuring mortality in the Democratic Republic of Congo' (2007), accessed at www.rescue.org/sites/default/files/resource-file/IRC_DRCMortalityFacts.pdf on February 28, 2017.

INTERPOL News, 'Annual Report 2012', accessed at www.interpol.int/News-and-media/Publications#n627 on March 1, 2017.

— 'INTERPOL announces formation of dedicated environmental crime team in Africa' (October 7, 2014), accessed at www.interpol.int/News-and-media/News/2014/N2014-196 on March 1, 2017.

IRIN News, 'Guinea-Bissau: Images of a crack cocaine rehabilitation centre' (March 5, 2008).

— 'Cape Verde: Deported youth offenders face drugs, unemployment' (November 26, 2008).

— 'Guinea-Bissau: Lowering the light weapon load' (May 22, 2009).

— 'Sierra Leone: A ballooning drug problem' (April 7, 2010).

Jackson, Robert, *Quasi-States: Sovereignty, International Relations, and the Third World* (Cambridge: Cambridge University Press, 1990).

Jamison, Dean, Joel Breman, Anthony Measham, *et al.*, *Priorities in Health* (Washington, DC: The World Bank, 2006).

Johnson, Toni, *Boko Haram* (Washington, DC: Council on Foreign Relations, December 27, 2011), accessed at www.cfr.org/africa/boko-haram/p25739 on February 26, 2017.

Kaplan, Robert, 'The coming anarchy', *The Atlantic Monthly* (February 1994).

Kaplan, Seth, 'Rethinking state-building in a failed state', *The Washington Quarterly*, 33:1 (2010).

Kasaija, Apuuli, 'The UN-led Djibouti peace process for Somalia 2008–2009: Results and problems', *Journal of Contemporary African Studies* 28:3 (2010).

Kaufman, Stuart, 'Social identity and the roots of future conflict' (NIC 2020 discussion paper, October 2003), accessed at www.au.af.mil/au/awc/awcgate/cia/nic2020/kaufman_panel2_nov6.pdf on February 24, 2017.

Keilberth, Mirco and Christoph Reuter, 'A threat to Europe: The Islamic State's dangerous gains in Libya', *Spiegel Online* (February 23, 2015), accessed at www.spiegel.de/international/world/islamic-state-advance-in-libya-could-present-threat-to-europe-a-1019976.html on February 26, 2017.

Ki-moon, Ban, 'An agenda for prosperity and peace' (Remarks to the Summit of the African Union, Addis Ababa, January 31, 2010), accessed at www.un.org/sg/statements/index.asp?nid=4368 on February 27, 2017.

Kingsbury, Damien, 'Environment and development', in Damien Kingsbury, John McKay, Janet Hunt, et al. (eds), *International Development: Issues and Challenges*, 2nd edn (Basingstoke: Palgrave Macmillan, 2012).

Klare, Michael, *Resource Wars* (New York: Henry Holt and Co., 2001).

Kozyulin, Vadim, 'Conventional arms transfers, illicit arms trade: An overview and implications for the region' (PRI Center lecture, circa 2004), accessed at www.pircenter.org/data/news/kozyulin091104lect.pdf on February 27, 2017.

KPMG Africa, 'Expenditure on healthcare in Africa' (December 12, 2012), accessed at www.blog.kpmgafrica.com/expenditure-on-healthcare-in-africa/ on February 23, 2017.

Kriesberg, Louis, *Social Inequity* (Hemel Hempstad: Prentice Hall, 1979).

Labrousse, Alain, 'Sub-Saharan Africa facing the challenge of drugs' (Ottawa, Canada: Parliament of Canada, February 2001), accessed at www.parl.gc.ca/Content/SEN/Committee/371/ille/presentation/labrousse1-e.htm on February 27, 2017.

Lamb, Guy, '"Under the gun": An assessment of firearm crime and violence in South Africa' (Report complied for the Office of the President, Pretoria, March 2008).

Lamb, Robert, *Ungoverned Areas and Threats from Safe Havens* (Washington, DC: Office of the Under Secretary of Defense for Policy, January 2008).

Lawrence, Kendall, 'The world's ten most fragile states in 2014' (June 2014), accessed at http://library.fundforpeace.org/fsi14-fragile10 on February 28, 2017.

Leao, Ana, 'Weapons in Mozambique: Reducing arms availability and demand', *ISS Monograph*, 94 (Pretoria: Institute for Security Studies, January 3, 2004).

Le Billon, Phillip (ed.), *The Geopolitics of Resource Wars: Resource Dependence, Governance and Violence* (Abingdon: Frank Cass, 2005).

Legum, Colin, 'The organisation of African unity—success or failure?' *International Affairs*, 51:2 (1975).

Lentz, Carola, 'Tribalism and ethnicity in Africa: A review of four decades of Anglophone research', *Cahiers des Sciences Humaines*, 31:2 (1995).

Le Sage, Andre, 'Terrorism threats and vulnerabilities in Africa', in Andre Le Sage (ed.), *African Counterterrorism Cooperation* (Washington, DC: National Defense University Press, 2007).

Levitt, Jeremy, 'The Peace and Security Council of the African Union: The known unknowns', *Transnational Law and Contemporary Problems*, 13:109 (Summer 2003).

Local, 'Germany wants key role in Africa security' (April 3, 2014), accessed at www.thelocal.de/20140601/germany-will-be-a-motor-in-un-africa-plan on March 1, 2017

Lonsdale, John, 'Moral and political argument in Kenya', in Bruce Berman, Dickson Eyoh, and Will Kymlicka (eds), *Ethnicity and Democracy in Africa* (Oxford: James Currey Publishers, 2004).

— 'Moral ethnicity and political tribalism' (April 21, 2008), accessed at http://kenyaimagine.com/index/php?view=article&catid=266%3Aintern on February 24, 2017.

Los Angeles Times, 'African continent tormented by tribal conflicts' (March 23, 1986).

Mail & Guardian, 'Ten things about guns in South Africa' (February 22, 2013), accessed at http://mg.co.za/article/2013-02-22-00-ten-things-about-guns-in-south-africa on February 27, 2017.

Mair, Stefan, 'The new world of privatized violence', *International Politik und Gesellschaft* (2003).

Mamdani, Mahmood, *Citizen and Subject: Contemporary Africa and the Legacy of Late Colonialism* (Princeton, NJ: Princeton University Press, 1996).

Mantzikos, Ioannis, 'The absence of the state in northern Nigeria: The case of Boko Haram', *African Renaissance*, 7:1 (2010).

McGowan, Patrick, 'African military coups d'etat, 1956–2001: Frequency, trends and distribution', *Journal of Modern African Studies*, 41:3.

McRae, Rob and Don Hubert (eds), *Human Security and the New Diplomacy: Protecting People, Promoting Peace* (Montreal, Canada: McGill-Queen's University Press, 2001.

Meleagrou-Hitchens, Alexander, 'Terrorist tug-of-war', *Foreign Affairs.com* (October 8, 2015), accessed at www.foreignaffairs.com/articles/kenya/2015-10-08/terrorist-tug-war on February 26, 2017.

Melly, Paul and Vincent Darracq, *A New Way to Engage? French Policy in Africa from Sarkozy to Hollande* (London: Chatham House, May 2013).

Menkhaus, Ken, 'The crisis in Somalia: Tragedy in five acts', *African Affairs*, 106:204 (2007).

— 'Violent Islamic extremism: Al-Shabaab recruitment in America' (Hearing before the Committee on Homeland Security and Governmental Affairs, United States Senate, Washington, DC, March 11, 2009).

Meyer, Angela, *Regional Integration and Security in Central Africa—Assessment and Perspectives 10 Years After the Revival* (Brussels, Belgium: Egmont—The Royal Institute for International Relations, December 2008).

— *Peace and Security Cooperation in Central Africa* (Uppsala, Sweden: Nordiska Afrikainstitutet, 2011).

Michel, Serge, Michel Beuret, and Paolo Woods, *China Safari: On the Trail of Beijing's Expansion in Africa* (New York: Nation Books, 2009).

Molatole, Raymond and Steven Thaga, 'Interventions against HIV/AIDS in the Botswana Defence Force', in Martin Rupiya (ed.), *The Enemy Within:*

Southern African Militaries' Quarter-Century Battle with HIV/AIDS (Pretoria: Institute for Security Studies, 2006).

Møller, Bjorn, 'The African Union as security actor: African solutions to African problems?' *Crisis States* (Working Papers Series 2:57, London: Crisis States Research Centre, August 2009).

Moyo, Ambrose, 'Religion in Africa', in April Gordon and Donald Gordon (eds), *Understanding Contemporary Africa*, 4th edn (Boulder, CO: Lynne Rienner, 2007).

Mukandavire, Zindoga, Shu Liao, Jin Wang, et al., 'Estimating the reproductive numbers in the 2008–2009 cholera outbreaks in Zimbabwe', *Proceedings of the National Academy of Sciences*, 108:21 (May 24, 2011).

Murdock, George, *Africa: Its Peoples and Their Culture History* (New York: McGraw-Hill, 1959).

Naim, Moises, *Illicit: How Smugglers, Traffickers, and Copycats are Hijacking the Global Economy* (New York: Anchor Books, 2006).

National Intelligence Council, *Global Trends 2025: A Transformed World*. Washington: US Government Printing Office. November 2008.

— *Global Trend 2030: Alternative Worlds* (2012), accessed at www.dni.gov/nic/globaltrends on February 28, 2017.

National Public Radio, 'Documenting the paradox of oil, poverty in Nigeria', *Weekend Edition Sunday* (July 6, 2008), accessed at www.npr.org/templates/story/story.php?storyId=92155119 on February 22, 2017.

NBC News, 'U.S. aims to root out "ungoverned spaces" as hotbeds of terrorism' (August 23, 2014).

Newsweek, 'As ISIS flees Sirte in Libya, Tunisia faces greater threat from returning jihadis' (October 27, 2016).

— 'Trump Expands U.S. Military Campaign in Africa with Somalia Offensive' (March 31, 2017).

New Yorker, 'China in Africa: The new imperialist?' (June 12, 2013).

New York Times, 'Former exile holds power in West African nation' (May 25, 2010).

— 'Brazil gains business and influence as it offers aid and loans in Africa' (August 7, 2012).

— 'U.S. sting that snared African ex-admiral shines light on drug trade' (April 15, 2013).

NGO Working Group for Women, Peace and Security, 'About us', accessed at www.womenpeacesecurity.org/about/ on March 1, 2017.

The Nile Basin Initiative, accessed at www.nilebasin.org/newsite/index.php?option=com_content&view=article&id=139%3Aabout-the-nbi&catid=34%3Anbi-background-facts&Itemid=74&lang=en&limitstart=2 on February 28, 2017.

Nyerere, Julius, 'A United States of Africa', *Journal of Modern African Studies* 1:1 (1963).

OECD, 'Development aid rose in 2009 and most donors will meet 2010 aid targets', *Financing for Sustainable Development* (Development Co-operation

Directorate, April 14, 2010), accessed at www.oecd.org/document/0,3445 ,en_2649_34447_44981579_1_1_1_1,00.html on February 22, 2017.
— 'Fragile States 2014', accessed at www.oecd.org/dac/incaf/FSR-2014.pdf on March 1, 2017.
— 'Sub-Saharan Africa and the OECD', accessed at www.oecd.org/africa/africa-focusedbodies.htm on March 1, 2017.
Office of the Coordinator for Counterterrorism, 'Designation of al-Shabaab' (US Department of State, 18 March 2008), www.state.gov/j/ct/rls/other/des/143205.htm.
— *Patterns of Terrorism 2009* (Washington, DC: US Department of State, August 2010).
Ogata, Sadako, 'Inclusion or exclusion: Social development challenges for Asia and Europe' (Statement of Mrs Sadako Ogata, U.N. High Commissioner for Refugees at the Asian Development Bank, April 27, 1998), accessed at www.unhcr.ch/refworld/unhcr/hcspeech/27ap1998.htm on February 23, 2017.
ONE, 'Water & sanitation', accessed at www.one.org/international/issues/water-and-sanitation on February 28, 2017.
Opalo, Ken, 'The consequences of the U.S. war on terrorism in Africa' *Al Jazeera America* (June 2, 2014), accessed at http://america.aljazeera.com/opinions/2014/6/africom-u-s-war-onterrorisminafricaalshabaabbokoharam.html on March 1, 2017.
O'Regan, D. and P. Thompson, 'Advancing stability and reconciliation in Guinea-Bissau: Lessons from Africa's first nacro-state', *ACSS Special Report No. 2* (Washington, DC: Africa Center for Strategic Studies, June 2013).
The Oxford Essential Quotations Dictionary—American Edition (New York: Berkley Books, 1998).
Oxfam International, 'Shooting down the MDGs: How irresponsible arms transfers undermine development goals' (2008), accessed at www.oxfam.org/en/research/shooting-down-mdgs on February 27, 2017.
Page, Edward, 'What's the point of environmental security?' (Paper presented for the SGIR at the 7th Pan-European International Relations Conference, Stockholm, September 10, 2010), accessed at www.academia.edu/2745855/What_s_the_Point_of_Environmental_Security on February 28, 2017.
Pargeter, Alison 'Islamist militant groups in post-Qadhafi Libya' (February 20, 2013), accessed at www.ctc.usma.edu/posts/islamist-militant-groups-in-post-qadhafi-libya on February 26, 2017.
Patrick, Stewart, 'Are "ungoverned spaces" a threat?' (Council on Foreign Relations, January 11, 2010), accessed at www.cfr.org/somalia/ungoverned-spaces-threat/p21165 on February 25, 2017.
Pennock, J. Roland, 'Political development, political systems, and political goods', *World Politics* (XVIII, 1966).
Pew Forum on Religion and Public Life, 'Tolerance and tension: Islam and Christianity in sub-Saharan Africa' (April 15, 2010), accessed at www.pewforum.org/datasets/tolerance-and-tension-islam-and-christianity-in-sub-saharan-africa/ on February 24, 2017.

— 'The global religious landscape' (December 18, 2012) accessed at www.pewforum.org/2012/12/18/global-religious-landscape-exec/ on February 24, 2017.

— 'The future of world religions: Population growth projections 2010–2050' (April 2, 2015), accessed at www.pewforum.org/2015/04/02/sub-saharan-africa/ on February 24, 2017.

Ploch, Lauren, *Countering Terrorism in East Africa: The U.S. Response* (Washington, DC: Congressional Research Service, November 3, 2010).

— 'Africa command: U.S. strategic interests and the role of the U.S. military in Africa' (Washington, DC: Congressional Research Service, July 22, 2011).

Porch, David, *The Conquest of the Sahara* (New York: Fromm International, 1986).

Powell, Kristiana, 'The African Union and the regional mechanisms for conflict prevention, management and resolution', in Kristiana Powell, *The African Union's Emerging Peace and Security Regime* (ISS Monograph Series No. 119, Pretoria: Institute for Security Studies, May 2005).

Preiss, B. and C. Brunner (eds), *Democracy in Crisis* (Munster, Germany: LIT Verlag, 2013).

Premier L. Keqiang, 'Bring about a better future for China-Africa cooperation' (Speech at the AU Conference Center, Addis Ababa, May 5, 2014), accessed at www.fmprc.gov.cn/mfa_eng/wjdt_665385/zyjh_665391/t1154397.shtml on March 1, 2017.

President's Emergency Plan for AIDS Relief, 'PEPFAR funding: Investments that save lives and promote security' (June 2011), accessed at www.pepfar.gov/press/80064.htm on February 23, 2017.

— '2014 PEPFAR latest results—fact sheet', accessed at www.pepfar.gov/documents/organization/234738.pdf on March 1, 2017.

— 'Budget information', accessed at www.pepfar.gov/funding/budget/index.htm on March 1, 2017.

— 'Executive summary of PEPFAR's strategy', accessed at www.pepfar.gov/about/strategy/document/133244.htm on March 1, 2017.

— 'PEPFAR funding' accessed at http://pepfar.gov/documents/organization/252516.pdf on February 23, 2017.

Puddington, Arch, 'Freedom in retreat: Is the tide turning?' *Freedom in the World 2008*, p. 10, accessed at https://freedomhouse.org/report/freedom-world-2008/essay-freedom-retreat on February 22, 2017.

PureMadi, accessed at www.puremadi.org/ on March 1, 2017.

Rabasa, Angel, *Radical Islam in East Africa* (Santa Monica, CA: RAND Corporation, 2009).

Reliefweb, 'Estimated number of people killed in inter-communal violence in Plateau and Kaduna states, Nigeria, January 2010–November 2013', accessed at http://reliefweb.int/map/nigeria/estimated-number-people-killed-inter-communal-violence-plateau-and-kaduna-states-nigeria on February 24, 2017.

— 'Nigeria: Escalating communal violence' (April 14, 2014).

Reuters, 'Drugs trafficking triggers abuse in W. Africa' (May 17, 2011).

— 'Special report: In the land of gangster-jihadists' (October 25, 2012).
— 'In Africa: U.S. promotes security, China does business' (May 30, 2014).
— 'Guinea-Bissau's ex-navy chief pleads guilty in U.S. drug case' (June 3, 2014).
— 'Egypt's Sisi issues decree widening scope of security crackdown' (February 24, 2015).
— 'As heroin trade grows, a sting in Kenya' (March 5, 2015).
— 'U.N. chief fears genocide about to start in South Sudan' (December 16, 2016).
Rice, Susan, *Testimony before the US House Committee on International Relations* (November 2001), accessed at http://commdocs.house.gov/committees/intlrel/hfa76191.000/hfa76191_0f.htm on February 25, 2017.
Roll Back Malaria, 'Economic costs of malaria', accessed at www.rollbackmalaria.org/files/files/toolbox/RBM%20Economic%20Costs%20of%20Malaria.pdf on February 28, 2017.
Rotberg, Robert, 'Failed states, collapsed states, weak states: Causes and indicators', in Robert Rotberg (ed.), *State Failure and State Weakness in a Time of Terror* (Washington DC: Brookings Institution Press, 2003).
Rothman, Jay, *Resolving Identity-Based Conflict in Nations, Organizations, and Communities* (San Francisco: Jossey-Bass Publishers, 1997).
SABC News, 'Human trafficking on the rise in SA' (December 8, 2014).
Saferworld, *China's Growing Role in African Peace and Security* (London: Saferworld, January 2011), accessed at www.saferworld.org.uk/resources/view-resource/500-chinas-growing-role-in-african-peace-and-security on March 1, 2017.
Salvation Army International, 'Our work', accessed at www.salvationarmy.org/ihq/ourwork on March 1, 2017.
Sany, Joseph and Sameeksha Desai, 'Transnational ethnic groups and conflict: The Zaghawa in Chad and Sudan', *Conflict Trends*, 2 (ACCORD, 2008).
ScienceDaily, 'MRSA strain linked to high death rates' (October 31, 2009), accessed at www.sciencedaily.com/releases/2009/10/0091031222347.htm on February 28, 2017.
Selassie, Haile, 'Towards African unity', *Journal of Modern African Studies*, 1:3 (1963).
Serafino, Nina, *The Global Peace Operations Initiative: Background and Issues for Congress* (Washington, DC: Congressional Research Service, Updated 3 October 2006).
Shank, Michael, 'Understanding political Islam in Somalia', *Contemporary Islam* 1:1 (2009).
Shaxson, Nicholas, *Poisoned Wells: The Dirty Politics of African Oil* (New York: Palgrave Macmillian, 2007).
Shinn, David, 'China in Africa Symposium' (Indiana University at Bloomington, March 6–7, 2009).
— 'Chinese involvement in African conflict zones', *China Brief*, 9 (The Jamestown Foundation, April 2, 2009).
— and J. Eisenman, *China and Africa: A Study of Engagement* (Philadelphia: University of Pennsylvania Press, 2012).

Simpson, Melissa, 'An Islamic solution to state failure in Somalia', *Geopolitics of the Middle East*, 2:1 (2009), 31–49.
Small Arms Survey, *Small Arms Survey 2003* (Oxford: Oxford University Press, 2003).
— *Small Arms Survey 2006* (Oxford: Oxford University Press, 2006).
— *Small Arms Survey 2007* (Cambridge: Cambridge University Press, 2007).
— 'Supply and demand: Arms flow and holdings in Sudan', *Sudan Issue Brief*, 15 (December 2009).
— *Small Arms Survey 2009* (Cambridge: Cambridge University Press, 2009).
— *Small Arms Survey 2010* (Cambridge: Cambridge University Press, 2010).
— *Small Arms Survey 2014* (Cambridge: Cambridge University Press, 2014).
— 'Missing missiles: The proliferation of man-portable air defense systems in North Africa.' *Issue Brief 2* (June 2015).
— *Small Arms Survey 2015* (Cambridge: Cambridge University Press, 2015).
— 'Stockpiles' (2015) accessed at www.smallarmssurvey.org/weapons-and-markets/stockpiles.html on February 27, 2017.
Smith, Karen, 'Has Africa got anything to say? African contributions to the theoretical development of International Relations', *The Roundtable: The Commonwealth Journal of International Affairs*, 98:402 (2009).
Snyder, Craig, 'Regional security structures', in Craig Snyder (ed.), *Contemporary Security and Strategy* (Basingstoke: Macmillan, 1999).
Soderbaum, Fredrik and Rodrigo Tavares, *Regional Organizations in African Security* (New York: Routledge, 2011).
Solomon, Hussein, 'The role and place of the African Standby Force within the African Peace and Security Architecture', *ISS Paper 209* (Institute for Security Studies, January 2010).
— 'Counter-terrorism in Nigeria: Responding to Boko Haram', *The RUSI Journal*, 157:4 (August/September 2012).
— 'South Africa and the Islamic State', *Research on Islam and Muslims in Africa* (RIMA Occasional Papers 3:3 (April 2015), accessed at https://muslimsinafrica.wordpress.com/2015/04/09/south-africa-and-the-islamic-state-professor-hussein-solomon on February 26, 2017.
— 'Somalia's Al Shabaab: Evolving tactics', *Research on Islam and Muslims in Africa* (RIMA Occasional Papers 3:3, May 2015).
— 'What to do about Libya?' *Research on Islam and Muslims in Africa* (RIMA Policy Papers, 3:3, June 2015), accessed at https://muslimsinafrica.word press.com/2015/06/02/what-to-do-about-libya-professor-hussein-solomon on February 26, 2017.
— *Terrorism and Counter-Terrorism in Africa* (Basingstoke: Palgrave Macmillan, 2015).
South African Department of Defence, 'White paper on national defence for the Republic of South Africa' (May 1996), accessed at www.dod.mil/za/docu ments/WhitePaperonDef/whitepaper%20on%20defence1996.pdf on February 23, 2017.

Speeches and Statements by the Prime Minister, 'The Africa that joins in partnership with Japan is brighter still' (Opening Session of the Fifth Tokyo International Conference on African Development, June 1, 2013), accessed at http://japan.kantei.go.jp/96_abe/statement/201306/01speech_e.html on March 1, 2017.

Stockholm International Peace Research Institute, 'SIPRI fact sheet: Trends in international arms transfers, 2014' (March 2015), *and SIPRI Arms Transfer Database*, accessed at www.sipri.org/databases/armstransfers on February 27, 2017.

Stolte, Christina, *Brazil in Africa: Just Another BRICS Country Seeking Resources?* (London: Chatham House, November 2012).

Straus, Scott, 'Wars do end: Why conflict in Africa is falling' (January 28, 2013), accessed at http://africanarguments.org/2013/01/28/wars-do-end-why-conflict-in-africa-is-falling-by-scott-straus/ on February 28, 2017.

Styan, David, *Djibouti: Changing Influence in the Horn's Strategic Hub* (London: Chatham House, April 2013).

Sunday Times (South Africa), 'Declaring war on the arms trade' (September 1, 2009).

Tadjbakhsh, S. and A. Chenoy, *Human Security: Concepts and Implications* (New York: Routledge, 2007).

Taylor, Ian, *China's New Role in Africa* (Boulder, CO: Lynne Rienner, 2010).

TB Facts.org, 'TB statistics/global, regional, high burden & MDR', accessed at www.tbfacts.org/tb-statistics/ on February 28, 2017.

The Telegraph (UK), 'Revealed: How Saharan caravans of cocaine help to fund al-Qaeda in terrorists' North African domain' (January 26, 2013).

— 'Isil recruiting "army of poor" with $1,000 sign-up bonus' (February 1, 2016).

Thakur, Ramesh, 'From national to human security', in S. Harris and A. Mack (eds) *Asia-Pacific Security* (Sydney: Allen & Unwin, 1997).

Thomson, Alex, *An Introduction to African Politics*, 2nd edn (New York: Routledge, 2009).

Times Books, 'Africa', in Times Books, *The Times Comprehensive Atlas of the World* (New York: Harper-Collins, 12th edn, 2008).

TimesLive (South Africa), 'Al-Qaeda at the gates' (February 2015), accessed at www.timeslive.co.za/thetimes/2015/02/20/al-qaeda-at-the-gates on February 26, 2017.

Transparency International, 'Corruption perception index 2014: Results', *Corruption Perception Index*, accessed at www.transparency.org/cpi2014/results on February 27, 2017.

UNAIDS, 'UNAIDS report on the global AIDS epidemic, 2010', *Global Report* (Geneva: UNAIDS, 2010).

— 'World AIDS day report 2011' (Geneva: UNAIDS, 2011).

— 'The Gap Report' (September 2014), accessed at www3.imperial.ac.uk/schisto/whatwedo/whatarentds on February 28, 2017.

— 'Fact Sheet 2014: Global statistics', accessed at www.unaids.org/sites/default/files/en/media/unaids/contentassets/documents/factsheet/2014/20140716_FactSheet_en.pdf on February 28, 2017.

— 'Global AIDS update' (January 2016), accessed at www.unaids.org/sites/default/files/media_asset/global-AIDS-update-2016_en.pdf on February 28, 2017.

— 'Global HIV statistics', *UNAIDS Fact Sheet* (November 2016) accessed at www.unaids.org/sites/default/files/media_asset/UNAIDS_FactSheet_en.pdf on February 22, 2017.

UNICEF, 'MD Goal: Combat HIV/AIDS, malaria and other diseases', accessed at www.unicef.org/mdg/disease.html on February 28, 2017.

— 'Water, sanitation and hygiene (WASH)', accessed at www.unicef.org/media/media_45481.html on February 28, 2017.

— 'Child labor: Down by a third since 2000' (September 30, 2013).

United Nations, 'Addressing the Security Council, Secretary-General says international community must revere global proliferation of small arms' (September 24, 1999).

— 'Illicit small arms trade in Africa fuels conflict, contributes to poverty, stalls development', *United Nations Information Service DC/3032* (June 27, 2006).

— 'Millennium Development Goals, Goal 6: Combat HIV/AIDS, malaria, and other disease', accessed at www.un.org/millenniumgoals/aids.shtml on March 1, 2017.

— 'Under-five mortality rankings', *UNData*, accessed at http://data.un.org on February 22, 2017.

United Nations Department of Economic and Social Affairs, Population Division, Population Estimates and Projection Section, accessed at http://esa.un.org/unpd/wpp/unpp/panel_population.htm on February 28, 2017.

— *World Mortality 2009* (New York: United Nations, 2009).

— *World Population Prospects: The 2010 Revision* (New York: United Nations, 2010).

— *World Population Prospects: The 2012 Revision* (New York: United Nations, 2013).

— *Excel Tables—Population Data 2015* (New York: United Nations, 2015) accessed at http://esa.un.org/unpd/wpp/Excell-Data/population.htm on February 22, 2017.

— '*World Population Prospects: The 2012 Revision*' (New York: United Nations, 2015), accessed at http://esa.un.org/wpp/unpp/p2k0data.asp on February 24, 2017.

United Nations Department of Peacekeeping Operations, 'United Nations Peacekeeping Operations Factsheet (as of December 31, 2015)', accessed at www.un.org/en/peacekeeping/resources/statistics/factsheet.shtml on March 1, 2017.

— 'Conflict and resources', accessed at www.un.org/en/peacekeeping/issues/environment/resources.shtml on February 28, 2017.

— 'Troops and police contributors', accessed at www.un.org/en/peacekeeping/resources/statistics/contributors.shtml on March 1, 2017.
United Nations Development Programme, *Human Development Report 1994* (New York: Oxford University Press, 1994).
— *UN Development Index 2015*, accessed at http://hdr.undp.org/en/countries on February 28, 2017.
— *Human Development Report 2015*, accessed at http://hdr.undp.org/en/data on February 28, 2017.
United Nations Economic Commission for Africa, *MDG Report 2015: Assessing Progress Toward the Millennium Development Goals* (Addis Ababa: Economic Commission for Africa, 2015).
United Nations Environment Programme, *Declaration of the United Nations Conference on the Human Environment* (21st plenary meeting, June 16, 1972), accessed at www.unep.org/Documents.Multilingual/Default.asp?DocumentID=97&ArticleID=1503 on February 28, 2017.
— 'From conflict to peacebuilding: The role of natural resources and environment' (Nairobi: UN Environment Programme, February 2009).
United Nations General Assembly, 'Political declaration' (June 8–10, 1998).
— 'Towards an arms treaty: Establishing common international standards for the import, export and transfer of conventional arms' (Issues at AMUN, First Committee: Disarmament and International Security, 2010).
United Nations Inter-agency Group for Child Mortality Estimation, *Levels & Trends in Child Mortality, Report 2011* (New York: UN Children's Fund, 2011).
— *Levels & Trends in Child Mortality, Report 2015* (New York: UN Children's Fund, 2015).
UN Office on Drugs and Crime, *Transnational Organized Crime in the West African Region* (New York: United Nations Publication, 2005).
— *Trafficking in Persons: Global Patterns 2006* (New York: United Nations Publication, April 2006).
— *World Drug Report 2006: Volume 2. Statistics* (New York: United Nations Publication, 2006).
— *Cocaine Trafficking in West Africa: The Threat to Stability and Development'* (New York: United Nations Publication, December 2007).
— *Transnational Trafficking and the Rule of Law in West Africa: A Threat Assessment* (New York: United Nations Publication, July 2009).
— *Crime and Instability: Case Studies of Transnational Threats* (New York: United Nations Publication, February 2010).
— *World Drug Report 2010* (New York: United Nations Publication, 2010).
— *West Africa: 2012 ATS Situation Report* (New York: United Nations Publication, June 2012).
— *Transnational Organized Crime in West Africa: A Threat Assessment* (New York: United Nations Publication, February 2013).
— *Transnational Organized Crime in East Africa: A Threat Assessment* (New York: United Nations Publication, September 2013).

— *World Drug Report 2013* (New York: United Nations Publication, 2013).
— *The Illicit Drug Trade through South-Eastern Europe* (New York: United Nations Publication, March 2014).
— 'Twenty-fourth meeting of heads of national drug law enforcement agencies, Africa' (Addis Ababa, September 15–19, 2014).
— *World Drug Report 2015* (New York: United Nations Publication, 2015).
— *World Drug Report 2016* (New York: United Nations Publication, 2016).
United Nations Security Council, 'Small arms—Report of the Secretary-General, S/2008/258' (April 17, 2008), accessed at www.poa-iss.org/DocsUpcomingEvents/S-2008-258.pdf on February 27, 2017.
— 'Report of panel of experts established pursuant to resolution 1591 (2005) concerning Sudan' (October 27, 2009).
United States Agency for International Development, *USAID Anti-Trafficking in Persons Programs in Africa: A Review* (Washington, DC: USAID, April 2007).
— *Fiscal Year 2014: Safeguarding the World's Water* (Washington, DC: USAID, July 15, 2015).
United States Department of State, *Country Reports on Terrorism 2009* (Kenya), accessed at www.state.gov/documents/organization/141114.pdf on February 26, 2017.
— *Independent States in the World* (Washington, DC: Bureau of Intelligence and Research, 2012), accessed at www.state.gov/s/inr/rls/4250.htm on February 25, 2017.
— 'African Contingency Operations Training and Assistance (ACOTA) Program', *Fact Sheet* (Washington, DC, February 6, 2013), accessed at www.state.gov/r/pa/prs/ps/2013/02/203841.htm on March 1, 2017.
— 'Counterterrorism programs and initiatives', accessed at www.state.gov/j/ct/programs/index.htm on March 1, 2017.
United States Government, 'US strategy toward sub-Saharan Africa' (Washington, DC: The White House, June 2012).
United States Government Accounting Office, 'Combating terrorism: Actions needed to enhance implementation of trans-Sahara counterterrorism partnership', *GAO Report-08-860* (Washington, DC: Government Accounting Office, July 31, 2008).
UN News Center, 'UN official shines spotlight on hunger and malnutrition in Africa' (May 6, 2010), accessed at www.un.org/apps/news/story.asp?NewsID=34616&Cr=fao&Cr1=africa# on February 28, 2017.
USA Today, 'How China is taking over Africa' (May 19, 2014).
van Dijk, Meine (ed.), *The New Presence of China in Africa* (Amsterdam: Amsterdam University Press, 2009).
Vanguard, 'Nigeria: Country's per capita income drops, now $2,748' (February 15, 2010).
Vincent, Leonard, *Guinea-Bissau: Cocaine and Coups Haunt Gagged Nation* (Paris: Reporters Without Borders, November 2007).

Vines, Alex, 'China in Africa: A mixed blessing?' *Current History* 106:700 (May 2007).
Vinograd, Cassandra, 'The revenge of Salva Kiir', *Foreign Policy.com* (January 2, 2017) accessed at http://foreignpolicy.com/2017/01/02/the-revenge-of-salva-kiir-south-sudan-genocide-ethnic-cleansing/ on February 28, 2017.
Vogler, John, 'Environmental issues', in John Baylis, Steve Smith, and Patricia Owens (eds), *The Globalization of World Politics: An Introduction to World Politics* (Oxford: Oxford University Press, 2008).
Voice of America, 'WHO: Waterborne disease is world's leading killer' (October 29, 2009).
Washington Post, 'Around the world, freedom is in peril' (July 5, 2010).
— 'How other countries are scrambling for Africa alongside the U.S.' (August 5, 2014).
— 'Foreign fighters flow into Syria' (January 27, 2015).
— 'The brutal toll of Boko Haram's attacks on civilians' (April 3, 2016).
— 'Islamic State loses its stronghold in Libya, but more chaos could soon follow' (December 7, 2016).
Washington Times, 'Analysis: Quiet on terror's "new front"' (May 13, 2005).
Weiss, Caleb, 'AQIM claims two attacks in northern Mali', *Long War Journal* (November 30, 2016), accessed at www.longwarjournal.org/archives/2016/11/aqim-claims-two-attacks-in-northern-mali.php on February 26, 2017.
Werbuer, Roger and Terence Ranger, *Postcolonial Identities in Africa* (Cape Town: University of Cape Town Press, 1997).
The White House, *National Security Strategy of the United States of America* (Washington, DC: The White House, 2002), accessed at www.state.gov/documents/organization/63562.pdf on February 25, 2017.
— 'President Obama's global development policy and global health initiative', accessed at www.whitehouse.gov/sites/default/files/Global_Health_Fact_Sheet.pdf on March 1, 2017.
Wiebe, Kristin, 'The Nile River: Potential for conflict and cooperation in the face of water degradation', *Natural Resources Journal*, 41:3 (2001), 731–54.
Williams, Paul, 'From non-intervention to non-indifference: The origins and development of the African Union's security culture', *African Affairs* 106:423 (2007).
— *War & Conflict in Africa* (Cambridge: Polity Press, 2011).
— 'Peace operations in Africa: Lessons learned since 2000', *Africa Security Brief*, 25 (Washington, DC: Africa Center for Strategic Studies, July 2013).
World Bank, *World Development Indicators 2006* (Washington, DC: The International Bank for Reconstruction and Development/World Bank, April 18, 2006), accessed at www.pdwb.de/archiv/weltbank/gdp04.pdf on February 28, 2017.
— 'Global output totals $59 trillion' (April 11, 2008).
— *World Development Indicators 2010* (Washington, DC: The International Bank for Reconstruction and Development/World Bank, April 2010),

accessed at http://data.worldbank.org/data-catalog/world-development-indicators/wdi-2010 on February 27, 2017.
— *World Development Report 2011* (Washington, DC: The International Bank for Reconstruction and Development/World Bank, April 2011).
— *World Development Indicators 2015* (Washington, DC: World Bank Publications, January 2017), accessed at http://wdi.worldbank.org/tables on February 27, 2017.
— 'Gross domestic product 2015', *World Development Indicators Database* (October 2016), accessed at http://databank.worldbank.org/data/download/GDP.pdf on February 22, 2017.
— *Global Economic Prospects* (Washington, DC: World Bank Publications, January 2017).
— 'Poverty' accessed at www.worldbank.org/en/topic/poverty/overview on February 28, 2017.
World Commission on Environment and Development, *Our Common Future* (Oxford: Oxford University Press, 1987).
World Food Programme, 'Hunger', accessed at www.wfp.org/hunger on February 28, 2017.
— 'Strategic Plan', accessed at www.wfp.org/about/strategic-plan on March 1, 2017.
World Health Organization, *World Health Report 2007* (Geneva: World Health Organization, 2007).
— *World Health Report 2010* (Geneva: World Health Organization, 2010).
— 'Global status report on noncommunicable disease 2010' (Geneva: World Health Organization).
— 'Millennium Development Goals: Progress towards the health-related Millennium Development Goals', *Fact Sheet*, 290 (May 2011), accessed at www.who.int/mediacentre/factsheets/fs290/en/index.html on February 28, 2017.
— *Global Tuberculosis Control 2011* (Geneva: World Health Organization, 2011).
— 'Health situation analysis in the Africa region: Atlas of health statistics, 2011' (Brazzaville, Republic of Congo: Regional Office for Africa, 2011).
— *World Malaria Report 2011* (Geneva: World Health Organization, 2011).
— 'Executive summary', *Trends in Maternal Mortality: 1990 to 2013* (Geneva: World Health Organization, 2014).
— *Atlas of African Health Statistics, 2014* (Brazzaville, Republic of Congo: Regional Office for Africa, 2014).
— *World Malaria Report 2014* (Geneva: World Health Organization, 2014).
— 'Factsheet on the World Malaria Report 2014' (December 2014), accessed at www.who.int/malaria/media/world_malaria_report_2014/en/ on February 28, 2017.
— 'Millennium Development Goals fact sheet no. 290' (updated May 2015), accessed at www.who.int/mediacentre/factsheets/fs290/en/ on February 28, 2017.

- *World Health Statistics 2015* (Geneva: World Health Organization, 2015).
- 'Children—reducing mortality', *Fact Sheet* (January 2016), accessed at www.who.int/mediacentre/factsheets/fs178/en/ on February 23, 2017.
- 'Deaths from NCDs', *Global Health Observatory data*, accessed at www.who.int/gho/ncd/mortality_morbidity/ncd_total_text/en/ on February 28, 2017.
- 'Noncommunicable diseases (NCD)', *Global Health Observatory data*, accessed at www.who.int/gho/ncd/en/index.html on February 28, 2017.
- 'Number of deaths due to HIV/AIDS', *Global Health Observatory data*, accessed at www.who.int/gho/hiv/epidemic_status/deaths_text/en on February 23, 2017.
- 'Nutrition', accessed at www.who.int/nutrition/topics/en/ on February 28, 2017.

World Health Organization-UNICEF, 'Millennium Development Goal drinking water target met' (Press release, March 6, 2012), accessed at www.who.int/mediacentre/news/releases/2012/drinking_water_20120306/en/index.html on February 28, 2017.

World Health Organization Media Centre, 'Emergence of XDR-TB' (September 5, 2006).

- 'New WHO study details low-cost solutions to help curb the tide on non-communicable diseases' (September 18, 2011), accessed at www.who.int/mediacentre/news/releases/2011/NCDs_solutions_20110918/en/ on February 28, 2017.
- 'Three-year study identifies key interventions to reduce maternal, newborn and child deaths' (December 15, 2011), accessed at www.who.int/mediacentre/news/releases/2011/reduce_maternal_deaths_20111215/en/ on February 28, 2017.
- 'Child mortality rates plunge by more than half since 1990 but global MDG target missed by wide margin' (September 9, 2015), accessed at www.who.int/mediacentre/news/releases/2015/child-mortality-report/en/# on February 28, 2017.
- 'WHO remove Nigeria from polio-endemic list' (September 25, 2015), accessed at www.who.int/mediacentre/news/releases/2015/nigeria-polio/en/# on February 28, 2017.

WorldHunger.org, '2015 world hunger and poverty facts and statistics', accessed at www.worldhunger.org/articles/Learn/world%20hunger%20facts%202002.htm on February 28, 2017.

Wyler, Liana and Nicolas Cook, *Illegal Drug Trade in Africa: Trends and U.S. Policy* (Washington, DC: Congressional Research Service, September 30, 2009).

Young, Crawford, 'Deciphering disorder in Africa: Is identity the key?' *World Politics*, 54 (July 2002).

- *Ethnicity and Politics in Africa* (Boston: Boston University African Studies Center, 2002).

Young, Laura and Korir Sing' Oei, 'Land, livelihoods and identities: Inter-community conflicts in East Africa' (Minority Rights Group International, 2011), accessed at www.minorityrights.org/download.php@id=1076 on February 28, 2017.

Zakaria, Fareed, 'The year of microterrorism', *Time* (December 17, 2010–January 3, 2011).

Zartman, William, 'Introduction: Posing the problem of state collapse', in William Zartman (ed.), *Collapsed States: The Disintegration and Restoration of Legitimate Authority* (Boulder, CO: Lynne Rienner Publishers, 1995).

— 'Life goes on and business as usual: The challenge of failed states', in *The (Un)Making of Failing States: Profits, Risks, and Measures of Failure* (Berlin: Heinrich Böll Foundation, Fall/Winter 2008/9), accessed at www.boell.org/downloads/hbf_failed_states_talk_series_William_Zartman.pdf on February 25, 2017.

Index

Note: page numbers in italics refer to figures, maps or tables

Afghanistan 98–9, 118, 121
African National Congress (ANC) 29–30, 89, 108
African nationalism 197
African Standby Force (ASF) 200–2, 233
African Union 1, 78, 80, 93, 194–6, 199–205 *passim*, 227, 250
   Mission in Somalia (AMISOM) 75–6, 201, 223, 228, 229
   Peace and Security Council (AUPSC) 199–202
Algeria 8, 18, 30, 45, 69, 96, 98–9, 101, 105, 107, 110, 223, 225
al-Qaeda in the Islamic Maghreb (AQIM) 92, 93, 96, 97, 101–2, 125–6, 253
al-Shabaab 47, 74–6, 93, 96, 97–8, 100, 106, 108, 201, 222, 253
AMISOM *see* African Union, Mission in Somalia
Annan, Kofi 23, 127, 239
AQIM *see* al-Qaeda in the Islamic Maghreb
Arab Spring 31, 91, 99, 106, 109, 111, 123
AUPSC *see* African Union, Peace and Security Council

Barre, Siad 53–4, 71–3
Boko Haram 8, 45, 78–9, 93–4, 96, 98, 100, 107, 224, 253
   see also Chad; Niger; Nigeria
Brazil 174, 235–7
Burundi 21, 31, 49, 75, 81, 204, 226, 227–8

Canada 25, 230, 254
Casamance 21, 49, 56
   see also Senegal
Central African Republic (CAR) 5, 128–9, 201, 204, 221, 225–6, 227, 239
Central Intelligence Agency (CIA) *19*, 67, 74, 78, 104
Chad 5, 6, 41, 52–3, 92, 179, 188, 199, 204, 223–4, 228
   Boko Haram and 79, 94, 96, *96*, 107
   see also Deby, Idriss
child and maternal mortality rates 147, 151, 162
China 146, 190, 217, 228, 231, 234, 255
   arms sales 119, 128, 235
   Forum on China-Africa Cooperation 232
   see also peacekeeping
Christian–Muslim 44, 108
civil liberties 7, 31, 66, 89, 106, 107, 108, 111, 225, 234
civil society 9, 26–31 *passim*, 54–8 *passim*, 68, 69, 73, 80, 130–1, 194, 195, 207–8, 210–11, 218, 219, 233, 238–9, 241–2, 244, 253, 256
civil war 49, 56, 72, 92, 171, 195
   see also ethnicity, ethnic violence; resource competition
clan 53–4, 70–3, 75, 87, 208
   see also Somalia
clean water 29, 144, 157, 162, 207, 209, 229, 231, 241–2

climate change 175, 178, 186, 188, 190, 207, 210–11, 220
  "carbon-sink effect" 174
  deforestation and desertification 174, 177
  environmental degradation 11, 23, 27, 169, 170, 179, 180, 185–90 *passim*, 206, 237, 252, 254, 258
Cold War 2, 4, 10, 56, 89, 107, 127, 128, 206, 233, 253
  post-Cold War 23, 25, 46, 49, 62, 127, 184, 197, 206
colonial rule 21, 37, 206
  apartheid 29, 41–2, 49, 88–9
  liberation struggle 20, 42, 90, 91, 232
Combined Joint Task Force – Horn of Africa (CJTF-HOA) 78, 104, 105, 222
  see also United States
communal violence 5, 36, 48, 50, 52, 177
  see also Nigeria; Uganda
conflict minerals 176, 179, 185
  see also Democratic Republic of the Congo; Sierra Leone
Cote d'Ivoire 45, 67, 227
coups 4, 71–2, 74, 106, 124, 126, 195, 224

Darfur 5–6, 52–3, 100, 172, 177, 186, 227
Deby, Idriss 52–3
Democratic Republic of the Congo (DRC) 2, 5, 44, 63, 156, 169, 179, 185, 233, 227, 235
  eastern DRC 4, 50, 70, 79, 81, 100, 150, 161, 176, 185, 187, 204
disarmament, demobilization and reintegration (DDR) 129
Djibouti 71, 106, 222, 233
  see also Combined Joint Task Force – Horn of Africa (CJTF-HOA)
drug trafficking 9, 11, 117, 119, 120–6, 135, 207, 238
  cocaine trafficking 120–1, 124
  Colombian drug 121, 123
  heroin trafficking 122

Eastern Europe 119, 128
Ebola 144, 150, 158, 209, 229, 240

Economic Community of Central African States (ECCAS) 204
Economic Community of West African States (ECOWAS) 2, 81, 196, 200, 202–3, 212, 219, 226
economics of war 185
ECOWAS *see* Economic Community of West African States
Egypt 7, 41, 43, 58, 69, 95, 96, 97, 99, 105, 107–8, 122, 180–3, 204, 227, 228, 281
environmental security 24, 170, 181, 184, 186, 190, 196
Eritrea 6, 43, 74
  see also Ethiopia; Somalia
Ethiopia 1, 18, 56, 63, 71, 74, 97, 104, 122, 180–3, 212, 227, 228
  Somalia and 6, 21, 161
  see also United States, war on terror
ethnicity 5, 37–9, 45, 49, 54, 56, 70
  ethnic violence 21, 26, 53, 252
  political tribalism 38, 40

failed states 65, 82, 137
France 18, 70, 119, 196, 229, 230
  see also P3+1
Fund for Peace 6, 63

G-8 3, 226
gender 153, 186, 240
Germany 119, 217, 219–21, 230
  see also P3+1
Ghana 122, 131, 228
global economic crisis 116
globalization 8–11, 36, 46, 57, 90, 98, 102, 109, 116–17, 120, 132, 136–7, 144, 148, 151, 158, 163, 174, 187, 191, 231, 243, 250, 253, 258
globalized security architecture 11
grassroots security 205–9
Great Lakes district 128
  see also Burundi; Democratic Republic of the Congo (DRC); Rwanda; Uganda
Groupe Islamique Arme (GIA) 101
Guinea 122–4
Guinea-Bissau 121, 123–6, 128, 136
  "Africa's first narco-state" 137
Gulf of Guinea 3, 178

Heavily Indebted Poor Countries (HIPC) 3
human security construct 25, 27, 32, 83, 144, 184, 196, 210–11, 216–17, 241, 254, 259

India 227, 228, 235, 237
infectious diseases 27, 145, 147, 153, 229
 cholera 149–50, 157
 Global Fund 230, 234
 HIV/AIDS 8, 27–8, 41, 146–8, 152–3, 159–60, 162–3, 236, 242
 malaria 8, 28, 148–9, 152–3, 154, 155, 159, 162, 234
 smallpox 147, 149
 tuberculosis (TB) 8, 149, 153, 155–6, 159, 162
 see also United States, President's Emergency Program for AIDS Relief (PEPFAR)
Intergovernmental Authority on Development (IGAD) 202–3
International Monetary Fund (IMF) 3
INTERPOL 240, 254
Islamic State 5, 8, 92–5, 96, 97–100, 106, 108, 111, 223–4, 253

Japan 230, 254
 aid to Africa 231
 see also peacekeeping

Kenya 8, 39, 41, 58, 63, 71, 75, 93, 96, 97, 102, 106–8, 118, 122–3, 130, 133, 137, 161, 177, 179, 201, 203, 208, 223, 226, 228, 238
 see also al-Shabaab; peacekeeping
Ki-moon, Ban 50, 120, 125, 252

legitimacy 24, 40, 47–8, 62–3, 66, 68–9, 74–7 passim, 82–3, 94, 119, 134, 160–1, 178, 188, 210–11, 256
Liberia 18, 49, 67–8, 79, 124, 128–9, 176, 202, 226, 227
Libya 5, 47, 50, 52, 57, 78, 81, 92, 94–5, 96, 97, 100, 204, 209, 224, 240
 armed militias 102, 223
lootable commodities 178

Mali 5, 42, 56, 78, 92, 96, 97, 100, 107, 124–6, 129, 136, 188, 201, 221, 223, 224, 228, 229, 239
 see also peacekeeping
malnutrition 27, 145, 152, 156–7, 160, 163, 185, 229
Mano River Basin 5, 79, 128, 186
Mauritania 42, 92, 94, 96, 105–6, 124, 126, 179, 188, 223
migration 5, 28, 39, 187–8, 211
 International Organization for Migration 240, 254
Millennium Development Goals (MDGs) 28, 145, 162
Morocco 99, 204, 223
Mozambique 20, 42–3, 49, 178, 203, 236
 Operation Rachel 129
Mugabe, Robert 22, 108, 238

nation-state 3, 20, 62, 83, 184, 196, 206, 217
negative sovereignty 64
Niger 41–2, 56, 79, 94, 96, 100, 106–7, 125, 176, 188, 223
 see also Boko Haram
Nigeria 2–3, 21, 37, 43–5, 47, 50–2, 58, 63, 69, 78–9, 86, 93–4, 96, 97, 100, 106–7, 109, 120, 122, 126, 133, 136, 149–50, 156, 169, 177–8, 202–3, 220, 223–4, 227, 236, 253
 see also Boko Haram
Nile River Basin 180–2
Nkurunziza, Pierre 81
non-governmental organizations (NGOs) 26, 129, 145, 218
non-state actors 8, 22, 62, 67, 76–7, 98, 119, 187, 190, 195–6, 219, 253
Nyerere, Julius 198

Organization of African Unity (OAU) 88, 198–9

P3+1 219, 222, 225
 see also Economic Community of West African States (ECOWAS); France; Germany; United Kingdom, British; United States
pan-Africanism 197

pan-Sahel 45, 78, 92, 98, 102, 104–6, 224
peacekeeping 31, 77–8, 108, 126, 172, 201–4, 208, 211, 219, 222, 224–6, 227, 229, 233, 236–7
  see also African Union, Mission in Somalia (AMISOM); African Union, Peace and Security Council (AUPSC); Economic Community of West African States (ECOWAS)
Peace of Westphalia 63
political goods 64–6
poor governance 2, 29, 56, 58, 103, 172, 176, 178, 185, 187, 211, 252, 258
population 2, 8–9, 18, 21, 23–4, 36–7, 41, 57–8, 68, 79, 88, 94, 153, 155, 161, 170–3, 177, 181, 186, 188
  demographic trends 2, 43
positive sovereignty 63–5, 76

Qadhafi, Muammar 22, 94, 129, 223
quasi-states 67

refugees 9, 29, 108, 150, 179, 186
regional economic communities (RECs) 81, 196, 198, 201–5
resource competition 28, 50, 172, 176–7, 184–5, 187, 189–90, 252
  illicit trade 179, 186, 188
  land and water 52, 169–70, 172, 175, 177, 186, 189, 207, 210, 240
  oil 169, 171, 176, 178, 185
resource exploitation 169–72, 178, 188, 207
rule of law 55, 132, 134–5, 199, 201
Russia, Soviet Union 36, 64, 66, 72, 73, 118–9, 228, 238
  see also Cold War
Rwanda 21, 31, 49–50, 57, 67, 150, 161, 199, 203–4, 207–8, 227, 228

Salafist Group for Preaching and Combat (GSPC) 92, 101
  see also Algeria; al-Qaeda in the Islamic Maghreb (AQIM)
securitization 144, 170, 174

security
  bottom up approach 9, 23–4, 83, 111, 208
  human security paradigm 22–5, 82, 206–7, 218, 258
  non-traditional 1, 7–8, 11, 25–6, 30, 32, 55, 179, 195, 207, 211, 237, 239, 241, 255, 258
  regime 20, 22, 25, 31, 80, 82–3, 110, 206, 212, 255, 257
  state 11, 20, 27, 56, 118–9, 196, 206, 211, 255
  top down approach 77, 195, 206
Senegal 39, 67, 227
  see also Casamance; drug trafficking
separatism 78, 171, 178, 183–4
Sierra Leone 68, 77, 126, 128–9, 169, 176, 179, 199, 202, 217, 221
small arms 8, 29, 116–38, 224, 234–5, 237, 239–40, 242, 254
  fueling violence 5, 132, 136, 234
  illicit trade 119–20, 126, 132, 134
  man-portable air defense systems (MANPADS) 129
  Programme of Action on Small Arms and Light Weapons 209
  proliferation challenge 5, 9, 172, 207, 209, 234, 238
Somalia 4, 6, 10, 47, 50, 53–4, 57, 63, 66, 68–76, 78–9, 92, 96, 97, 100–1, 111, 130, 161, 201, 208–9, 222, 225, 228
  Kenya and 108, 203, 226
  piracy 219, 222, 233, 237, 239
  Somaliland 70–1, 73, 81
  Union of Islamic Courts (UIC) 74–5, 92
  see also African Union, Mission in Somalia (AMISOM); al-Shabaab; clan; Ethiopia
South Africa 29–30, 43, 45–6, 68, 89, 91, 99, 108, 122–3, 126, 129–30, 133, 137, 153–4, 157, 201, 203, 208, 226, 227, 237, 242
  South African National Defence Force (SANDF) 29
  see also African National Congress (ANC); colonial rule, apartheid; peacekeeping
Southern African Development Community (SADC) 196, 200, 202–3, 209

South Sudan 2, 6, 10, 35, 41–2, 44, 47, 50, 63, 78, 128, 129, 133, 172, 178, 180, 225, 228, 237, 252
  see also ethnicity; resource competition
sustainable development 183, 184, 190

Taylor, Charles 176
  see also Liberia
terrorism (definitions) 86–90
  Counterterrorism Initiative 78, 104, 217
  high profile attacks 53, 93
  state terrorism 88, 98
  ungoverned spaces 77
  see also United States, war on terror
transnational criminal activity 120, 188
tribalism *see* ethnicity, political tribalism

Uganda 5, 31, 41, 74, 129, 133, 154, 177, 180, 201, 203, 212, 225–6, 228
  Lord's Resistance Army 100
  see also al-Shabaab; peacekeeping
United Kingdom, British 19, 25, 37, 51, 70, 129, 182, 217, 219, 221, 223–4, 226, 229–31
  see also colonial rule; Economic Community of West African States (ECOWAS); P3+1; peacekeeping
United Nations (UN) 2, 8, 41, 119–20, 125, 129, 133, 157, 169, 173, 198, 201, 217, 219, 224–5, 227, 228, 233, 235, 238–9
  Conference on the Human Environment (UNCHE) 173
  Development Index 178
  Environmental Programme (UNEP) 174
  High Commissioner for Refugees (UNHCR) 186
  Office on Drugs and Crime (UNODC) 117, 118, 121, 124, 126
  see also drugs; peacekeeping; small arms
United States 1, 12, 28, 30, 74, 77, 87, 89–91, 104–7, 110, 119, 150, 171, 196, 216–17, 221, 224–5, 229, 231, 244, 255, 257, 259
  Department of State 87, 97, 222–3, 226, 244
  humanitarian assistance 27, 105, 161, 240–1
  National Intelligence Council 2, 177
  President's Emergency Program for AIDS Relief (PEPFAR) 163, 217, 230
  US Africa Command (AFRICOM) 220
  war on terror 87, 90, 97, 99, 104–7, 110, 220, 222–5, 242
  see also cold war; Combined Joint Task Force – Horn of Africa (CJTF-HOA); drugs; Economic Community of West African States (ECOWAS); P3+1; peacekeeping; small arms; terrorism
United States of Africa 198
urbanization 46, 153, 175, 177

violence against refugees 179

Western Sahara 204, *228*
World Health Organization (WHO) 28, 145–7, 149–53 *passim*, 155, 158

xenophobia 179

Zimbabwe 20, 22, 40, 69, 89, 108, 157, 161, 235, 238
  see also Mugabe, Robert
zones of conflict 5, 225